Texas Legislative Almanac

TEXAS LEGISLATIVE ALMANAC 1999

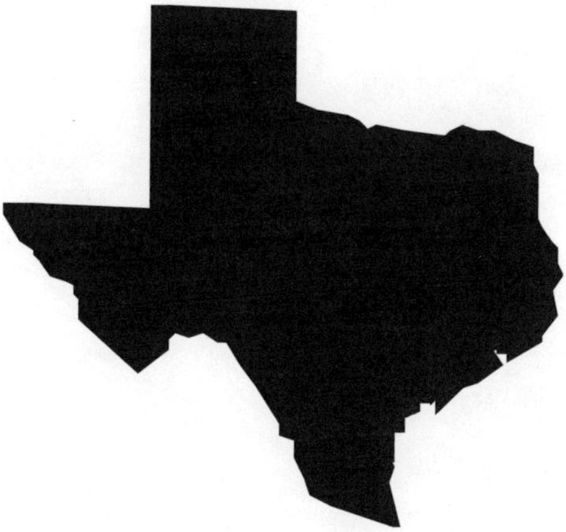

Harvey J. Tucker
Gary M. Halter

Texas A&M University Press
College Station

Manufactured in the United States of America

First edition

The paper used in this book meets the minimum requirements
of the American National Standard for Permanence
of Paper for Printed Library Materials, Z-39.48-1984.
Binding materials have been chosen for durability.

ISSN: 1092-9843

CONTENTS

PREFACE TO THE 1999 EDITION

The 1997 edition of the *Texas Legislative Almanac* went to press several weeks after the beginning of the 1997 legislative session and was available midway through the session. In order to make the 1999 edition available at the beginning of the legislative session, it went to press immediately after the November 1998 election. As a result, information on committee assignments and much information from the 1998 election for individual legislative districts was not yet available to us. In the section on introductory material, we have identified internet sites where these and other data will be published.

The most controversial element of the 1997 *Texas Legislative Almanac* was the information on bill introduction passage. Those data were taken from printed reports of the Texas Legislative Council. Numerous legislators and staff encouraged us to include more information on activity and success to provide a more complete picture of legislative work. We asked them to help us by making the job of collecting comprehensive information more manageable. Probably by coincidence, the Texas Legislature Online internet site began to offer a complex bill searching service that makes it possible to identify many legislative activities by individual member. We are happy to include data on amendments introduced and passed as an additional measure of legislative work in this volume.

Unfortunately, we are not able to include other indicators of work and success suggested by some legislators. Many have pointed out that some or all of the content of their "failed" bills was incorporated into bills passed by the legislature even though their names do not appear as bill authors or sponsors or proposers of amendments. Others claim that they played major roles in passing important legislation without these roles being identified in official records. We agree with these points and those who make them. However, we are limiting information on legislative work and success to data we can collect comprehensively for all legislators from official state sources.

A faculty research minigrant from Texas A&M University supported some of Tucker's research and data collection that appears here. We want to thank Charles A. Johnson for support of this project from the department of political science at Texas A&M University. Avis Munson scanned photographs for us. Student workers Amanda Green, Shamika Fulson and Abbie Conlee helped with data collection and other tasks.

We are grateful for the professionalism and support of the Texas A&M University Press. Mary Ann Jacob designed the layout and cover for this book. Karol Murrah copyedited the volume. Mary Lenn Dixon was the managing editor for the *Texas Legislative Almanac* project.

Finally, we would like to thank the members and staff of the 75th and 76th Texas Legislatures. We also thank candidates who were unsuccessful in their efforts to win seats in the 76th Texas Legislature. Some provided us with photographs and biographical information. Others reviewed draft material and helped us identify omissions and correct errors. Almost all of them were simultaneously conducting their election campaigns. We could not have produced this book without their generous help.

PREFACE TO THE 1997 EDITION

The 1997 edition of the *Texas Legislative Almanac* grew out of independent research projects the two of us were conducting at Texas A&M University on the Texas State Legislature. There was a wealth of readily available information on Texas legislators and legislative districts. Much of what one used to have to gather from a variety of official state documents was becoming available on state Gopher and World Wide Web sites on the Internet. However, the data we thought most important were still scattered across numerous information sources. The goal of this volume is to provide a reference of broad scope that is still small enough to be carried in a briefcase.

We have benefited from the wise counsel of Sally Reynolds, head of the Legislative Reference Library in the state capitol. Sally and her outstanding staff of reference librarians first helped us identify the kind of information most pertinent for the *Texas Legislative Almanac*, and then advised us on appropriate sources.

Texas is second to no state in the quantity and quality of official legislative information available on the Internet. Much of the data and text that follows is taken or adapted from Internet sites maintained by the Texas Legislative Council. Kay Huffman conferred with us about these sites. Tom Kelley helped us identify and acquire information from Internet and other sources. Alan Ware gave us access to 1996 election data by legislative district.

A grant to develop a course on the Texas Legislature from the Office of Honors and Academic Programs at Texas A&M University partially supported some of Tucker's research and data collection that appears here. We want to thank Charles A. Johnson for support of this project from the department of political science at Texas A&M University. Ellyn Perrone encouraged and advised us when we were contemplating this project. We also thank Mary Ann Jacob, who designed the layout, and Karol Murrah, who copyedited this volume. We gratefully acknowledge the contributions of our student assistants Amanda Green, Adam Warber, Kristi Thomas, Chris Diaz, and Lucy Xie.

Finally, we would like to thank the members of the 75th Texas Legislature and their office staff who reviewed draft material and helped us identify omissions and correct errors. They also made a variety of suggestions aimed at improving the content of the *Texas Legislative Almanac*. Limitations of time and space prevented us from taking advantage of all of their ideas. The responsibility for remaining inaccuracies is ours.

PART I
Introductory Material

OVERVIEW OF MEMBERSHIP IN THE TEXAS LEGISLATURE

Several generalizations about the men and women who serve in the Texas Legislature can be drawn from the data included in this volume. These generalizations are helpful in understanding the overall nature and characteristics of these public servants.

REPRESENTATION

The Texas Legislature comprises 181 men and women selected locally by voters in single-member districts. There are 150 members of the Texas House of Representatives and 31 members of the Texas Senate. In some respects these men and women represent the diversity of the population of the state and in other respects they do not. Only 3 of 31 senators are women and only 24 of 150 house members are women. While African Americans make up 13.4 percent of the state's population they hold only 9.3 percent of House seats and .06 percent of Senate seats. Hispanics make up 25 percent of the state's population and hold 19.3 percent of House seats and 22.5 percent of Senate seats.

OCCUPATION

The Texas Legislature meets for 140 days in regular session every two years and pays members an annual salary of only $7,200 ($600 per month). Partly because of low pay and biennial sessions, most members of the Texas Legislature do not consider themselves to be full time legislators. Texas is one of seven states (Arkansas, Kentucky, Montana, Nevada, North Dakota and Oregon) that still meets in biennial sessions. Most large, industrial states pay members of their legislatures more than Texas and meet in annual sessions.

Table 1 compares Texas legislators' occupations with legislators in the other 49 states. Several observations are worth noting. First, Texas has a higher number of attorneys than most states—about 35 percent compared with about 15 percent nationwide. Also, members of the Texas Legislature are drawn from selected occupational groups and are not a cross-section of the population of the state. Service is limited to individuals who can afford to serve in the legislature. The low pay is also a contributing factor in limiting the ability of many citizens to serve in the legislature.

Table 1
Occupation of State Legislators
In Percent

	All States			Texas	
	1986	**1993**	**1995**	**1997**	**1999**
Full-time Leg.	11.5	14.9	8.2	3.9	4.4
Retired	6.7	7.2	2.7	1.1	1.6
Attorney	16.4	16.5	32.5	31.5	35.3
Business Owner	13.8	10.0	18.4	16.1	17.6
Business/Ex. Mgr.	5.8	6.2	3.8	11.6	9.3
Business/Non Mgr.	4.6	5.1	0.0	0.0	1.6
Consultant/Prof.	3.0	3.5	3.8	7.1	4.9
Real Estate	4.2	3.2	8.8	8.2	3.3
Insurance	3.4	3.2	3.8	5.0	7.7
Farmer/Rancher	9.9	7.9	4.4	3.9	3.3
Education K-12	5.7	6.2	0.0	2.2	1.1
Educator/College	2.0	2.0	0.5	1.1	1.6
Communications/Arts	2.0	2.4	0.0	0.0	0.0
Medical	1.8	2.4	2.7	3.9	2.2
Govt. Employee Local	1.3	2.1	0.5	1.1	0.5
Govt. Employee State	0.1	0.4	0.0	0.0	0.0
Homemaker	1.0	1.3	0.0	0.0	0.5
Engineer/Architect	1.0	1.2	1.1	1.6	2.7
Accountant	0.7	0.7	1.1	1.1	0.0
Clergy	0.4	0.4	0.0	0.0	0.0
Labor Union	0.3	0.3	0.0	0.0	0.0
Student	0.3	0.3	0.0	0.0	0.0
Not Available	0.1	0.2	0.0	0.0	0.0
Insufficient Information	3.1	2.4	7.7	0.5	1.6

Source: For all states, National Conference of State Legislatures (NCSL) *Legislator's Occupations.* Denver, Colo.: NCSL, 1995. Percentages may vary due to different interpretations of self-reported data.

PAY OF STATE LEGISLATORS

As indicated above, the pay for Texas legislators is rather low when compared with the other large, industrial states. Listed below are the annual salaries of these states by population.

Table 2
Legislative Salaries in the Ten Most Populous States

State	Annual Salary
California	$75,600
Texas	7,200
New York	57,500

Florida	24,912
Pennsylvania	57,367
Illinois	47,039
Ohio	42,426
Michigan	51,895
North Carolina	14,951
Georgia	11,374

Source: Council of State Governments, *The Book of the States 1998-99* (Lexington, Ky.: Council of State Governments, 1998), p. 81, Table 3.9.

YEARS OF SERVICE IN THE LEGISLATURE

In recent years, term limits for members of legislative bodies has been a topic of concern. From 1990 to 1996, 21 states imposed term limits on the members of their legislatures. Most of these states limit members to between 8 and 12 years of service. While Texas is not among those states with formal term limits, other factors seem to limit legislative service. Few members serve longer than 10 years. Most voluntarily retire from office because of the demands the office takes on their other occupations and their family and the demands imposed by campaigning for office and low pay. Only 25 members of the 76th Legislature have served more than 12 years, 36 have served longer than 10 years, and 57 have served more than 8 years. While turnover in the membership of the legislature may provide for new ideas, experience is also an important factor in the legislative process. Texas seems to have a balance between turnover and experience.

Table 3
Years of Service of Members of the Texas Legislature
1999 Session

	House		Senate	
First Service	**Number**	**Percent**	**Number**	**Percent**
1979 or before	9	6.1	1	3.2
1981-85	11	7.4	3	9.6
1987-89	16	10.6	4	13.0
1991	21	14.0	5	16.1
1993	24	16.0	6	19.4
1995	19	12.7	4	13.0
1997	25	16.6	6	19.4
1999	25	16.6	2	6.4

PARTY COMPOSITION OF THE TEXAS LEGISLATURE

In 1997 the Republican party gained majority control of the Texas Senate for the first time in 121 years. Republicans will maintain majority control of the Texas Senate by one seat in the 1999 session. There will be a Republican Lieutenant Governor presiding over the Texas Senate in 1999, the first since Reconstruction. Republicans had hoped to gain control of the Texas House in 1999. However, Democrats won a slim majority of eight seats. This is a net gain for the Republicans of three seats in the House from 1997.

Republicans have been gaining seats in both chambers since the mid-1970s. This change is part of a trend in southern states: increasing Republican strength and change from one-party Democratic control. Texas is very much a part of this pattern. Table 4 shows the change in party composition in the Texas Legislature since 1975.

Table 4
Party Composition of the Texas Legislature
1975-99

	Senate		House	
Year	Dem	Rep	Dem	Rep
1975	28	3	133	17
1977	28	3	132	18
1979	27	4	126	24
1981	24	7	114	36
1983	26	5	115	35
1985	25	6	98	52
1987	25	6	94	56
1989	23	8	93	57
1991	23	8	93	57
1993	18	13	92	58
1995	17	14	90	60
1997	14	17	82	68
1999	15	16	79	71

LEGISLATIVE CONTINUITY AND TURNOVER

There are two new senators and twenty-three new representatives in the 76th Texas Legislature. Table 5 summarizes continuity and turnover from the 75th to the 76th Texas Legislature. As in the past, incumbents seeking reelection were highly successful. Turnover of legislators was most often voluntary. They gave up their seats to seek other office or to retire. Incumbent defeat was rare, and occurred more often in primary elections than in general elections.

Table 5
Continuity and Turnover from 1997 to 1999

	Senate	**House**
Continuity		
Seat not up for reelection	15	0
Incumbent won reelection	14	127
Turnover		
Died	0	1
Retired	0	13
Sought other office	1	3
Lost primary election	0	5
Lost general election	1	1

DISTRICT AND MEMBER PAGE DEFINITIONS AND DATA SOURCES

DISTRICT MAP AND COUNTIES

Each district page presents a list of counties entirely or partially in the legislative district. An accompanying map of Texas identifies those counties. The maps are intended to show the approximate locations of districts. They do not document precise boundaries.

DEMOGRAPHIC INFORMATION

District page data on total population, race and ethnicity, education, age, wealth and urbanization employment and household types were taken or developed from information provided by the Texas Legislative Council on its Texas Legislature Online internet site, *http://www.capitol.state.tx.us*.. The original source of data was the 1990 Census of Population from the U. S. Bureau of the Census.

OVERLAPPING HOUSE AND SENATE DISTRICTS

Each senate district page identifies house district numbers and incumbents within or overlapping the senate district. Each house district page identifies corresponding information about senate districts and incumbents.

DISTRICT ELECTION DATA

Each district page presents information on the results of the 1996 election within the district for the legislative seat. The major party vote in the presidential election of 1996 is reported. The composite party vote for 1994 is the average vote in the district for state offices contested on a statewide basis. Data are also presented for total registered voters, total turnout, and percent of registered voting in the 1996 election. These data were taken or developed from information provided by the Texas Legislative Council on its Texas Legislature Online site, *http://www.capitol.state.tx.us*.

Each district page presents information on the results of the 1998 election for the legislative seat within the district. These data were taken or developed from early election results reported by the Texas Secretary of State's Office. Comprehensive results from the 1998 general election by state legislative district are to be posted and linked to the Texas Legislature Online, Texas Senate, and Texas House of Representative internet home pages. The respective addresses for these sites are: *http://www.capitol.state.tx.us*, *http://www.senate.state.tx.us*, and *http://www.house.state.tx.us*. For election results from the 1998 primary and general elections and earlier elections in Texas, see the internet home page of the Texas Office of the Secretary of State, *http://www.sos.state.tx.us*.

MEMBER NAME

There is no single official name roster of members of the Texas Legislature. The various multiple lists vary in their use of formal names, informal names, or both. There are also differences with respect to middle names and initials, "Jr.," and "III." The primary sources of names for this volume are state election ballots and reports of election results. For cases in which other sources were consistent in listing another name, the more frequent listing was used.

CAPITOL AND DISTRICT OFFICE INFORMATION

Each member page identifies capitol office telephone number(s) and district office addresses and telephone number(s). Electronic mail addresses are given for members if one or more official state listing suggests they use electronic mail. Capitol mailing addresses and proper forms of address for communicating with members of the Texas Legislature are presented later in this introductory section.

Capitol offices and chamber desk locations are assigned on the basis of seniority. They can change during a legislative session if one or more members leave and other members want to relocate. Senate and House capitol office telephone numbers are district specific and do not change when incumbents or office locations do.

PERSONAL INFORMATION

Personal information was collected from surveys conducted of legislators by the Texas Legislative Council and kept in the Legislative Reference Library. We requested this information by mail from new members of the legislature. All members were asked to review draft material to correct errors and omissions.

For most members state legislative service identifies the year in which the member's first session met. For members originally elected in a regular election held in an even numbered year, the first year of service is the following odd numbered year. For members originally elected in special elections, the first year of legislative service is the year of that election.

COMMITTEE ASSIGNMENT HISTORY

Assignments to standing committees made at the beginning of each session are reported for each member. Some members are originally chosen in special elections but do not serve during a regular or special session for that term of office. Those individuals do not serve on committees for that term of office, and the item is not applicable (NA). The history of assignments to special or interim committees, subcommittees, and committees of the whole are not reported on member pages.

BILL PASSAGE RATES, 1997

Data on bill passage rates come from two reports issued by the Texas Legislative Council: *List of Bills by Author/Sponsor, Master List of Bills for the 75th Regular Session, 1995* (June 2, 1997), and *List of Bills Passed by Author/Sponsor* (July 11, 1997). We summarize information on Senate and House bills only, not on resolutions. The reports give credit for bill authorship and sponsorship to all single and joint authors. The author is defined as the legislator who files a bill and guides it through the legislative process. A maximum of five joint authors can be identified at introduction. The sponsor is defined as the legislator who guides the bill through the legislative process after the bill has passed the originating chamber. The sponsor must be a member of the opposite chamber of the one in which the bill was filed. A maximum of five joint sponsors can be identified for each bill. Bill sponsors must be identified before floor action in the second chamber, but may be identified earlier in the legislative process. Bills approved by the legislature—that is, bills that pass both chambers and are sent to the governor—are counted as passed, even if they are vetoed by the governor.

In the 75th Regular Session of 1997, the average number of bills singly or jointly authored by senators was 68. The average number of authored bills passed was 23; the average percent passed was 33. The average number of bills singly or jointly sponsored by senators was 31. The average number of sponsored bills passed was 28; the average percent passed was 91.

In the 75th Regular Session of 1997, the average number of bills singly or jointly authored by house members was 32. The average number of authored bills passed was 8.7; the average percent passed was 28. The average number of bills singly or jointly sponsored by house members was 6.6. The average number of sponsored bills passed was

5.2; the average percent passed was 79.

Many legislators are able to incorporate all or part of their bills that do not pass as amendments to other bills. Data on amendments proposed and passed were gathered for each member by executing bill searches by member and action taken on the Texas Legislature Online internet site. The average number of amendments proposed by senators in the 1997 session was 34.4. The average number passed by senators was 30.5; the average percent passed was 87. The average number of amendments proposed by house members was 12.8. The average number passed by house menbers was 10.6; the average percent passed was 83.

As many legislative members and their staff have communicated to us, these accounts of bills proposed and passed are incomplete and imperfect measures of legislative work or success. They are incomplete because they do not include coauthors or cosponsors; legislators authorized by the primary author(s) or sponsor(s) to join in authorship or sponsorship after the original author(s) or sponsor(s) have been named. They are incomplete because they do not include credit for those whose defeated bills are included, wholly or in part, in other bills without their names appearing in the legislative record. They are incomplete because they do not include other important legislation, such as joint resolutions to propose amendments to the Texas Constitution, to ratify amendments to the U.S. Constitution, or to request a convention to propose amendments to the U.S. Constitution.

The bill introduction and passage information is imperfect because it does not distinguish major bills from minor bills, more important from less important bills. It does not differentiate between bills that die immediately after introduction and those that fall just short of passing. It does not single out companion bills—identical bills introduced in both chambers. Although such bills have authors in each chamber, only one is given authorship credit if one of the bills is passed. However, companion bill authors are typically sponsors of the identical bill in the opposite chamber.

Bill introduction and passage information is also imperfect because it does not measure what some members view as a most important part of legislative activity: preventing "bad" bills from being passed. There is no formal accounting of effort and success in killing bills.

We present this information as important, albeit incomplete, imperfect, and potentially misleading indicators of legislative work and success.

ELECTORAL HISTORY IN CURRENT DISTRICT

Information is provided on competition in primary and general elections since 1994 for each member for each term served. For general elections, the entry indicates the party or parties of those who unsuccessfully challenged the member. An entry of NA (Not Applicable) means the member either was not a candidate in a primary or general election or did not win the general election.

SENATE MEMBERS IN ALPHABETIC ORDER

Senate Members	Party	District
Kenneth L. Armbrister	D	18
Gonzalo Barrientos	D	14
David Bernsen	D	4
Teel Bivins	R	31
J. E. (Buster) Brown	R	17
David Cain	D	2
John J. Carona	R	16
Robert Duncan	R	28
Rodney Ellis	D	13
Troy Fraser	R	24
Mario V. Gallegos, Jr.	D	6
Chris Harris	R	10
Tom Haywood	R	30
Mike Jackson	R	11
Jon Lindsay	R	7
Eddie Lucio, Jr.	D	27
Gregory Luna	D	26
Frank Madla	D	19
Mike Moncrief	D	12
Jane Nelson	R	9
Drew Nixon	R	3
Steve Ogden	R	5
Bill Ratliff	R	1
Florence Shapiro	R	8
Eliot Shapleigh	D	29
David Sibley	R	22
Carlos F. Truan	D	20
Jeff Wentworth	R	25
Royce West	D	23
John Whitmire	D	15
Judith Zaffirini	D	21

SENATE STANDING COMMITTEES

Senate standing committees for the 76th Texas Legislature will be established by rules adopted at the beginning of the session in January, 1999. They will be listed on the Senate internet site, *http://www.senate.state.tx.us*. Listed below are the standing Senate committees from the 75th Texas Legislature. They are likely to continue in the 76th Legislature.

Administration

Criminal Justice

Economic Development

Education

Finance

Health and Human Services

Intergovernmental Relations

International Relations, Trade and Technology

Jurisprudence

Natural Resources

Natural Resources Subcommittee on Agriculture

Natural Resources Subcommittee on Water

Nominations

State Affairs

Committee of the Whole on Legislative and Congressional Redistricting

General Investigating

Veteran Arrairs and Military Installations

HOUSE MEMBERS IN ALPHABETIC ORDER

House Members	Party	Dist.
Clyde Alexander	D	12
Ray Allen	R	106
Leo G. Alvarado	D	116
Kip Averitt	R	56
Kevin Bailey	D	140
Leo Berman	R	6
Dennis Bonnen	R	25
Fred M. Bosse	D	128
Kenneth (Kim) Brimer	R	96
Betty Brown	R	4
Fred Brown	R	14
Lon Burnam	D	90
Jaime L. Capelo, Jr.	D	34
Bill G. Carter	R	91
Norma Chavez	D	76
Warren Chisum	D	88
Wayne Christian	R	9
Ron Clark	R	62
Garnet F. Coleman	D	147
Robert L. Cook	D	28
Frank J. Corte	R	123
David Counts	D	70
Joe Crabb	R	127
Tom Craddick	R	82
Ronny Crownover	R	64
Henry Cuellar	D	42
John Culberson	R	130
Debra Danberg	D	137
John Davis	R	129
Yvonne Davis	D	111
Dianne White Delisi	R	55
Mary Denny	R	63
Joseph D. Deshotel	D	22
Joe Driver	R	113
Dawnna M. Dukes	D	50
Jim Dunham	D	57
Harold V. Dutton	D	142
Al Edwards	D	146
Harryette Ehrhardt	D	107
Craig Eiland	D	24
Gary Elkins	R	135
Dan Ellis	D	18

House Members	Party	Dist.
David Farabee	D	69
Jessica Christina Farrar	D	148
Ismael (Kino) Flores	D	36
Pete P. Gallego	D	74
Domingo Garcia	D	104
Kenn George	R	108
Helen Giddings	D	109
Bob Glaze	D	5
Toby Goodman	R	93
Tony Goolsby	R	102
Patricia Gray	D	23
Sherri Greenberg	D	48
Kent Grusendorf	R	94
Roberto Gutierrez	D	41
Pat Haggerty	R	78
Peggy Hamric	R	126
Rick Hardcastle	R	68
Will Hartnett	R	114
Judy Hawley	D	31
Talmadge L. Heflin	R	149
Paul J. Hilbert	R	150
Harvey Hilderbran	R	53
Fred Hill	R	112
Juan (Chuy) Hinojosa	D	40
Scott Hochberg	D	132
Terri Hodge	D	100
Mark Homer	D	3
Ruben Hope	R	16
Charlie Howard	R	26
Bob Hunter	R	71
Suzanna Gratia Hupp	R	54
Carl H. Isett	R	84
Kyle Janek	R	134
Charles B. Jones	R	13
Delwin Jones	R	83
Jesse Jones	D	110
Robert Junell	D	72
Terry Keel	R	47
Jim Keffer	R	60
Phil King	R	61
Tracy O. King	D	43
Mike Krusee	R	52

House Members	Party	Dist.
Edmund Kuempel	R	45
James E. (Pete) Laney	D	85
David Lengefeld	D	59
Glenn O. Lewis	D	95
Ron E. Lewis	D	19
John A. Longoria	D	117
Vilma Luna	D	33
Jerry Madden	R	67
Ken Marchant	R	99
Glenn Maxey	D	51
Brian McCall	R	66
Ruth Jones McClendon	D	120
Jim McReynolds	D	17
Tommy Merritt	R	7
Joe Moreno	D	143
Paul C. Moreno	D	77
Geanie W. Morrison	R	30
Anna Mowery	R	97
Elliott Naishtat	D	49
Manny Najera	D	75
Joe Nixon	R	133
Rick Noriega	D	145
Rene O. Oliveira	D	37
Dora Olivo	D	27
Sue Palmer	R	89
Joseph C. Pickett	D	79
Jim Pitts	R	10
Robert R. Puente	D	119
Tom Ramsay	D	2
Irma Rangel	D	35
Arthur (Art) Reyna	D	125
Elivra Reyna	R	101
Alec Rhodes	D	46
Allan B. Ritter	D	21
Paul Sadler	D	8
Ignacio Salinas	D	44
Eugene (Gene) R. Seaman	R	32
John H. Shields	R	122
Bill Siebert	R	121
Todd Smith	R	92
John Smithee	R	86
Jim Solis	D	38
Juan F. Solis, III	D	124
Burt Solomons	R	65
Todd Staples	R	11
David Swinford	R	87
Robert E. Talton	R	144
Barry B. Telford	D	1

House Members	Party	Dist.
Senfronia Thompson	D	141
Dale B. Tillery	D	105
Vicki Truitt	R	98
Robert R. (Bob) Turner	D	73
Sylvester Turner	D	139
D. R. (Tom) Uher	D	29
Carlos Uresti	D	118
Leticia Van de Putte	D	115
Gary L. Walker	R	80
G. E. (Buddy) West	R	81
Thomas Williams	R	15
Ron Wilson	D	131
Miguel David Wise	D	39
Arlene Wohlgemuth	R	58
Steven Wolens	D	103
Beverly Woolley	R	136
Ken Yarbrough	D	138
Zeb Zbranek	D	20

HOUSE STANDING AND SPECIAL COMMITTEES

House standing committees for the 76th Texas Legislature will be established by rules adopted at the beginning of the session in January, 1999. They will be listed on the House internet site, *http://www.house.state.tx.us*. Listed below are the House committees from the 75th Texas Legislature. They are likely to continue in the 76th Legislature.

Agriculture and Livestock

Appropriations

Business and Industry

Calendars

Civil Practices

Corrections

County Affairs

Criminal Jurisprudence

Economic Development

Elections

Energy Resources

Environmental Regulation

Financial Institutions

General Investigating

Higher Education

House Administration

Human Services

Insurance

Judicial Affairs

Juvenile Justice and Family Issues

Licensing and Administrative Procedures

Land and Resource Management

Local and Consent Calendars

Natural Resources

Pensions and Investments

Public Education

Public Safety

Redistricting

State Affairs

State, Federal and International Relations

State Recreational Resources

Rules and Resolutions

Transportation

Urban Affairs

Ways and Means

Select Committee on Revenue and Public Education Funding (Special)

COMMUNICATING WITH TEXAS STATE LEGISLATORS

UNITED STATES MAIL

Correspondence to members of the legislature sent through the U.S. mail should be addressed to their respective district or capitol office addresses. District office addresses are provided on individual member pages. Some members relocate or close their district offices between legislative sessions. Mail sent to capitol offices between sessions is forwarded to members. Capitol office addresses are post office boxes identified below.

Examples of proper forms of Senate and House addresses are:

The Honorable (Full Name)
Texas Senate
P.O. Box 12068
Austin, Texas 78769

Dear Senator __________,

The Honorable (Full Name)
Texas House of Representatives
P.O. Box 2910
Austin, Texas 78769

Dear Representative __________,

ELECTRONIC MAIL

Many members of the Senate and House communicate through e-mail. Individual member pages indicate e-mail addresses for members who list them on the House and Senate internet pages.

Senate addresses take the following form:
firstname.lastname@senate.state.tx.us

House addresses take the following form:
firstname.lastname@house.state.tx.us

TELEPHONE

Telephone numbers for capitol and district offices are provided on individual member pages. Many members list numbers for both voice and fax communications. Senate capitol office voice telephone numbers reflect senate district numbers. Each Senate capitol office number is (512) 463-01 followed by the number of the district. For example, (512) 463-0101 is Senate district number one.

FINDING YOUR WAY AROUND THE CAPITOL

Offices of legislators are located in the capitol building or in the capitol extension. Capitol building office numbers take the form "Floor, Wing, Number." Room 1E.9 Capitol Building indicates the first floor, east wing, number 9. Other Capitol Building office examples:

GE.7	ground floor, east wing, office number 7
1W.10	first floor, west wing, office number 10
2 S.2	second floor, south wing, office number 2
3 N.5	third floor, north wing, office number 5

Capitol extension office numbers take the form "E, Level, Number." Room E2.706 indicates capitol extension, second level, office number 706.

Most (100) Representative offices are located in the capitol extension. Most Senate Offices are located in the main capitol complex.

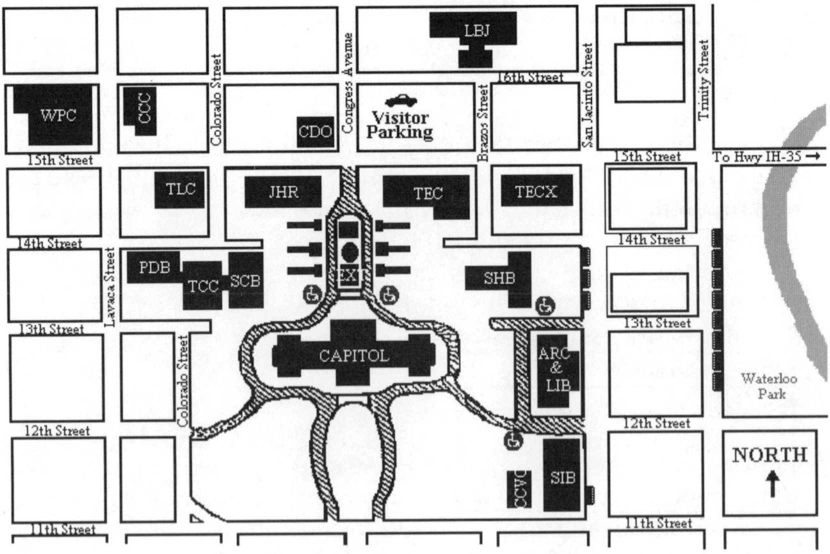

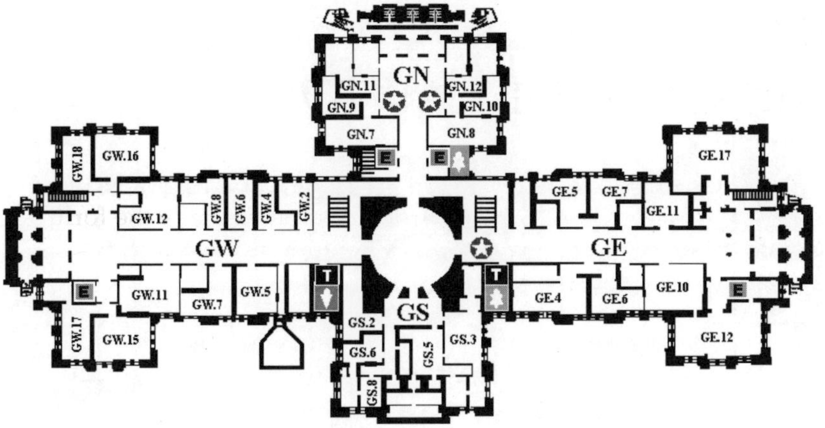

KEY TO SYMBOLS

HISTORICAL EXHIBIT	WOMENS ROOM
ELEVATORS	MENS ROOM
TELEPHONES	SECURITY (DPS)

State Capitol
Ground (Basement) Floor

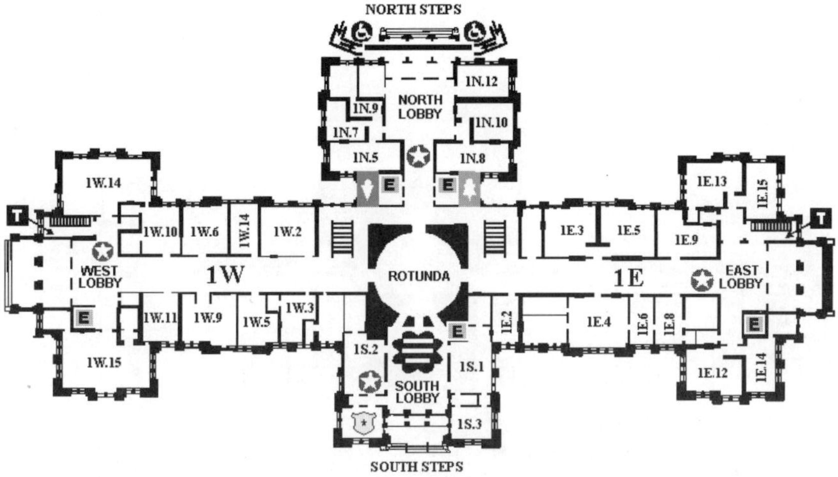

KEY TO SYMBOLS

HISTORICAL EXHIBIT	WOMENS ROOM
ELEVATORS	MENS ROOM
TELEPHONES	SECURITY (DPS)

State Capitol
First Floor

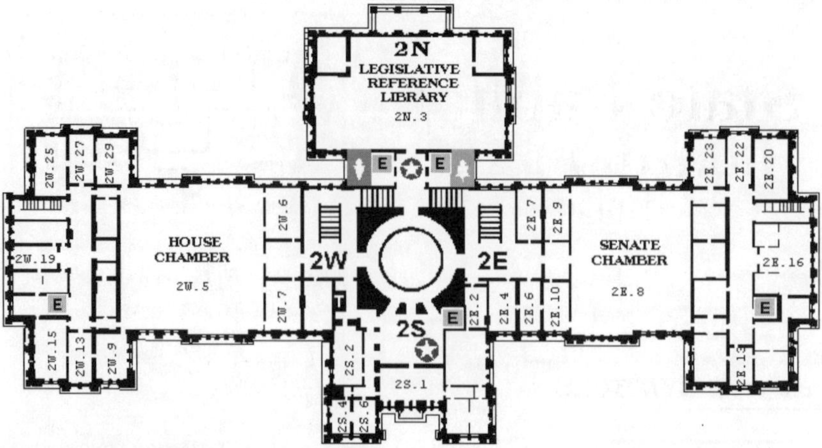

KEY TO SYMBOLS

- HISTORICAL EXHIBIT
- ELEVATORS
- TELEPHONES
- WOMENS ROOM
- MENS ROOM
- SECURITY (DPS)

State Capitol
Second Floor

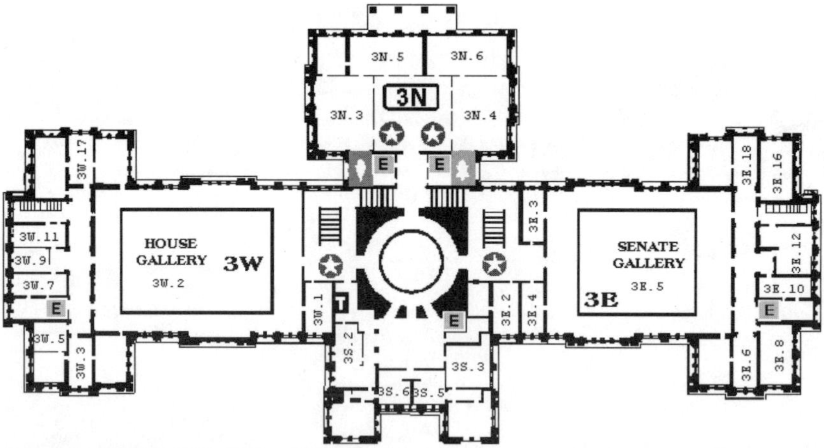

KEY TO SYMBOLS

- HISTORICAL EXHIBIT
- ELEVATORS
- TELEPHONES
- WOMENS ROOM
- MENS ROOM
- SECURITY (DPS)

State Capitol
Third Floor

State Capitol
Fourth Floor

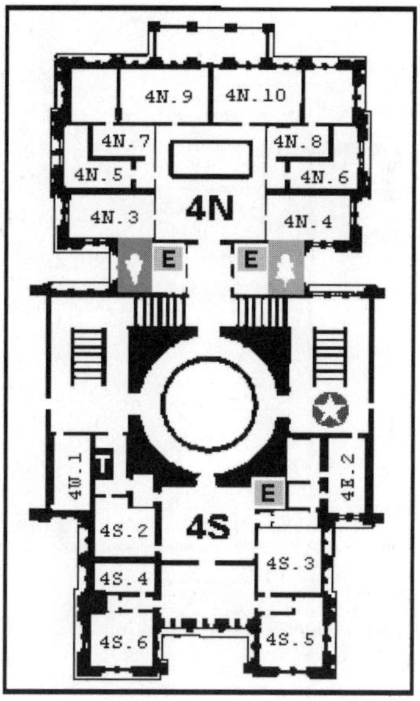

KEY TO SYMBOLS

- HISTORICAL EXHIBIT
- E ELEVATORS
- T TELEPHONES
- WOMENS ROOM
- MENS ROOM
- SECURITY (DPS)

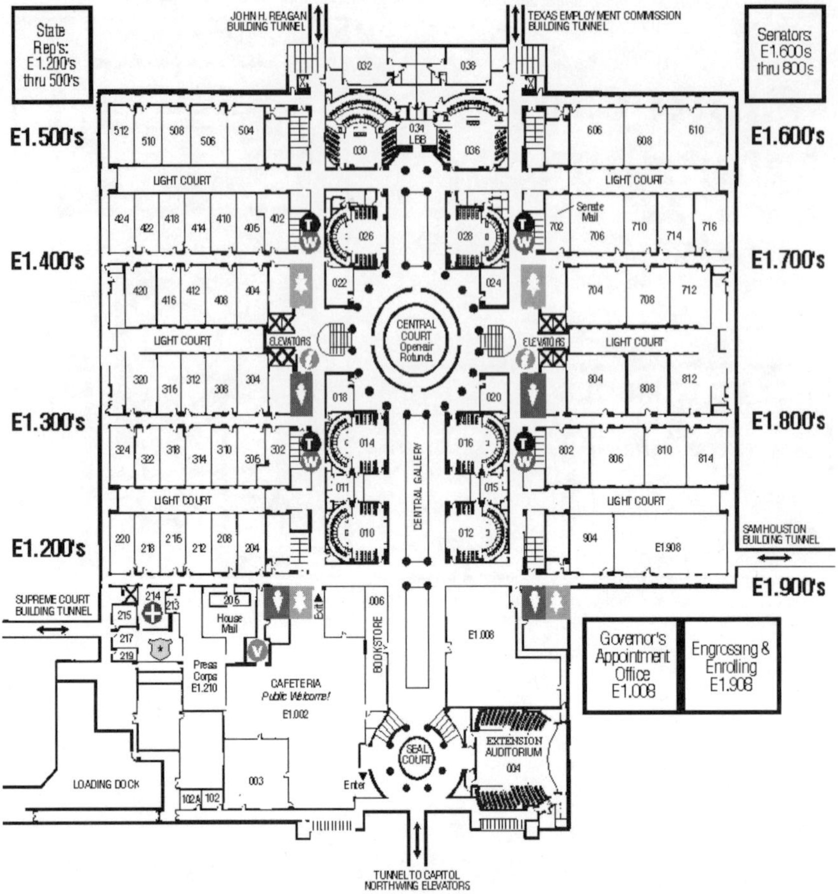

KEY TO SYMBOLS	
BUILDING DIRECTORY	SECURITY (DPS)
VENDING MACHINES & Bank of America ATM	FIRST AID
TELEPHONES	WOMENS ROOM
WATER FOUNTAINS	MENS ROOM

MEETING ROOMS CROSS REFERENCE	
010 House Hearing Room 1	012 Senate Hearing Room 1
014 House Hearing Room 2	016 Senate Hearing Room 2
026 House Hearing Room 3	028 Senate Hearing Room 3
030 House Hearing Room 4 (House Committee on Appropriations)	036 Senate Hearing Room 4 (Senate Finance Committee)
018 House Conference Room A	020 Senate Conference Room A
022 House Conference Room B	024 Senate Conference Room B

NORTH

Capitol Extension Guide

LEVEL E1

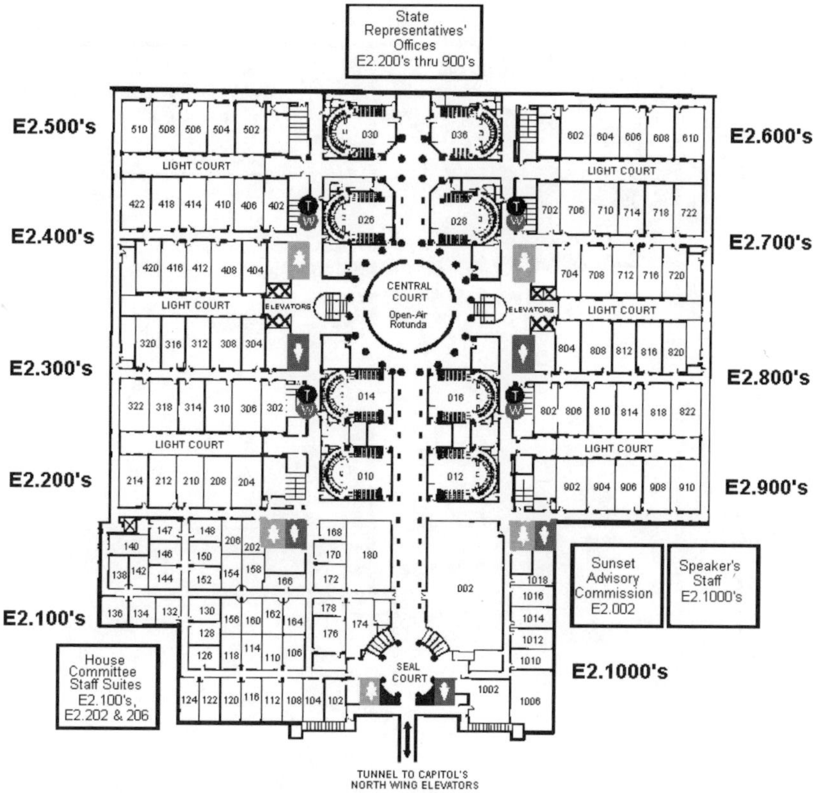

KEY TO SYMBOLS	ACCESSIBILITY	MEETING ROOMS CROSS REFERENCE	NORTH
WOMENS ROOM MENS ROOM TELEPHONES WATER FOUNTAIN	All facilities are accessible to persons with disabilities. For assistance call 463-0063.	010 House Hearing Room 5 014 House Hearing Room 6 026 House Hearing Room 7 030 House Hearing Room 8 036 House Hearing Room 9 028 House Hearing Room 10 016 House Hearing Room 11 012 House Hearing Room 12 018 House Conference Room C 022 House Conference Room D 024 House Conference Room E 020 House Conference Room F	

Capitol Extension Guide

LEVEL E2

Exhibit Space

Capitol Extension Level E2

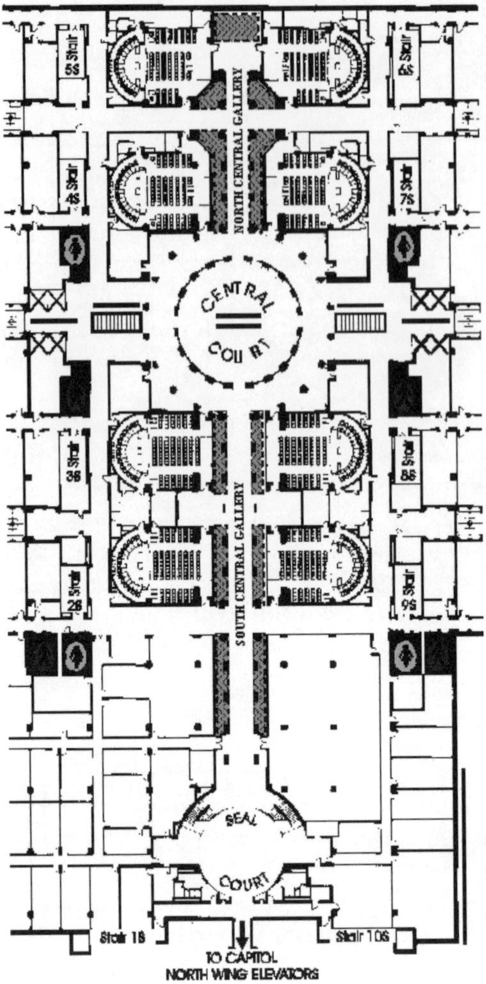

KEY

Areas Available for Exhibits

Public Restrooms

WHAT'S NEW IN THE 1999 LEGISLATURE

Since the mid-1970s, when the Republicans began to increase their strength in the Texas Legislature and gained control of the governor's office, the Texas House and Senate have operated on a bipartisan basis. Even though the Republicans were in a minority, many served as chairs of standing committees. Cooperation between the Democratic legislative leaders and Republican governors and legislators has been common. While these men and women were of different political parties, philosophically most were conservatives, and this fact made cooperation easier.

As was noted previously, the 75th session (1997) of the Texas Legislature marked the first time in over 100 years that the Republican party had controlled the Senate. In 1999, the Republicans retained control of the Senate by a single seat, down one seat from the 1997 session. The more significant change is that, for the first time in 123 years, there is a Republican Lt. Governor, Rick Perry. Most of the power of the Lt. Governor is derived from Senate rules adopted at the beginning of each legislative session. In the past, Senate rules have given the Lt. Governor a great deal of influence in shaping state policy and influencing laws that may be passed by the Senate. Senate rules have given the Lt. Governor the power to set up standing and special committees, to name committee members and chairs, to assign bills to committees for consideration, and to decide all parliamentary questions. An important issue for the new Texas Senate to decide is how much of the traditional powers of the Lt. Governor will be given to the new Republican Lt. Governor. A number of senators have indicated that they are inclined to continue to give the Lt. Governor most, if not all, of these powers.

During the 1997 session, under Lt. Governor Bob Bullock, the Senate operated on a bipartisan basis. Bullock gave Republicans a majority of the seats on 10 of 13 standing committees. Republicans were chairs of 5 of these 13 committees. It remains to be seen whether Lt. Governor Perry will continue the practice of bipartisan leadership and cooperation.

The leader of the Texas House of Representative is the 26-year veteran Democrat Pete Laney, who is serving his fourth term as Speaker. House rules give the Speaker tremendous powers to appoint committee chairs and the membership of committees and to assign bills to committees. Speaker Laney has appointed Republicans to significant committee positions in past sessions. However, bipartisan cooperation may have been strained by Republican electoral challenges to the Speaker and significant Democratic leaders in 1996 and 1998. Only time will tell if the degree of bipartisan cooperation that has characterized past

House sessions will prevail in the 76th session.

During the 1995 and 1997 sessions, cooperation between Senate and House leadership and the governor was noteworthy. Some have characterized these sessions as two of the least controversial and most cooperative in memory. This was due, in part, to the noncontroversial agenda outlined by newly elected Governor Bush. In 1995 he called for strengthening local control of schools, getting tough on juvenile crime, and implementing welfare and lawsuit reforms. These were agenda items easily embraced by legislators, largely because the governor let them determine the details of legislation.

In 1997, Governor Bush proposed reducing taxes as a key use of a $1.7 billion budget surplus. The legislature passed part of the Governor Bush's proposal. This tax reform led to a reduction in local school property taxes for some homeowners. However, actions taken by a number of school districts resulted in an increase in property taxes for other homeowners.

Governor Bush's agenda for the 1999 session will again propose using much of a projected $3.1 budget surplus to improve primary and secondary education and to reduce local property taxes. Most candidates for statewide office and most candidates for the Texas House and Senate emphasized that improving local schools was the most important issue in Texas. Most also included fiscal responsibility among their campaign pledges. Thus, it is likely that increased funding for education and some form of tax reduction will be passed in the 1999 session.

Governor Bush won 69 percent of the popular vote in the 1998 election. His coattails and a very low voter turnout helped Republicans sweep all the statewide positions on the ballot. However, the partisan composition of the 1999 Texas Legislature does not reflect the Republican success in 1998. This is because the large majority of legislative districts are drawn to favor strongly one political party: some to favor Democrats, others to favor Republicans. Of 15 senators elected in 1998, 11 faced no opponent from the other major party in the general election. The large majority of house candidates, 97 of 150, also faced no opponent from the other major party. Members of the 1999 Texas Legislature were elected, in the main, from safe and highly partisan districts. Within each of the two chambers, there are nearly equal numbers of Republicans and Democrats. Were the Texas Legislature to operate exclusively on a strictly partisan basis, the result would probably be organizational gridlock. Texas Legislators value highly their traditions of bipartisan leadership and cooperation. They will seek to continue these practices in 1999.

PART II
District and Member Pages

The Texas Senate

STATE OF TEXAS

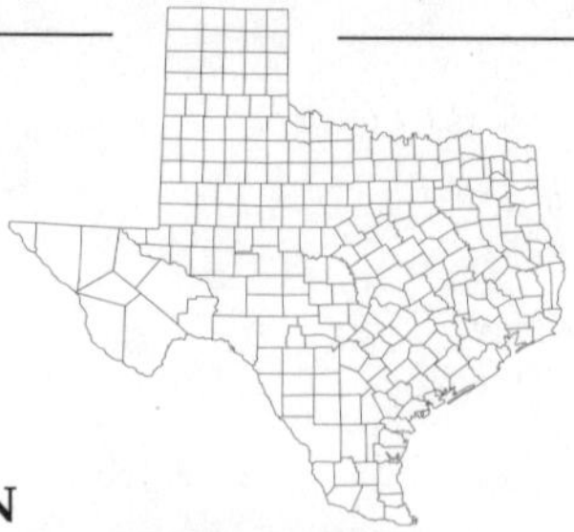

DEMOGRAPHIC INFORMATION

Population

Total	16,940,580
Anglo	59.7%
Black	13.4%
Hispanic	25.1%
Others	2.2%

Education

High School Graduates	72.1%
College Graduates	20.3%

Age of Population

5 years or less	9.8%
6-17 years	18.7%
18-64 years	61.5%
65 or older	10.1%

Wealth and Urbanization

Per capita Income	$12,904
Avg. House Value	$73,543
Percent Poverty	18.1%
Public Assistance	6.7%
Percent Urban	80.3%

Employed

Percent Employed	92.9%
Private Sector	76.7%

Household Types

Family households	85.8%
Non-family households	11.9%
Single-parent families	21.5%
Both parents working	61.0%

STATE ELECTION DATA

Lt. Governor 1996

NA

President 1996

Bill Clinton (D)	47.3%
Bob Dole (R)	52.7%

Composite Party Vote 1996

Democratic	46.4%
Republican	52.9%

Registered Voters 1996	**10,554,082**
Turnout	5,611,644
Percent of registered voting	53.2%

Lt. Governor 1998

John Sharp (D)	48.0%
Rick Perry (R)	50.9%
Anthony Garcia (L)	1.8%

Governor 1998

Gary Mauro (D)	30.9%
George W. Bush (R)	68.6%
Lester. R. Turlington, Jr. (L)	0.6%
Susan Lee Solar (W-I)	0.0%

Registered Voters 1998	**11,538,235**
Turnout	3,745,925
Percent of registered voting	32.5%

Lt. Governor
Rick Perry (R)

Senate Office
Room 2E.13, Capitol Building
Austin, Texas 78701
(512) 463-0001

Personal

Year of birth	1951
Family	Married to Anita Perry, two children
Education	Texas A&M University, B.S.
Occupation	Rancher/Lt. Governor
Religion	Methodist
State legislative service	House 1973 to 1978

ELECTORAL HISTORY

	1994	1996	1998
Primary Election Opponent(s)	NA	NA	No
General Election Opponent(s)	NA	NA	Dem

Senate District 1

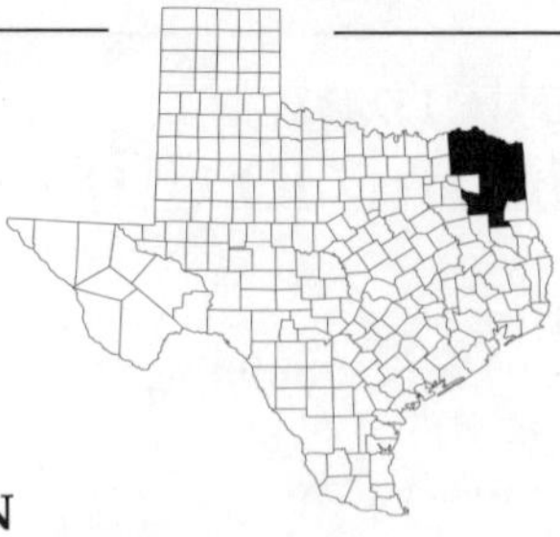

COUNTIES IN DISTRICT

Bowie, Camp, Cass, Delta, Franklin, Gregg, Harrison, Hopkins, Lamar, Marion, Morris, Red River, Rusk, Smith (part), Titus, Upshur

DEMOGRAPHIC INFORMATION

Population	
Total	566,151
Anglo	78.4%
Black	18.0%
Hispanic	15.5%
Others	2.9%

Wealth and Urbanization	
Per capita Income	$11,467
Avg. House Value	$55,039
Percent Poverty	18.3%
Public Assistance	8.2%
Percent Urban	51.8%

Education	
High School Graduates	70.9%
College Graduates	14.5%

Employed	
Percent Employed	92.9%
Private Sector	75.5%

Age of Population	
5 years or less	8.6%
6-17 years	18.9%
18-64 years	57.7%
65 or older	15.2%

Household Types	
Family households	87.0%
Non-family households	11.1%
Single-parent families	20.8%
Both parents working	61.9%

HOUSE DISTRICTS IN SENATORIAL DISTRICT

Dist 1 Barry B. Telford (D)
Dist 2 Tom Ramsay (D)
Dist 3 Mark Homer (D)
Dist 5 Bob Glaze (D)
Dist 6 Leo Berman (R)
Dist 7 Tommy Merritt (R)
Dist 8 Paul Sadler (D)

DISTRICT ELECTION DATA

Senate 1996

NA

Senate 1998

Bill Ratliff (R)	100%

President 1996	
Bill Clinton (D)	45.9%
Bob Dole (R)	54.1%

Composite Party Vote 1994	
Democratic	49.6%
Republican	50.4%

Registered Voters 1996	371,500
Turnout	206,188
Percent of registered voting	55.5%

Senate District 1
Senator Bill Ratliff (R)

Senate Office
(512) 463-0101

District Office
110 South Madison
Mount Pleasant, Texas 75456
(903) 572-1887

Personal

Year of birth	1936
Family	Married to Sally Ratliff, three children
Education	University of Texas, B.S.
Occupation	Consulting engineer
Religion	Methodist
State legislative service	Senate 1989 to present

COMMITTEE ASSIGNMENT HISTORY

1997 Administration, Education, Finance (Chair), International Relations, Trade and Technology
1995 Education (Chair), Finance, Natural Resources
1993 Education (Chair), Finance, Natural Resources
1991 Education, Finance, Natural Resources
1989 Economic Development, Intergovernmental Relations, Natural Resources

BILL PASSAGE RATES, 1997

	Total	Passed Legislature	Pct. Passed Legislature
Authored	48	22	46%
Sponsored	34	31	91%
Amendments	24	19	79%

ELECTORAL HISTORY IN CURRENT DISTRICT

	1994	1996	1998
Primary Election Opponent(s)	No	NA	No
General Election Opponent(s)	Dem	NA	No

Senate District 2

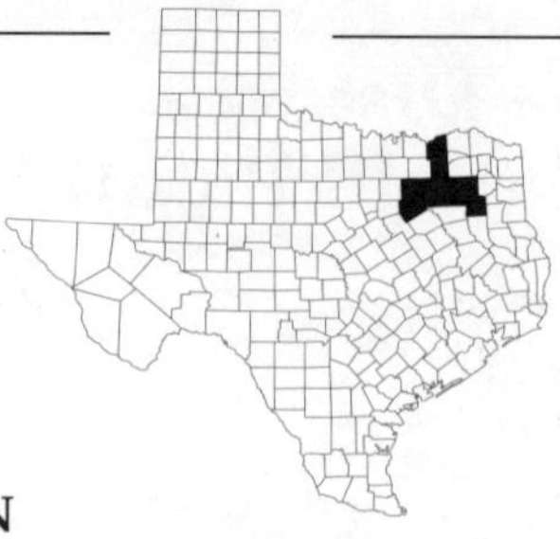

COUNTIES IN DISTRICT

Dallas (part), Ellis (part), Fannin, Hunt, Kaufman, Rains, Rockwall (part), Smith (part), Van Zant, Wood

DEMOGRAPHIC INFORMATION

Population

Total	566,981
Anglo	66.8%
Black	16.4%
Hispanic	15.5%
Others	1.6%

Education

High School Graduates	65.8%
College Graduates	14.6%

Age of Population

5 years or less	9.4%
6-17 years	17.8%
18-64 years	60.3%
65 or older	12.5%

Wealth and Urbanization

Per capita Income	$11,454
Avg. House Value	$61,545
Percent Poverty	19.3%
Public Assistance	6.9%
Percent Urban	63.6%

Employed

Percent Employed	92.5%
Private Sector	78.8%

Household Types

Family households	84.2%
Non-family households	13.6%
Single-parent families	23.2%
Both parents working	62.8%

HOUSE DISTRICTS IN SENATORIAL DISTRICT

Dist 2 Tom Ramsay (D)
Dist 3 Mark Homer (D)
Dist 4 Betty Brown (R)
Dist 5 Bob Glaze (D)
Dist 6 Leo Berman (R)
Dist 10 Jim Pitts (R)
Dist 63 Mary Denny (R)
Dist 100 Terri Hodge (D)
Dist 103 Steven Wolens (D)
Dist 104 Domingo Garcia (D)
Dist 105 Dale B. Tillery (D)
Dist 107 Harryette Ehrhardt (D)
Dist 109 Helen Giddings (D)

DISTRICT ELECTION DATA

Senate 1996

David Cain (D)	52.2%
Bob Reese (R)	47.8%

President 1996

Bill Clinton (D)	51.9%
Bob Dole (R)	48.1%

Composite Party Vote 1994

Democratic	52.9%
Republican	46.4%

Registered Voters 1996	**322,216**
Turnout	166,684
Percent of registered voting	51.7%

Senate 1998

NA

Senate District 2
Senator David Cain (D)

Senate Office
(512) 463-0102
(512) 463-7202 (Fax)

District Office
6301 Gaston Avenue, Suite 355
Dallas, Texas 75214
(214) 826-0160

Personal

Year of birth	1947
Family	Married to Sally Cain, two children
Education	University of Texas, J.D.
Occupation	Attorney
Religion	Methodist
State legislative service	House 1977-94; Senate 1995 to present

COMMITTEE ASSIGNMENT HISTORY

1997 Economic Development (Vice-Chair), Intergovernmental Relations, Jurisprudence, State Affairs

1995 Intergovernmental Relations, International Relations, Trade and Technology, Jurisprudence, State Affairs

BILL PASSAGE RATES, 1997

	Total	Passed Legislature	Pct. Passed Legislature
Authored	76	28	37%
Sponsored	49	47	96%
Amendments	25	24	96%

ELECTORAL HISTORY IN CURRENT DISTRICT

	1994	1996	1998
Primary Election Opponent(s)	No	No	NA
General Election Opponent(s)	Rep	Rep	NA

Senate District 3

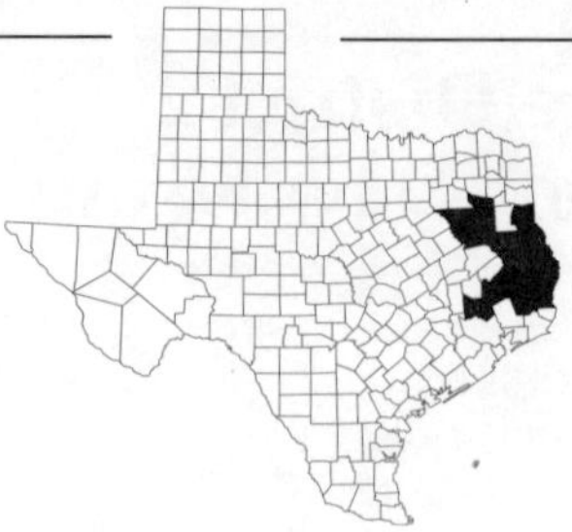

COUNTIES IN DISTRICT

Anderson, Angelina, Cherokee, Hardin, Henderson, Jasper, Montgomery (part), Nacogdoches, Newton, Panola, Polk, Sabine, San Augustine, San Jacinto, Shelby, Smith (part), Tyler

DEMOGRAPHIC INFORMATION

Population		**Wealth and Urbanization**	
Total	566,895	Per capita Income	$10,663
Anglo	80.3%	Avg. House Value	$55,989
Black	14.2%	Percent Poverty	19.3%
Hispanic	4.9%	Public Assistance	8.1%
Others	0.7%	Percent Urban	31.4%

Education		**Employed**	
High School Graduates	66.3%	Percent Employed	92.7%
College Graduates	11.7%	Private Sector	72.6%

Age of Population		**Household Types**	
5 years or less	8.1%	Family households	85.6%
6-17 years	18.8%	Non-family households	10.5%
18-64 years	58.7%	Single-parent families	20.1%
65 or older	15.2%	Both parents working	58.6%

HOUSE DISTRICTS IN SENATORIAL DISTRICT

Dist 6 Leo Berman (R)	Dist 12 Clyde Alexander (D)	Dist 18 Dan Ellis (D)
Dist 8 Paul Sadler (D)	Dist 15 Thomas Williams (R)	Dist 19 Ron E. Lewis (D)
Dist 9 Wayne Christian (R)	Dist 16 Ruben Hope (R)	Dist 20 Zeb Zbranek (D)
Dist 11 Todd Staples (R)	Dist 17 Jim McReynolds (D)	Dist 100 Terri Hodge (D)

DISTRICT ELECTION DATA

Senate 1996	
Jerry K. Johnson (D)	49.9%
Drew Nixon (R)	50.2%

President 1996	
Bill Clinton (D)	44.9%
Bob Dole (R)	55.1%

Composite Party Vote 1994	
Democratic	49.8%
Republican	50.2%

Registered Voters 1996	**394,530**
Turnout	220,798
Percent of registered voting	56.0%

Senate 1998

NA

Senate District 3
Senator Drew Nixon (R)

Senate Office
(512) 463-0103
Drew.Nixon@senate.state.tx.us

District Office
1509 West Panola Street
Carthage, Texas 75633
(903) 694-2047

Personal

Year of birth	1959
Family	Married to Cheryl Nixon, no children
Education	Stephen F. Austin State University, B.B.A.
Occupation	CPA, securities/insurance agency, real estate
Religion	Baptist
State legislative service	Senate 1995 to present

COMMITTEE ASSIGNMENT HISTORY

1997 Health and Human Services, Natural Resources, Nominations, State Affairs (Vice-Chair)
1995 Health and Human Services, Natural Resources, State Affairs

BILL PASSAGE RATES, 1997

	Total	Passed Legislature	Pct. Passed Legislature
Authored	31	4	13%
Sponsored	11	11	100%
Amendments	42	38	90%

ELECTORAL HISTORY IN CURRENT DISTRICT

	1994	1996	1998
Primary Election Opponent(s)	No	No	NA
General Election Opponent(s)	Dem	Dem	NA

Senate District 4

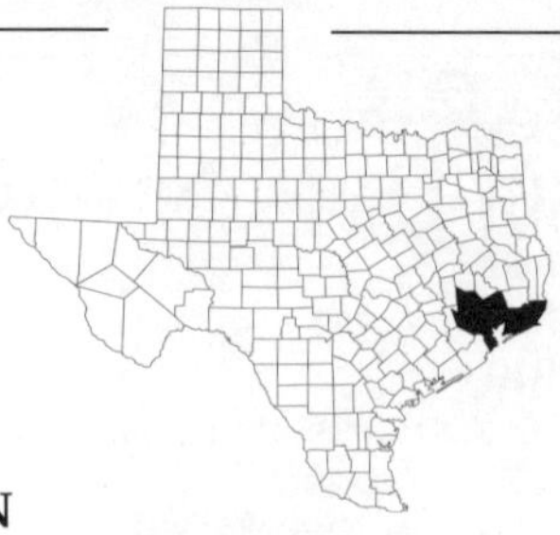

COUNTIES IN DISTRICT
Chambers, Galveston (part), Harris (part), Jefferson, Liberty, Montgomery (part), Orange

DEMOGRAPHIC INFORMATION

Population

Total	551,901
Anglo	75.9%
Black	17.4%
Hispanic	5.3%
Others	1.6%

Wealth and Urbanization

Per capita Income	$12,687
Avg. House Value	$58,651
Percent Poverty	15.9%
Public Assistance	7.2%
Percent Urban	64.6%

Education

High School Graduates	73.8%
College Graduates	15.8%

Employed

Percent Employed	92.9%
Private Sector	80.2%

Age of Population

5 years or less	9.3%
6-17 years	19.5%
18-64 years	60.0%
65 or older	11.2%

Household Types

Family households	89.0%
Non-family households	9.7%
Single-parent families	20.1%
Both parents working	58.0%

HOUSE DISTRICTS IN SENATORIAL DISTRICT

Dist 15 Thomas Williams (R)
Dist 16 Ruben Hope (R)
Dist 19 Ron E. Lewis (D)
Dist 20 Zeb Zbranek (D)
Dist 21 Allan B. Ritter (D)
Dist 22 Joseph D. Deshotel (D)
Dist 23 Patricia Gray (D)

DISTRICT ELECTION DATA

Senate 1996
NA

Senate 1998

David Bernsen (D)	52.1%
Michael Galloway (R)	47.9%

President 1996

Bill Clinton (D)	46.8%
Bob Dole (R)	53.2%

Composite Party Vote 1994

Democratic	44.4%
Republican	55.2%

Registered Voters 1996	**377,575**
Turnout	205,231
Percent of registered voting	54.4%

Senate District 4
Senator David Bernsen (D)

Senate Office
(512) 463-0104

District Office
P.O. Box 822
Beaumont, Texas 77704-0822
(409) 839-4444

Personal

Year of birth	1950
Family	Married to Dinah Bernsen, two children
Education	Lamar University, B.B.A.
	St. Mary's University, J.D.
Occupation	Attorney
Religion	Methodist
State legislative service	Senate 1999 to present

COMMITTEE ASSIGNMENT HISTORY

BILL PASSAGE RATES, 1997

	Total	Passed Legislature	Pct. Passed Legislature
Authored	NA	NA	NA
Sponsored	NA	NA	NA
Amendments	NA	NA	NA

ELECTORAL HISTORY IN CURRENT DISTRICT

	1994	1994	1996
Primary Election Opponent(s)	NA	NA	No
General Election Opponent(s)	NA	NA	Rep

Senate District 5

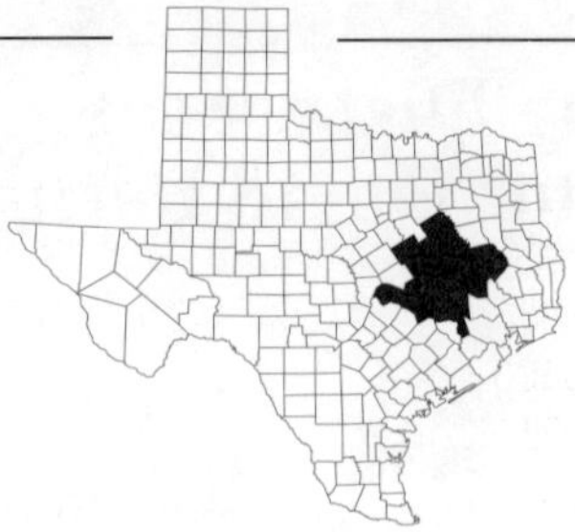

COUNTIES IN DISTRICT

Brazos, Burleson, Falls, Freestone, Grimes, Houston, Lee, Leon, Limestone, McLennan (part), Madison, Milam, Navarro, Robertson, Trinity, Walker, Waller, Washington, Williamson (part)

DEMOGRAPHIC INFORMATION

Population	
Total	551,652
Anglo	70.4%
Black	17.2%
Hispanic	11.3%
Others	1.4%

Wealth and Urbanization	
Per capita Income	$10,413
Avg. House Value	$57,067
Percent Poverty	22.1%
Public Assistance	7.6%
Percent Urban	56.5%

Education	
High School Graduates	68.2%
College Graduates	17.0%

Employed	
Percent Employed	93.8%
Private Sector	65.7%

Age of Population	
5 years or less	8.5%
6-17 years	16.5%
18-64 years	61.8%
65 or older	13.2%

Household Types	
Family households	77.5%
Non-family households	14.1%
Single-parent families	20.7%
Both parents working	67.3%

HOUSE DISTRICTS IN SENATORIAL DISTRICT

Dist 11 Todd Staples (R)
Dist 12 Clyde Alexander (D)
Dist 13 Charles B. Jones (R)
Dist 14 Fred Brown (R)
Dist 15 Thomas Williams (R)
Dist 17 Jim McReynolds (D)
Dist 18 Dan Ellis (D)
Dist 52 Mike Krusee (R)
Dist 53 Harvey Hilderbran (R)
Dist 56 Kip Averitt (R)
Dist 57 Jim Dunnam (D)

DISTRICT ELECTION DATA

Senate 1996

NA

Senate 1998	
Mary M. Moore (D)	44.4%
Steve Ogden (R)	55.6%

President 1996	
Bill Clinton (D)	46.5%
Bob Dole (R)	53.5%

Composite Party Vote 1994	
Democratic	50.4%
Republican	49.6%

Registered Voters 1996	**341,188**
Turnout	191,868
Percent of registered voting	56.2%

Senate District 5
Senator Steve Ogden (R)

Senate Office
(512) 463-0105
(512) 463-0216 (Fax)

District Office
2700 East Bypass #1400
College Station, Texas 77845
(409) 694-2609

Personal

Year of birth	1950
Family	Married to Beverly Ogden, three children
Education	United States Naval Academy, B.S., Foreign Affairs Texas A&M University, M.B.A.
Occupation	Oil and gas producer
Religion	Catholic
State legislative service	House 1991-97; Senate 1997 to present

COMMITTEE ASSIGNMENT HISTORY

1997 Intergovernmental Relations, International Relations, Trade and Technology, Jurisprudence, Natural Resources

BILL PASSAGE RATES, 1997

	Total	Passed Legislature	Pct. Passed Legislature
Authored	31	8	26%
Sponsored	11	11	100%
Amendments	41	36	88%

ELECTORAL HISTORY IN CURRENT DISTRICT

	1994	1997	1998
Primary Election Opponent(s)	NA	NA	No
General Election Opponent(s)	NA	NA	Dem
Special Election Opponent(s)	NA	Dem	NA

Senate District 6

COUNTIES IN DISTRICT

Harris (part)

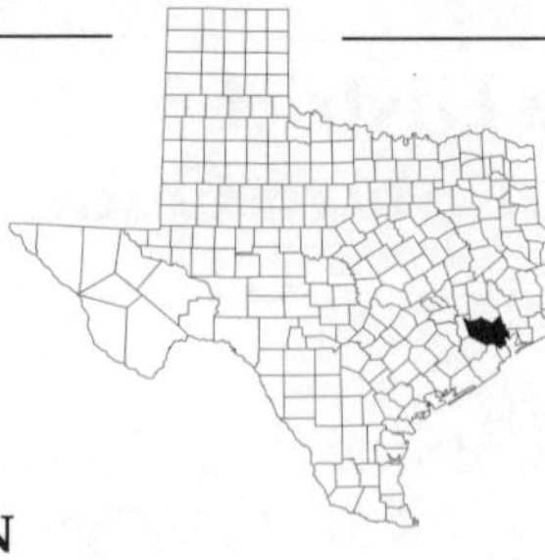

DEMOGRAPHIC INFORMATION

Population	
Total	512,552
Anglo	27.7%
Black	10.3%
Hispanic	60.4%
Others	2.1%

Wealth and Urbanization	
Per capita Income	$9,151
Avg. House Value	$49,025
Percent Poverty	28.2%
Public Assistance	8.4%
Percent Urban	100.0%

Education	
High School Graduates	48.0%
College Graduates	10.6%

Employed	
Percent Employed	90.3%
Private Sector	85.3%

Age of Population	
5 years or less	11.7%
6-17 years	19.9%
18-64 years	60.5%
65 or older	7.9%

Household Types	
Family households	86.9%
Non-family households	12.5%
Single-parent families	24.4%
Both parents working	49.4%

HOUSE DISTRICTS IN SENATORIAL DISTRICT

Dist 128	Fred M. Bosse (D)	Dist 137	Debra Danburg (D)	Dist 143	Gerard Torres (D)
Dist 129	John Davis (R)	Dist 138	Ken Yarbrough (D)	Dist 144	Robert E. Talton (R)
Dist 133	Joe M. Nixon (R)	Dist 140	Kevin Bailey (D)	Dist 145	Rick Noriega (D)
Dist 134	Kyle Janek (R)	Dist 141	Senfronia Thompson (D)	Dist 147	Garnet F. Coleman (D)
Dist 136	Beverly Woolley (R)	Dist 142	Harold V. Dutton Jr. (D)	Dist 148	Jessica Cristina Farrar (D)

DISTRICT ELECTION DATA

Senate 1996

NA

Senate 1998	
Mario V. Gallegos, Jr. (D)	100%

President 1996	
Bill Clinton (D)	67.2%
Bob Dole (R)	32.8%

Composite Party Vote 1994	
Democratic	61.7%
Republican	36.9%

Registered Voters 1996	**208,214**
Turnout	93,747
Percent of registered voting	45.0%

Senate District 6
Senator Mario V. Gallegos, Jr. (D)

Senate Office
(512) 463-0106
(512) 463-0346 (Fax)
Mario.Gallegos@senate.state.tx.us

District Office
P.O. Box 41
2205 Clinton Drive
Galena Park, Texas 77547
(713) 678-8600
(713) 678-7080 (Fax)

Personal

Year of birth	1950
Family	Married to Theresa Gallegos, three children
Education	University of Houston
Occupation	Senior captain, Houston Fire Department
Religion	Catholic
State legislative service	House 1991-94, Senate 1995 to present

COMMITTEE ASSIGNMENT HISTORY

1997 Health and Human Services, Intergovernmental Relations, Nominations, State Affairs

1995 Health and Human Services, Intergovernmental Relations, International Relations, Trade and Technology, State Affairs

BILL PASSAGE RATES, 1997

	Total	Passed Legislature	Pct. Passed Legislature
Authored	63	13	21%
Sponsored	22	15	68%
Amendments	16	13	81%

ELECTORAL HISTORY IN CURRENT DISTRICT

	1994	1996	1998
Primary Election Opponent(s)	Yes	NA	No
General Election Opponent(s)	No	NA	No

Senate District 7

COUNTIES IN DISTRICT

Harris (part)

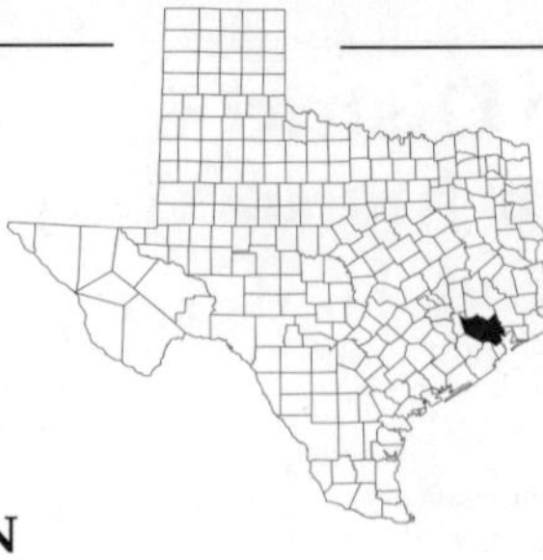

DEMOGRAPHIC INFORMATION

Population

Total	566,682
Anglo	82.6%
Black	5.1%
Hispanic	10.0%
Others	4.1%

Education

High School Graduates	90.3%
College Graduates	37.8%

Age of Population

5 years or less	10.4%
6-17 years	19.5%
18-64 years	65.6%
65 or older	4.6%

Wealth and Urbanization

Per capita Income	$20,597
Avg. House Value	$113,504
Percent Poverty	5.2%
Public Assistance	1.9%
Percent Urban	88.4%

Employed

Percent Employed	96.0%
Private Sector	83.3%

Household Types

Family households	89.6%
Non-family households	9.9%
Single-parent families	15.4%
Both parents working	63.0%

HOUSE DISTRICTS IN SENATORIAL DISTRICT

Dist 126 Peggy Hamric (R)
Dist 127 Joe Crabb (R)
Dist 130 John Culberson (R)
Dist 133 Joe M. Nixon (R)
Dist 134 Kyle Janek (R)
Dist 135 Gary Elkins (R)
Dist 136 Beverly Woolley (R)
Dist 141 Senfronia Thompson (D)
Dist 142 Harold V. Dutton Jr. (D)
Dist 148 Jessica Cristina Farrar (D)
Dist 150 Paul J. Hilbert (R)

DISTRICT ELECTION DATA

Senate 1996

Jon Lindsay (R)	100.0%

President 1996

Bill Clinton (D)	27.0%
Bob Dole (R)	73.0%

Composite Party Vote 1994

Democratic	24.8%
Republican	73.7%

Registered Voters 1996	**390,044**
Turnout	242,429
Percent of registered voting	62.2%

Senate 1998

NA

Senate District 7
Senator Jon Lindsay (R)

Senate Office
(512) 463-0107

District Office
15531 Kuykendahl
Houston, Texas 77090

Personal

Year of birth	1935
Family	Married to Tony Lindsay, two children
Education	New Mexico State, B.S., Engineering
Occupation	Consultant
Religion	Methodist
State legislative service	Senate 1997 to present

COMMITTEE ASSIGNMENT HISTORY

1997 Intergovernmental Relations, International Relations, Trade and Technology, Natural Resources, State Affairs

BILL PASSAGE RATES, 1997

	Total	Passed Legislature	Pct. Passed Legislature
Authored	30	16	53%
Sponsored	19	18	95%
Amendments	21	18	86%

ELECTORAL HISTORY IN CURRENT DISTRICT

	1994	1996	1998
Primary Election Opponent(s)	NA	Yes	NA
General Election Opponent(s)	NA	No	NA

Senate District 8

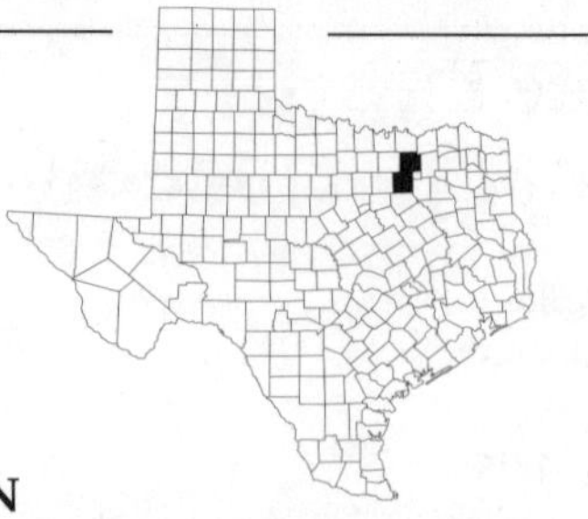

COUNTIES IN DISTRICT
Collin (part), Dallas (part)

DEMOGRAPHIC INFORMATION

Population	
Total	565,408
Anglo	81.5%
Black	4.7%
Hispanic	10.2%
Others	3.8%

Education	
High School Graduates	88.5%
College Graduates	42.5%

Age of Population	
5 years or less	9.0%
6-17 years	15.5%
18-64 years	67.9%
65 or older	7.6%

Wealth and Urbanization	
Per capita Income	$23,972
Avg. House Value	$160,121
Percent Poverty	6.9%
Public Assistance	1.9%
Percent Urban	94.0%

Employed	
Percent Employed	96.0%
Private Sector	83.3%

Household Types	
Family households	89.6%
Non-family households	9.9%
Single-parent families	15.4%
Both parents working	63.0%

HOUSE DISTRICTS IN SENATORIAL DISTRICT

Dist 63 Mary Denny (R)
Dist 66 Brian McCall (R)
Dist 67 Jerry Madden (R)
Dist 99 Ken Marchant (R)
Dist 100 Terri Hodge (D)
Dist 102 Tony Goolsby (R)
Dist 103 Steve Wolens (D)
Dist 106 Ray Allen (R)
Dist 107 Harryette Ehrhardt (D)
Dist 108 Kenn George (R)
Dist 112 Fred Hill (R)
Dist 114 Will Hartnett (R)

DISTRICT ELECTION DATA

Senate 1996	
Florence Shapiro (R)	89.8%
Randal Morgan (L)	10.2%

Senate 1998
NA

President 1996	
Bill Clinton (D)	32.1%
Bob Dole (R)	67.9%

Composite Party Vote 1994	
Democratic	30.9%
Republican	68.4%

Registered Voters 1996	**423,701**
Turnout	252,295
Percent of registered voting	59.5%

Senate District 8
Senator Florence Shapiro (R)

Senate Office
(512) 463-0108

District Office
3700 West 15th Street, Suite 100-C
Plano, Texas 75075
(214) 964-5585

Personal

Year of Birth	1948
Family	Married to Howard Shapiro, three children
Education	University of Texas, B.S., Secondary Education
Occupation	Co-owner & President, Shapiro, Small & Associates
Religion	Jewish
State legislative service	Senate 1993 to present

COMMITTEE ASSIGNMENT HISTORY

1997 Criminal Justice (Vice-Chair), Economic Development, Intergovernmental Relations, Nominations (Vice-Chair), State Affairs

1995 Criminal Justice (Vice-Chair), Economic Development, Intergovernmental Relations, Administration

1993 Economic Development, Education, Intergovernmental Relations, Administration

BILL PASSAGE RATES, 1997

	Total	Passed Legislature	Pct. Passed Legislature
Authored	69	23	33%
Sponsored	33	31	94%
Amendments	40	35	88%

ELECTORAL HISTORY IN CURRENT DISTRICT

	1994	1996	1998
Primary Election Opponent(s)	No	No	NA
General Election Opponent(s)	Lib, Ind	Lib	NA

Senate District 9

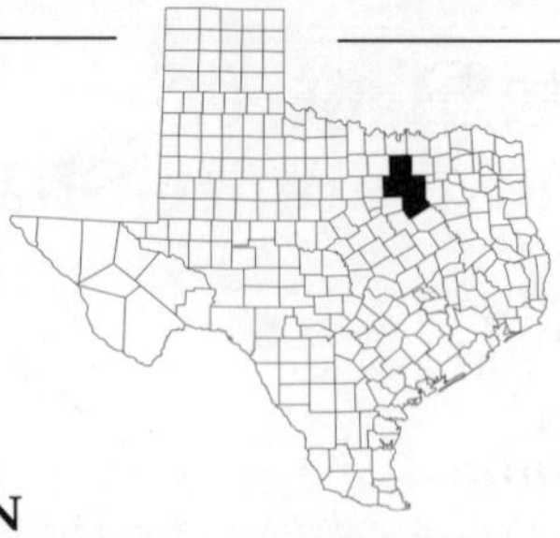

COUNTIES IN DISTRICT

Dallas (part), Denton (part), Ellis (part), Tarrant (part)

DEMOGRAPHIC INFORMATION

Population		**Wealth and Urbanization**	
Total	565,689	Per capita Income	$17,240
Anglo	81.8%	Avg. House Value	$102,506
Black	5.6%	Percent Poverty	5.8%
Hispanic	9.4%	Public Assistance	2.0%
Others	3.4%	Percent Urban	91.4%

Education		**Employed**	
High School Graduates	86.3%	Percent Employed	95.8%
College Graduates	29.8%	Private Sector	83.8%

Age of Population		**Household Types**	
5 years or less	10.5%	Family households	86.0%
6-17 years	17.2%	Non-family households	13.2%
18-64 years	67.5%	Single-parent families	15.5%
65 or older	4.7%	Both parents working	69.1%

HOUSE DISTRICTS IN SENATORIAL DISTRICT

Dist 10	Jim Pitts (R)	Dist 93	Toby Goodman (R)	Dist 106	Ray Allen (R)
Dist 63	Mary Denny (R)	Dist 98	Nancy Moffat (R)	Dist 109	Helen Giddings (D)
Dist 64	Ronny Crownover (R)	Dist 99	Ken Marchant (R)	Dist 110	Jesse Jones (D)
Dist 65	Burt Solomons (R)	Dist 103	Steven Wolens (D)	Dist 111	Yvonne Davis (D)
Dist 89	Sue Palmer (R)	Dist 104	Domingo Garcia (D)	Dist 114	Will Hartnett (R)
Dist 92	Todd Smith (R)	Dist 105	Dale B. Tillery (D)		

DISTRICT ELECTION DATA

Senate 1996

Jane Nelson (R)	100.0%

Senate 1998

NA

President 1996

Bill Clinton (D)	34.9%
Bob Dole (R)	65.1%

Composite Party Vote 1994

Democratic	32.2%
Republican	67.3%

Registered Voters 1996	**416,383**
Turnout	228,012
Percent of registered voting	54.8%

Senate District 9
Senator Jane Nelson (R)

Senate Office
(512) 463-0109

District Office
3700 Forums, Suite 107
Flower Mound, Texas 75028
(214) 724-0520

Personal

Year of birth	1951
Family	Married to J. Michael Nelson, five children
Education	University of North Texas, B.S.
Occupation	Businesswoman, former teacher
Religion	Methodist
State legislative service	Senate 1993 to present

COMMITTEE ASSIGNMENT HISTORY

1997 Criminal Justice, Finance, Health and Human Services (Vice-Chair), State Affairs
1995 Education, Health and Human Services (Vice-Chair), State Affairs, Nominations
1993 Criminal Justice, Health and Human Services, State Affairs

BILL PASSAGE RATES, 1997

	Total	Passed Legislature	Pct. Passed Legislature
Authored	76	18	24%
Sponsored	15	11	73%
Amendments	7	5	71%

ELECTORAL HISTORY IN CURRENT DISTRICT

	1994	1996	1998
Primary Election Opponent(s)	No	No	NA
General Election Opponent(s)	No	No	NA

Senate District 10

COUNTIES IN DISTRICT

Johnson (part), Parker (part), Tarrant (part)

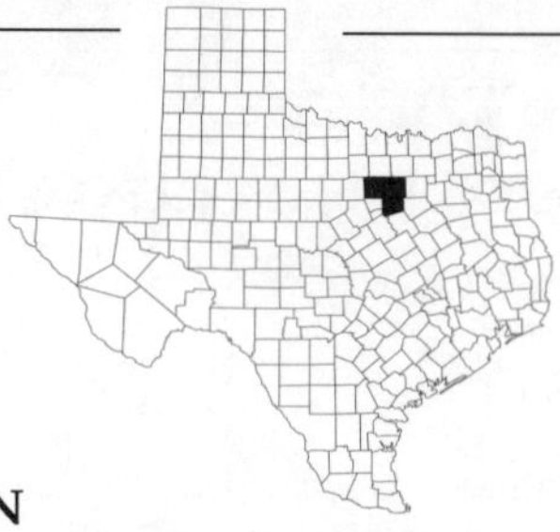

DEMOGRAPHIC INFORMATION

Population	
Total	563,436
Anglo	84.0%
Black	5.9%
Hispanic	6.9%
Others	3.3%

Education	
High School Graduates	87.3%
College Graduates	28.2%

Age of Population	
5 years or less	10.1%
6-17 years	17.2%
18-64 years	67.3%
65 or older	5.5%

Wealth and Urbanization	
Per capita Income	$16,897
Avg. House Value	$99,977
Percent Poverty	6.7%
Public Assistance	2.4%
Percent Urban	92.5%

Employed	
Percent Employed	95.4%
Private Sector	82.8%

Household Types	
Family households	86.2%
Non-family households	13.1%
Single-parent families	17.8%
Both parents working	68.3%

HOUSE DISTRICTS IN SENATORIAL DISTRICT

Dist 58 Arlene Wohlgemuth (R)
Dist 61 Phil King (R)
Dist 91 Bill G. Carter (R)
Dist 92 Todd Smith (R)
Dist 93 Toby Goodman (R)
Dist 94 Kent Grusendorf (R)
Dist 96 Kenneth(Kim) Brimer (R)
Dist 97 Anna Mowery (R)
Dist 98 Nancy Moffat (R)

DISTRICT ELECTION DATA

Senate 1996	
Chris Harris (R)	100.0%

President 1996	
Bill Clinton (D)	37.3%
Bob Dole (R)	62.7%

Composite Party Vote 1994	
Democratic	35.2%
Republican	64.8%

Registered Voters 1996	**389,096**
Turnout	219,302
Percent of registered voting	56.4%

Senate 1998

NA

Senate District 10
Senator Chris Harris (R)

Senate Office
(512) 463-0110

District Office
1309-A West Abram
Arlington, Texas 76013
(817) 261-5396

Personal

Year of birth	1948
Family	Married to Tammy Harris, four children
Education	Texas Christian University Baylor School of Law, J.D.
Occupation	Attorney
Religion	Episcopalian
State legislative service	House 1985-90, Senate 1991 to present

COMMITTEE ASSIGNMENT HISTORY

1997 Administration (Chair), Economic Development, Health and Human Services, Jurisprudence (Vice-Chair)
1995 Economic Development, Education, Jurisprudence, Administration (Chair)
1993 Economic Development, Education, International Relations, Trade and Technology, Jurisprudence (Vice-Chair)
1991 Criminal Justice, Economic Development, Health and Human Services

BILL PASSAGE RATES, 1997

	Total	Passed Legislature	Pct. Passed Legislature
Authored	125	46	37%
Sponsored	36	33	92%
Amendments	55	55	100%

ELECTORAL HISTORY IN CURRENT DISTRICT

	1994	1996	1998
Primary Election Opponent(s)	No	Yes	NA
General Election Opponent(s)	No	No	NA

Senate District 11

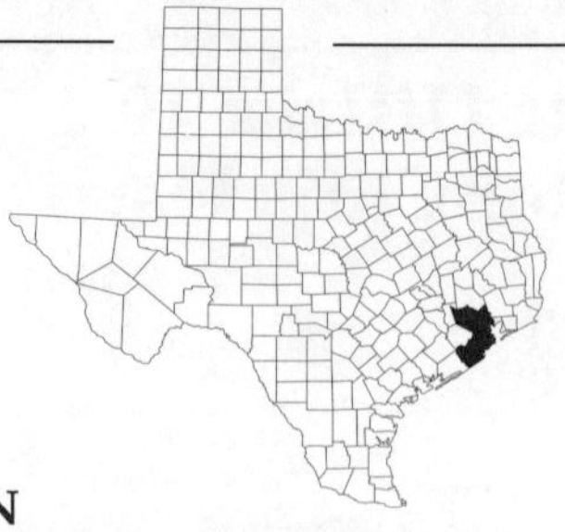

COUNTIES IN DISTRICT
Brazoria (part), Galveston (part), Harris (part)

DEMOGRAPHIC INFORMATION

Population

Total	566,744
Anglo	67.5%
Black	12.6%
Hispanic	17.8%
Others	2.4%

Wealth and Urbanization

Per capita Income	$13,873
Avg. House Value	$65,967
Percent Poverty	13.2%
Public Assistance	5.3%
Percent Urban	93.6%

Education

High School Graduates	76.1%
College Graduates	17.3%

Employed

Percent Employed	93.5%
Private Sector	79.2%

Age of Population

5 years or less	9.8%
6-17 years	19.1%
18-64 years	62.8%
65 or older	8.4%

Household Types

Family households	87.4%
Non-family households	11.6%
Single-parent families	21.9%
Both parents working	60.7%

HOUSE DISTRICTS IN SENATORIAL DISTRICT

Dist 23 Patricia Gray (D)
Dist 24 Craig Eiland (D)
Dist 25 Dennis Bonnen (R)
Dist 29 D. R. (Tom) Uher (D)
Dist 127 Joe Crabb (R)
Dist 128 Fred M. Bosse (D)
Dist 129 John Davis (R)
Dist 143 Gerard Torres (D)
Dist 144 Robert E. Talton (R)
Dist 145 Rick Noriega (D)
Dist 146 Al Edwards (D)
Dist 147 Garnet F. Coleman (D)

DISTRICT ELECTION DATA

Senate 1996
NA

Senate 1998

Edward Wesley (D)	43.0%
Mike Jackson (R)	57.0%

President 1996

Bill Clinton (D)	47.3%
Bob Dole (R)	52.7%

Composite Party Vote 1994

Democratic	42.8%
Republican	56.3%

Registered Voters 1996	**349,823**
Turnout	185,078
Percent of registered voting	52.9%

Senate District 11
Senator Mike Jackson (R)

Senate Office
(512) 463-0111

District Office
1350 NASA Rd. #1, Ste. 212
Houston, Texas 77058
(281) 333-1350

Personal

Year of birth	1953
Family	Married to Vickie Jackson, two children
Education	Attended Louisiana Tech University Attended Louisiana State University
Occupation	General contractor
Religion	Methodist
State legislative service	House 1989 to 1999; Senate 1999 to present

COMMITTEE ASSIGNMENT HISTORY
1997 NA

BILL PASSAGE RATES, 1997

	Total	Passed Legislature	Pct. Passed Legislature
Authored	NA	NA	NA
Sponsored	NA	NA	NA
Amendments	NA	NA	NA

ELECTORAL HISTORY IN CURRENT DISTRICT

	1994	1996	1998
Primary Election Opponent(s)	NA	NA	No
General Election Opponent(s)	NA	NA	Dem

Senate District 12

COUNTIES IN DISTRICT

Tarrant (part)

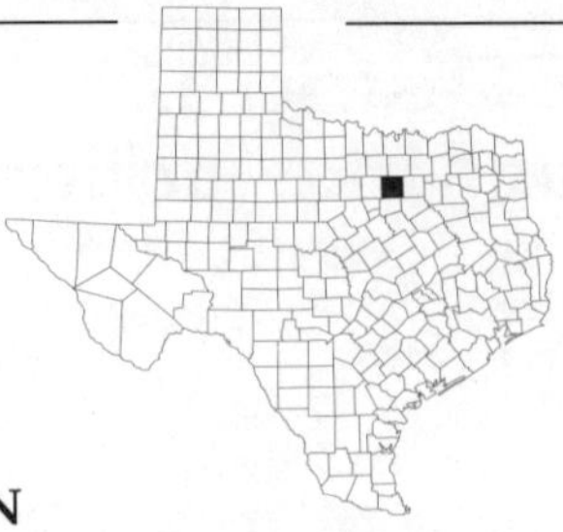

DEMOGRAPHIC INFORMATION

Population		**Wealth and Urbanization**	
Total	535,857	Per capita Income	$12,983
Anglo	61.3%	Avg. House Value	$70,579
Black	19.0%	Percent Poverty	16.4%
Hispanic	17.6%	Public Assistance	5.8%
Others	2.5%	Percent Urban	99.9%

Education		**Employed**	
High School Graduates	71.5%	Percent Employed	92.6%
College Graduates	19.0%	Private Sector	81.6%

Age of Population		**Household Types**	
5 years or less	10.0%	Family households	83.6%
6-17 years	16.8%	Non-family households	13.7%
18-64 years	61.6%	Single-parent families	26.0%
65 or older	11.5%	Both parents working	63.6%

HOUSE DISTRICTS IN SENATORIAL DISTRICT

Dist 89 Sue Palmer (R)
Dist 90 Lon Burnam (D)
Dist 91 Bill G. Carter (R)
Dist 92 Todd Smith (R)
Dist 95 Glenn O. Lewis (D)
Dist 96 Kenneth (Kim) Brimer (R)
Dist 97 Anna Mowery (R)
Dist 98 Nancy Moffat (R)

DISTRICT ELECTION DATA

Senate 1996

Mike Moncrief (D)	100.0%

Senate 1998

NA

President 1996

Bill Clinton (D)	56.2%
Bob Dole (R)	43.8%

Composite Party Vote 1994

Democratic	54.3%
Republican	45.7%

Registered Voters 1996	**301,972**
Turnout	163,372
Percent of registered voting	54.1%

Senate District 12
Senator Mike Moncrief (D)

Senate Office
(512) 463-0112
Mike.Moncrief@senate.state.tx.us

District Office
1701 River Run Road, Suite 504, Box 54
Fort Worth, Texas 76107
(817) 338-9420

Personal

Year of birth	1943
Family	Married to Rosie Moncrief, two children
Education	Tarleton State University
Occupation	Businessman
Religion	Methodist
State legislative service	House 1970-72, Senate 1991 to present

COMMITTEE ASSIGNMENT HISTORY

1997 Administration, Finance, Health and Human Services, Intergovernmental Relations

1995 Criminal Justice, Finance, Health and Human Services, Administration (Vice-Chair)

1993 Finance, Health and Human Services, Intergovernmental Relations, Administration (Vice-Chair)

1991 Health and Human Services, Intergovernmental Relations, State Affairs

BILL PASSAGE RATES, 1997

	Total	Passed Legislature	Pct. Passed Legislature
Authored	75	36	48%
Sponsored	33	31	94%
Amendments	60	55	92%

ELECTORAL HISTORY IN CURRENT DISTRICT

	1994	1996	1998
Primary Election Opponent(s)	No	No	NA
General Election Opponent(s)	No	No	NA

Senate District 13

COUNTIES IN DISTRICT

Fort Bend (part), Harris (part)

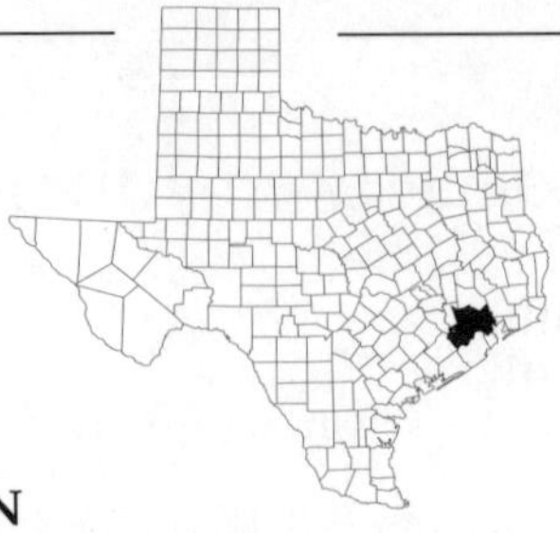

DEMOGRAPHIC INFORMATION

Population	
Total	524,038
Anglo	29.7%
Black	52.4%
Hispanic	14.8%
Others	4.0%

Education	
High School Graduates	74.0%
College Graduates	28.0%

Age of Population	
5 years or less	9.4%
6-17 years	16.2%
18-64 years	65.8%
65 or older	8.6%

Wealth and Urbanization	
Per capita Income	$14,257
Avg. House Value	$83,494
Percent Poverty	22.8%
Public Assistance	9.1%
Percent Urban	99.8%

Employed	
Percent Employed	90.2%
Private Sector	78.3%

Household Types	
Family households	79.0%
Non-family households	17.7%
Single-parent families	38.8%
Both parents working	66.6%

HOUSE DISTRICTS IN SENATORIAL DISTRICT

Dist 26 Charlie Howard (R)
Dist 27 Dora Olivo (D)
Dist 131 Ron Wilson (D)
Dist 132 Scott Hochberg (D)
Dist 133 Joe M. Nixon (R)
Dist 134 Kyle Janek (R)
Dist 136 Beverly Woolley (R)
Dist 137 Debra Danburg (D)
Dist 140 Kevin Bailey (D)
Dist 141 Senfronia Thompson (D)
Dist 142 Harold V. Dutton Jr. (D)
Dist 143 Gerard Torres (D)
Dist 146 Al Edwards (D)
Dist 147 Garnet F. Coleman (D)
Dist 148 Jessica Cristina Farrar (D)
Dist 149 Talmadge L. Heflin (R)

DISTRICT ELECTION DATA

Senate 1996

NA

President 1996	
Bill Clinton (D)	75.1%
Bob Dole (R)	24.9%

Composite Party Vote 1994	
Democratic	70.7%
Republican	27.9%

Registered Voters 1996	**322,282**
Turnout	162,859
Percent of registered voting	50.5%

Senate 1998	
Rodney Ellis (D)	100%

Senate District 13
Senator Rodney Ellis (D)

Senate Office
(512) 463-0113

District Office
440 Louisiana, Suite 575
Houston, Texas 77002
(713) 236-0306

Personal

Year of birth	1954
Family	Single, one child
Education	Texas Southern University, B.A.
	LBJ School of Public Affairs, M.P.A.
	University of Texas Law School, J.D.
Occupation	Director, Apex Securities, Inc.; attorney
Religion	Protestant
State legislative service	Senate 1991 to present

COMMITTEE ASSIGNMENT HISTORY

1997 Economic Development, Jurisprudence (Chair), State Affairs
1995 Economic Development, Finance, Intergovernmental Relations (Chair)
1993 Economic Development, Finance, Health and Human Services (Vice-Chair), Administration, Nominations
1991 Criminal Justice, Intergovernmental Relations, State Affairs

BILL PASSAGE RATES, 1997

	Total	Passed Legislature	Pct. Passed Legislature
Authored	160	44	28%
Sponsored	60	50	83%
Amendments	54	47	87%

ELECTORAL HISTORY IN CURRENT DISTRICT

	1994	1996	1998
Primary Election Opponent(s)	No	NA	No
General Election Opponent(s)	No	NA	No

Senate District 14

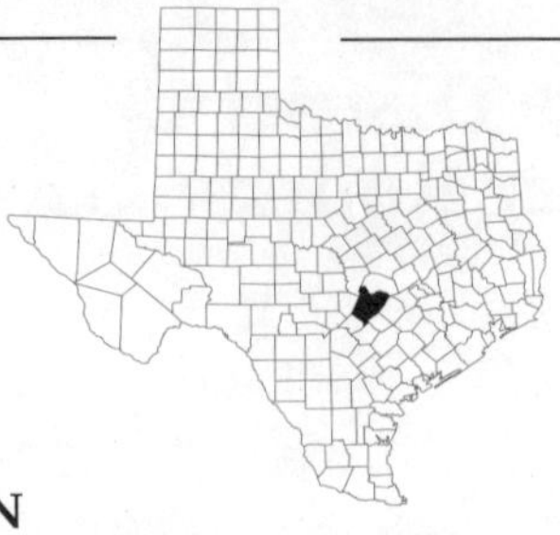

COUNTIES IN DISTRICT
Hays (part), Travis (part)

DEMOGRAPHIC INFORMATION

Population	
Total	567,088
Anglo	63.3%
Black	11.3%
Hispanic	22.6%
Others	3.2%

Education	
High School Graduates	74.0%
College Graduates	28.0%

Age of Population	
5 years or less	9.4%
6-17 years	16.2%
18-64 years	65.8%
65 or older	8.6%

Wealth and Urbanization	
Per capita Income	$14,348
Avg. House Value	$83,494
Percent Poverty	16.7%
Public Assistance	4.4%
Percent Urban	99.8%

Employed	
Percent Employed	93.9%
Private Sector	67.1%

Household Types	
Family households	74.3%
Non-family households	22.1%
Single-parent families	26.3%
Both parents working	70.0%

HOUSE DISTRICTS IN SENATORIAL DISTRICT

Dist 46 Alec Rhodes (D)
Dist 47 Terry Keel (R)
Dist 48 Sherri Greenberg (D)
Dist 49 Elliott Naishtat (D)
Dist 50 Dawnna M. Dukes (D)
Dist 51 Glen Maxey (D)

DISTRICT ELECTION DATA

Senate 1996	
Gonzalo Barrientos (D)	84.9%
Sandra L. BonSell (NLP)	15.1%

President 1996	
Bill Clinton (D)	58.9%
Bob Dole (R)	41.1%

Composite Party Vote 1994	
Democratic	60.3%
Republican	39.7%

Registered Voters 1996	**436,562**
Turnout	231,613
Percent of registered voting	53.1%

Senate 1998
NA

Senate District 14
Senator Gonzalo Barrientos (D)

Senate Office
(512) 463-0114
(512) 463-5949 (Fax)

District Office
105 Center Street
Kyle, Texas 78640
(512) 268-1358

Personal

Year of birth	1941
Family	Married to Emma Barrientos, five children
Education	University of Texas, attended three years
Occupation	Advertising and State Legislative relations
Religion	Catholic
State legislative service	House 1975-85, Senate 1985 to present

COMMITTEE ASSIGNMENT HISTORY

1997 Education, Finance, Natural Resources (Vice-Chair), Nominations
1995 Education, Finance, Natural Resources, Nominations
1993 Education, Finance, International Relations, Trade & Technology (Vice-Chair), Natural Resources, Nominations (Chair)
1991 Administration, Education, Finance (Vice-Chair), Natural Resources, Nominations (Chair)
1989 Education, Finance, Intergovernmental Relations
1987 Education, Intergovernmental Relations, State Affairs
1985 Education, Health and Human Services, Intergovernmental Relations

BILL PASSAGE RATES, 1997

	Total	Passed Legislature	Pct. Passed Legislature
Authored	106	24	23%
Sponsored	35	32	91%
Amendlments	52	44	85%

ELECTORAL HISTORY IN CURRENT DISTRICT

	1994	1996	1998
Primary Election Opponent(s)	No	No	NA
General Election Opponent(s)	Lib	NLP	NA

Senate District 15

COUNTIES IN DISTRICT

Harris (part)

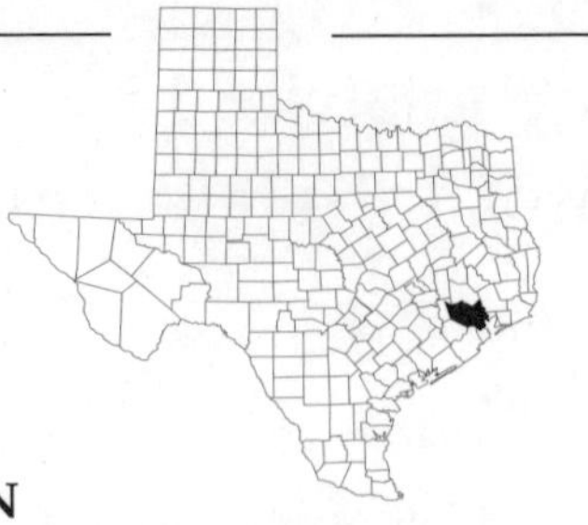

DEMOGRAPHIC INFORMATION

Population

Total	565,833
Anglo	49.8%
Black	28.1%
Hispanic	19.1%
Others	3.7%

Education

High School Graduates	70.2%
College Graduates	14.1%

Age of Population

5 years or less	10.5%
6-17 years	19.2%
18-64 years	63.5%
65 or older	6.8%

Wealth and Urbanization

Per capita Income	$11,796
Avg. House Value	$56,528
Percent Poverty	16.5%
Public Assistance	6.8%
Percent Urban	96.4%

Employed

Percent Employed	92.1%
Private Sector	82.6%

Household Types

Family households	87.8%
Non-family households	11.7%
Single-parent families	28.5%
Both parents working	63.9%

HOUSE DISTRICTS IN SENATORIAL DISTRICT

Dist 126 Peggy Hamric (R)
Dist 127 Joe Crabb (R)
Dist 128 Fred M. Bosse (D)
Dist 129 John Davis (R)
Dist 135 Gary Elkins (R)
Dist 136 Beverly Woolley (R)
Dist 137 Debra Danburg (D)
Dist 138 Ken Yarbrough (D)
Dist 139 Sylvester Turner (D)
Dist 140 Kevin Bailey (D)
Dist 141 Senfronia Thompson (D)
Dist 142 Harold V. Dutton Jr. (D)
Dist 143 Gerard Torres (D)
Dist 148 Jessica Cristina Farrar (D)
Dist 150 Paul J. Hilbert (R)

DISTRICT ELECTION DATA

Senate 1996

John Whitmire (D)	62.0%
Tom Kelly (R)	38.0%

President 1996

Bill Clinton (D)	59.4%
Bob Dole (R)	40.6%

Composite Party Vote 1994

Democratic	54.5%
Republican	44.1%

Registered Voters 1996	**289,606**
Turnout	145,001
Percent of registered voting	50.1%

Senate 1998

NA

Senate District 15
Senator John Whitmire (D)

Senate Office
(512) 463-0115

District Office
803 Yale Street
Houston, Texas 77007
(713) 864-8701

Personal

Year of birth	1949
Family	Married to Becki Whitmire, two children
Education	University of Houston, B.A. Bates College of Law
Occupation	Attorney
Religion	Protestant
State legislative service	House 1973-82, Senate 1983 to present

COMMITTEE ASSIGNMENT HISTORY

1997 Criminal Justice (Chair), Intergovernmental Relations, State Affairs
1995 Criminal Justice (Chair), Intergovernmental Relations, State Affairs
1993 Criminal Justice (Chair), Intergovernmental Relations, State Affairs, Nominations
1991 Administration, Economic Development, Education, Intergovernmental Relations (Chair), State Affairs
1989 Economic Development, Health and Human Services, Intergovernmental Relations
1987 Health and Human Services, Intergovernmental Relations, Natural Resources
1985 Health and Human Services, Intergovernmental Relations, Jurisprudence
1983 Administration, Health and Human Services, Intergovernmental Relations

BILL PASSAGE RATES, 1997

	Total	Passed Legislature	Pct. Passed Legislature
Authored	26	10	38%
Sponsored	38	27	71%
Amendments	23	22	96%

ELECTORAL HISTORY IN CURRENT DISTRICT

	1994	1996	1998
Primary Election Opponent(s)	No	No	NA
General Election Opponent(s)	No	Rep	NA

Senate District 16

COUNTIES IN DISTRICT
Dallas (part), Rockwall (part)

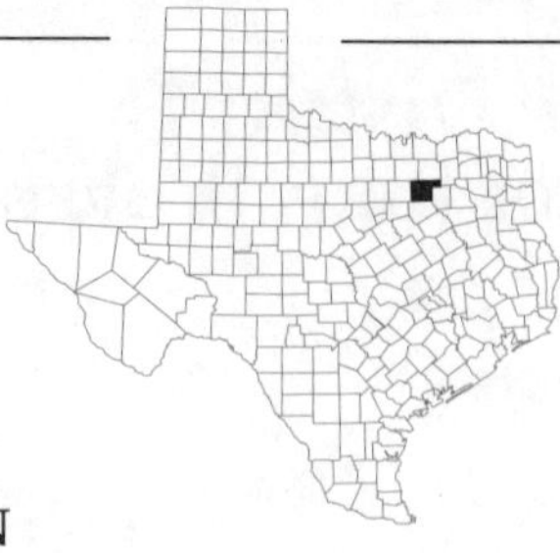

DEMOGRAPHIC INFORMATION

Population

Total	566,225
Anglo	78.2%
Black	8.9%
Hispanic	9.0%
Others	4.1%

Wealth and Urbanization

Per capita Income	$18,004
Avg. House Value	$100,389
Percent Poverty	7.0%
Public Assistance	2.5%
Percent Urban	99.4%

Education

High School Graduates	86.1%
College Graduates	30.6%

Employed

Percent Employed	95.5%
Private Sector	83.0%

Age of Population

5 years or less	9.8%
6-17 years	16.0%
18-64 years	66.4%
65 or older	7.7%

Household Types

Family households	83.7%
Non-family households	15.7%
Single-parent families	20.0%
Both parents working	61.0%

HOUSE DISTRICTS IN SENATORIAL DISTRICT

Dist 63 Mary Denny (R)
Dist 100 Terri Hodge (D)
Dist 101 Elvira Reyna (R)
Dist 102 Tony Goolsby (R)
Dist 105 Dale B. Tillery (D)
Dist 107 Harryette Ehrhardt (D)
Dist 108 Kenn George (R)
Dist 112 Fred Hill (R)
Dist 113 Joe Driver (R)

DISTRICT ELECTION DATA

Senate 1996
NA

Senate 1998

John Carona (R)	100.0%

President 1996

Bill Clinton (D)	40.7%
Bob Dole (R)	59.3%

Composite Party Vote 1994

Democratic	35.9%
Republican	62.8%

Registered Voters 1996	**343,835**
Turnout	190,106
Percent of registered voting	55.3%

Senate District 16
Senator John J. Carona (R)

Senate Office
(512) 463-0116

District Office
1919 S. Shiloh Rd., Suite 103
Garland, Texas 75042
(972) 864-2255

Personal

Year of birth	1955
Family	Married to Debbie Carona, three children
Education	University of Texas, B.B.A. in Insurance, Real Estate
Occupation	President, Principal Management Group
Religion	Baptist
State legislative service	House 1991-96; Senate 1996 (part) to present

COMMITTEE ASSIGNMENT HISTORY

1997 Health and Human Services, Intergovernmental Relations, International Relations, Trade and Technology (Vice-Chair), State Affairs
1996 Economic Development, Intergovernmental Relations, State Affairs

BILL PASSAGE RATES, 1997

	Total	Passed Legislature	Pct. Passed Legislature
Authored	42	18	43%
Sponsored	26	25	96%
Amendments	22	20	91%

ELECTORAL HISTORY IN CURRENT DISTRICT

	1994	1996	1996
Primary Election Opponent(s)	NA	NA	No
General Election Opponent(s)	NA	NA	No
Special Election Opponent(s)	NA	Dem, Rep	NA

Senate District 17

COUNTIES IN DISTRICT

Brazoria (part), Fort Bend (part), Harris (part)

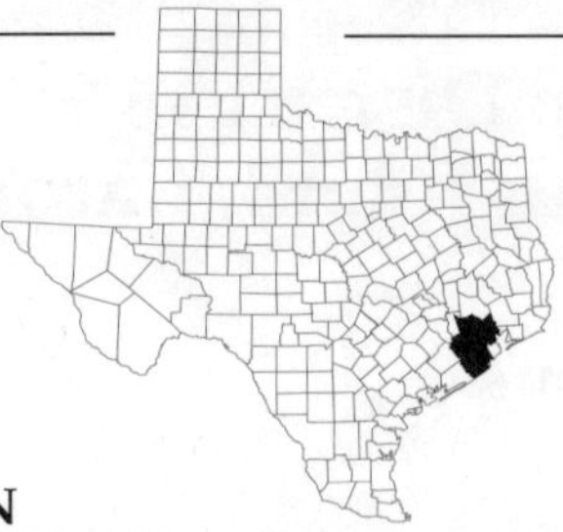

DEMOGRAPHIC INFORMATION

Population	
Total	566,201
Anglo	72.6%
Black	7.5%
Hispanic	12.9%
Others	7.3%

Education	
High School Graduates	87.8%
College Graduates	36.9%

Age of Population	
5 years or less	9.2%
6-17 years	16.6%
18-64 years	67.5%
65 or older	6.7%

Wealth and Urbanization	
Per capita Income	$20,182
Avg. House Value	$106,944
Percent Poverty	7.0%
Public Assistance	2.3%
Percent Urban	90.1%

Employed	
Percent Employed	95.9%
Private Sector	82.1%

Household Types	
Family households	82.1%
Non-family households	16.0%
Single-parent families	17.6%
Both parents working	64.7%

HOUSE DISTRICTS IN SENATORIAL DISTRICT

Dist 25 Dennis Bonnen (R)
Dist 26 Charlie Howard (R)
Dist 27 Dora Olivo (D)
Dist 29 D. R. (Tom) Uher (D)
Dist 127 Joe Crabb (R)
Dist 129 John Davis (R)
Dist 130 John Culberson (R)
Dist 131 Ron Wilson (D)
Dist 132 Scott Hochberg (D)
Dist 133 Joe M. Nixon (R)
Dist 134 Kyle Janek (R)
Dist 136 Beverly Woolley (R)
Dist 137 Debra Danburg (D)
Dist 146 Al Edwards (D)
Dist 147 Garnet F. Coleman (D)
Dist 149 Talmadge L. Heflin (R)

DISTRICT ELECTION DATA

Senate 1996

NA

Senate 1998	
Ronnie Ellen Harrison (D)	29.4%
J. E. (Buster) Brown (R)	70.6%

President 1996	
Bill Clinton (D)	35.4%
Bob Dole (R)	64.6%

Composite Party Vote 1994	
Democratic	32.9%
Republican	66.0%

Registered Voters 1996	**369,413**
Turnout	223,406
Percent of registered voting	60.5%

Senate District 17
Senator J. E. (Buster) Brown (R)

Senate Office
(512) 463-0117

District Office
490 This Way, Post Office Box 888
Lake Jackson, Texas 77566
(409) 297-5261

Personal

Year of birth	1940
Family	Married to Jill Brown, three children
Education	Southwest Texas State University Texas A&I University, B.S. University of Texas, L.L.B., J.D.
Occupation	Attorney
Religion	Methodist
State legislative service	Senate 1981 to present

COMMITTEE ASSIGNMENT HISTORY

1997 Administration, Finance, Natural Resources (Chair), Nominations
1995 Criminal Justice, Finance (Vice-Chair), Natural Resources
1993 Criminal Justice (Vice-Chair), International Relations, Trade and Technology, Jurisprudence, Natural Resources
1991 Criminal Justice (Vice-Chair), Intergovernmental Relations, Natural Resources
1989 Criminal Justice (Vice-Chair), Intergovernmental Relations, Natural Resources
1987 Intergovernmental Relations, Natural Resources, Jurisprudence
1985 Intergovernmental Relations, Natural Resources, Jurisprudence (Vice-Chair)
1983 Administration (Vice-Chair), Natural Resources
1981 Administration, Human Resources, Natural Resources

BILL PASSAGE RATES, 1997

	Total	Passed Legislature	Pct. Passed Legislature
Authored	98	40	41%
Sponsored	41	41	100%
Amendments	56	51	91%

ELECTORAL HISTORY IN CURRENT DISTRICT

	1994	1996	1998
Primary Election Opponent(s)	No	NA	No
General Election Opponent(s)	Dem	NA	Dem

Senate District 18

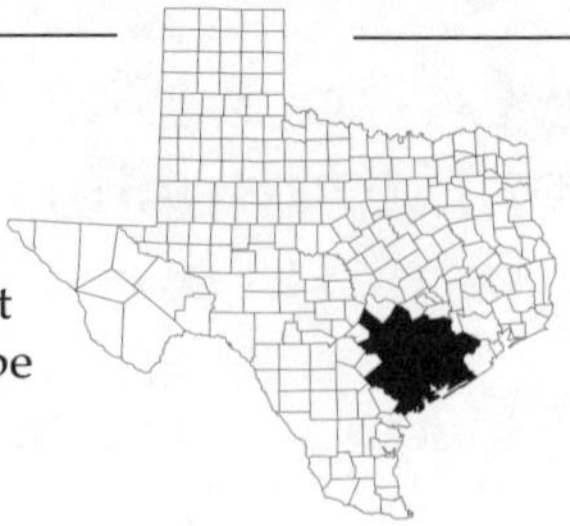

COUNTIES IN DISTRICT

Aransas, Austin, Bastrop, Caldwell, Calhoun, Colorado, DeWitt, Fayette, Fort Bend (part), Goliad, Gonzales, Guadalupe (part), Hays (part), Jackson, Karnes, Lavaca, Matagorda, Refugio, Victoria, Wharton

DEMOGRAPHIC INFORMATION

Population

Total	563,032
Anglo	63.2%
Black	9.4%
Hispanic	25.6%
Others	2.1%

Wealth and Urbanization

Per capita Income	$11,418
Avg. House Value	$62,855
Percent Poverty	19.5%
Public Assistance	7.6%
Percent Urban	54.4%

Education

High School Graduates	66.1%
College Graduates	15.4%

Employed

Percent Employed	93.6%
Private Sector	73.0%

Age of Population

5 years or less	9.6%
6-17 years	19.3%
18-64 years	58.1%
65 or older	12.9%

Household Types

Family households	86.6%
Non-family households	10.3%
Single-parent families	17.7%
Both parents working	62.9%

HOUSE DISTRICTS IN SENATORIAL DISTRICT

Dist 13 Charles B. Jones (R)
Dist 26 Charlie Howard (R)
Dist 27 Dora Olivo (D)
Dist 28 Robert L. Cook (D)
Dist 29 D. R. (Tom) Uher (D)
Dist 30 Geanie W. Morrison (R)
Dist 31 Judy Hawley (D)
Dist 32 Eugene (Gene) Seaman (R)
Dist 45 Edmund Kuempel (R)
Dist 46 Alec Rhodes (D)

DISTRICT ELECTION DATA

Senate 1996

NA

Senate 1998

Kenneth L. Armbrister (D)	59.4%
Reese Turner (R)	40.6%

President 1996

Bill Clinton (D)	43.4%
Bob Dole (R)	56.6%

Composite Party Vote 1994

Democratic	47.3%
Republican	52.7%

Registered Voters 1996	**360,494**
Turnout	205,931
Percent of registered voting	57.1%

Senate District 18
Senator Kenneth L. Armbrister (D)

Senate Office
(512) 463-0118
(512) 475-3736 (Fax)

District Office
3205 East Mockingbird
Victoria, Texas 77904
(512) 572-8061

Personal

Year of birth	1947
Family	Married to Susie Armbrister, no children
Education	Sam Houston State University FBI National Academy
Occupation	Businessman
Religion	Catholic
State legislative service	House 1983-86, Senate 1987 to present

COMMITTEE ASSIGNMENT HISTORY

1997 Administration, Finance, International Relations, Trade and Technology, State Affairs (Chair)
1995 Education, International Relations, Trade and Technology, Natural Resources, State Affairs (Chair)
1993 Finance, Intergovernmental Relations (Chair), Natural Resources, Nominations
1991 Finance, Intergovernmental Relations, Natural Resources, Nominations
1989 Intergovernmental Relations, Natural Resources, Nominations, State Affairs
1987 Economic Development, Intergovernmental Relations, Natural Resources

BILL PASSAGE RATES, 1997

	Total	Passed Legislature	Pct. Passed Legislature
Authored	118	51	43%
Sponsored	59	57	97%
Amendments	69	59	86%

ELECTORAL HISTORY IN CURRENT DISTRICT

	1994	1996	1998
Primary Election Opponent(s)	No	NA	No
General Election Opponent(s)	No	NA	Rep

Senate District 19

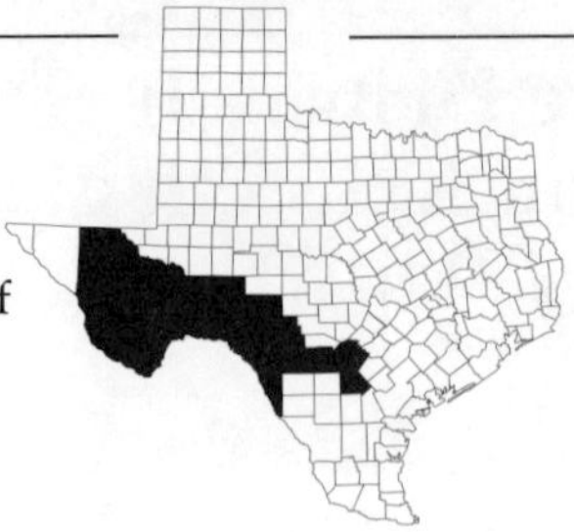

COUNTIES IN DISTRICT

Atascosa (part), Bexar (part), Brewster, Crockett, Culberson (part), Edwards, Jeff Davis, Kinney, Maverick, Medina (part), Pecos, Presidio, Real, Reeves (part), Sutton (part), Terrell, Uvalde (part), Val Verde

DEMOGRAPHIC INFORMATION

Population

Total	512,424
Anglo	28.3%
Black	7.9%
Hispanic	62.8%
Others	1.2%

Education

High School Graduates	57.1%
College Graduates	8.4%

Age of Population

5 years or less	10.7%
6-17 years	21.9%
18-64 years	57.7%
65 or older	9.8%

Wealth and Urbanization

Per capita Income	$7,736
Avg. House Value	$42,399
Percent Poverty	29.4%
Public Assistance	12.9%
Percent Urban	82.0%

Employed

Percent Employed	87.9%
Private Sector	69.5%

Household Types

Family households	89.6%
Non-family households	7.0%
Single-parent families	23.9%
Both parents working	53.2%

HOUSE DISTRICTS IN SENATORIAL DISTRICT

Dist 43 Tracy O. King (D)
Dist 44 Richard Raymond (D)
Dist 73 Robert R. (Bob) Turner (D)
Dist 74 Pete P. Gallego (D)
Dist 80 Gary L. Walker (R)
Dist 117 John A. Longoria (D)
Dist 118 Carlos Uresti (D)
Dist 119 Robert R. Puente (D)
Dist 120 Ruth Jones McClendon (D)
Dist 121 Bill Siebert (R)
Dist 124 Juan F. Solis, III (D)

DISTRICT ELECTION DATA

Senate 1996

NA

President 1996

Bill Clinton (D)	66.2%
Bob Dole (R)	33.8%

Composite Party Vote 1994

Democratic	63.7%
Republican	36.3%

Registered Voters 1996	**277,466**
Turnout	135,589
Percent of registered voting	48.9%

Senate 1998

Frank Madla (D)	100.0%

Senate District 19
Senator Frank Madla (D)

Senate Office
(512) 463-0119

District Office
1313 Southeast Military Drive, Suite 101
San Antonio, Texas 78214
(210) 927-9464

Personal

Year of birth	1937
Family	Married to Helen Madla, two children
Education	St. Mary's University, B.A., M.A.
Occupation	Real estate and insurance broker, part-time college instructor, Home Health Agency
Religion	Catholic
State legislative service	House 1973-92, Senate 1993 to present

COMMITTEE ASSIGNMENT HISTORY

1997 Economic Development, Health and Human Services, Intergovernmental Relations, Nominations (Chair)
1995 Economic Development, Health and Human Services, Intergovernmental Relations, Nominations (Vice-Chair)
1993 Economic Development, Health and Human Services, Intergovernmental Relations

BILL PASSAGE RATES, 1997

	Total	Passed Legislature	Pct. Passed Legislature
Authored	90	34	38%
Sponsored	29	28	97%
Amendments	49	45	92%

ELECTORAL HISTORY IN CURRENT DISTRICT

	1994	1996	1998
Primary Election Opponent(s)	No	NA	No
General Election Opponent(s)	No	NA	No

Senate District 20

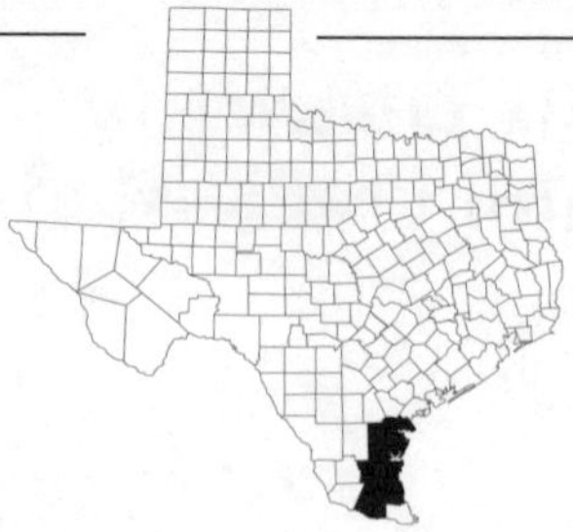

COUNTIES IN DISTRICT

Brooks, Hidalgo (part), Jim Wells, Kenedy, Kleberg, Nueces, San Patricio, Willacy

DEMOGRAPHIC INFORMATION

Population

Total	534,542
Anglo	34.9%
Black	2.8%
Hispanic	61.5%
Others	0.9%

Education

High School Graduates	62.6%
College Graduates	14.5%

Age of Population

5 years or less	10.2%
6-17 years	21.7%
18-64 years	57.9%
65 or older	10.2%

Wealth and Urbanization

Per capita Income	$9,840
Avg. House Value	$55,555
Percent Poverty	26.6%
Public Assistance	11.5%
Percent Urban	81.4%

Employed

Percent Employed	90.4%
Private Sector	72.4%

Household Types

Family households	90.0%
Non-family households	8.5%
Single-parent families	21.9%
Both parents working	54.5%

House Districts in Senatorial District

Dist 31 Judy Hawley (D)
Dist 32 Eugene (Gene) Seaman (R)
Dist 33 Vilma Luna (D)
Dist 34 Jaime L. Capelo, Jr. (D)
Dist 35 Irma Rangel (D)
Dist 36 Ismael (Kino) Flores (D)
Dist 39 Miguel David Wise (D)
Dist 40 Juan (Chuy) Hinojosa (D)
Dist 41 Roberto Gutierrez (D)
Dist 44 Richard Raymond (D)

DISTRICT ELECTION DATA

Senate 1996

NA

Senate 1998

Carlos F. Truan (D)	58.1%
Joe Gardner (R)	41.9%

President 1996

Bill Clinton (D)	60.6%
Bob Dole (R)	39.4%

Composite Party Vote 1994

Democratic	60.4%
Republican	39.6%

Registered Voters 1996	**330,132**
Turnout	161,845
Percent of registered voting	48.7%

Senate District 20
Senator Carlos F. Truan (D)

Senate Office
(512) 463-0120

District Office
4531 Ayers, Suite 402
Corpus Christi, Texas 78467
(512) 853-2693

Personal

Year of birth	1935
Family	Married to Elvira Truan, four children
Education	Texas A&I University, B.B.A.
Occupation	Life insurance
Religion	Catholic
State legislative service	House 1969-76, Senate 1977 to present

COMMITTEE ASSIGNMENT HISTORY

1997 Administration (Vice-Chair), Finance (Vice-Chair), International Relations, Trade and Technology (Chair), Natural Resources

1995 Finance, Health and Human Services, International Relations, Trade and Technology (Chair), Natural Resources (Vice-Chair), Administration

1993 Finance, Health and Human Services, International Relations, Trade and Technology (Chair), Natural Resources (Vice-Chair), Administration

1991 Finance, Health and Human Services (Vice-Chair), Natural Resources (Vice-Chair)

1989 Education (Vice-Chair), Finance, Health and Human Services

1987 Education (Vice-Chair), Finance, Health and Human Services

1985 Education (Vice-Chair), Health and Human Services, Natural Resources

1983 Education (Vice-Chair), Health and Human Services, Natural Resources

1981 Education (Vice-Chair), Human Resources, Natural Resources

1979 Education, Human Resources, Natural Resources

1977 Economic Development, Human Resources Natural Resources

BILL PASSAGE RATES, 1997

	Total	Passed Legislature	Pct. Passed Legislature
Authored	65	15	23%
Sponsored	23	22	96%
Amendments	28	22	79%

ELECTORAL HISTORY IN CURRENT DISTRICT

	1994	1996	1998
Primary Election Opponent(s)	No	NA	No
General Election Opponent(s)	Rep	NA	Rep

Senate District 21

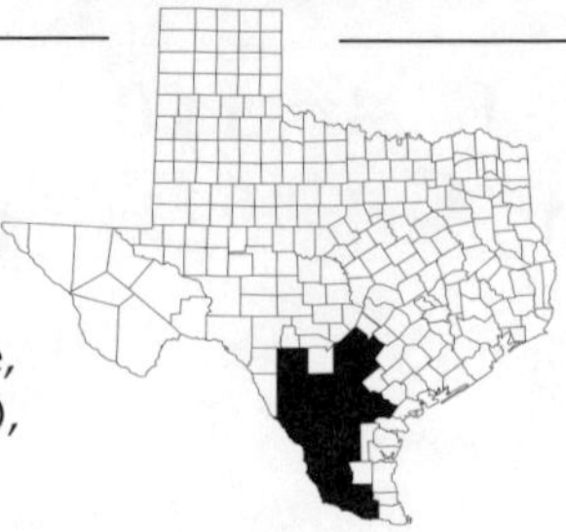

COUNTIES IN DISTRICT

Atascosa (part), Bee, Bexar (part), Comal (part), Dimmit, Duval, Frio, Guadalupe (part), Hidalgo (part), Jim Hogg, La Salle, Live Oak, McMullen, Starr, Uvalde (part), Webb, Wilson, Zapata, Zavala

DEMOGRAPHIC INFORMATION

Population	
Total	512,389
Anglo	33.6%
Black	2.6%
Hispanic	63.0%
Others	1.0%

Wealth and Urbanization	
Per capita Income	$8,432
Avg. House Value	$52,101
Percent Poverty	31.1%
Public Assistance	12.6%
Percent Urban	71.6%

Education	
High School Graduates	58.8%
College Graduates	12.4%

Employed	
Percent Employed	89.9%
Private Sector	68.5%

Age of Population	
5 years or less	10.8%
6-17 years	23.1%
18-64 years	57.0%
65 or older	9.2%

Household Types	
Family households	92.6%
Non-family households	6.2%
Single-parent families	18.7%
Both parents working	52.9%

HOUSE DISTRICTS IN SENATORIAL DISTRICT

Dist 31 Judy Hawley (D)
Dist 35 Irma Rangel (D)
Dist 36 Ismael (Kino) Flores (D)
Dist 40 Juan (Chuy) Hinojosa (D)
Dist 42 Henry Cuellar (D)
Dist 43 Tracy O. King (D)
Dist 44 Richard Raymond (D)
Dist 45 Edmund Kuempel (R)
Dist 118 Carlos Uresti (D)
Dist 119 Robert R. Puente (D)
Dist 120 Ruth Jones McClendon (D)
Dist 121 Bill Siebert (R)
Dist 122 John H. Shields (R)

DISTRICT ELECTION DATA

Senate 1996	
Judith Zaffirini (D)	66.2%
James C. Whitworth (R)	33.8%

Senate 1998

NA

President 1996	
Bill Clinton (D)	58.5%
Bob Dole (R)	41.5%

Composite Party Vote 1994	
Democratic	55.2%
Republican	44.8%

Registered Voters 1996	**316,160**
Turnout	157,125
Percent of registered voting	49.7%

Senate District 21
Senator Judith Zaffirini (D)

Senate Office
(512) 463-0121

District Office
1407 Washington Street
Laredo, Texas 78042
(210) 722-2293

Personal

Year of birth	1946
Family	Married to Carlos M. Zaffirini, one child
Education	University of Texas, B.S., M.A., Ph.D.
Occupation	Communications specialist
Religion	Catholic
State legislative service	Senate 1987 to present

COMMITTEE ASSIGNMENT HISTORY

1997 Education, Finance, Health and Human Services (Chair)
1995 Education, Finance, Health and Human Services (Chair)
1993 Education, Finance, Health and Human Services (Chair)
1991 Education, Health and Human Services, Natural Resources
1989 Education, Health and Human Services, Natural Resources
1987 Health and Human Services, Intergovernmental Relations, Natural Resources

BILL PASSAGE RATES, 1997

	Total	Passed Legislature	Pct. Passed Legislature
Authored	82	56	68%
Sponsored	31	31	100%
Amendments	25	25	100%

ELECTORAL HISTORY IN CURRENT DISTRICT

	1994	1996	1998
Primary Election Opponent(s)	No	No	NA
General Election Opponent(s)	Rep	Rep	NA

Senate District 22

COUNTIES IN DISTRICT

Bosque, Comanche, Denton (part), Eastland, Erath, Hamilton, Hill, Hood, Jack, Johnson (part), McLennan (part), Palo Pinto, Parker (part), Somervell, Tarrant (part), Wise

DEMOGRAPHIC INFORMATION

Population	
Total	535,596
Anglo	82.2%
Black	7.3%
Hispanic	9.6%
Others	1.1%

Wealth and Urbanization	
Per capita Income	$11,023
Avg. House Value	$55,374
Percent Poverty	18.8%
Public Assistance	6.5%
Percent Urban	58.0%

Education	
High School Graduates	68.2%
College Graduates	13.6%

Employed	
Percent Employed	92.8%
Private Sector	74.6%

Age of Population	
5 years or less	8.6%
6-17 years	17.0%
18-64 years	59.2%
65 or older	15.2%

Household Types	
Family households	82.2%
Non-family households	13.5%
Single-parent families	19.6%
Both parents working	61.9%

HOUSE DISTRICTS IN SENATORIAL DISTRICT

Dist 10 Jim Pitts (R)
Dist 56 Kip Averitt (R)
Dist 57 Jim Dunnam (D)
Dist 58 Arlene Wohlgemuth (R)
Dist 59 David Lengefeld (D)
Dist 60 Jim Keffer (R)
Dist 61 Phil King (R)
Dist 63 Mary Denny (R)
Dist 64 Ronny Crownover (R)
Dist 65 Burt Solomons (R)
Dist 68 Rick Hardcastle (R)
Dist 89 Sue Palmer (R)

DISTRICT ELECTION DATA

Senate 1996

NA

Senate 1998

David Sibley (R)	100%

President 1996	
Bill Clinton (D)	47.4%
Bob Dole (R)	52.6%

Composite Party Vote 1994	
Democratic	51.2%
Republican	48.8%

Registered Voters 1996	**336,003**
Turnout	184,415
Percent of registered voting	54.9%

Senate District 22
Senator David Sibley (R)

Senate Office
(512) 463-0122
David.Sibley@senate.state.tx.us

District Office
801 Austin Ave., Suite 1020
Waco, Texas 76701
(817) 756-0122
(817) 756-0123 (Fax)

Personal

Year of birth	1947
Family	Married to Pam Sibley, three children
Education	Baylor University Baylor College of Dentistry Baylor College of Law
Occupation	Attorney
Religion	Baptist
State legislative service	Senate 1991 to present

COMMITTEE ASSIGNMENT HISTORY

1997 Administration, Economic Development (Chair), Education, Finance, International Relations, Trade and Technology
1995 Economic Development (Chair), Education, Finance, International Relations, Trade and Technology
1993 Criminal Justice, Education, State Affairs, Nominations (Vice-Chair)
1991 Criminal Justice, Intergovernmental Relations, Natural Resources

BILL PASSAGE RATES, 1997

	Total	Passed Legislature	Pct. Passed Legislature
Authored	75	26	35%
Sponsored	37	34	92%
Amendments	37	34	92%

ELECTORAL HISTORY IN CURRENT DISTRICT

	1994	1996	1998
Primary Election Opponent(s)	No	NA	No
General Election Opponent(s)	Dem	NA	No

Senate District 23

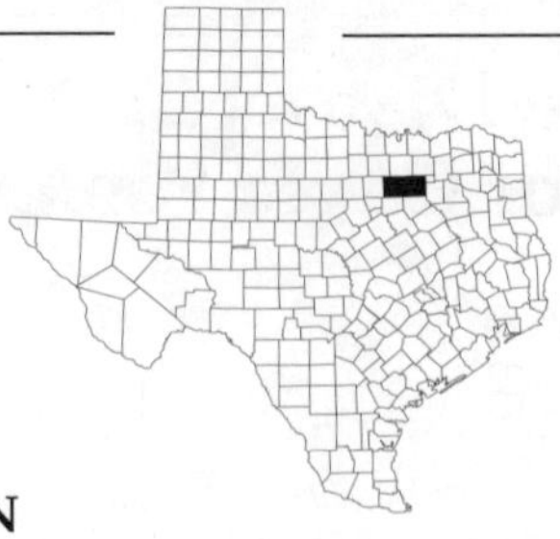

COUNTIES IN DISTRICT
Dallas (part), Tarrant (part)

DEMOGRAPHIC INFORMATION

Population	
Total	520,839
Anglo	27.3%
Black	46.9%
Hispanic	25.1%
Others	1.5%

Education	
High School Graduates	68.2%
College Graduates	13.6%

Age of Population	
5 years or less	8.6%
6-17 years	17.0%
18-64 years	59.2%
65 or older	15.2%

Wealth and Urbanization	
Per capita Income	$9,797
Avg. House Value	$63,521
Percent Poverty	23.5%
Public Assistance	10.2%
Percent Urban	58.0%

Employed	
Percent Employed	89.7%
Private Sector	80.5%

Household Types	
Family households	87.9%
Non-family households	10.4%
Single-parent families	35.6%
Both parents working	64.7%

HOUSE DISTRICTS IN SENATORIAL DISTRICT

Dist 93 Toby Goodman (R)
Dist 100 Terri Hodge (D)
Dist 103 Steve Wolens (D)
Dist 104 Domingo Garcia (D)
Dist 105 Dale B. Tillery (D)
Dist 106 Ray Allen (R)
Dist 107 Harryette Ehrhardt (D)
Dist 109 Helen Giddings (D)
Dist 110 Jesse Jones (D)
Dist 111 Yvonne Davis (D)

DISTRICT ELECTION DATA

Senate 1996
NA

Senate 1998	
Royce West (D)	100.0%

President 1996	
Bill Clinton (D)	79.8%
Bob Dole (R)	22.1%

Composite Party Vote 1994	
Democratic	70.2%
Republican	27.3%

Registered Voters 1996	**264,633**
Turnout	125,975
Percent of registered voting	47.6%

Senate District 23
Senator Royce West (D)

Senate Office
(512) 463-0123
Royce.West@senate.state.tx.us

District Office
5787 S. Hampton Road, Suite 385
Dallas, Texas 75232
(214) 467-0123

Personal

Year of birth	1952
Family	Married to Carol Richard, seven children
Education	University of Texas at Arlington, B.A., M.A. University of Houston, J.D.
Occupation	Senior partner, law firm of Robinson, West & Gooden, P.C.
Religion	Baptist
State legislative service	Senate 1993 to present

COMMITTEE ASSIGNMENT HISTORY

1997 Criminal Justice, Education, Finance, Health and Human Services
1995 Criminal Justice, Jurisprudence (Vice-Chair), State Affairs, Administration
1993 Criminal Justice, Jurisprudence, State Affairs

BILL PASSAGE RATES, 1997

	Total	Passed Legislature	Pct. Passed Legislature
Authored	66	27	41%
Sponsored	18	13	72%
Amendments	32	28	88%

ELECTORAL HISTORY IN CURRENT DISTRICT

	1994	1996	1998
Primary Election Opponent(s)	No	NA	No
General Election Opponent(s)	No	NA	No

Senate District 24

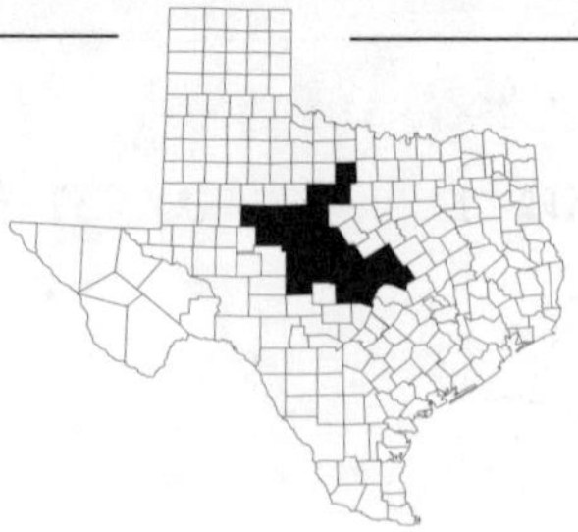

COUNTIES IN DISTRICT

Bell, Brown, Burnet, Callahan, Coke, Coleman, Concho, Coryell, Lampasas, Llano (part), McCulloch, Menard, Mills, Mitchell, Nolan, Runnels, San Saba, Shackelford, Stephens, Taylor (part), Young

DEMOGRAPHIC INFORMATION

Population	
Total	540,782
Anglo	73.4%
Black	11.1%
Hispanic	13.8%
Others	2.0%

Education	
High School Graduates	72.4%
College Graduates	14.3%

Age of Population	
5 years or less	9.8%
6-17 years	17.5%
18-64 years	59.3%
65 or older	13.3%

Wealth and Urbanization	
Per capita Income	$10,416
Avg. House Value	$52,608
Percent Poverty	17.3%
Public Assistance	6.6%
Percent Urban	71.1%

Employed	
Percent Employed	92.1%
Private Sector	68.0%

Household Types	
Family households	83.6%
Non-family households	10.2%
Single-parent families	18.7%
Both parents working	63.0%

HOUSE DISTRICTS IN SENATORIAL DISTRICT

Dist 53 Harvey Hilderbran (R)
Dist 54 Suzanna Gratia Hupp (R)
Dist 55 Dianne White Delisi (R)
Dist 59 David Lengefeld (D)
Dist 60 Jim Keffer (R)
Dist 68 Rick Hardcastle (R)
Dist 70 David Counts (D)
Dist 71 Bob Hunter (R)
Dist 72 Robert Junell (D)
Dist 73 Robert R. (Bob) Turner (D)

DISTRICT ELECTION DATA

Senate 1996	
Rick Rhodes (D)	48.1%
Troy Fraser (R)	51.9%

President 1996	
Bill Clinton (D)	42.4%
Bob Dole (R)	57.6%

Composite Party Vote 1994	
Democratic	50.6%
Republican	49.4%

Registered Voters 1996	**324,184**
Turnout	176,157
Percent of registered voting	54.3%

Senate 1998

NA

Senate District 24
Senator Troy Fraser (R)

Senate Office
(512) 463-0124

District Office
1920 North Main, Suite 101
Belton, Texas 76513
(817) 939-3562

Personal

Year of birth	1949
Family	Married to Linda Cochran, three children
Education	San Angelo State University University of Texas at Arlington
Occupation	Business executive with Fraser Industries
Religion	Methodist
State legislative service	House 1987-91; Senate 1997 to present

COMMITTEE ASSIGNMENT HISTORY
1997 Education, Natural Resources, State Affairs

BILL PASSAGE RATES, 1997

	Total	Passed Legislature	Pct. Passed Legislature
Authored	20	6	30%
Sponsored	19	17	89%
Amendments	13	11	85%

ELECTORAL HISTORY IN CURRENT DISTRICT

	1994	1996	1998
Primary Election Opponent(s)	NA	Yes	NA
General Election Opponent(s)	NA	Yes	NA

Senate District 25

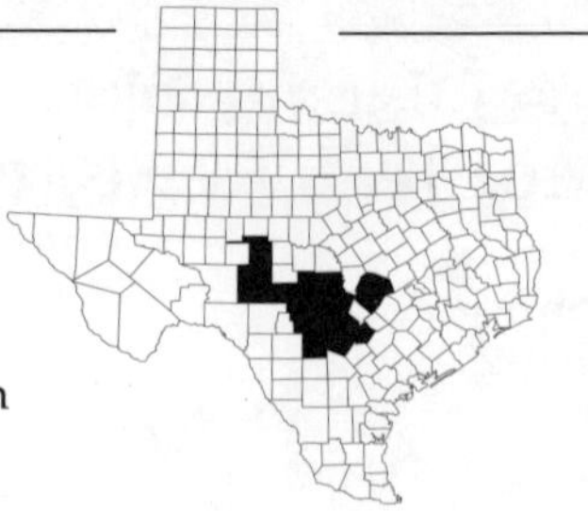

COUNTIES IN DISTRICT

Bandera, Bexar (part), Blanco, Comal (part), Gillespie, Guadalupe (part), Kendall, Kerr, Kimble, Llano (part), Mason, Medina (part), Schleicher, Sutton (part), Tom Green (part), Travis (part), Williamson (part)

DEMOGRAPHIC INFORMATION

Population		**Wealth and Urbanization**	
Total	567,045	Per capita Income	$17,778
Anglo	81.9%	Avg. House Value	$105,525
Black	2.1%	Percent Poverty	8.8%
Hispanic	14.6%	Public Assistance	3.0%
Others	1.5%	Percent Urban	73.8%

Education		**Employed**	
High School Graduates	86.3%	Percent Employed	95.4%
College Graduates	32.3%	Private Sector	71.4%

Age of Population		**Household Types**	
5 years or less	8.4%	Family households	85.5%
6-17 years	16.8%	Non-family households	12.5%
18-64 years	62.3%	Single-parent families	16.3%
65 or older	12.4%	Both parents working	68.0%

HOUSE DISTRICTS IN SENATORIAL DISTRICT

Dist 43 Tracy O. King (D)	Dist 73 Robert R. (Bob) Turner (D)	Dist 121 Bill Siebert (R)
Dist 45 Edmund Kuempel (R)	Dist 115 Leticia Van de Putte (D)	Dist 122 John H. Shields (R)
Dist 47 Terry Keel (R)	Dist 116 Leo G. Alvarado Jr. (D)	Dist 123 Frank J. Corte (R)
Dist 52 Mike Krusee (R)	Dist 117 John A. Longoria (D)	Dist 124 Juan F. Solis, III (D)
Dist 53 Harvey Hilderbran (R)	Dist 120 Ruth Jones McClendon (D)	Dist 125 Arthur (Art) Reyna (D)
Dist 72 Robert Junell (D)		

DISTRICT ELECTION DATA

Senate 1996		**Senate 1998**
		NA
Jeff Wentworth (R)	100.0%	

President 1996	
Bill Clinton (D)	31.4%
Bob Dole (R)	68.6%

Composite Party Vote 1994	
Democratic	32.3%
Republican	67.7%

Registered Voters 1996	**477,984**
Turnout	297,380
Percent of registered voting	62.2%

Senate District 25
Senator Jeff Wentworth (R)

Senate Office
(512) 463-0125
jeff.wentworth@senate.state.tx.us

District Office
1250 NE Loop 410, Suite 720
San Antonio, Texas 78209
(210) 826-7800

Personal

Year of birth	1940
Family	Married to Karla Wentworth, two children
Education	Texas A&M University, B.A.
	Texas Tech University School of Law, J.D.
Occupation	Attorney and realtor
Religion	Christian Scientist
State legislative service	House 1988-92, Senate 1993 to present

COMMITTEE ASSIGNMENT HISTORY

1997 Finance, Jurisprudence, Natural Resources
1995 Intergovernmental Relations, Jurisprudence, State Affairs (Vice-Chair), Nominations
1993 Economic Development, Health and Human Services, Intergovernmental Relations, International Relations, Trade and Technology

BILL PASSAGE RATES, 1997

	Total	Passed Legislature	Pct. Passed Legislature
Authored	75	20	27%
Sponsored	46	44	96%
Amendments	43	41	95%

ELECTORAL HISTORY IN CURRENT DISTRICT

	1994	1996	1998
Primary Election Opponent(s)	Yes	Yes	NA
General Election Opponent(s)	Dem	No	NA

Senate District 26

COUNTIES IN DISTRICT

Bexar (part)

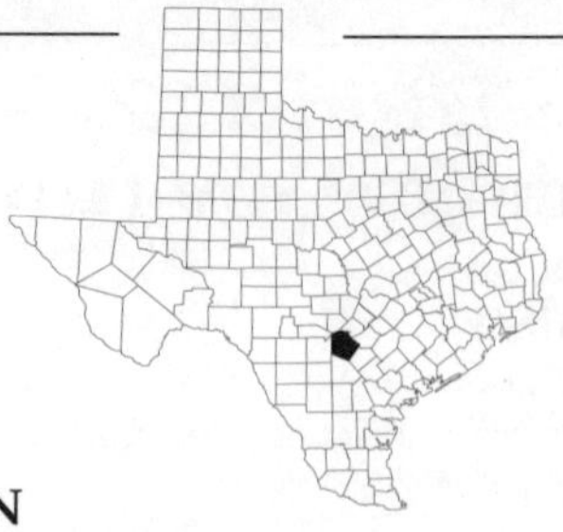

DEMOGRAPHIC INFORMATION

Population		**Wealth and Urbanization**	
Total	512,469	Per capita Income	$9,196
Anglo	28.8%	Avg. House Value	$52,401
Black	6.2%	Percent Poverty	25.9%
Hispanic	63.9%	Public Assistance	11.3%
Others	1.4%	Percent Urban	98.8%

Education		**Employed**	
High School Graduates	65.5%	Percent Employed	90.1%
College Graduates	14.6%	Private Sector	72.4%

Age of Population		**Household Types**	
5 years or less	11.0%	Family households	86.4%
6-17 years	19.1%	Non-family households	11.5%
18-64 years	59.5%	Single-parent families	29.1%
65 or older	10.3%	Both parents working	57.1%

HOUSE DISTRICTS IN SENATORIAL DISTRICT

Dist 115 Leticia Van de Putte (D)
Dist 116 Leo G. Alvarado Jr. (D)
Dist 117 John A. Longoria (D)
Dist 119 Robert R. Puente (D)
Dist 120 Ruth Jones McClendon (D)
Dist 122 John H. Shields (R)
Dist 123 Frank J. Corte (R)
Dist 124 Juan F. Solis, III (D)
Dist 125 Arthur (Art) Reyna (D)

DISTRICT ELECTION DATA

Senate 1996	
Gregory Luna (D)	67.5%
Andrew Longaker (R)	32.5%

Senate 1998

NA

President 1996	
Bill Clinton (D)	65.0%
Bob Dole (R)	35.0%

Composite Party Vote 1994	
Democratic	60.5%
Republican	39.5%

Registered Voters 1996	**301,335**
Turnout	135,196
Percent of registered voting	44.9%

Senate District 26
Senator Gregory Luna (D)

Senate Office
(512) 463-0126

District Office
318 West Houston, Suite 302
San Antonio, Texas 78205
(210) 226-2626

Personal

Year of birth	1932
Family	Married to Helen Luna, four children
Education	Trinity University, B.A.
	St. Mary's School of Law, J.D.
Occupation	Attorney
Religion	Catholic
State legislative service	House 1985-92, Senate 1993 to present

COMMITTEE ASSIGNMENT HISTORY

1997 Education (Vice-Chair), Jurisprudence, State Affairs
1995 Education (Vice-Chair), Jurisprudence, State Affairs
1993 Education, Jurisprudence, State Affairs

BILL PASSAGE RATES, 1997

	Total	Passed Legislature	Pct. Passed Legislature
Authored	33	10	30%
Sponsored	10	9	90%
Amendments	14	10	71%

ELECTORAL HISTORY IN CURRENT DISTRICT

	1994	1996	1998
Primary Election Opponent(s)	No	No	NA
General Election Opponent(s)	Rep	Rep	NA

Senate District 27

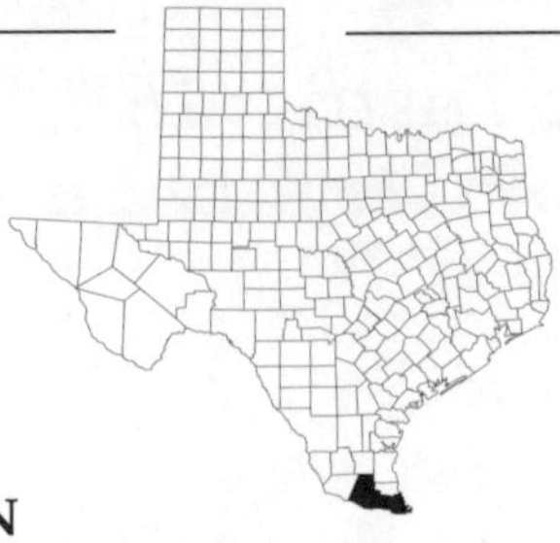

COUNTIES IN DISTRICT

Cameron, Hidalgo (part)

DEMOGRAPHIC INFORMATION

Population	
Total	538,234
Anglo	16.2%
Black	0.3%
Hispanic	83.1%
Others	0.5%

Wealth and Urbanization	
Per capita Income	$7,096
Avg. House Value	$47,925
Percent Poverty	39.8%
Public Assistance	17.5%
Percent Urban	83.8%

Education	
High School Graduates	49.1%
College Graduates	12.4%

Employed	
Percent Employed	86.4%
Private Sector	71.2%

Age of Population	
5 years or less	10.8%
6-17 years	24.6%
18-64 years	54.1%
65 or older	10.5%

Household Types	
Family households	93.3%
Non-family households	5.2%
Single-parent families	22.1%
Both parents working	50.3%

HOUSE DISTRICTS IN SENATORIAL DISTRICT

Dist 36 Ismael (Kino) Flores (D)
Dist 37 Rene O. Oliveira (D)
Dist 38 Jim Solis (D)
Dist 39 Miguel David Wise (D)
Dist 40 Juan (Chuy) Hinojosa (D)
Dist 41 Roberto Gutierrez (D)

DISTRICT ELECTION DATA

Senate 1996	
Eddie Lucio, Jr. (D)	100.0%

Senate 1998

NA

President 1996	
Bill Clinton (D)	67.5%
Bob Dole (R)	32.5%

Composite Party Vote 1994	
Democratic	62.4%
Republican	37.6%

Registered Voters 1996	271,625
Turnout	120,934
Percent of registered voting	44.5%

Senate District 27
Senator Eddie Lucio, Jr. (D)

Senate Office
(512) 463-0127

District Office
32 North Park Plaza
Brownsville, Texas 78521
(210) 548-0227

Personal

Year of birth	1946
Family	Married to Minnie Lucio, two children
Education	Pan American University, B.S.
Occupation	Advertising executive
Religion	Catholic
State legislative service	House 1986-90, Senate 1991 to present

COMMITTEE ASSIGNMENT HISTORY

1997 Economic Development, Finance, Intergovernmental Relations (Chair), Natural Resources
1995 Economic Development, Finance, International Relations, Trade and Technology, Natural Resources
1993 Economic Development (Vice-Chair), International Relations, Trade and Technology, Natural Resources, State Affairs
1991 Intergovernmental Relations, Natural Resources, State Affairs

BILL PASSAGE RATES, 1997

	Total	Passed Legislature	Pct. Passed Legislature
Authored	80	12	15%
Sponsored	43	37	86%
Amendments	45	43	96%

ELECTORAL HISTORY IN CURRENT DISTRICT

	1994	1996	1998
Primary Election Opponent(s)	Yes	Yes	NA
General Election Opponent(s)	Rep	No	NA

Senate District 28

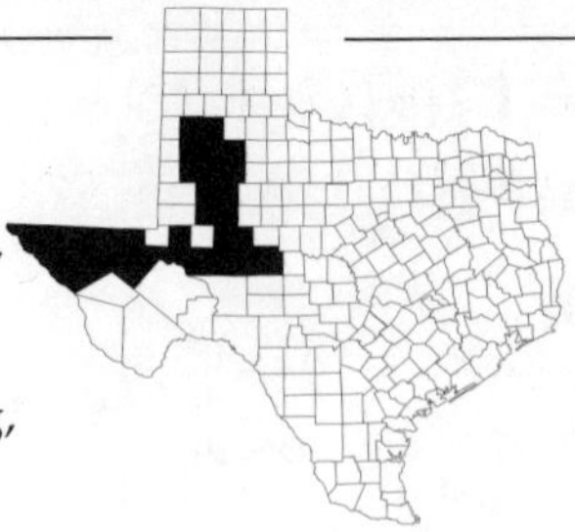

COUNTIES IN DISTRICT

Borden, Crane, Crosby, Culberson (part), Dawson, Ector (part), El Paso (part), Garza, Glasscock, Hale, Hockley, Howard, Hudspeth, Irion, Lamb, Loving, Lubbock, Lynn, Martin, Reagan, Reeves (part), Sterling, Terry, Tom Green (part), Upton, Ward

DEMOGRAPHIC INFORMATION

Population

Total	558,712
Anglo	59.0%
Black	6.5%
Hispanic	33.4%
Others	1.2%

Wealth and Urbanization

Per capita Income	$10,603
Avg. House Value	$51,638
Percent Poverty	21.8%
Public Assistance	7.6%
Percent Urban	78.4%

Education

High School Graduates	66.8%
College Graduates	16.0%

Employed

Percent Employed	92.5%
Private Sector	71.6%

Age of Population

5 years or less	10.3%
6-17 years	19.6%
18-64 years	59.4%
65 or older	10.7%

Household Types

Family households	85.7%
Non-family households	10.6%
Single-parent families	18.7%
Both parents working	56.9%

HOUSE DISTRICTS IN SENATORIAL DISTRICT

Dist 70 David Counts (D)
Dist 72 Robert Junell (D)
Dist 73 Robert R. Turner (D)
Dist 74 Pete P. Gallego (D)
Dist 75 Manny Najera (D)
Dist 78 Pat Haggerty (R)
Dist 79 Joseph C. Pickett (D)
Dist 80 Gary L. Walker (R)
Dist 81 G. E. (Buddy) West (R)
Dist 82 Tom Craddick (R)
Dist 83 Delwin Jones (R)
Dist 84 Carl H. Isett (R)
Dist 85 James E. (Pete) Laney (D)

DISTRICT ELECTION DATA

Senate 1996

NA

President 1996

Bill Clinton (D)	39.8%
Bob Dole (R)	60.2%

Composite Party Vote 1994

Democratic	44.8%
Republican	55.2%

Registered Voters 1996	**319,104**
Turnout	169,971
Percent of registered voting	53.3%

Senate 1998

Robert Duncan (R)	100.0%

Senate District 28
Senator Robert Duncan (R)

Senate Office
(512) 463-0128

District Office
1001 Main Street, Suite 602
Lubbock, Texas 79401
(806) 762-1122

Personal

Year of birth	1953
Family	Married to Lynne Duncan, two children
Education	Texas Tech University, B.A., J.D.
Occupation	Attorney
Religion	Protestant
State legislative service	House 1993-96, Senate 1997 to present

COMMITTEE ASSIGNMENT HISTORY
1997 Criminal Justice, Economic Development, Jurisprudence

BILL PASSAGE RATES, 1997

	Total	Passed Legislature	Pct. Passed Legislature
Authored	58	21	36%
Sponsored	42	39	93 %
Amendments	38	34	89%

ELECTORAL HISTORY IN CURRENT DISTRICT

	1994	1996	1998
Primary Election Opponent(s)	NA	NA	No
General Election Opponent(s)	NA	NA	No
Special Election Opponent(s)	NA	Dem, Rep	NA

Senate District 29

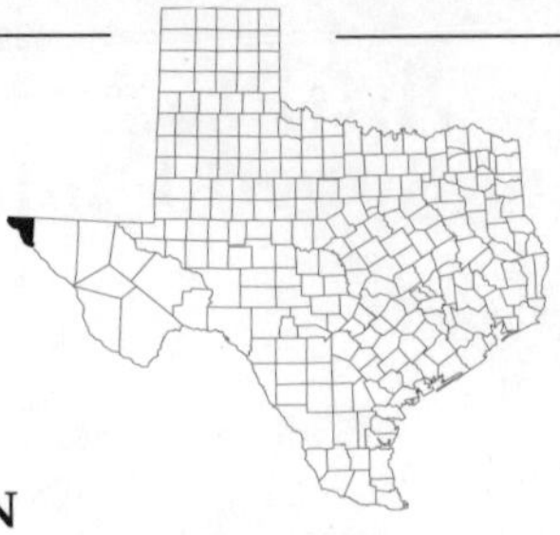

COUNTIES IN DISTRICT

El Paso (part)

DEMOGRAPHIC INFORMATION

Population	
Total	544,605
Anglo	24.4%
Black	3.2%
Hispanic	71.3%
Others	1.3%

Education	
High School Graduates	62.4%
College Graduates	15.0%

Age of Population	
5 years or less	10.5%
6-17 years	21.7%
18-64 years	59.2%
65 or older	8.6%

Wealth and Urbanization	
Per capita Income	$9,132
Avg. House Value	$67,199
Percent Poverty	27.5%
Public Assistance	10.5%
Percent Urban	98.3%

Employed	
Percent Employed	89.2%
Private Sector	73.8%

Household Types	
Family households	91.5%
Non-family households	7.2%
Single-parent families	24.5%
Both parents working	51.7%

HOUSE DISTRICTS IN SENATORIAL DISTRICT

Dist 75 Manny Najera (D)
Dist 76 Norma Chavez (D)
Dist 77 Paul C. Moreno (D)
Dist 78 Pat Haggerty (R)
Dist 79 Joseph C. Pickett (D)

DISTRICT ELECTION DATA

Senate 1996	
Eliot Shapleigh (D)	73.7%
Randy Berry (R)	26.3%

President 1996	
Bill Clinton (D)	66.6%
Bob Dole (R)	33.4%

Composite Party Vote 1994	
Democratic	59.0%
Republican	41.0%

Registered Voters 1996	270,499
Turnout	126,741
Percent of registered voting	46.9%

Senate 1998

NA

Senate District 29
Senator Eliot Shapleigh (D)

Senate Office
(512) 463-0129

District Office
800 Wyoming, Suite A
El Paso, Texas 79902
(915) 544-1990

Personal

Year of birth	1952
Family	Married to Lee Shapleigh, two children
Education	Rice University, B.A.
	University of Texas, J.D.
Occupation	Attorney
Religion	Episcopalian
State legislative service	Senate 1997 to present

COMMITTEE ASSIGNMENT HISTORY

1997 Criminal Justice, Economic Development, Education, International Relations, Trade and Technology

BILL PASSAGE RATES, 1997

	Total	Passed Legislature	Pct. Passed Legislature
Authored	34	10	29%
Sponsored	21	20	95%
Amendments	30	27	90%

ELECTORAL HISTORY IN CURRENT DISTRICT

	1994	1996	1998
Primary Election Opponent(s)	NA	Yes	NA
General Election Opponent(s)	NA	Rep	NA

Senate District 30

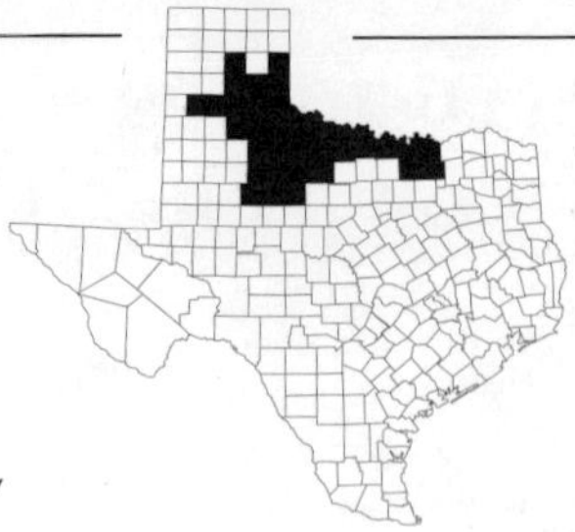

COUNTIES IN DISTRICT

Archer, Armstrong, Baylor, Briscoe, Carson, Castro, Childress, Clay, Collin (part), Collingsworth, Cooke, Cottle, Denton (part), Dickens, Donley, Fisher, Floyd, Foard, Grayson, Hall, Hardeman, Haskell, Jones, Kent, King, Knox, Montague, Motley, Scurry, Stonewall, Swisher, Taylor (part), Throckmorton, Wheeler, Wichita, Wilbarger

DEMOGRAPHIC INFORMATION

Population

Total	534,550
Anglo	82.7%
Black	6.1%
Hispanic	10.0%
Others	1.3%

Education

High School Graduates	70.8%
College Graduates	15.7%

Age of Population

5 years or less	8.8%
6-17 years	17.9%
18-64 years	58.0%
65 or older	15.3%

Wealth and Urbanization

Per capita Income	$11,540
Avg. House Value	$52,206
Percent Poverty	16.5%
Public Assistance	6.4%
Percent Urban	63.9%

Employed

Percent Employed	94.1%
Private Sector	70.9%

Household Types

Family households	84.8%
Non-family households	11.7%
Single-parent families	18.0%
Both parents working	64.7%

HOUSE DISTRICTS IN SENATORIAL DISTRICT

Dist 61	Phil King (R)	Dist 65	Burt Solomons (R)	Dist 71	Bob Hunter (R)
Dist 62	Ron Clark (R)	Dist 68	Rick Hardcastle (R)	Dist 85	James E. (Pete) Laney (D)
Dist 63	Mary Denny (R)	Dist 69	David Farabee (D)	Dist 86	John Smithee (R)
Dist 64	Ronny Crownover (R)	Dist 70	David Counts (D)	Dist 88	Warren Chisum (R)

DISTRICT ELECTION DATA

Senate 1996

NA

Senate 1998

Greg Underwood (D)	37.4%
Tom Haywood (R)	62.6%

President 1996

Bill Clinton (D)	43.1%
Bob Dole (R)	56.9%

Composite Party Vote 1994

Democratic	49.2%
Republican	50.8%

Registered Voters 1996	**342,964**
Turnout	192,612
Percent of registered voting	56.2%

Senate District 30
Senator Tom Haywood (R)

Senate Office
(512) 463-0130

District Office
2525 Kell, Suite 305
Wichita Falls, Texas 76308
(817) 767-3073

Personal

Year of birth	1939
Family	Married to Pat Haywood, four children
Education	University of Texas at Arlington, B.S.
	University of North Texas, M.S.
	University of Alberta (Canada), Ph.D.
Occupation	Businessman
Religion	Methodist
State legislative service	Senate 1995 to present

COMMITTEE ASSIGNMENT HISTORY

1997 Economic Development, Education, Natural Resources, Nominations
1995 Economic Development, Education, Natural Resources

BILL PASSAGE RATES, 1997

	Total	Passed Legislature	Pct. Passed Legislature
Authored	65	19	29%
Sponsored	18	17	94%
Amendments	17	12	71%

ELECTORAL HISTORY IN CURRENT DISTRICT

	1994	1996	1998
Primary Election Opponent(s)	Yes	NA	No
General Election Opponent(s)	Dem	NA	Dem

Senate District 31

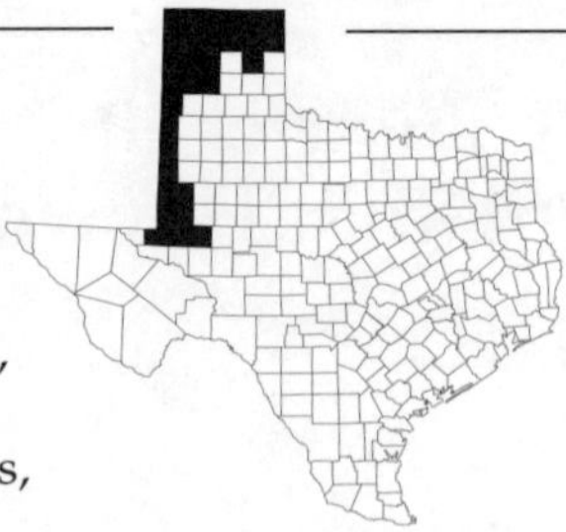

COUNTIES IN DISTRICT

Andrews, Bailey, Cochran, Dallam, Deaf Smith, Ector (part), Gaines, Gray, Hansford, Hartley, Hemphill, Hutchison, Lipscomb, Midland, Moore, Ochiltree, Oldham, Parmer, Potter, Randall, Roberts, Sherman, Winkler, Yoakum

DEMOGRAPHIC INFORMATION

Population

Total	541,958
Anglo	74.4%
Black	4.2%
Hispanic	19.9%
Others	1.6%

Education

High School Graduates	72.3%
College Graduates	17.1%

Age of Population

5 years or less	10.2%
6-17 years	20.1%
18-64 years	58.7%
65 or older	11.0%

Wealth and Urbanization

Per capita Income	$12,595
Avg. House Value	$58,264
Percent Poverty	16.3%
Public Assistance	5.2%
Percent Urban	80.4%

Employed

Percent Employed	94.0%
Private Sector	75.5%

Household Types

Family households	88.1%
Non-family households	10.7%
Single-parent families	18.5%
Both parents working	59.3%

HOUSE DISTRICTS IN SENATORIAL DISTRICT

Dist 80 Gary L. Walker (R)
Dist 81 G. E. (Buddy) West (R)
Dist 82 Tom Craddick (R)
Dist 85 James E. (Pete) Laney (D)
Dist 86 John Smithee (R)
Dist 87 David Swinford (R)
Dist 88 Warren Chisum (R)

DISTRICT ELECTION DATA

Senate 1996

NA

Senate 1998

Teel Bivins (R)	100.0%

President 1996

Bill Clinton (D)	29.3%
Bob Dole (R)	70.7%

Composite Party Vote 1994

Democratic	36.1%
Republican	63.9%

Registered Voters 1996	**313,559**
Turnout	183,272
Percent of registered voting	58.4%

Senate District 31
Senator Teel Bivins (R)

Senate Office
(512) 463-0131
Teel.Bivins@senate.state.tx.us

District Office
203 West 8th Street, Suite 301
Amarillo, Texas 79101
(806) 374-8994

Personal

Year of birth	1947
Family	Married to Nancy Bivins, three children
Education	Tulane University, B.A.
	Southern Methodist University, J.D.
Occupation	Businessman, cattleman
Religion	Episcopalian
State legislative service	Senate 1989 to present

COMMITTEE ASSIGNMENT HISTORY

1997 Education (Chair), Finance, International Relations, Trade and Technology, Natural Resources
1995 Education, Finance, Natural Resources, Nominations (Chair)
1993 Education, Finance, International Relations, Trade and Technology, Natural Resources
1991 Education, Finance, Intergovernmental Relations
1989 Economic Development, Jurisprudence, Natural Resources

BILL PASSAGE RATES, 1997

	Total	Passed Legislature	Pct. Passed Legislature
Authored	70	28	40%
Sponsored	35	32	91%
Amendments	29	26	90%

ELECTORAL HISTORY IN CURRENT DISTRICT

	1994	1996	1998
Primary Election Opponent(s)	No	NA	No
General Election Opponent(s)	No	NA	No

The Texas House of Representatives

House District 1

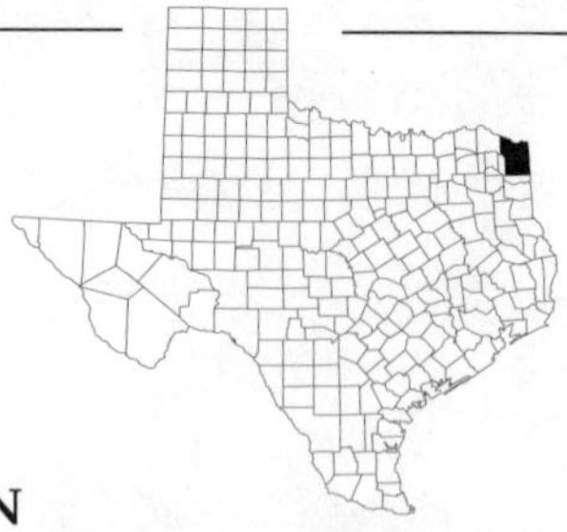

COUNTIES IN DISTRICT
Bowie, Cass

DEMOGRAPHIC INFORMATION

Population	
Total	111,647
Anglo	76.5%
Black	21.4%
Hispanic	1.5%
Others	0.7%

Wealth and Urbanization	
Per capita Income	$11,186
Avg. House Value	$51,957
Percent Poverty	18.7%
Public Assistance	9.1%
Percent Urban	50.4%

Education	
High School Graduates	70.6%
College Graduates	12.9%

Employed	
Percent Employed	93.0%
Private Sector	66.8%

Age of Population	
5 years or less	8.4%
6-17 years	18.9%
18-64 years	57.6%
65 or older	15.1%

Household Types	
Family households	87.0%
Non-family households	10.6%
Single-parent families	23.5%
Both parents working	64.5%

SENATE DISTRICTS IN HOUSE DISTRICT
Dist 1 Bill Ratliff (R)

DISTRICT ELECTION DATA

House 1996	
Barry B. Telford (D)	73.8%
George Lavender (R)	36.2%

House 1998	
Barry B. Telford (D)	100.0%

President 1996	
Bill Clinton (D)	53.5%
Bob Dole (R)	46.5%

Composite Party Vote 1994	
Democratic	56.2%
Republican	43.8%

Registered Voters 1996	**71,073**
Turnout	40,462
Percent of registered voting	56.9%

House District 1
Rep. Barry B. Telford (D)

House Office
(512) 463-0692

District Office
206 Northwest Front Street
DeKalb, Texas 75559
(903) 667-5514

Personal

Year of birth	1946
Family	Married to Marsha Telford, two children
Education	University of North Texas, B.S., Education
Occupation	Businessman
Religion	Baptist
State legislative service	House 1987 to present

COMMITTEE ASSIGNMENT HISTORY

1997 House Administration, Pensions and Investments (Chair), Ways and Means
1995 Corrections, House Administration, Pensions and Investments (Chair)
1993 Appropriations, Corrections, Local and Consent Calendars (Vice-Chair)
1991 Appropriations, Corrections
1989 Corrections, Public Safety
1987 Corrections, Public Safety

BILL PASSAGE RATES, 1997

	Total	Passed Legislature	Pct. Passed Legislature
Authored	25	11	44%
Sponsored	8	8	100%
Amendments	9	9	100%

ELECTORAL HISTORY IN CURRENT DISTRICT

	1994	1996	1998
Primary Election Opponent(s)	No	No	No
General Election Opponent(s)	No	Rep	No

House District 2

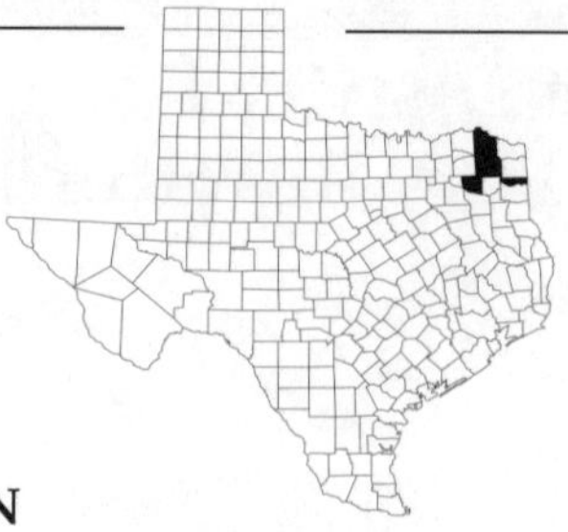

COUNTIES IN DISTRICT

Camp, Franklin, Marion, Morris, Red River, Titus, Wood

DEMOGRAPHIC INFORMATION

Population	
Total	108,596
Anglo	78.9%
Black	16.2%
Hispanic	4.5%
Others	0.5%

Wealth and Urbanization	
Per capita Income	$10,443
Avg. House Value	$46,284
Percent Poverty	21.8%
Public Assistance	9.0%
Percent Urban	27.8%

Education	
High School Graduates	88.2%
College Graduates	9.9%

Employed	
Percent Employed	92.4%
Private Sector	74.0%

Age of Population	
5 years or less	8.0%
6-17 years	17.9%
18-64 years	55.2%
65 or older	19.0%

Household Types	
Family households	87.1%
Non-family households	10.8%
Single-parent families	20.5%
Both parents working	59.8%

SENATE DISTRICTS IN HOUSE DISTRICT

Dist 1 Bill Ratliff (R)

Dist 2 David Cain (D)

DISTRICT ELECTION DATA

House 1996	
Tom Ramsay (D)	100.0%

House 1998	
Tom Ramsay (D)	54.5%
Debe McGuire (R)	45.5%

President 1996	
Bill Clinton (D)	52.8%
Bob Dole (R)	47.2%

Composite Party Vote 1994	
Democratic	55.8%
Republican	44.2%

Registered Voters 1996	**69,836**
Turnout	40,557
Percent of registered voting	58.1%

House District 2
Rep. Tom Ramsay (D)

House Office
(512) 463-0680

District Office
P.O. Box 663
Mount Vernon, Texas 75457
(903) 537-4711

Personal

Year of birth	1939
Family	Married to Laurie Manning, four children
Education	Southern Methodist University, B.B.S.
Occupation	Realtor
Religion	Baptist
State legislative service	House 1993 to present

COMMITTEE ASSIGNMENT HISTORY
1997 State Affairs, Ways and Means (Vice-Chair)
1995 Energy Resources, State Affairs
1993 Economic Development, Energy Resources

BILL PASSAGE RATES, 1995

	Total	Passed Legislature	Pct. Passed Legislature
Authored	20	5	25%
Sponsored	8	7	88%
Amendments	6	6	100%

ELECTORAL HISTORY IN CURRENT DISTRICT

	1994	1996	1998
Primary Election Opponent(s)	No	No	No
General Election Opponent(s)	No	No	Rep

House District 3

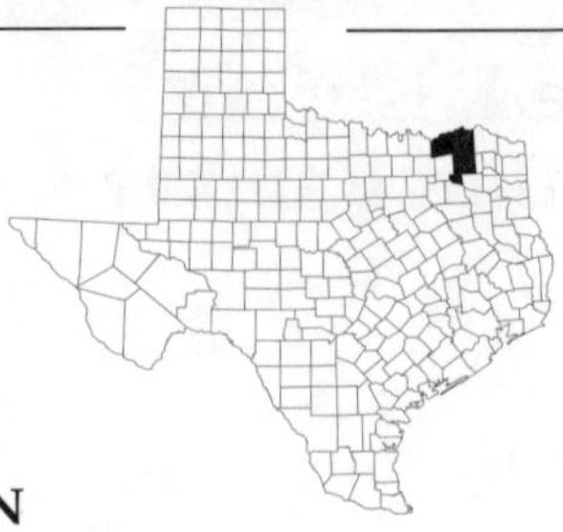

COUNTIES IN DISTRICT
Delta, Fannin, Hopkins, Lamar, Rains

DEMOGRAPHIC INFORMATION

Population	
Total	109,158
Anglo	86.4%
Black	10.3%
Hispanic	2.4%
Others	1.0%

Education	
High School Graduates	87.8%
College Graduates	11.7%

Age of Population	
5 years or less	8.4%
6-17 years	17.1%
18-64 years	56.1%
65 or older	18.3%

Wealth and Urbanization	
Per capita Income	$10,588
Avg. House Value	$44,846
Percent Poverty	19.2%
Public Assistance	9.0%
Percent Urban	41.6%

Employed	
Percent Employed	92.8%
Private Sector	72.8%

Household Types	
Family households	86.7%
Non-family households	11.1%
Single-parent families	17.8%
Both parents working	64.8%

SENATE DISTRICTS IN HOUSE DISTRICT
Dist 1 Bill Ratliff (R)
Dist 2 David Cain (D)

DISTRICT ELECTION DATA

House 1996	
L. P. (Pete) Patterson (D)	100.0%

House 1998	
Mark Homer (D)	57.0%
Sue Fancher (R)	43.0%

President 1996	
Bill Clinton (D)	51.3%
Bob Dole (R)	48.7%

Composite Party Vote 1994	
Democratic	56.4%
Republican	43.6%

Registered Voters 1996	**69,498**
Turnout	37,373
Percent of registered voting	53.8%

House District 3
Rep. Mark Homer (D)

House Office
(512) 463-0650

District Office
P.O. Box 6128
Paris, Texas 75461
(903) 737-9949

Personal

Year of birth	1962
Family	Married to Jennifer Homer, one child
Education	Texas A&M University, B. A.
	Angelo State University, B.B.A.
Occupation	Sonic Drive In Franchisee
Religion	Christian
State legislative service	House 1999 to present

COMMITTEE ASSIGNMENT HISTORY

BILL PASSAGE RATES, 1997

	Total	Passed Legislature	Pct. Passed Legislature
Authored	NA	NA	NA
Sponsored	NA	NA	NA
Amendments	NA	NA	NA

ELECTORAL HISTORY IN CURRENT DISTRICT

	1994	1996	1998
Primary Election Opponent(s)	NA	NA	Yes
General Election Opponent(s)	NA	NA	Rep

House District 4

COUNTIES IN DISTRICT
Hunt, Kaufman

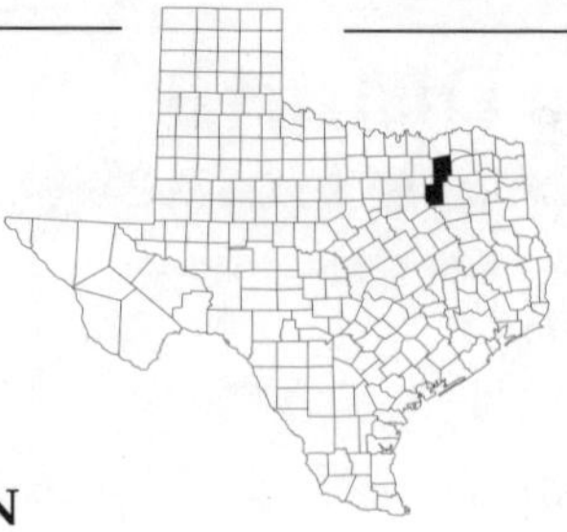

DEMOGRAPHIC INFORMATION

Population	
Total	116,563
Anglo	81.8%
Black	12.1%
Hispanic	5.3%
Others	0.9%

Education	
High School Graduates	68.6%
College Graduates	13.7%

Age of Population	
5 years or less	8.8%
6-17 years	18.9%
18-64 years	59.3%
65 or older	13.0%

Wealth and Urbanization	
Per capita Income	$11,720
Avg. House Value	$58,034
Percent Poverty	15.5%
Public Assistance	6.8%
Percent Urban	44.4%

Employed	
Percent Employed	93.3%
Private Sector	74.7%

Household Types	
Family households	87.8%
Non-family households	9.7%
Single-parent families	19.4%
Both parents working	65.4%

SENATE DISTRICTS IN HOUSE DISTRICT

Dist 2 David Cain (D)

DISTRICT ELECTION DATA

House 1996	
Keith Oakley (D)	52.9%
Betty Brown (R)	47.1%

House 1998	
Bruce Wood (D)	46.7%
Betty Brown (R)	53.3%

President 1996	
Bill Clinton (D)	45.4%
Bob Dole (R)	54.6%

Composite Party Vote 1994	
Democratic	48.6%
Republican	51.4%

Registered Voters 1996	**76,332**
Turnout	39,954
Percent of registered voting	52.3%

House District 4
Rep. Betty Brown (R)

House Office
(512) 463-0458

District Office
P.O. Box 1477
Terrell, Texas 75160
(972) 524-9499

Personal

Year of birth	1939
Family	Married to Ron Brown, three children
Education	Attended Southern Methodist University
Occupation	Rancher and homemaker
Religion	Christian
State legislative service	House 1999 to present

COMMITTEE ASSIGNMENT HISTORY

BILL PASSAGE RATES, 1997

	Total	Passed Legislature	Pct. Passed Legislature
Authored	NA	NA	NA
Sponsored	NA	NA	NA
Amendments	NA	NA	NA

ELECTORAL HISTORY IN CURRENT DISTRICT

	1994	1996	1998
Primary Election Opponent(s)	NA	NA	Yes
General Election Opponent(s)	NA	NA	Dem

House District 5

COUNTIES IN DISTRICT
Smith (part), Upshur,Van Zandt

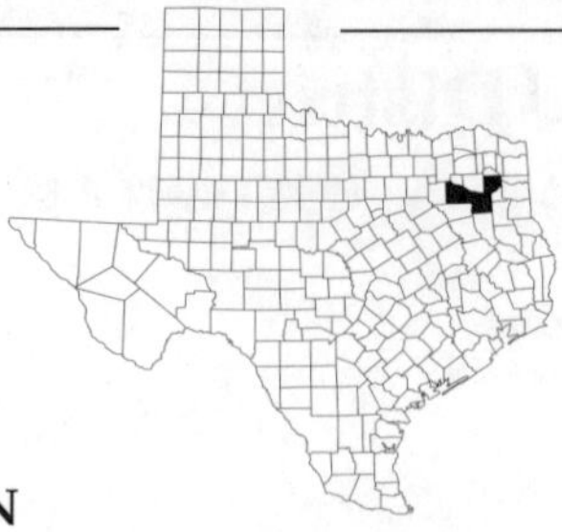

DEMOGRAPHIC INFORMATION

Population

Total	110,972
Anglo	69.7%
Black	23.5%
Hispanic	6.5%
Others	0.5%

Education

High School Graduates	63.6%
College Graduates	9.3%

Age of Population

5 years or less	8.7%
6-17 years	19.0%
18-64 years	56.8%
65 or older	15.5%

Wealth and Urbanization

Per capita Income	$9,709
Avg. House Value	$46,422
Percent Poverty	21.2%
Public Assistance	8.88%
Percent Urban	35.5%

Employed

Percent Employed	90.9%
Private Sector	75.6%

Household Types

Family households	88.7%
Non-family households	9.4%
Single-parent families	20.6%
Both parents working	59.4%

SENATE DISTRICTS IN HOUSE DISTRICT

Dist 1 Bill Ratliff (R)

Dist 2 David Cain (D)

DISTRICT ELECTION DATA

House 1996

Bob Glaze (D)	59.5%
Dan Flynn (R)	40.5%

President 1996

Bill Clinton (D)	52.8%
Bob Dole (R)	47.2%

Composite Party Vote 1994

Democratic	56.4%
Republican	43.6%

Registered Voters 1996	**69,312**
Turnout	36,923
Percent of registered voting	53.3%

House 1998

Bob Glaze (D)	55.4%
Dan Flynn (R)	44.6%

House District 5
Rep. Bob Glaze (D)

House Office
(512) 463-0580

District Office
P.O. Box 1210
Gilmer, Texas 75644
(903) 843-5792

Personal

Year of birth	1927
Family	Married to Jean Glaze, three children
Education	Texas Chiropractic College, D.C.
Occupation	Chiropractor
Religion	Baptist
State legislative service	House 1991 to present

COMMITTEE ASSIGNMENT HISTORY

1997 Appropriations, Public Health, Redistricting (Vice-Chair)
1995 Appropriations, Public Health, Redistricting
1993 Appropriations, Public Health, Redistricting
1991 Cultural and Historical Resources, Public Health

BILL PASSAGE RATES, 1997

	Total	Passed Legislature	Pct. Passed Legislature
Authored	21	12	57%
Sponsored	3	3	100%
Amendments	1	1	100%

ELECTORAL HISTORY IN CURRENT DISTRICT

	1994	1996	1998
Primary Election Opponent(s)	No	No	No
General Election Opponent(s)	Rep	Rep	Rep

House District 6

COUNTIES IN DISTRICT
Smith (part)

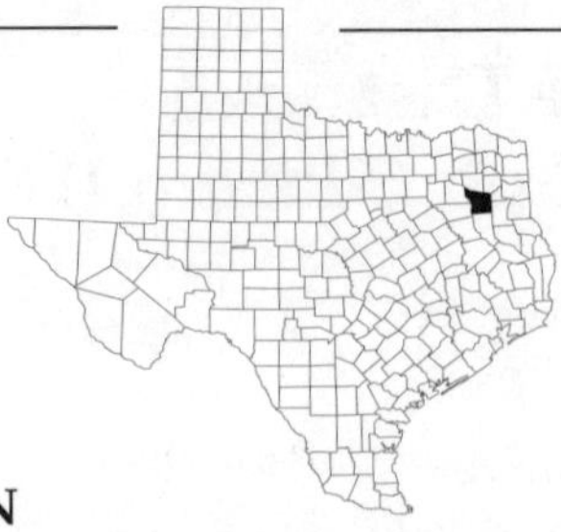

DEMOGRAPHIC INFORMATION

Population		**Wealth and Urbanization**	
Total	109,651	Per capita Income	$15,206
Anglo	85.7%	Avg. House Value	$84,076
Black	9.9%	Percent Poverty	10.0%
Hispanic	3.6%	Public Assistance	4.3%
Others	0.9%	Percent Urban	54.6%

Education		**Employed**	
High School Graduates	83.9%	Percent Employed	95.2%
College Graduates	25.4%	Private Sector	77.0%

Age of Population		**Household Types**	
5 years or less	8.4%	Family households	86.1%
6-17 years	16.7%	Non-family households	12.4%
18-64 years	60.6%	Single-parent families	15.9%
65 or older	14.2%	Both parents working	62.8%

SENATE DISTRICTS IN HOUSE DISTRICT

Dist 1 Bill Ratliff (R)
Dist 2 David Cain (D)
Dist 3 Drew Nixon (R)

DISTRICT ELECTION DATA

House 1996		**House 1998**	
Ted Kamel (R)	100.0%	Leo Berman (R)	100.0%

President 1996

Bill Clinton (D)	28.4%
Bob Dole (R)	71.6%

Composite Party Vote 1994

Democratic	35.0%
Republican	65.0%

Registered Voters 1996	**70,617**
Turnout	44,307
Percent of registered voting	62.7%

House District 6
Rep. Leo Berman (R)

House Office
(512) 463-0584

District Office
815 South College
Tyler, Texas 75701
(903) 597-8206

Personal

Year of birth	1935
Family	Married to Cara Sue Berman, four children
Education	Southern Methodist University, B.A.
Occupation	Retired
Religion	United Methodist
State legislative service	House 1999 to present

COMMITTEE ASSIGNMENT HISTORY

BILL PASSAGE RATES, 1997

	Total	Passed Legislature	Pct. Passed Legislature
Authored	NA	NA	NA
Sponsored	NA	NA	NA
Amendments	NA	NA	NA

ELECTORAL HISTORY IN CURRENT DISTRICT

	1994	1996	1998
Primary Election Opponent(s)	NA	NA	Yes
General Election Opponent(s)	NA	NA	No

House District 7

COUNTIES IN DISTRICT

Gregg, Rusk (part)

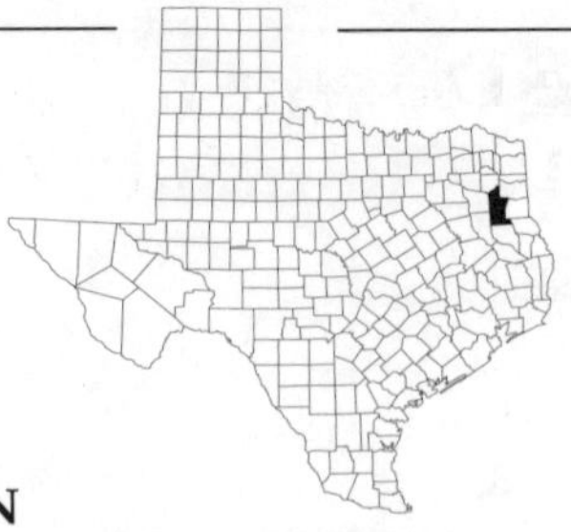

DEMOGRAPHIC INFORMATION

Population		**Wealth and Urbanization**	
Total	110,188	Per capita Income	$12,437
Anglo	77.0%	Avg. House Value	$61,977
Black	18.7%	Percent Poverty	16.7%
Hispanic	3.5%	Public Assistance	6.4%
Others	0.9%	Percent Urban	82.8%

Education		**Employed**	
High School Graduates	75.9%	Percent Employed	93.0%
College Graduates	17.5%	Private Sector	82.0%

Age of Population		**Household Types**	
5 years or less	9.0%	Family households	85.4%
6-17 years	18.0%	Non-family households	12.4%
18-64 years	59.6%	Single-parent families	22.8%
65 or older	13.4%	Both parents working	61.7%

SENATE DISTRICTS IN HOUSE DISTRICT

Dist 1 Bill Ratliff (R)

DISTRICT ELECTION DATA

House 1996		**House 1998**	
Tommy Merritt (R)	100.0%	Tommy Merritt (R)	100.0%

President 1996	
Bill Clinton (D)	38.5%
Bob Dole (R)	61.5%

Composite Party Vote 1994	
Democratic	42.4%
Republican	57.6%

Registered Voters 1996	**76,238**
Turnout	39,409
Percent of registered voting	51.7%

House District 7
Rep. Tommy Merritt (R)

House Office
(512) 463-0750
(513) 463-9085 fax

District Office
201 Estes Drive
Longview, Texas 75603
(903) 238-9100
(903) 238-9102 (Fax)

Personal

Year of birth	1948
Family	Married to Janet Merritt, three children
Education	Texas Christian University, B.B.A.
Occupation	President, Gregg Industrial Insulators
Religion	Baptist
State legislative service	House 1997 to present

COMMITTEE ASSIGNMENT HISTORY

1997 Energy Resources, State Recreational Resources

BILL PASSAGE RATES, 1997

	Total	Passed Legislature	Pct. Passed Legislature
Authored	17	4	24%
Sponsored	1	1	100%
Amendments	0	0	NA

ELECTORAL HISTORY IN CURRENT DISTRICT

	1994	1996	1996
Primary Election Opponent(s)	NA	Yes	No
General Election Opponent(s)	NA	No	No

House District 8

COUNTIES IN DISTRICT

Harrison, Panola, Rusk (part)

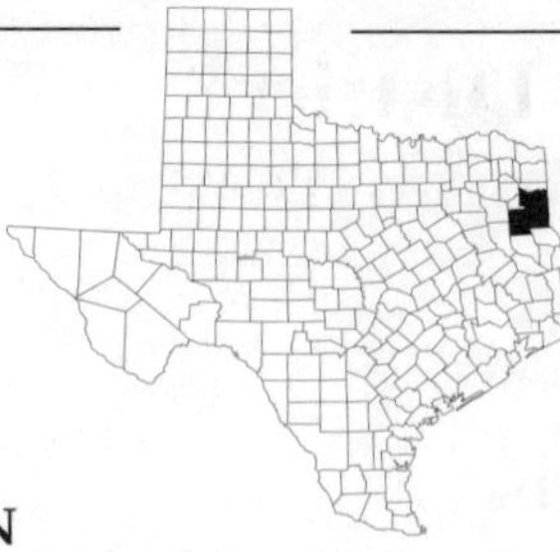

DEMOGRAPHIC INFORMATION

Population

Total	110,013
Anglo	77.0%
Black	18.7%
Hispanic	3.5%
Others	0.9%

Education

High School Graduates	68.1%
College Graduates	11.8%

Age of Population

5 years or less	8.5%
6-17 years	20.0%
18-64 years	56.3%
65 or older	15.3%

Wealth and Urbanization

Per capita Income	$10,247
Avg. House Value	$49,843
Percent Poverty	20.7%
Public Assistance	9.7%
Percent Urban	37.1%

Employed

Percent Employed	91.8%
Private Sector	76.5%

Household Types

Family households	88.1%
Non-family households	10.0%
Single-parent families	20.3%
Both parents working	59.1%

SENATE DISTRICTS IN HOUSE DISTRICT

Dist 1 Bill Ratliff (R)

Dist 3 Drew Nixon (R)

DISTRICT ELECTION DATA

House 1996

Paul Sadler (D)	61.1%
Gene Barron (R)	38.9%

President 1996

Bill Clinton (D)	48.5%
Bob Dole (R)	51.5%

Composite Party Vote 1994

Democratic	51.4%
Republican	48.6%

Registered Voters 1996	**78,013**
Turnout	44,590
Percent of registered voting	57.2%

House 1998

Paul Sadler (D)	61.6%
Gene Barron (R)	38.4%

House District 8
Rep. Paul Sadler (D)

House Office
(512) 463-0626

District Office
200 W. Houston
Marshall, Texas 75670
(903) 935-1141

Personal

Year of birth	1955
Family	Married to Sherri Sadler, five children
Education	Baylor University, B.B.A., J.D.
Occupation	Attorney
Religion	Methodist
State legislative service	House 1991 to present

COMMITTEE ASSIGNMENT HISTORY

1997 Calendars, Pensions and Investments, Public Education (Chair)
1995 Civil Practices, Public Education (Chair)
1993 Judicial Affairs, Local and Consent Calendars, Public Education
1991 House Administration, Human Services, Judiciary

BILL PASSAGE RATES, 1997

	Total	Passed Legislature	Pct. Passed Legislature
Authored	13	2	15%
Sponsored	10	4	40%
Amendments	3	3	100%

ELECTORAL HISTORY IN CURRENT DISTRICT

	1994	1996	1998
Primary Election Opponent(s)	No	No	No
General Election Opponent(s)	No	Rep	Rep

House District 9

COUNTIES IN DISTRICT

Jasper, Nacogdoches, Sabine, Shelby

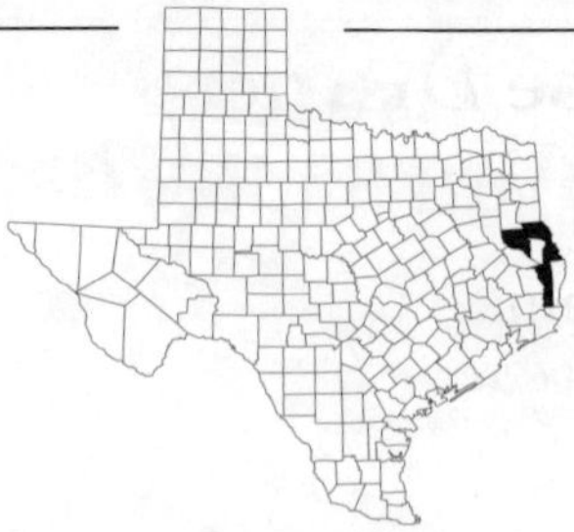

DEMOGRAPHIC INFORMATION

Population	
Total	117,475
Anglo	78.5%
Black	17.6%
Hispanic	3.4%
Others	0.6%

Wealth and Urbanization	
Per capita Income	$9,782
Avg. House Value	$51,572
Percent Poverty	23.2%
Public Assistance	9.4%
Percent Urban	36.4%

Education	
High School Graduates	64.8%
College Graduates	13.4%

Employed	
Percent Employed	92.7%
Private Sector	71.6%

Age of Population	
5 years or less	7.7%
6-17 years	17.4%
18-64 years	59.4%
65 or older	15.5%

Household Types	
Family households	81.6%
Non-family households	13.7%
Single-parent families	22.2%
Both parents working	57.0%

SENATE DISTRICTS IN HOUSE DISTRICT

Dist 3 Drew Nixon (R)

DISTRICT ELECTION DATA

House 1996	
Judy McDonald (D)	49.6%
Wayne Christian (R)	50.4%

House 1998	
Colin Strother (D)	42.2%
Wayne Christian (R)	57.8%

President 1996	
Bill Clinton (D)	47.8%
Bob Dole (R)	52.2%

Composite Party Vote 1994	
Democratic	51.3%
Republican	48.7%

Registered Voters 1996	**78,112**
Turnout	42,424
Percent of registered voting	54.3%

House District 9
Rep. Wayne Christian (R)

House Office
(512) 463-0556
Wayne.Christian@house.state.tx.us

District Office
204 Houston Street
Center, Texas 75935
(409) 598-9966

Personal

Year of birth	1950
Family	Married to Lisa Christian, three children
Education	Stephen F. Austin University, B.B.A.
Occupation	Investment counselor
Religion	Southern Baptist
State legislative service	House 1997 to present

COMMITTEE ASSIGNMENT HISTORY
1997 County Affairs, Human Services

BILL PASSAGE RATES, 1997

	Total	Passed Legislature	Pct. Passed Legislature
Authored	13	6	46%
Sponsored	1	1	100%
Amendments	4	4	100%

ELECTORAL HISTORY IN CURRENT DISTRICT

	1994	1996	1998
Primary Election Opponent(s)	NA	NA	No
General Election Opponent(s)	NA	Dem	Dem

House District 10

COUNTIES IN DISTRICT
Ellis, Hill

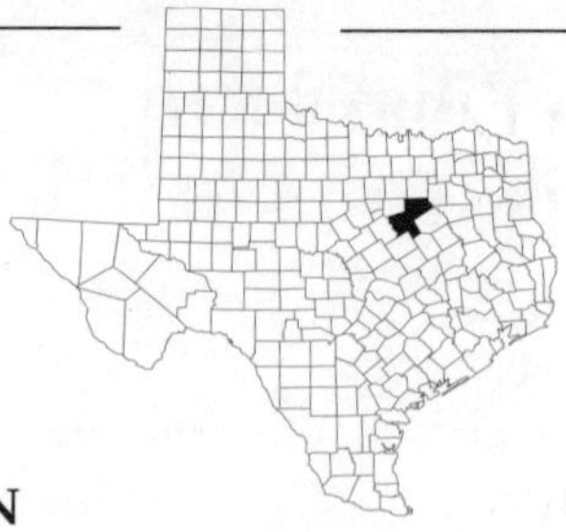

DEMOGRAPHIC INFORMATION

Population		**Wealth and Urbanization**	
Total	112,313	Per capita Income	$11,838
Anglo	77.6%	Avg. House Value	$66,765
Black	9.8%	Percent Poverty	14.8%
Hispanic	12.0%	Public Assistance	6.7%
Others	0.7%	Percent Urban	41.9%

Education		**Employed**	
High School Graduates	69.1%	Percent Employed	93.5%
College Graduates	12.7%	Private Sector	76.9%

Age of Population		**Household Types**	
5 years or less	9.9%	Family households	89.7%
6-17 years	19.5%	Non-family households	8.5%
18-64 years	57.8%	Single-parent families	16.6%
65 or older	12.8%	Both parents working	64.4%

SENATE DISTRICTS IN HOUSE DISTRICT

Dist 2 David Cain (D)
Dist 9 Jane Nelson (R)
Dist 22 David Sibley (R)

DISTRICT ELECTION DATA

House 1996		**House 1998**	
Jim Pitts (R)	100.0%	Jim Pitts (R)	100.0%

President 1996	
Bill Clinton (D)	42.0%
Bob Dole (R)	58.0%

Composite Party Vote 1994	
Democratic	44.7%
Republican	55.3%

Registered Voters 1996	**73,768**
Turnout	39,512
Percent of registered voting	53.6%

House District 10
Rep. Jim Pitts (R)

House Office
(512) 463-0516

District Office
200 North Rogers
Waxahachie, Texas 75165
(972) 938-9392

Personal

Year of birth	1947
Family	Married to Evelyn Pitts, three children
Education	Southern Methodist University, B.B.A., M.B.A., J.D.
Occupation	Attorney
Religion	Catholic
State legislative service	House 1993 to present

COMMITTEE ASSIGNMENT HISTORY

1997 Appropriations, State, Federal and International Relations
1995 Corrections, Criminal Jurisprudence
1993 Economic Development, Transportation

BILL PASSAGE RATES, 1997

	Total	Passed Legislature	Pct. Passed Legislature
Authored	30	6	20%
Sponsored	8	6	75%
Amendments	11	10	91%

ELECTORAL HISTORY IN CURRENT DISTRICT

	1994	1996	1998
Primary Election Opponent(s)	No	No	No
General Election Opponent(s)	No	No	No

House District 11

COUNTIES IN DISTRICT
Anderson, Cherokee, Leon, Robertson

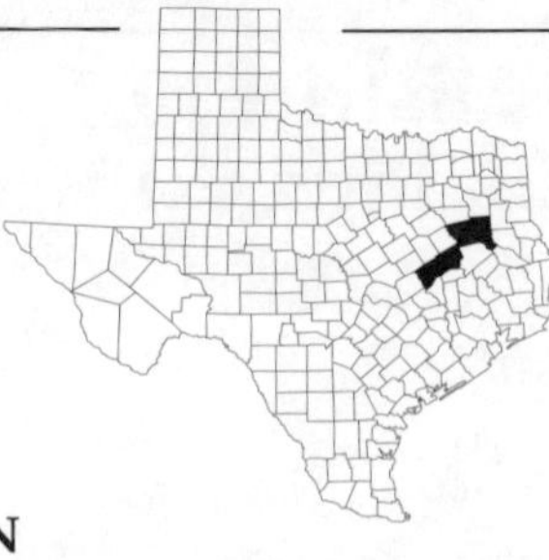

DEMOGRAPHIC INFORMATION

Population

Total	117,249
Anglo	71.4%
Black	20.4%
Hispanic	7.7%
Others	0.6%

Wealth and Urbanization

Per capita Income	$9,468
Avg. House Value	$47,581
Percent Poverty	21.4%
Public Assistance	9.3%
Percent Urban	34.4%

Education

High School Graduates	64.6%
College Graduates	9.8%

Employed

Percent Employed	93.1%
Private Sector	67.1%

Age of Population

5 years or less	8.2%
6-17 years	17.1%
18-64 years	58.6%
65 or older	16.1%

Household Types

Family households	79.7%
Non-family households	9.7%
Single-parent families	22.3%
Both parents working	62.1%

SENATE DISTRICTS IN HOUSE DISTRICT

Dist 3 Drew Nixon (R)
Dist 5 Steve Ogden (R)

DISTRICT ELECTION DATA

House 1996

Doug Lowe (D)	43.8%
Todd Staples (R)	56.2%

House 1998

Todd Staples (R)	100.0%

President 1996

Bill Clinton (D)	47.5%
Bob Dole (R)	52.5%

Composite Party Vote 1994

Democratic	52.7%
Republican	47.3%

Registered Voters 1996	**67,512**
Turnout	37,186
Percent of registered voting	55.1%

House District 11
Rep. Todd Staples (R)

House Office
(512) 463-0592

District Office
118 E. Palestine Ave.
Palestine, Texas 75801
(903) 729-7717

Personal

Year of birth	1963
Family	Married to Janet Staples, four children
Education	Texas A&M University, B.S., Agricultural Economics
Occupation	Real estate appraiser
Religion	Baptist
State legislative service	House 1995 to present

COMMITTEE ASSIGNMENT HISTORY

1997 Juvenile Justice and Family Issues (Vice-Chair), Land and Resource Management
1995 Elections, Urban Affairs

BILL PASSAGE RATES, 1997

	Total	Passed Legislature	Pct. Passed Legislature
Authored	14	4	29%
Sponsored	5	5	100%
Amendments	21	17	81%

ELECTORAL HISTORY IN CURRENT DISTRICT

	1994	1995	1996	1998
Primary Election Opponent(s)	NA	NA	No	No
General Election Opponent(s)	NA	NA	Dem	No
Special Election Opponent(s)	NA	Dem, Dem	NA	NA

House District 12

COUNTIES IN DISTRICT

Freestone, Henderson, Navarro

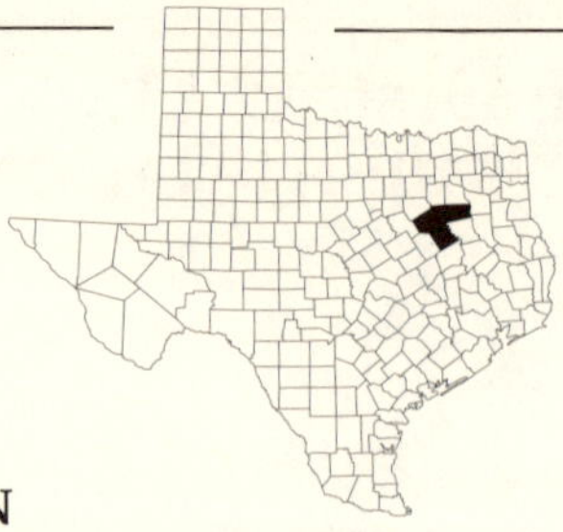

DEMOGRAPHIC INFORMATION

Population		**Wealth and Urbanization**	
Total	114,287	Per capita Income	$10,620
Anglo	80.8%	Avg. House Value	$56,291
Black	13.4%	Percent Poverty	18.8%
Hispanic	5.1%	Public Assistance	7.5%
Others	0.7%	Percent Urban	38.4%

Education		**Employed**	
High School Graduates	64.8%	Percent Employed	92.0%
College Graduates	11.0%	Private Sector	74.6%

Age of Population		**Household Types**	
5 years or less	8.0%	Family households	86.6%
6-17 years	17.5%	Non-family households	11.1%
18-64 years	56.0%	Single-parent families	19.8%
65 or older	18.5%	Both parents working	65.1%

SENATE DISTRICTS IN HOUSE DISTRICT

Dist 3 Drew Nixon (R)

Dist 5 Steve Ogden (R)

DISTRICT ELECTION DATA

House 1996		**House 1998**	
Clyde Alexander (D)	63.9%	Clyde Alexander (D)	62.8%
Jerry Moon (R)	36.1%	Jeffrey L. Weinstein (R)	37.2%

President 1996	
Bill Clinton (D)	50.4%
Bob Dole (R)	49.6%

Composite Party Vote 1994	
Democratic	52.4%
Republican	47.6%

Registered Voters 1996	**73,296**
Turnout	41,728
Percent of registered voting	56.9%

House District 12
Rep. Clyde Alexander (D)

House Office
(512) 463-0730

District Office
P.O. Box 750
Athens, Texas 75751
(903) 675-1990

Personal

Year of birth	1946
Family	Single, two children
Education	University of Denver, B.S., Economics
Occupation	Rancher, businessman
Religion	Methodist
State legislative service	House 1989 to present

COMMITTEE ASSIGNMENT HISTORY

1997 Corrections, Transportation (Chair)
1995 Land and Resource Management, Transportation (Chair)
1993 Appropriations, Local and Consent Calendars, Ways and Means
1991 Appropriations, Environmental Affairs, House Administration
1989 Criminal Jurisprudence, Environmental Affairs, Local and Consent Calendars

BILL PASSAGE RATES, 1997

	Total	Passed Legislature	Pct. Passed Legislature
Authored	27	10	37%
Sponsored	2	2	100%
Amendments	18	18	100%

ELECTORAL HISTORY IN CURRENT DISTRICT

	1994	1996	1998
Primary Election Opponent(s)	No	No	No
General Election Opponent(s)	No	Rep	Rep

House District 13

COUNTIES IN DISTRICT

Austin, Brazos (part), Burleson, Lee, Milam, Washington

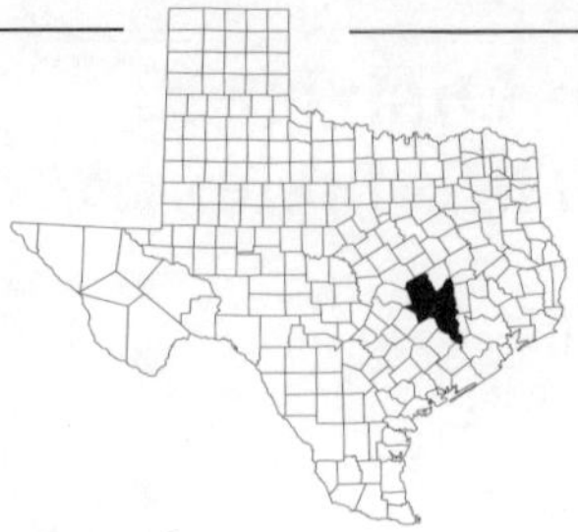

DEMOGRAPHIC INFORMATION

Population		**Wealth and Urbanization**	
Total	107,623	Per capita Income	$10,706
Anglo	74.5%	Avg. House Value	$57,166
Black	15.1%	Percent Poverty	19.4%
Hispanic	10.0%	Public Assistance	8.6%
Others	0.5%	Percent Urban	37.3%

Education		**Employed**	
High School Graduates	61.8%	Percent Employed	94.2%
College Graduates	12.5%	Private Sector	69.5%

Age of Population		**Household Types**	
5 years or less	8.7%	Family households	86.0%
6-17 years	18.6%	Non-family households	11.0%
18-64 years	55.6%	Single-parent families	18.0%
65 or older	17.1%	Both parents working	66.2%

SENATE DISTRICTS IN HOUSE DISTRICT

Dist 5 Steve Ogden (R)

Dist 18 Kenneth L. Armbrister (D)

DISTRICT ELECTION DATA

House 1996		**House 1998**	
Dan Kubiak (D)	59.4%	Theodora V. Boehm (D)	49.0%
James T. Hartley (R)	40.6%	Charles B. Jones (R)	51.0%

President 1996	
Bill Clinton (D)	43.3%
Bob Dole (R)	56.7%

Composite Party Vote 1994	
Democratic	49.2%
Republican	50.8%

Registered Voters 1996	**68,170**
Turnout	39,321
Percent of registered voting	57.7%

House District 13
Rep. Charles B. Jones (R)

House Office
(512) 463-0600

District Office
11054 Nunn Jones
College Station, Texas 77845
(409) 822-0797

Personal

Year of birth	1930
Family	Married to Jeannette Jones, three children
Education	Texas A&M University, B.S., M.S., Agricultural Education Texas A&M University, Ph.D. Educational Administration
Occupation	Rancher/Administrator
Religion	Baptist
State legislative service	1998 to present

COMMITTEE ASSIGNMENT HISTORY

BILL PASSAGE RATES, 1997

	Total	Passed Legislature	Pct. Passed Legislature
Authored	NA	NA	NA
Sponsored	NA	NA	NA
Amendments	NA	NA	NA

ELECTORAL HISTORY IN CURRENT DISTRICT

	1994	1996	1998
Primary Election Opponent(s)	NA	NA	No
General Election Opponent(s)	NA	NA	Dem
Special Election Opponent(s)	NA	NA	Dem, AMC

House District 14

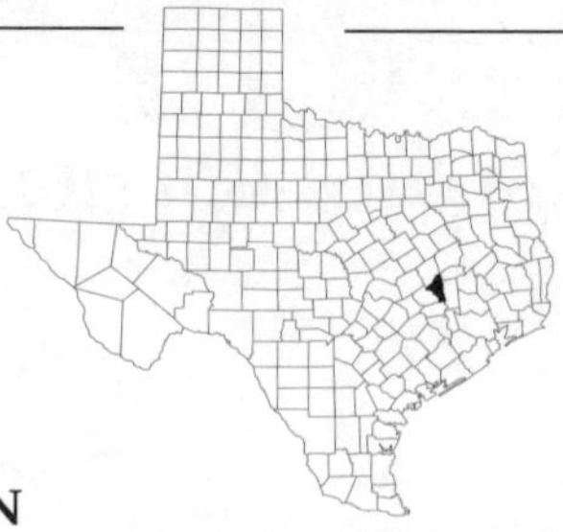

COUNTIES IN DISTRICT

Brazos (part)

DEMOGRAPHIC INFORMATION

Population		Wealth and Urbanization	
Total	109,650	Per capita Income	$10,215
Anglo	70.4%	Avg. House Value	$71,861
Black	11.5%	Percent Poverty	29.3%
Hispanic	14.2%	Public Assistance	4.2%
Others	4.1%	Percent Urban	98.0%

Education		Employed	
High School Graduates	80.9%	Percent Employed	94.3%
College Graduates	38.0%	Private Sector	57.3%

Age of Population		Household Types	
5 years or less	7.8%	Family households	62.2%
6-17 years	12.2%	Non-family households	25.8%
18-64 years	73.4%	Single-parent families	24.0%
65 or older	6.6%	Both parents working	67.7%

SENATE DISTRICTS IN HOUSE DISTRICT

Dist 5 Steve Ogden (R)

DISTRICT ELECTION DATA

House 1996		House 1998	
Steve Ogden (R)	100.0%	Fred Brown (R)	100.0%

President 1996	
Bill Clinton (D)	39.2%
Bob Dole (R)	60.8%

Composite Party Vote 1994	
Democratic	41.4%
Republican	58.6%

Registered Voters 1996	**62,009**
Turnout	22,982
Percent of registered voting	37.1%

House District 14
Rep. Fred Brown (R)

House Office
(512) 463-0698

District Office
3100 Briarcrest Drive
Bryan, TX 77802
(409) 776-7600

Personal

Year of birth	1954
Family	Married to Jane Brown, two children
Education	Attended Texas A&M University
Occupation	BMW, Mazda, VW, Ford Dealer
Religion	Baptist
State legislative service	1999 to present

COMMITTEE ASSIGNMENT HISTORY

BILL PASSAGE RATES, 1997

	Total	Passed Legislature	Pct. Passed Legislature
Authored	NA	NA	NA
Sponsored	NA	NA	NA
Amendments	NA	NA	NA

ELECTORAL HISTORY IN CURRENT DISTRICT

	1994	1996	1998
Primary Election Opponent(s)	NA	NA	Yes
General Election Opponent(s)	NA	NA	No

House District 15

COUNTIES IN DISTRICT

Grimes, Madison, Montgomery (part), Waller

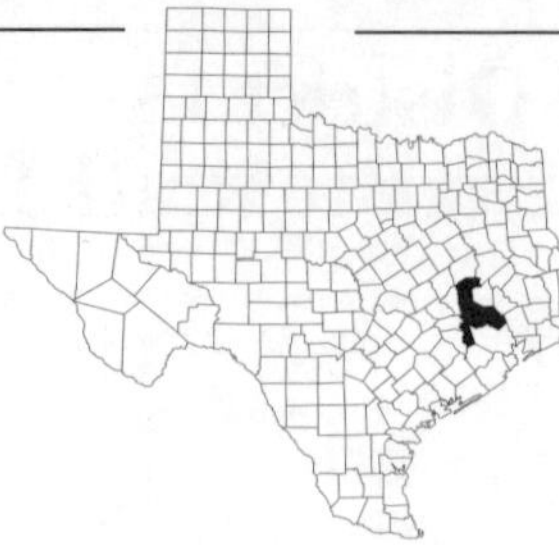

DEMOGRAPHIC INFORMATION

Population		**Wealth and Urbanization**	
Total	117,946	Per capita Income	$13,799
Anglo	75.5%	Avg. House Value	$87,015
Black	14.8%	Percent Poverty	14.2%
Hispanic	8.7%	Public Assistance	5.9%
Others	0.9%	Percent Urban	46.5%

Education		**Employed**	
High School Graduates	75.0%	Percent Employed	94.2%
College Graduates	22.2%	Private Sector	76.4%

Age of Population		**Household Types**	
5 years or less	9.2%	Family households	84.3%
6-17 years	18.7%	Non-family households	8.8%
18-64 years	62.5%	Single-parent families	16.5%
65 or older	9.6%	Both parents working	60.3%

SENATE DISTRICTS IN HOUSE DISTRICT

Dist 3 Drew Nixon (R)
Dist 4 David Bernsen (D)
Dist 5 Steve Ogden (R)

DISTRICT ELECTION DATA

House 1996		**House 1998**	
Peter B. Plotts (D)	31.0%	Larry R. Hickman (D)	28.8%
Thomas Williams (R)	69.0%	Thomas Williams (R)	71.2%

President 1996	
Bill Clinton (D)	34.7%
Bob Dole (R)	65.3%

Composite Party Vote 1994	
Democratic	36.9%
Republican	63.1%

Registered Voters 1996	**91,520**
Turnout	53,778
Percent of registered voting	58.8%

House District 15
Rep. Thomas Williams (R)

House Office
(512) 463-0550

District Office
P.O. Box 8069
The Woodlands, Texas 77387
(281) 296-0023
(281) 296-0449 (Fax)

Personal

Year of birth	1956
Family	Married to Marsha Williams, two children
Education	Texas A&M University, B.B.A.
Occupation	Insurance and financial services
Religion	Methodist
State legislative service	House 1997 to present

COMMITTEE ASSIGNMENT HISTORY

1997 Juvenile Justice and Family Issues, Pensions and Investments, Rules and Resolutions

BILL PASSAGE RATES, 1997

	Total	Passed Legislature	Pct. Passed Legislature
Authored	19	4	21%
Sponsored	3	2	67%
Amendments	3	3	100%

ELECTORAL HISTORY IN CURRENT DISTRICT

	1994	1996	1998
Primary Election Opponent(s)	NA	Yes	No
General Election Opponent(s)	NA	Dem	Dem

House District 16

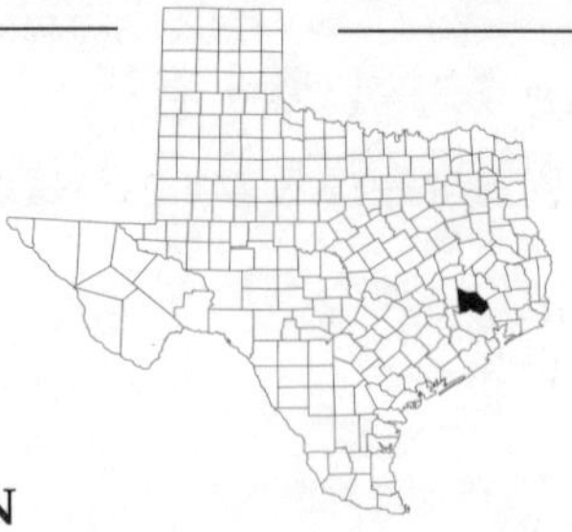

COUNTIES IN DISTRICT

Montgomery (part)

DEMOGRAPHIC INFORMATION

Population		Wealth and Urbanization	
Total	117,404	Per capita Income	$12,554
Anglo	85.9%	Avg. House Value	$69,262
Black	5.3%	Percent Poverty	14.8%
Hispanic	8.0%	Public Assistance	6.1%
Others	0.9%	Percent Urban	26.8%

Education		Employed	
High School Graduates	70.5%	Percent Employed	93.7%
College Graduates	13.6%	Private Sector	77.2%

Age of Population		Household Types	
5 years or less	9.4%	Family households	90.2%
6-17 years	19.9%	Non-family households	8.7%
18-64 years	61.2%	Single-parent families	18.2%
65 or older	9.5%	Both parents working	56.4%

SENATE DISTRICTS IN HOUSE DISTRICT

Dist 3 Drew Nixon (R)

Dist 4 David Bernsen (D)

DISTRICT ELECTION DATA

House 1996		House 1998	
Bob Rabuck (R)	100.0%	Ruben Hope (R)	100.0%

President 1996	
Bill Clinton (D)	31.4%
Bob Dole (R)	68.6%

Composite Party Vote 1994	
Democratic	32.7%
Republican	67.3%

Registered Voters 1996	**80,679**
Turnout	42,620
Percent of registered voting	52.8%

House District 16
Rep. Ruben Hope (R)

House Office
(512) 463-0726

District Office
P.O. Box 3188
Conroe, Texas 77304
(409) 760-1628

Personal

Year of birth	1937
Family	Married to Francine Hope, three children
Education	University of Texas, B.B.A., J.D.
Occupation	Attorney
Religion	Baptist
State legislative service	House 1999 to present

COMMITTEE ASSIGNMENT HISTORY

BILL PASSAGE RATES, 1997

	Total	Passed Legislature	Pct. Passed Legislature
Authored	NA	NA	NA
Sponsored	NA	NA	NA
Amendments	NA	NA	NA

ELECTORAL HISTORY IN CURRENT DISTRICT

	1994	1996	1998
Primary Election Opponent(s)	NA	NA	Yes
General Election Opponent(s)	NA	NA	W-I

House District 17

COUNTIES IN DISTRICT

Angelina, Houston, San Augustine, Trinity

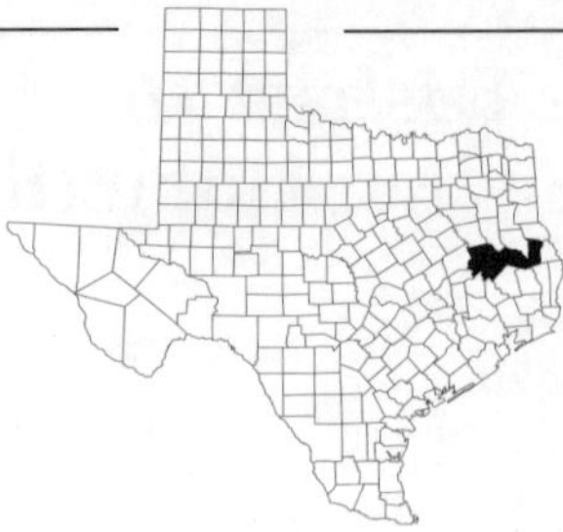

DEMOGRAPHIC INFORMATION

Population		Wealth and Urbanization	
Total	110,703	Per capita Income	$10,607
Anglo	74.0%	Avg. House Value	$49,532
Black	18.9%	Percent Poverty	21.4%
Hispanic	6.7%	Public Assistance	9.6%
Others	0.6%	Percent Urban	40.0%

Education		Employed	
High School Graduates	63.9%	Percent Employed	93.1%
College Graduates	11.7%	Private Sector	71.7%

Age of Population		Household Types	
5 years or less	8.7%	Family households	86.8%
6-17 years	18.6%	Non-family households	9.9%
18-64 years	56.9%	Single-parent families	22.8%
65 or older	15.8%	Both parents working	60.0%

SENATE DISTRICTS IN HOUSE DISTRICT

Dist 3 Drew Nixon (R)

Dist 5 Steve Ogden (R)

DISTRICT ELECTION DATA

House 1996		House 1998	
Jim McReynolds (D)	51.3%	Jim McReynolds (D)	63.6%
Billy Clemons (R)	48.7%	Les R. Chambers (R)	36.4%

President 1996	
Bill Clinton (D)	51.1%
Bob Dole (R)	48.9%

Composite Party Vote 1994	
Democratic	58.3%
Republican	41.7%

Registered Voters 1996	**76,230**
Turnout	42,113
Percent of registered voting	55.2%

House District 17
Rep. Jim McReynolds (D)

House Office
(512) 463-0490

District Office
210 South First
Lufkin, Texas 75904
(409) 634-9786

Personal

Year of birth	1942
Family	Married to Judy McReynolds, two children
Education	Abilene Christian, B.A.
	Lamar University, M.A.
	Texas Tech University, Ph.D., History
Occupation	Petroleum land man and rancher
Religion	Church of Christ
State legislative service	House 1997 to present

COMMITTEE ASSIGNMENT HISTORY

1997 Human Services, Juvenile Justice and Family Issues

BILL PASSAGE RATES, 1997

	Total	Passed Legislature	Pct. Passed Legislature
Authored	14	6	43%
Sponsored	3	3	100%
Amendments	6	6	100%

ELECTORAL HISTORY IN CURRENT DISTRICT

	1994	1996	1996
Primary Election Opponent(s)	NA	Yes	No
General Election Opponent(s)	NA	Rep	Rep

House District 18

COUNTIES IN DISTRICT

Polk, San Jacinto, Tyler, Walker

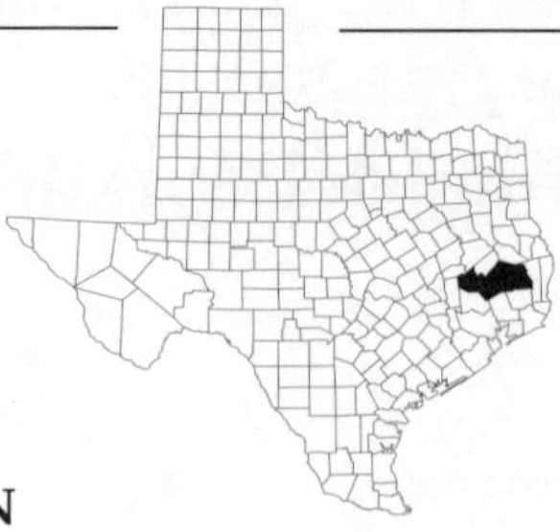

DEMOGRAPHIC INFORMATION

Population

Total	114,622
Anglo	74.3%
Black	18.1%
Hispanic	6.7%
Others	1.2%

Education

High School Graduates	65.7%
College Graduates	12.9%

Age of Population

5 years or less	7.1%
6-17 years	15.6%
18-64 years	62.7%
65 or older	14.6%

Wealth and Urbanization

Per capita Income	$9,945
Avg. House Value	$53,001
Percent Poverty	21.6%
Public Assistance	8.7%
Percent Urban	31.0%

Employed

Percent Employed	92.4%
Private Sector	61.5%

Household Types

Family households	75.3%
Non-family households	11.9%
Single-parent families	20.3%
Both parents working	60.5%

SENATE DISTRICTS IN HOUSE DISTRICT

Dist 3 Drew Nixon (R)

Dist 5 Steve Ogden (R)

DISTRICT ELECTION DATA

House 1996

Allen Ross Hightower Jr. (D)	60.1%
Richard S. Ohendalski (R)	39.9%

President 1996

Bill Clinton (D)	48.9%
Bob Dole (R)	51.1%

Composite Party Vote 1994

Democratic	53.4%
Republican	46.6%

Registered Voters 1996	**77,969**
Turnout	42,509
Percent of registered voting	54.5%

House 1998

Dan Ellis (D)	51.3%
Ben Bius (R)	48.7%

House District 18
Rep. Dan Ellis (D)

NO PHOTO AVAILABLE

House Office
(512) 463-0570

District Office
1032 12th Street
Huntsville, Texas 77340
(409) 295-5925

Personal

Year of birth	1959
Family	Bea Ellis, two children
Education	Livingston High School
Occupation	Office Manager
Religion	Baptist
State legislative service	House 1999

COMMITTEE ASSIGNMENT HISTORY

BILL PASSAGE RATES, 1997

	Total	Passed Legislature	Pct. Passed Legislature
Authored	NA	NA	NA
Sponsored	NA	NA	NA
Amendments	NA	NA	NA

ELECTORAL HISTORY IN CURRENT DISTRICT

	1994	1996	1998
Primary Election Opponent(s)	NA	NA	Yes
General Election Opponent(s)	NA	NA	Rep

House District 19

COUNTIES IN DISTRICT
Jefferson (part), Newton, Orange

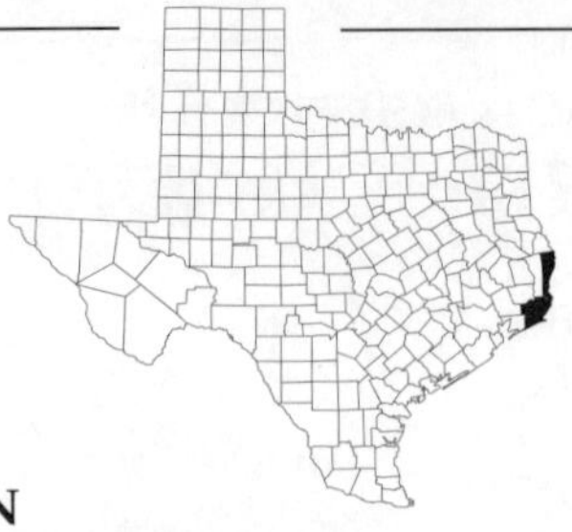

DEMOGRAPHIC INFORMATION

Population	
Total	109,072
Anglo	87.7%
Black	9.0%
Hispanic	2.4%
Others	0.8%

Wealth and Urbanization	
Per capita Income	$11,331
Avg. House Value	$49,708
Percent Poverty	16.1%
Public Assistance	6.9%
Percent Urban	53.6%

Education	
High School Graduates	72.0%
College Graduates	10.2%

Employed	
Percent Employed	92.0%
Private Sector	81.7%

Age of Population	
5 years or less	8.8%
6-17 years	19.8%
18-64 years	60.3%
65 or older	11.2%

Household Types	
Family households	90.7%
Non-family households	8.6%
Single-parent families	18.6%
Both parents working	54.3%

SENATE DISTRICTS IN HOUSE DISTRICT

Dist 3 Drew Nixon (R)
Dist 4 David Bernsen (D)

DISTRICT ELECTION DATA

House 1996	
Ron E. Lewis (D)	69.0%
Jeff VanFleet (R)	31.0%

House 1998	
Ron E. Lewis (D)	100.0%

President 1996	
Bill Clinton (D)	52.5%
Bob Dole (R)	47.5%

Composite Party Vote 1994	
Democratic	58.0%
Republican	42.0%

Registered Voters 1996	**72,620**
Turnout	40,367
Percent of registered voting	55.6%

House District 19
Rep. Ron E. Lewis (D)

House Office
(512) 463-0612

District Office
11867 Hwy. 62N
Mauriceville, Texas 77626
(409) 745-3644

Personal

Year of birth	1953
Family	Married to Tessa Lewis, one child
Education	Stephen F. Austin State University, B.A. Political Science
Occupation	Insurance
Religion	Catholic
State legislative service	House 1985 to present

COMMITTEE ASSIGNMENT HISTORY

1997 County Affairs (Chair), Natural Resources
1995 County Affairs (Chair), Natural Resources
1993 Environmental Regulation, Natural Resources
1991 Natural Resources (Chair), Transportation
1989 Appropriations, Calendars, Transportation
1987 Appropriations, Calendars, Science and Technology
1985 County Affairs, Ways and Means

BILL PASSAGE RATES, 1997

	Total	Passed Legislature	Pct. Passed Legislature
Authored	32	4	13%
Sponsored	11	7	64%
Amendments	29	27	93%

ELECTORAL HISTORY IN CURRENT DISTRICT

	1994	1996	1998
Primary Election Opponent(s)	No	No	No
General Election Opponent(s)	No	Rep	No

House District 20

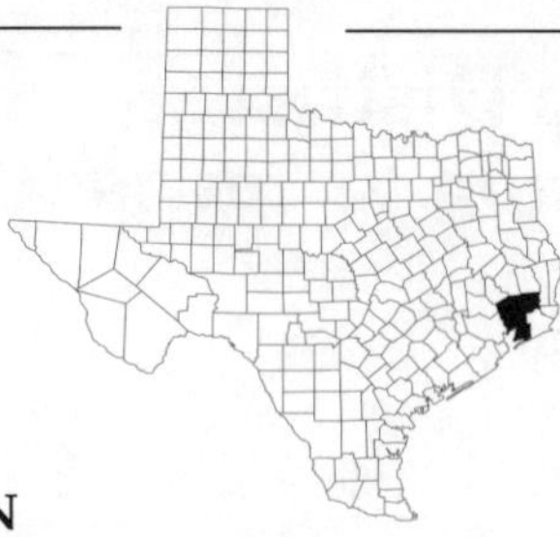

COUNTIES IN DISTRICT

Chambers, Hardin, Liberty

DEMOGRAPHIC INFORMATION

Population		**Wealth and Urbanization**	
Total	114,134	Per capita Income	$10,784
Anglo	84.0%	Avg. House Value	$51,865
Black	11.3%	Percent Poverty	16.0%
Hispanic	4.2%	Public Assistance	8.1%
Others	0.6%	Percent Urban	32.7%

Education		**Employed**	
High School Graduates	66.4%	Percent Employed	92.4%
College Graduates	9.2%	Private Sector	78.0%

Age of Population		**Household Types**	
5 years or less	8.9%	Family households	90.4%
6-17 years	20.7%	Non-family households	8.4%
18-64 years	59.1%	Single-parent families	15.1%
65 or older	11.3%	Both parents working	55.1%

SENATE DISTRICTS IN HOUSE DISTRICT

Dist 3 Drew Nixon (R)

Dist 4 David Bernsen (D)

DISTRICT ELECTION DATA

House 1996		**House 1998**	
Zeb Zbranek (D)	53.0%	Zeb Zbranek (D)	56.0%
Lent Batman (R)	47.0%	Eddie Shauberger (R)	44.0%

President 1996	
Bill Clinton (D)	45.3%
Bob Dole (R)	54.7%

Composite Party Vote 1994	
Democratic	49.7%
Republican	50.3%

Registered Voters 1996	**83,109**
Turnout	43,040
Percent of registered voting	51.8%

House District 20
Rep. Zeb Zbranek (D)

House Office
(512) 463-0488
(800) 438-6202

District Office
P.O. Box 2050
Liberty, Texas 77575
(409) 336-6454

Personal

Year of birth	1962
Family	Married to Angela Zbranek, two children
Education	University of Texas, B.S., Petroleum Engineering University of Houston, J.D.
Occupation	Attorney
Religion	Methodist
State legislative service	House 1993 to present

COMMITTEE ASSIGNMENT HISTORY
1997 Civil Practices, Judicial Affairs
1995 Civil Practices, Judicial Affairs
1993 County Affairs, Judicial Affairs

BILL PASSAGE RATES, 1997

	Total	Passed Legislature	Pct. Passed Legislature
Authored	22	5	23%
Sponsored	2	2	100%
Amendments	13	12	92%

ELECTORAL HISTORY IN CURRENT DISTRICT

	1994	1996	1998
Primary Election Opponent(s)	No	No	No
General Election Opponent(s)	No	Rep	Rep

House District 21

COUNTIES IN DISTRICT
Jefferson (part)

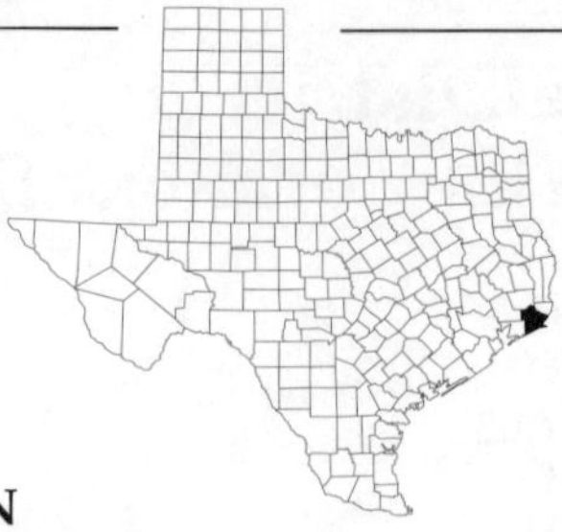

DEMOGRAPHIC INFORMATION

Population		**Wealth and Urbanization**	
Total	111,716	Per capita Income	$15,599
Anglo	83.7%	Avg. House Value	$62,770
Black	10.9%	Percent Poverty	9.5%
Hispanic	4.2%	Public Assistance	4.2%
Others	1.3%	Percent Urban	85.2%

Education		**Employed**	
High School Graduates	83.2%	Percent Employed	95.2%
College Graduates	21.0%	Private Sector	80.1%

Age of Population		**Household Types**	
5 years or less	8.9%	Family households	88.6%
6-17 years	17.4%	Non-family households	10.5%
18-64 years	61.4%	Single-parent families	16.9%
65 or older	12.3%	Both parents working	60.0%

SENATE DISTRICTS IN HOUSE DISTRICT

Dist 4 David Bernsen (D)

DISTRICT ELECTION DATA

House 1996		**House 1998**	
Mark W. Stiles (D)	87.6%	Allan B. Ritter (D)	53.1%
John Preston (NLP)	12.4%	Kent Adams (R)	46.9%

President 1996	
Bill Clinton (D)	44.9%
Bob Dole (R)	55.1%

Composite Party Vote 1994	
Democratic	49.6%
Republican	50.4%

Registered Voters 1996	**80,222**
Turnout	47,198
Percent of registered voting	58.8%

House District 21
Rep. Allan B. Ritter (D)

House Office
(512) 463-0706

District Office
P.O. Box 1265
Nederland, Texas 77727
(409) 729-3228

Personal

Year of birth	1954
Family	Married to Peggy Ritter, four children
Education	
Occupation	President of Ritter Lumber
Religion	Baptist
State legislative service	House 1999 to present

COMMITTEE ASSIGNMENT HISTORY

BILL PASSAGE RATES, 1997

	Total	Passed Legislature	Pct. Passed Legislature
Authored	NA	NA	NA
Sponsored	NA	NA	NA
Amendments	NA	NA	NA

ELECTORAL HISTORY IN CURRENT DISTRICT

	1994	1996	1998
Primary Election Opponent(s)	NA	NA	No
General Election Opponent(s)	NA	NA	Rep

House District 22

COUNTIES IN DISTRICT
Jefferson (part)

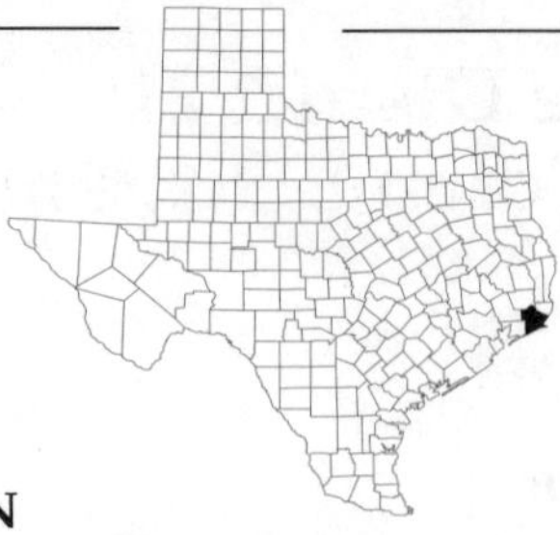

DEMOGRAPHIC INFORMATION

Population		Wealth and Urbanization	
Total	112,687	Per capita Income	$8,794
Anglo	35.2%	Avg. House Value	$34,358
Black	55.2%	Percent Poverty	30.8%
Hispanic	6.6%	Public Assistance	13.2%
Others	3.5%	Percent Urban	100%

Education		Employed	
High School Graduates	63.6%	Percent Employed	87.2%
College Graduates	9.8%	Private Sector	79.5%

Age of Population		Household Types	
5 years or less	9.3%	Family households	83.7%
6-17 years	18.8%	Non-family households	13.5%
18-64 years	55.7%	Single-parent families	38.1%
65 or older	16.2%	Both parents working	60.8%

SENATE DISTRICTS IN HOUSE DISTRICT
Dist 4 David Bernsen (D)

DISTRICT ELECTION DATA

House 1996		House 1996	
Al Price (D)	100.0%	Joseph D. Deshotel (D)	100.0%

President 1996	
Bill Clinton (D)	79.8%
Bob Dole (R)	20.2%

Composite Party Vote 1994	
Democratic	77.6%
Republican	22.4%

Registered Voters 1996	**68,972**
Turnout	32,297
Percent of registered voting	46.8%

House District 22
Rep. Joseph D. Deshotel (D)

House Office
(512) 463-0662

District Office
1310 Calvin
Beaumont, Texas 77707
(409) 842-4844

Personal

Year of birth	1951
Family	Married to Claudie Deshotel, one child
Education	Lamar University, B.S.
	Texas Southern University, J.D.
Occupation	Homebuilder/Attorney
Religion	Catholic
State legislative service	House 1999 to present

COMMITTEE ASSIGNMENT HISTORY

BILL PASSAGE RATES, 1995

	Total	Passed Legislature	Pct. Passed Legislature
Authored	NA	NA	NA
Sponsored	NA	NA	NA
Amendments	NA	NA	NA

ELECTORAL HISTORY IN CURRENT DISTRICT

	1994	1996	1998
Primary Election Opponent(s)	NA	NA	No
General Election Opponent(s)	NA	NA	No

House District 23

COUNTIES IN DISTRICT

Galveston (part)

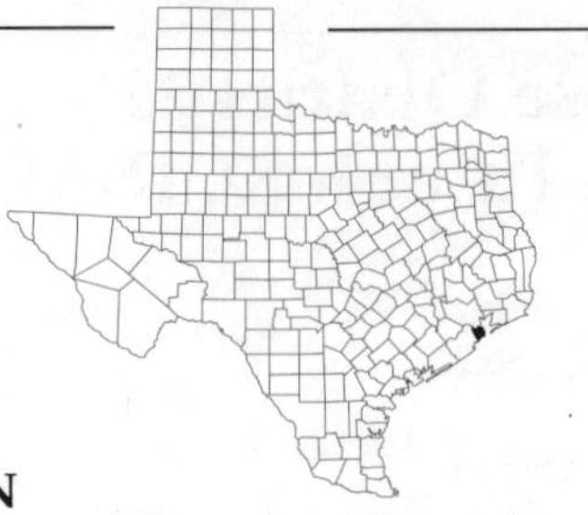

DEMOGRAPHIC INFORMATION

Population

Total	108,649
Anglo	63.8%
Black	18.0%
Hispanic	16.1%
Others	2.6%

Wealth and Urbanization

Per capita Income	$13,480
Avg. House Value	$67,979
Percent Poverty	17.5%
Public Assistance	7.1%
Percent Urban	96.4%

Education

High School Graduates	74.3%
College Graduates	19.6%

Employed

Percent Employed	92.6%
Private Sector	72.2%

Age of Population

5 years or less	9.3%
6-17 years	18.4%
18-64 years	61.6%
65 or older	10.7%

Household Types

Family households	83.9%
Non-family households	14.1%
Single-parent families	26.1%
Both parents working	60.4%

SENATE DISTRICTS IN HOUSE DISTRICT

Dist 4 David Bernsen (D)

Dist 11 Mike Jackson (R)

DISTRICT ELECTION DATA

House 1996

Patricia Gray (D)	57.7%
Dave Norman (R)	42.3%

House 1998

Patricia Gray (D)	56.0%
Dave Norman (R)	44.0%

President 1996

Bill Clinton (D)	52.9%
Bob Dole (R)	47.1%

Composite Party Vote 1994

Democratic	51.5%
Republican	48.5%

Registered Voters 1996	**76,457**
Turnout	39,238
Percent of registered voting	51.3%

House District 23
Rep. Patricia Gray (D)

House Office
(512) 463-0588

District Office
520 20th Street
Galveston, Texas 77550
(409) 765-8958
(800) 615-2525

Personal

Year of birth	1946
Family	Single, no children
Education	Mississippi State University, B.A., English; M.Ed. University of Texas, M.A. South Texas College of Law, J.D.
Occupation	Attorney
Religion	Episcopalian
State legislative service	House 1991 (part) to present

COMMITTEE ASSIGNMENT HISTORY

1997 Civil Practices (Chair), Corrections, General Investigating
1995 Appropriations, Corrections (Vice-Chair), General Investigating
1993 Corrections, Environmental Regulation
1991 NA

BILL PASSAGE RATES, 1997

	Total	Passed Legislature	Pct. Passed Legislature
Authored	40	20	50%
Sponsored	11	10	91%
Amendments	28	28	100%

ELECTORAL HISTORY IN CURRENT DISTRICT

	1994	1996	1998
Primary Election Opponent(s)	No	No	No
General Election Opponent(s)	Rep	Rep	Rep

House District 24

COUNTIES IN DISTRICT
Galveston (part)

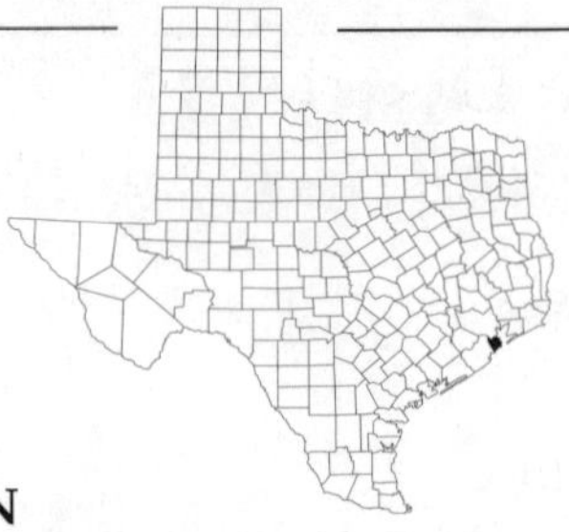

DEMOGRAPHIC INFORMATION

Population		**Wealth and Urbanization**	
Total	108,750	Per capita Income	$14,498
Anglo	77.2%	Avg. House Value	$73,565
Black	4.5%	Percent Poverty	13.5%
Hispanic	16.6%	Public Assistance	5.6%
Others	1.8%	Percent Urban	88.9%

Education		**Employed**	
High School Graduates	77.1%	Percent Employed	93.4%
College Graduates	19.1%	Private Sector	73.6%

Age of Population		**Household Types**	
5 years or less	8.9%	Family households	88.1%
6-17 years	18.8%	Non-family households	11.5%
18-64 years	62.2%	Single-parent families	23.9%
65 or older	10.0%	Both parents working	64.3%

SENATE DISTRICTS IN HOUSE DISTRICT

Dist 11 Mike Jackson (R)

DISTRICT ELECTION DATA

House 1996		**House 1998**	
Craig Eiland (D)	100.0%	Craig Eiland (D)	58.3%
		Larry Taylor (R)	41.7%

President 1996	
Bill Clinton (D)	51.5%
Bob Dole (R)	48.5%

Composite Party Vote 1994	
Democratic	51.4%
Republican	48.6%

Registered Voters 1996	**77,196**
Turnout	41,381
Percent of registered voting	53.6%

House District 24
Rep. Craig Eiland (D)

House Office
(512) 463-0502

District Office
225 FM 517 West, Suite 1
Dickinson, Texas 77539
(281) 534-4492

Personal

Year of birth	1962
Family	Married to Melissa Eiland, one child
Education	Baylor University, B.B.A.
	Baylor Law School, J.D.
Occupation	Attorney
Religion	Baptist
State legislative service	House 1995 to present

COMMITTEE ASSIGNMENT HISTORY

1997 Appropriations, Insurance
1995 Business and Industry, State, Federal & Intergovernmental Relations

BILL PASSAGE RATES, 1997

	Total	Passed Legislature	Pct. Passed Legislature
Authored	34	11	32%
Sponsored	9	7	78%
Amendments	18	17	94%

ELECTORAL HISTORY IN CURRENT DISTRICT

	1994	1996	1998
Primary Election Opponent(s)	Yes	No	No
General Election Opponent(s)	Rep	No	Rep

House District 25

COUNTIES IN DISTRICT

Brazoria (part)

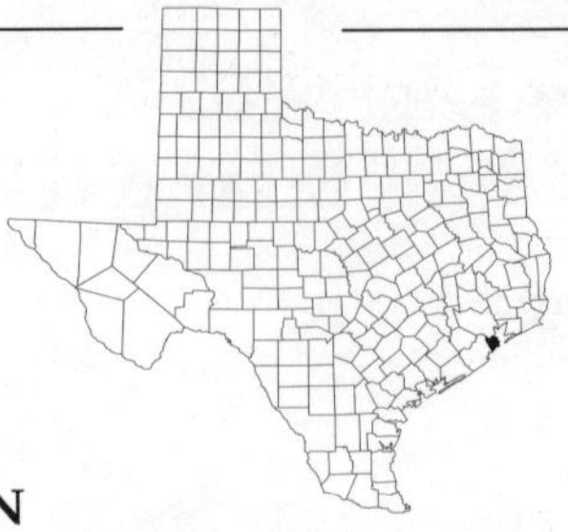

DEMOGRAPHIC INFORMATION

Population

Total	118,398
Anglo	77.2%
Black	4.5%
Hispanic	16.6%
Others	1.8%

Education

High School Graduates	80.0%
College Graduates	19.2%

Age of Population

5 years or less	10.1%
6-17 years	19.8%
18-64 years	62.8%
65 or older	7.3%

Wealth and Urbanization

Per capita Income	$14,922
Avg. House Value	$74,101
Percent Poverty	8.2%
Public Assistance	2.9%
Percent Urban	74.2%

Employed

Percent Employed	95.4%
Private Sector	79.8%

Household Types

Family households	90.3%
Non-family households	8.0%
Single-parent families	14.4%
Both parents working	61.6%

SENATE DISTRICTS IN HOUSE DISTRICT

Dist 11 Mike Jackson (R)

Dist 17 J. E. (Buster) Brown (R)

DISTRICT ELECTION DATA

House 1996

David S. Miller (D)	33.1%
Dennis Bonnen (R)	66.9%

President 1996

Bill Clinton (D)	35.0%
Bob Dole (R)	65.0%

Composite Party Vote 1994

Democratic	35.7%
Republican	64.3%

Registered Voters 1996	**80,637**
Turnout	46,414
Percent of registered voting	57.6%

House 1998

Dennis Bonnen (R)	100.0%

House District 25
Rep. Dennis Bonnen (R)

House Office
(512) 463-0564
dennis.bonnen@house.state.tx.us

District Office
122E. Myrtle
Angleton, Texas 77515
(409) 848-1770
(800)647-3809

Personal

Year of birth	1972
Family	Single
Education	St. Edwards, B.A.
Occupation	Small business
Religion	Catholic
State legislative service	House 1997 to present

COMMITTEE ASSIGNMENT HISTORY
1997 County Affairs, Insurance

BILL PASSAGE RATES, 1997

	Total	Passed Legislature	Pct. Passed Legislature
Authored	19	9	47%
Sponsored	2	1	50%
Amendments	2	2	100%

ELECTORAL HISTORY IN CURRENT DISTRICT

	1994	1996	1998
Primary Election Opponent(s)	NA	Yes	No
General Election Opponent(s)	NA	Dem	No

House District 26

COUNTIES IN DISTRICT

Fort Bend (part)

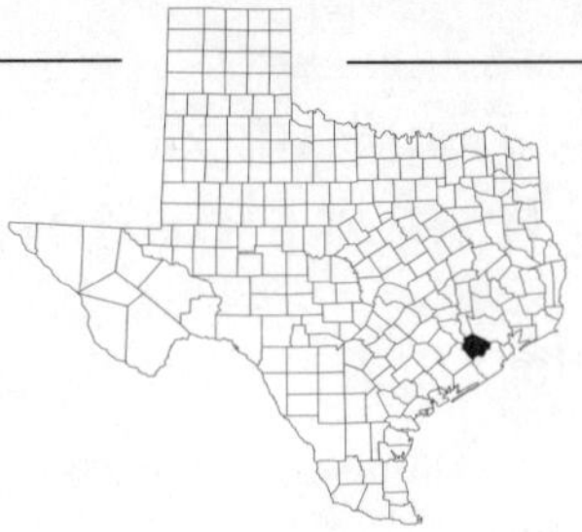

DEMOGRAPHIC INFORMATION

Population	
Total	116,332
Anglo	70.1%
Black	8.4%
Hispanic	11.3%
Others	10.4%

Education	
High School Graduates	91.0%
College Graduates	42.4%

Age of Population	
5 years or less	12.2%
6-17 years	20.4%
18-64 years	63.5%
65 or older	3.9%

Wealth and Urbanization	
Per capita Income	$20,265
Avg. House Value	$108,828
Percent Poverty	3.7%
Public Assistance	1.8%
Percent Urban	94.3%

Employed	
Percent Employed	96.7%
Private Sector	81.6%

Household Types	
Family households	92.4%
Non-family households	5.1%
Single-parent families	9.5%
Both parents working	63.9%

SENATE DISTRICTS IN HOUSE DISTRICT

Dist 13 Rodney Ellis (D)

Dist 17 J.E. (Buster) Brown (R)

Dist 18 Kenneth L. Armbrister (D)

DISTRICT ELECTION DATA

House 1996	
Diane Prather (NLP)	13.9%
Charlie Howard (R)	86.1%

President 1996	
Bill Clinton (D)	31.8%
Bob Dole (R)	68.2%

Composite Party Vote 1994	
Democratic	26.9%
Republican	73.1%

Registered Voters 1996	87,250
Turnout	58,328
Percent of registered voting	66.9%

House 1998	
Charlie Howard (R)	100.0%

House District 26
Rep. Charlie Howard (R)

House Office
(512) 463-0710

District Office
14100 SW Freeway, Suite 200
Sugar Land, Texas 77478
(281) 565-9500

Personal

Year of birth	1942
Family	Married to Jo Howard, two children
Education	Auburn University, B.S., Electrical Engineering Harvard Business School, M.B.A.
Occupation	Realtor, investor
Religion	Baptist
State legislative service	House 1995 to present

COMMITTEE ASSIGNMENT HISTORY

1997 Environmental Regulation, Land and Resource Management
1995 Environmental Regulation, Land and Resource Management

BILL PASSAGE RATES, 1997

	Total	Passed Legislature	Pct. Passed Legislature
Authored	35	8	23%
Sponsored	2	2	100%
Amendments	21	13	62%

ELECTORAL HISTORY IN CURRENT DISTRICT

	1994	1996	1998
Primary Election Opponent(s)	Yes	No	No
General Election Opponent(s)	Dem	NLP	No

House District 27

COUNTIES IN DISTRICT
Fort Bend (part)

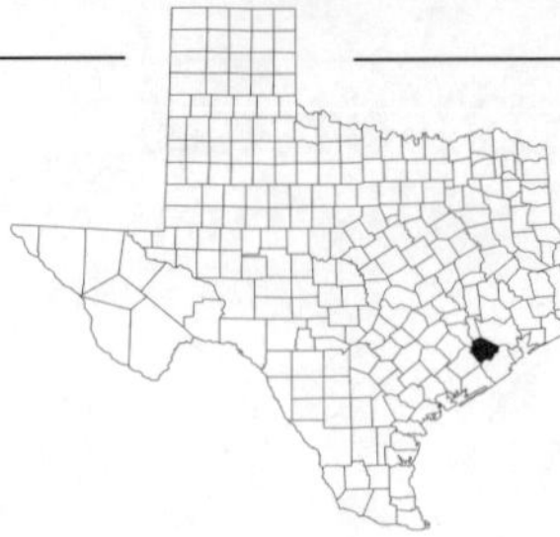

DEMOGRAPHIC INFORMATION

Population

Total	109,089
Anglo	36.4%
Black	33.8%
Hispanic	28.2%
Others	2.3%

Education

High School Graduates	69.5%
College Graduates	16.6%

Age of Population

5 years or less	11.1%
6-17 years	22.7%
18-64 years	60.4%
65 or older	5.8%

Wealth and Urbanization

Per capita Income	$11,519
Avg. House Value	$58,290
Percent Poverty	14.4%
Public Assistance	6.4%
Percent Urban	76.9%

Employed

Percent Employed	93.5%
Private Sector	75.1%

Household Types

Family households	92.3%
Non-family households	6.2%
Single-parent families	20.7%
Both parents working	72.0%

SENATE DISTRICTS IN HOUSE DISTRICT

Dist 13 Rodney Ellis (D)
Dist 17 J. E. (Buster) Brown (R)
Dist 18 Kenneth L. Armbrister (D)

DISTRICT ELECTION DATA

House 1996

Dora Olivo (D)	60.5%
Bobby E. Mills (R)	39.5%

President 1996

Bill Clinton (D)	62.6%
Bob Dole (R)	37.4%

Composite Party Vote 1994

Democratic	59.5%
Republican	40.5%

Registered Voters 1996	**76,959**
Turnout	35,083
Percent of registered voting	45.6%

House 1998

Dora Olivo (D)	100.0%

House District 27
Rep. Dora Olivo (D)

House Office
(512) 463-0494

District Office
P.O. Box 2910
Austin, Texas 78768
(512) 463-0494

Personal

Year of birth	1943
Family	Married to Victor M. Olivo, two children
Education	Texas A&M at Kingsville, B.S.
	University of Houston, M.S., J.D.
Occupation	Attorney
Religion	Catholic
State legislative service	House 1997 to present

COMMITTEE ASSIGNMENT HISTORY
1997 Insurance, Public Safety

BILL PASSAGE RATES, 1997

	Total	Passed Legislature	Pct. Passed Legislature
Authored	15	3	20%
Sponsored	5	5	100%
Amendments	4	4	100%

ELECTORAL HISTORY IN CURRENT DISTRICT

	1994	1996	1996
Primary Election Opponent(s)	NA	Yes	No
General Election Opponent(s)	NA	Rep	No

House District 28

COUNTIES IN DISTRICT
Bastrop, Colorado, Fayette, Wharton

DEMOGRAPHIC INFORMATION

Population

Total	116,696
Anglo	67.9%
Black	13.4%
Hispanic	18.5%
Others	0.5%

Wealth and Urbanization

Per capita Income	$10,602
Avg. House Value	$56,260
Percent Poverty	19.7%
Public Assistance	7.7%
Percent Urban	38.7%

Education

High School Graduates	62.3%
College Graduates	11.6%

Employed

Percent Employed	93.7%
Private Sector	68.8%

Age of Population

5 years or less	9.0%
6-17 years	19.2%
18-64 years	55.6%
65 or older	16.1%

Household Types

Family households	87.3%
Non-family households	10.4%
Single-parent families	19.0%
Both parents working	67.7%

SENATE DISTRICTS IN HOUSE DISTRICT

Dist 18 Kenneth L. Armbrister (D)

DISTRICT ELECTION DATA

House 1996

Robert L. Cook (D)	54.9%
Chip Rayburn (R)	45.1%

House 1998

Robert L. Cook (D)	64.6%
Michael Franks (R)	35.4%

President 1996

Bill Clinton (D)	47.1%
Bob Dole (R)	52.9%

Composite Party Vote 1994

Democratic	53.5%
Republican	46.5%

Registered Voters 1996	**69,995**
Turnout	41,980
Percent of registered voting	60.0%

House District 28
Rep. Robert L. Cook (D)

House Office
(512) 463-0682

District Office
P.O. Box 217
Eagle Lake, Texas 77434
(409) 234-2493

Personal

Year of birth	1962
Family	Married to Mary Kay Cook, two children
Education	Southwest Texas State University
Occupation	Rice farmer
Religion	Catholic
State legislative service	House 1997 to present

COMMITTEE ASSIGNMENT HISTORY

1997 Agriculture and Livestock, Local and Consent Calendars, Natural Resources

BILL PASSAGE RATES, 1997

	Total	Passed Legislature	Pct. Passed Legislature
Authored	10	9	90%
Sponsored	2	2	100%
Amendments	5	5	100%

ELECTORAL HISTORY IN CURRENT DISTRICT

	1994	1996	1998
Primary Election Opponent(s)	NA	Yes	No
General Election Opponent(s)	NA	Rep	Rep

House District 29

COUNTIES IN DISTRICT
Brazoria (part), Matagorda

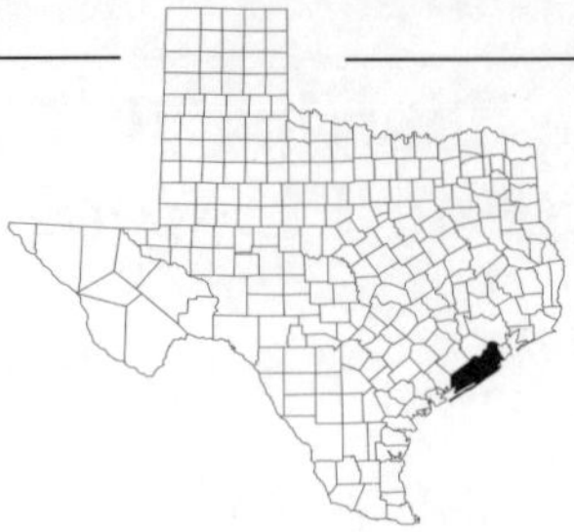

DEMOGRAPHIC INFORMATION

Population		**Wealth and Urbanization**	
Total	110,237	Per capita Income	$11,261
Anglo	63.6%	Avg. House Value	$55,527
Black	14.3%	Percent Poverty	16.7%
Hispanic	21.1%	Public Assistance	6.6%
Others	1.4%	Percent Urban	52.9%

Education		**Employed**	
High School Graduates	67.7%	Percent Employed	93.4%
College Graduates	10.2%	Private Sector	80.7%

Age of Population		**Household Types**	
5 years or less	9.7%	Family households	84.6%
6-17 years	19.5%	Non-family households	8.8%
18-64 years	61.4%	Single-parent families	17.5%
65 or older	9.4%	Both parents working	56.0%

SENATE DISTRICTS IN HOUSE DISTRICT

Dist 11 Mike Jackson (R)
Dist 17 J. E. (Buster) Brown (R)
Dist 18 Kenneth L. Armbrister (D)

DISTRICT ELECTION DATA

House 1996		**House 1998**	
D. R. (Tom) Uher (D)	53.4%	D. R. (Tom) Uher (D)	65.2%
Donna Coleman (R)	46.6%	Edward T. Garcia (R)	34.8%

President 1996	
Bill Clinton (D)	47.5%
Bob Dole (R)	52.5%

Composite Party Vote 1994	
Democratic	49.6%
Republican	50.4%

Registered Voters 1996	**61,613**
Turnout	33,314
Percent of registered voting	54.1%

House District 29
Rep. D. R. (Tom) Uher (D)

House Office
(512) 463-0724

District Office
2219 Avenue G.
Bay City, Texas 77414
(409) 245-6542

Personal

Year of birth	1937
Family	Married to Ann Uher, three children
Education	University of Texas, B.B.A., J.D.
Occupation	Attorney
Religion	Presbyterian
State legislative service	House 1968 (part) to present

COMMITTEE ASSIGNMENT HISTORY

1997 General Investigating, Public Education, Transportation
1995 General Investigating, Public Education, Transportation
1993 Human Services, Ways and Means
1991 Higher Education, Judiciary, Redistricting (Chair)
1989 Higher Education, Judicial Affairs, Redistricting (Chair)
1987 Appropriations, Higher Education
1985 Appropriations, Calendars, Higher Education
1983 Agriculture and Livestock; Regions, Compacts and Districts (Chair)
1981 Criminal Jurisprudence, State Affairs (Chair)
1979 State Affairs (Chair)
1977 State Affairs (Chair)
1975 Insurance, State Affairs (Chair)
1973 Agriculture and Livestock, Insurance, State Affairs
1971 Criminal Jurisprudence, Liquor Regulation, Public Health (Vice-Chair), State Affairs, Revenue and Taxation
1969 Banks and Banking, Constitutional Amendments, Criminal Jurisprudence, Liquor Regulation, State Affairs
1968 House Administration, Insurance, Banks and Banking, Parks and Wildlife, Revenue and Taxation

BILL PASSAGE RATES, 1997

	Total	Passed Legislature	Pct. Passed Legislature
Authored	54	11	20%
Sponsored	12	8	67%
Amendments	18	12	67%

ELECTORAL HISTORY IN CURRENT DISTRICT

	1994	1996	1998
Primary Election Opponent(s)	No	No	No
General Election Opponent(s)	No	Rep	Rep

House District 30

COUNTIES IN DISTRICT
De Witt, Goliad, Lavaca, Victoria

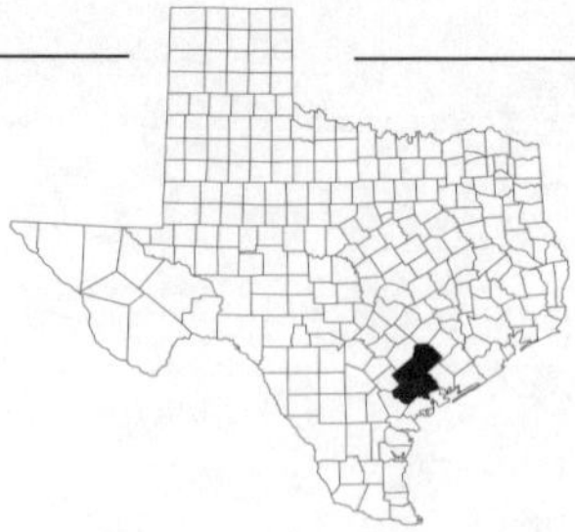

DEMOGRAPHIC INFORMATION

Population		**Wealth and Urbanization**	
Total	117,871	Per capita Income	$11,406
Anglo	63.8%	Avg. House Value	$55,949
Black	7.4%	Percent Poverty	18.9%
Hispanic	28.6%	Public Assistance	9.0%
Others	0.6%	Percent Urban	59.5%

Education		**Employed**	
High School Graduates	64.7%	Percent Employed	93.8%
College Graduates	12.1%	Private Sector	76.0%

Age of Population		**Household Types**	
5 years or less	9.3%	Family households	88.4%
6-17 years	19.6%	Non-family households	10.3%
18-64 years	56.4%	Single-parent families	18.5%
65 or older	14.8%	Both parents working	61.4%

SENATE DISTRICTS IN HOUSE DISTRICT

Dist 18 Kenneth L. Armbrister (D)

DISTRICT ELECTION DATA

House 1996		**House 1998**	
		Vernon Reaser (D)	47.3%
Steve Holzheauser (R)	100.0%	Geanie W. Morrison (R)	52.7%

President 1996	
Bill Clinton (D)	37.8%
Bob Dole (R)	62.2%

Composite Party Vote 1994	
Democratic	47.8%
Republican	52.2%

Registered Voters 1996	**76,041**
Turnout	41,266
Percent of registered voting	54.3%

House District 30
Rep. Geanie W. Morrison (R)

House Office
(512) 463-0456

District Office
808 Champions Row
Victoria, Texas 77904
(512) 578-2971

Personal

Year of birth	1950
Family	Married to Jack Morrison, Jr., two children
Education	
Occupation	Homemaker
Religion	Episcopalian
State legislative service	House 1999 to present

COMMITTEE ASSIGNMENT HISTORY

BILL PASSAGE RATES, 1997

	Total	Passed Legislature	Pct. Passed Legislature
Authored	NA	NA	NA
Sponsored	NA	NA	NA
Amendments	NA	NA	NA

ELECTORAL HISTORY IN CURRENT DISTRICT

	1994	1996	1998
Primary Election Opponent(s)	NA	NA	Yes
General Election Opponent(s)	NA	NA	Dem

House District 31

COUNTIES IN DISTRICT

Bee, Karnes, Live Oak, Refugio, San Patricio

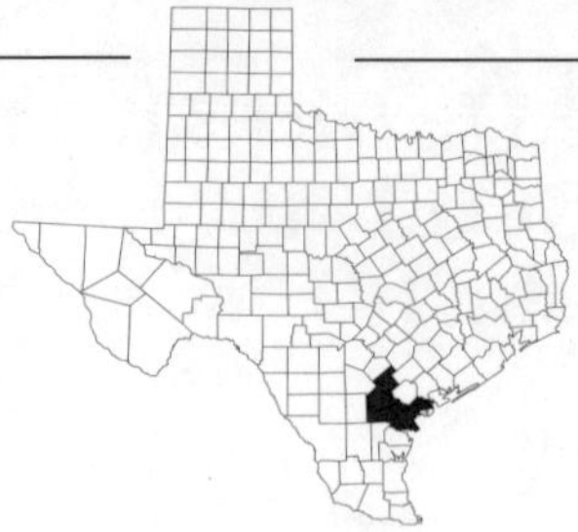

DEMOGRAPHIC INFORMATION

Population

Total	113,871
Anglo	48.6%
Black	2.4%
Hispanic	48.4%
Others	0.8%

Wealth and Urbanization

Per capita Income	$9,244
Avg. House Value	$47,829
Percent Poverty	26.6%
Public Assistance	11.4%
Percent Urban	56.5%

Education

High School Graduates	60.6%
College Graduates	11.2%

Employed

Percent Employed	90.7%
Private Sector	69.6%

Age of Population

5 years or less	9.7%
6-17 years	21.7%
18-64 years	56.4%
65 or older	12.2%

Household Types

Family households	90.7%
Non-family households	8.0%
Single-parent families	19.2%
Both parents working	51.3%

SENATE DISTRICTS IN HOUSE DISTRICT

Dist 18 Kenneth L. Armbrister (D)
Dist 20 Carlos F. Truan (D)
Dist 21 Judith Zaffirini (D)

DISTRICT ELECTION DATA

House 1996

Judy Hawley (D)	70.5%
Jim Gaines (R)	29.5%

House 1998

Judy Hawley (D)	100.0%

President 1996

Bill Clinton (D)	52.0%
Bob Dole (R)	48.0%

Composite Party Vote 1994

Democratic	55.6%
Republican	44.4%

Registered Voters 1996	**73,673**
Turnout	37,088
Percent of registered voting	50.3%

House District 31
Rep. Judy Hawley (D)

House Office
(512) 463-0512

District Office
611 8th Street, Suite C
Portland, Texas 78374
(512) 643-4755

Personal

Year of birth	1945
Family	Married to David Hawley, two children
Education	Knox College, B.A.
Occupation	State Representative
Religion	Methodist
State legislative service	House 1995 to present

COMMITTEE ASSIGNMENT HISTORY

1997 Energy Resources (Vice-Chair), House Administration, Transportation
1995 Agriculture and Livestock, Energy Resources

BILL PASSAGE RATES, 1997

	Total	Passed Legislature	Pct. Passed Legislature
Authored	31	15	48%
Sponsored	10	9	90%
Amendments	6	5	83%

ELECTORAL HISTORY IN CURRENT DISTRICT

	1994	1996	1998
Primary Election Opponent(s)	Yes	No	No
General Election Opponent(s)	Rep	Rep	No

House District 32

COUNTIES IN DISTRICT
Aransas, Calhoun, Jackson, Nueces (part)

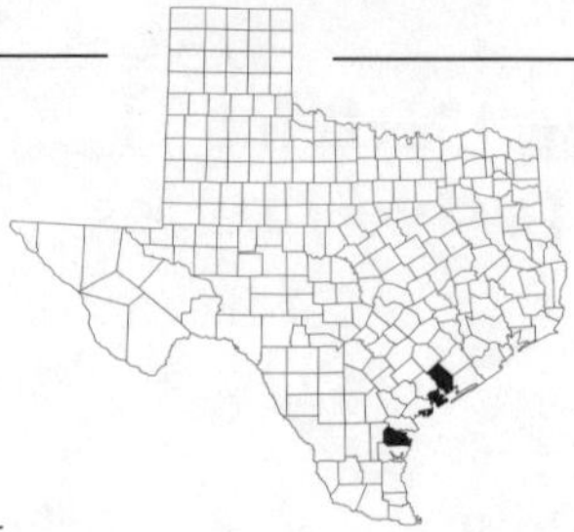

DEMOGRAPHIC INFORMATION

Population	
Total	118,562
Anglo	69.9%
Black	3.2%
Hispanic	24.6%
Others	2.4%

Wealth and Urbanization	
Per capita Income	$13,548
Avg. House Value	$73,991
Percent Poverty	15.8%
Public Assistance	5.5%
Percent Urban	72.7%

Education	
High School Graduates	75.7%
College Graduates	20.5%

Employed	
Percent Employed	93.5%
Private Sector	71.6%

Age of Population	
5 years or less	9.1%
6-17 years	18.2%
18-64 years	61.1%
65 or older	11.6%

Household Types	
Family households	87.3%
Non-family households	11.6%
Single-parent families	19.5%
Both parents working	61.1%

SENATE DISTRICTS IN HOUSE DISTRICT

Dist 18 Kenneth L. Armbrister (D)
Dist 20 Carlos F. Truan (D)

DISTRICT ELECTION DATA

House 1996	
Pat M. Eisenhauer (D)	49.1%
Eugene (Gene) Seaman (R)	50.9%

House 1998	
Eugene (Gene) Seaman (R)	100.0%

President 1996	
Bill Clinton (D)	41.8%
Bob Dole (R)	58.2%

Composite Party Vote 1994	
Democratic	47.0%
Republican	53.0%

Registered Voters 1996	**81,077**
Turnout	46,519
Percent of registered voting	57.4%

House District 32
Rep. Eugene (Gene) Seaman (R)

House Office
(512) 463-0672
(888) 436-3945

District Office
5866 S. Staples, Suite 313
Corpus Christi, Texas 78413
(512) 994-1996

Personal

Year of birth	1930
Family	Married to Ellen Brauer Seaman, five children
Education	American College, M.A.
Occupation	Insurance, real estate developer
Religion	Baptist
State legislative service	House 1997 to present

COMMITTEE ASSIGNMENT HISTORY

1997 Economic Development, Rules and Resolutions, State, Federal and International Relations

BILL PASSAGE RATES, 1997

	Total	Passed Legislature	Pct. Passed Legislature
Authored	33	9	27%
Sponsored	5	4	80%
Amendments	4	4	100%

ELECTORAL HISTORY IN CURRENT DISTRICT

	1994	1996	1998
Primary Election Opponent(s)	NA	Yes	No
General Election Opponent(s)	NA	Dem	No

House District 33

COUNTIES IN DISTRICT
Nueces (part)

DEMOGRAPHIC INFORMATION

Population	
Total	111,673
Anglo	34.4%
Black	3.3%
Hispanic	61.5%
Others	1.0%

Wealth and Urbanization	
Per capita Income	$10,607
Avg. House Value	$59,569
Percent Poverty	19.2%
Public Assistance	9.1%
Percent Urban	100%

Education	
High School Graduates	70.3%
College Graduates	14.8%

Employed	
Percent Employed	91.5%
Private Sector	73.4%

Age of Population	
5 years or less	10.1%
6-17 years	20.7%
18-64 years	60.1%
65 or older	9.1%

Household Types	
Family households	89.9%
Non-family households	9.3%
Single-parent families	25.4%
Both parents working	60.6%

SENATE DISTRICTS IN HOUSE DISTRICT

Dist 20 Carlos F. Truan (D)

DISTRICT ELECTION DATA

House 1996	
Vilma Luna (D)	100.0%

House 1998	
Vilma Luna (D)	70.3%
Arturo Granado (R)	29.7%

President 1996	
Bill Clinton (D)	64.6%
Bob Dole (R)	35.4%

Composite Party Vote 1994	
Democratic	62.4%
Republican	37.6%

Registered Voters 1996	**66,839**
Turnout	33,856
Percent of registered voting	50.7%

House District 33
Rep. Vilma Luna (D)

House Office
(512) 463-0484

District Office
4525 Gollihar #200
Corpus Christi, Texas 78411
(512) 854-9816

Personal

Year of birth	1957
Family	Married to Enrico Gonzalez, two children
Education	Southwest Texas State University, B.S.W. University of Houston, J.D.
Occupation	Attorney
Religion	Catholic
State legislative service	House 1993 (part) to present

COMMITTEE ASSIGNMENT HISTORY

1997 Economic Development, House Administration (Vice-Chair), Judicial Affairs
1995 Economic Development, Public Safety
1993 NA

BILL PASSAGE RATES, 1997

	Total	Passed Legislature	Pct. Passed Legislature
Authored	28	9	32%
Sponsored	1	1	100%
Amendments	10	9	90%

ELECTORAL HISTORY IN CURRENT DISTRICT

	1994	1996	1998
Primary Election Opponent(s)	Yes	No	No
General Election Opponent(s)	Rep	No	Rep

House District 34

COUNTIES IN DISTRICT

Nueces (part)

DEMOGRAPHIC INFORMATION

Population

Total	110,894
Anglo	32.3%
Black	6.6%
Hispanic	60.9%
Others	0.7%

Education

High School Graduates	56.1%
College Graduates	11.3%

Age of Population

5 years or less	10.1%
6-17 years	22.0%
18-64 years	56.5%
65 or older	11.4%

Wealth and Urbanization

Per capita Income	$9,284
Avg. House Value	$54,555
Percent Poverty	28.0%
Public Assistance	13.6%
Percent Urban	86.8%

Employed

Percent Employed	89.1%
Private Sector	75.2%

Household Types

Family households	88.4%
Non-family households	9.0%
Single-parent families	25.1%
Both parents working	52.0%

SENATE DISTRICTS IN HOUSE DISTRICT

Dist 20 Carlos F. Truan (D)

DISTRICT ELECTION DATA

House 1996

Hugo Berlanga (D)	100.0%

President 1996

Bill Clinton (D)	64.5%
Bob Dole (R)	35.5%

Composite Party Vote 1994

Democratic	63.4%
Republican	36.6%

Registered Voters 1996	**66,657**
Turnout	31,796
Percent of registered voting	47.7%

House 1998

Jaime L. Capelo, Jr. (D)	67.3%
Rene De Alejandro (R)	32.7%

House District 34
Rep. Jaime L. Capelo, Jr. (D)

House Office
(512) 463-0462

District Office
719 S. Shoreline Blvd., Suite 301B
Corpus Christi, Texas 78404
(512) 882-2277

Personal

Year of birth	1962
Family	Married to Sandra Capelo, two children
Education	Yale University, B.A.
	Texas School of Law, J.D.
Occupation	Attorney
Religion	Catholic
State legislative service	House 1998 to present

COMMITTEE ASSIGNMENT HISTORY
1998 Pensions and Investments, Public Health

BILL PASSAGE RATES, 1995

	Total	Passed Legislature	Pct. Passed Legislature
Authored	NA	NA	NA
Sponsored	NA	NA	NA
Amendments	NA	NA	NA

ELECTORAL HISTORY IN CURRENT DISTRICT

	1994	1996	1998
Primary Election Opponent(s)	NA	NA	No
General Election Opponent(s)	NA	NA	Rep
Special Election Opponent(s)	NA	NA	Yes

House District 35

COUNTIES IN DISTRICT

Brooks, Jim Hogg, Kennedy, Kleberg, Starr, Willacy, Zapata

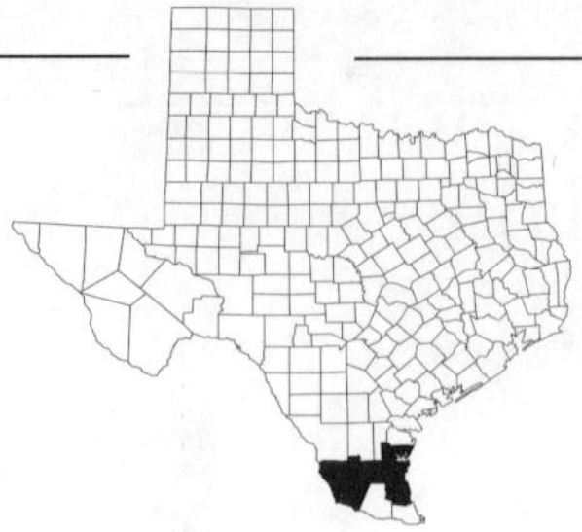

DEMOGRAPHIC INFORMATION

Population	
Total	111,549
Anglo	15.2%
Black	1.0%
Hispanic	83.1%
Others	0.7%

Education	
High School Graduates	46.0%
College Graduates	10.7%

Age of Population	
5 years or less	11.0%
6-17 years	23.9%
18-64 years	55.1%
65 or older	9.9%

Wealth and Urbanization	
Per capita Income	$6,455
Avg. House Value	$36,449
Percent Poverty	44.3%
Public Assistance	16.7%
Percent Urban	62.2%

Employed	
Percent Employed	85.7%
Private Sector	61.5%

Household Types	
Family households	92.2%
Non-family households	6.3%
Single-parent families	17.6%
Both parents working	46.2%

SENATE DISTRICTS IN HOUSE DISTRICT

Dist 20 Carlos F. Truan (D)

Dist 21 Judith Zaffirini (D)

DISTRICT ELECTION DATA

House 1996	
Irma Rangel (D)	100.0%

President 1996	
Bill Clinton (D)	76.2%
Bob Dole (R)	23.8%

Composite Party Vote 1994	
Democratic	74.1%
Republican	25.9%

Registered Voters 1996	67,899
Turnout	30,800
Percent of registered voting	45.4%

House 1998	
Irma Rangel (D)	100.0%

House District 35
Rep. Irma Rangel (D)

House Office
(512) 463-0666

District Office
P.O. Box 2910
Austin, Texas 78768
(512) 463-0666

Personal

Year of birth	1931
Family	Single, no children
Education	Texas A&I University, B.B.A.
	St. Mary's School of Law, J.D.
Occupation	Attorney (retired)
Religion	Catholic
State legislative service	House 1977 to present

COMMITTEE ASSIGNMENT HISTORY

1997 Higher Education (Chair), Pensions and Investments
1995 Higher Education (Chair), Pensions and Investments
1993 General Investigating, Higher Education (Vice-Chair), International and Cultural Relations (Vice-Chair)
1991 Higher Education, Judicial Affairs (Vice-Chair)
1989 Higher Education (Vice-Chair), House Administration, Judicial Affairs
1987 Higher Education, House Administration, Judicial Affairs (Vice-Chair)
1985 Higher Education, House Administration, Urban Affairs (Vice-Chair)
1983 Higher Education, Judicial Affairs (Vice-Chair)
1981 Judiciary, Transportation
1979 Judiciary, Security and Sanctions
1977 Business and Industry, Social Services

BILL PASSAGE RATES, 1997

	Total	Passed Legislature	Pct. Passed Legislature
Authored	23	8	35%
Sponsored	10	6	60%
Amendments	8	8	100%

ELECTORAL HISTORY IN CURRENT DISTRICT

	1994	1996	1998
Primary Election Opponent(s)	Yes	Yes	No
General Election Opponent(s)	No	No	No

House District 36

COUNTIES IN DISTRICT

Cameron (part), Hidalgo (part)

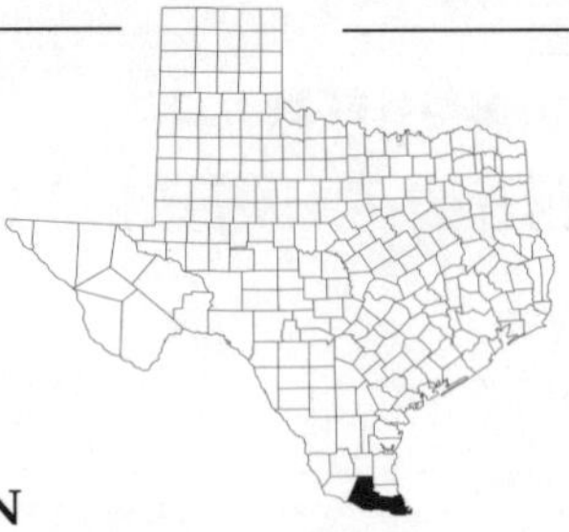

DEMOGRAPHIC INFORMATION

Population

Total	107,277
Anglo	18.8%
Black	0.3%
Hispanic	80.7%
Others	0.3%

Education

High School Graduates	48.8%
College Graduates	9.9%

Age of Population

5 years or less	11.4%
6-17 years	24.3%
18-64 years	53.1%
65 or older	11.2%

Wealth and Urbanization

Per capita Income	$6,804
Avg. House Value	$42,701
Percent Poverty	40.0%
Public Assistance	15.5%
Percent Urban	70.6%

Employed

Percent Employed	86.2%
Private Sector	72.8%

Household Types

Family households	95.1%
Non-family households	4.3%
Single-parent families	17.7%
Both parents working	47.7%

SENATE DISTRICTS IN HOUSE DISTRICT

Dist 20 Carlos F. Truan (D)
Dist 21 Judith Zaffirini (D)
Dist 27 Eddie Lucio Jr. (D)

DISTRICT ELECTION DATA

House 1996

Ismael (Kino) Florez (D)	61.3%
Kathleen Holton (R)	48.7%

President 1996

Bill Clinton (D)	63.5%
Bob Dole (R)	36.5%

Composite Party Vote 1994

Democratic	57.8%
Republican	42.2%

Registered Voters 1996	**54,634**
Turnout	25,566
Percent of registered voting	46.8%

House 1998

Ismael (Kino) Florez (D)	100.0%

House District 36
Rep. Ismael (Kino) Flores (D)

House Office
(512) 463-0704

District Office
P.O. Box 2910
Austin, Texas 78768
(512) 463-0704

Personal

Year of birth	1958
Family	Married to Debra Flores, no children
Education	Pan American University
Occupation	Businessman, accounting
Religion	Methodist
State legislative service	House 1997 to present

COMMITTEE ASSIGNMENT HISTORY

1997 Agriculture and Livestock, County Affairs

BILL PASSAGE RATES, 1997

	Total	Passed Legislature	Pct. Passed Legislature
Authored	31	13	42%
Sponsored	1	1	100%
Amendments	2	2	100%

ELECTORAL HISTORY IN CURRENT DISTRICT

	1994	1996	1998
Primary Election Opponent(s)	NA	Yes	No
General Election Opponent(s)	NA	Rep	No

House District 37

COUNTIES IN DISTRICT
Cameron (part)

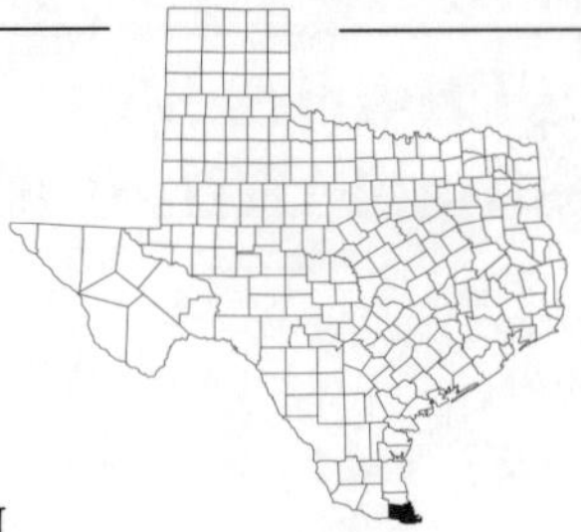

DEMOGRAPHIC INFORMATION

Population	
Total	107,273
Anglo	10.1%
Black	0.2%
Hispanic	89.5%
Others	0.4%

Education	
High School Graduates	43.0%
College Graduates	10.9%

Age of Population	
5 years or less	10.9%
6-17 years	26.2%
18-64 years	54.3%
65 or older	8.6%

Wealth and Urbanization	
Per capita Income	$5,874
Avg. House Value	$47,078
Percent Poverty	46.9%
Public Assistance	22.7%
Percent Urban	97.2%

Employed	
Percent Employed	83.8%
Private Sector	71.4%

Household Types	
Family households	93.6%
Non-family households	4.7%
Single-parent families	25.7%
Both parents working	47.0%

SENATE DISTRICTS IN HOUSE DISTRICT

Dist 27 Eddie Lucio Jr. (D)

DISTRICT ELECTION DATA

House 1996	
Rene O. Oliveira (D)	69.4%
Philip Thomas Cowen (R)	30.6%

President 1996	
Bill Clinton (D)	75.5%
Bob Dole (R)	24.5%

Composite Party Vote 1994	
Democratic	71.9%
Republican	28.1%

Registered Voters 1996	49,603
Turnout	20,587
Percent of registered voting	41.5%

House 1998	
Rene O. Oliveira (D)	100.0%

House District 37
Rep. Rene O. Oliveira (D)

House Office
(512) 463-0640

District Office
855 W. Price Drive, #22
Brownsville, Texas 78520
(210) 542-1828

Personal

Year of birth	1955
Family	Single, two children
Education	University of Texas, B.S., J.D.
Occupation	Attorney
Religion	Catholic
State legislative service	House 1981-85; 1991 to present

COMMITTEE ASSIGNMENT HISTORY
1997 Economic Development (Chair), Ways and Means
1995 Economic Development (Chair), Ways and Means
1993 Economic Development (Chair), Ways and Means
1991 Appropriations, Ways and Means
1985 Appropriations, Business and Commerce
1983 Cultural and Historical Resources, Higher Education
1981 Health Services, Insurance

BILL PASSAGE RATES, 1997

	Total	Passed Legislature	Pct. Passed Legislature
Authored	47	22	47%
Sponsored	11	6	55%
Amendments	23	21	91%

ELECTORAL HISTORY IN CURRENT DISTRICT

	1994	1996	1998
Primary Election Opponent(s)	Yes	No	Yes
General Election Opponent(s)	No	Rep	No

House District 38

COUNTIES IN DISTRICT

Cameron (part)

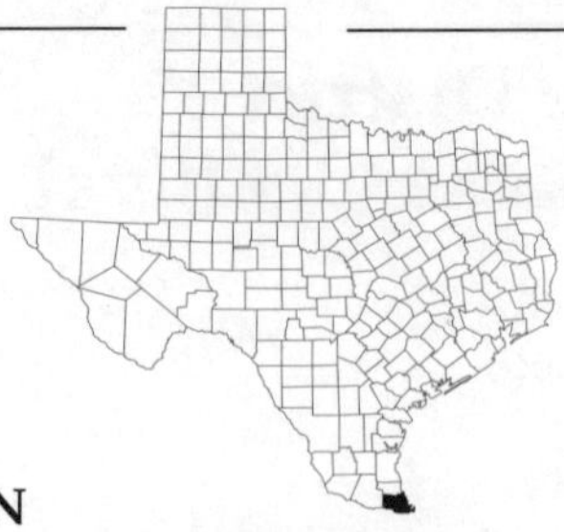

DEMOGRAPHIC INFORMATION

Population		**Wealth and Urbanization**	
Total	107,293	Per capita Income	$7,351
Anglo	20.1%	Avg. House Value	$46,058
Black	0.4%	Percent Poverty	36.6%
Hispanic	79.1%	Public Assistance	16.1%
Others	0.6%	Percent Urban	65.8%

Education		**Employed**	
High School Graduates	51.0%	Percent Employed	88.0%
College Graduates	12.1%	Private Sector	71.3%

Age of Population		**Household Types**	
5 years or less	10.8%	Family households	92.2%
6-17 years	24.5%	Non-family households	5.4%
18-64 years	53.7%	Single-parent families	20.7%
65 or older	11.0%	Both parents working	52.1%

SENATE DISTRICTS IN HOUSE DISTRICT

Dist 27 Eddie Lucio Jr. (D)

DISTRICT ELECTION DATA

House 1996		**House 1998**	
Jim Solis (D)	100.0%	Jim Solis (D)	100.0%

President 1996	
Bill Clinton (D)	63.3%
Bob Dole (R)	36.7%

Composite Party Vote 1994	
Democratic	59.4%
Republican	40.6%

Registered Voters 1996	**54,121**
Turnout	25,424
Percent of registered voting	47.0%

House District 38
Rep. Jim Solis (D)

House Office
(512) 463-0606

District Office
1706 E. Tyler, Suite 2
Harlingen, Texas 78550
(210) 421-4120

Personal

Year of birth	1963
Family	Single, no children
Education	Pan American University, B.B.A., Marketing Thurgood Marshall School of Law, J.D.
Occupation	Attorney
Religion	Catholic
State legislative service	House 1993 to present

COMMITTEE ASSIGNMENT HISTORY

1997 Higher Education (Vice-Chair), Judicial Affairs
1995 Criminal Jurisprudence, Judicial Affairs
1993 Criminal Jurisprudence, Transportation

BILL PASSAGE RATES, 1997

	Total	Passed Legislature	Pct. Passed Legislature
Authored	29	10	34%
Sponsored	0	0	NA
Amendments	14	13	93%

ELECTORAL HISTORY IN CURRENT DISTRICT

	1994	1996	1998
Primary Election Opponent(s)	No	No	No
General Election Opponent(s)	No	No	No

House District 39

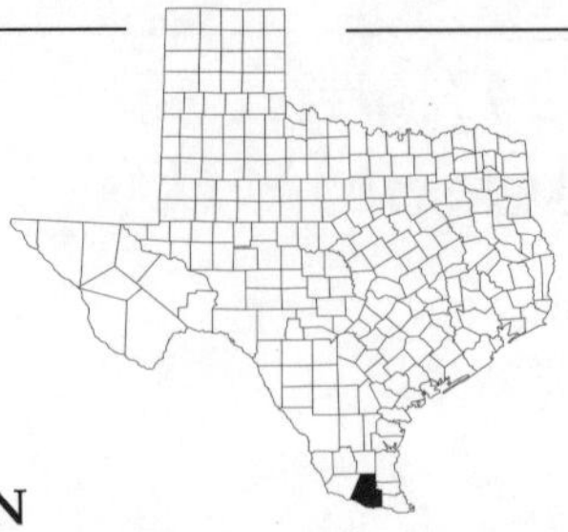

COUNTIES IN DISTRICT

Hidalgo (part)

DEMOGRAPHIC INFORMATION

Population

Total	107,283
Anglo	13.0%
Black	0.1%
Hispanic	86.5%
Others	0.4%

Education

High School Graduates	43.7%
College Graduates	8.4%

Age of Population

5 years or less	11.2%
6-17 years	25.3%
18-64 years	51.4%
65 or older	12.0%

Wealth and Urbanization

Per capita Income	$5,852
Avg. House Value	$36,629
Percent Poverty	43.1%
Public Assistance	19.0%
Percent Urban	74.4%

Employed

Percent Employed	82.9%
Private Sector	70.9%

Household Types

Family households	94.7%
Non-family households	4.5%
Single-parent families	21.3%
Both parents working	48.8%

SENATE DISTRICTS IN HOUSE DISTRICT

Dist 20 Carlos F. Truan (D)

Dist 27 Eddie Lucio Jr. (D)

DISTRICT ELECTION DATA

House 1996

Miguel David Wise (D)	100.0%

House 1998

Miguel David Wise (D)	100.0%

President 1996

Bill Clinton (D)	73.2%
Bob Dole (R)	26.8%

Composite Party Vote 1994

Democratic	66.8%
Republican	33.2%

Registered Voters 1996	**56,328**
Turnout	23,108
Percent of registered voting	41.0%

House District 39
Rep. Miguel David Wise (D)

House Office
(512) 463-0530

District Office
800 W. Railroad St., Bldg. W-4, Suite G3
Westlaco, Texas 78596
(210) 968-9600

Personal

Year of birth	1960
Family	Married to Erin Duffy Wise, three children
Education	St. Mary's University, B.A., J.D.
Occupation	Attorney
Religion	Catholic
State legislative service	House 1997 to present

COMMITTEE ASSIGNMENT HISTORY

1997 Insurance, State, Federal and International Relations

BILL PASSAGE RATES, 1997

	Total	Passed Legislature	Pct. Passed Legislature
Authored	78	14	18%
Sponsored	1	1	100%
Amendments	17	14	82%

ELECTORAL HISTORY IN CURRENT DISTRICT

	1994	1996	1998
Primary Election Opponent(s)	NA	Yes	No
General Election Opponent(s)	NA	No	No

House District 40

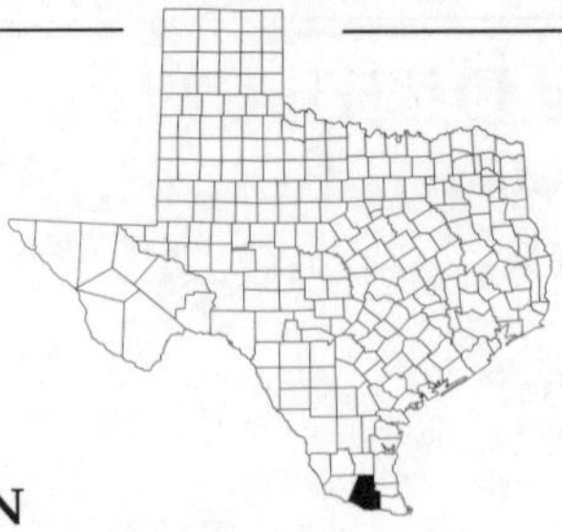

COUNTIES IN DISTRICT

Hidalgo (part)

DEMOGRAPHIC INFORMATION

Population

Total	107,266
Anglo	14.3%
Black	0.3%
Hispanic	84.9%
Others	0.6%

Education

High School Graduates	50.5%
College Graduates	14.7%

Age of Population

5 years or less	11.1%
6-17 years	24.7%
18-64 years	55.5%
65 or older	8.7%

Wealth and Urbanization

Per capita Income	$6,894
Avg. House Value	$50,312
Percent Poverty	39.5%
Public Assistance	16.6%
Percent Urban	75.1%

Employed

Percent Employed	87.7%
Private Sector	69.1%

Household Types

Family households	93.2%
Non-family households	5.1%
Single-parent families	21.6%
Both parents working	53.9%

SENATE DISTRICTS IN HOUSE DISTRICT

Dist 20 Carlos F. Truan (D)
Dist 21 Judith Zaffirini (D)
Dist 27 Eddie Lucio Jr. (D)

DISTRICT ELECTION DATA

House 1996

Juan (Chuy) Hinojosa (D)	71.4%
Emilio D. Santos (R)	28.6%

President 1996

Bill Clinton (D)	68.6%
Bob Dole (R)	31.4%

Composite Party Vote 1994

Democratic	64.9%
Republican	35.1%

Registered Voters 1996	**54,267**
Turnout	24,288
Percent of registered voting	44.8%

House 1998

Juan (Chuy) Hinojosa (D)	100.0%

House District 40
Rep. Juan (Chuy) Hinojosa (D)

House Office
(512) 463-0636

District Office
204 Cano, Ste. 111
Edinburg, Texas 78539
(956) 386-0639

Personal

Year of birth	1946
Family	Single, three children
Education	Pan American, B.S. Georgetown University, J.D.
Occupation	Attorney
Religion	Catholic
State legislative service	House 1997 to present

COMMITTEE ASSIGNMENT HISTORY
1997 Appropriations, Criminal Jurisprudence

BILL PASSAGE RATES, 1995

	Total	Passed Legislature	Pct. Passed Legislature
Authored	29	7	24%
Sponsored	4	2	50%
Amendments	3	3	100%

ELECTORAL HISTORY IN CURRENT DISTRICT

	1994	1996	1998
Primary Election Opponent(s)	NA	Yes	No
General Election Opponent(s)	NA	Rep	No

House District 41

COUNTIES IN DISTRICT
Hidalgo (part)

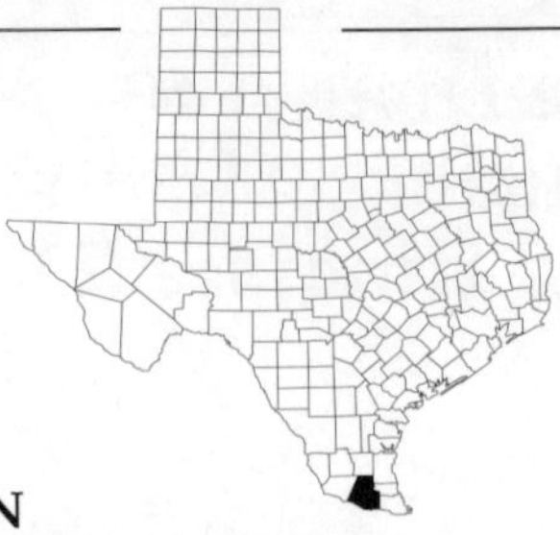

DEMOGRAPHIC INFORMATION

Population

Total	107,273
Anglo	16.7%
Black	0.2%
Hispanic	82.7%
Others	0.5%

Education

High School Graduates	49.2%
College Graduates	14.0%

Age of Population

5 years or less	10.5%
6-17 years	24.8%
18-64 years	54.0%
65 or older	10.8%

Wealth and Urbanization

Per capita Income	$7,874
Avg. House Value	$52,497
Percent Poverty	39.1%
Public Assistance	16.4%
Percent Urban	96.7%

Employed

Percent Employed	87.1%
Private Sector	72.9%

Household Types

Family households	94.1%
Non-family households	5.0%
Single-parent families	21.4%
Both parents working	49.2%

SENATE DISTRICTS IN HOUSE DISTRICT

Dist 20 Carlos F. Truan (D)
Dist 27 Eddie Lucio Jr. (D)

DISTRICT ELECTION DATA

House 1996

Roberto Gutierrez (D)	66.3%
Javier Perez (R)	33.7%

President 1996

Bill Clinton (D)	66.0%
Bob Dole (R)	34.0%

Composite Party Vote 1994

Democratic	60.8%
Republican	39.2%

Registered Voters 1996	**57,181**
Turnout	25,199
Percent of registered voting	44.1%

House 1998

Roberto Gutierrez (D)	100.0%

House District 41
Rep. Roberto Gutierrez (D)

House Office
(512) 463-0578

District Office
100 Savannah #270
McAllen, Texas 78503
(956) 618-0192

Personal

Year of birth	1936
Family	Married to Cecilia Gutierrez, three children
Education	Pan American University, B.A. and M.A., Education
Occupation	Petroleum products distributor, owner and president
Religion	Catholic
State legislative service	House 1991 to present

COMMITTEE ASSIGNMENT HISTORY

1997 County Affairs, Financial Institutions (Vice-Chair), Local and Consent Calendars
1995 County Affairs (Vice-Chair), Financial Institutions
1993 County Affairs (Vice-Chair), Investments and Banking
1991 Cultural and Historical Resources, Financial Institutions

BILL PASSAGE RATES, 1997

	Total	Passed Legislature	Pct. Passed Legislature
Authored	44	16	36%
Sponsored	5	3	60%
Amendments	11	10	91%

ELECTORAL HISTORY IN CURRENT DISTRICT

	1994	1996	1998
Primary Election Opponent(s)	No	No	No
General Election Opponent(s)	No	Rep	No

House District 42

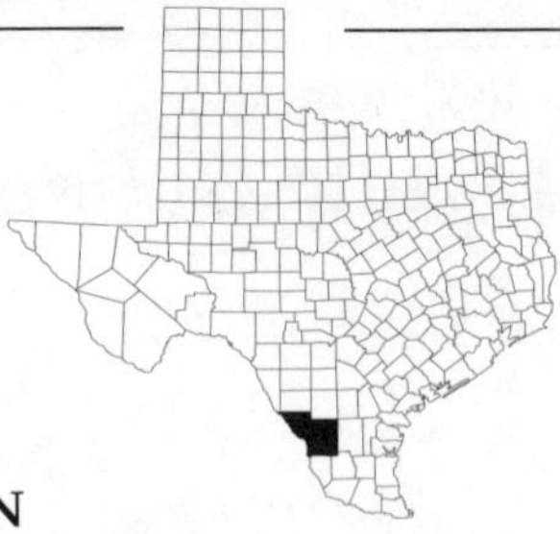

COUNTIES IN DISTRICT
Webb (part)

DEMOGRAPHIC INFORMATION

Population

Total	110,999
Anglo	6.1%
Black	0.1%
Hispanic	93.3%
Others	0.6%

Education

High School Graduates	51.0%
College Graduates	12.5%

Age of Population

5 years or less	11.6%
6-17 years	23.3%
18-64 years	56.6%
65 or older	8.6%

Wealth and Urbanization

Per capita Income	$7,423
Avg. House Value	$64,744
Percent Poverty	35.6%
Public Assistance	16.5%
Percent Urban	99.9%

Employed

Percent Employed	89.4%
Private Sector	70.1%

Household Types

Family households	93.9%
Non-family households	4.6%
Single-parent families	22.1%
Both parents working	49.6%

SENATE DISTRICTS IN HOUSE DISTRICT

Dist 21 Judith Zaffirini (D)

DISTRICT ELECTION DATA

House 1996

Henry Cuellar (D)	100.0%

House 1998

Henry Cuellar (D)	100.0%

President 1996

Bill Clinton (D)	79.2%
Bob Dole (R)	20.8%

Composite Party Vote 1994

Democratic	75.9%
Republican	24.1%

Registered Voters 1996	**57,752**
Turnout	21,796
Percent of registered voting	37.7%

House District 42
Rep. Henry Cuellar (D)

House Office
(512) 463-0558

District Office
P. O. Box 757
Laredo, Texas 78042
(956) 725-8988

Personal

Year of birth	1955
Family	Married to Imelda Rios, two children
Education	Georgetown University, B.S.F.S. Laredo State University, M.A. University of Texas, J.D.
Occupation	Attorney, customs broker
Religion	Catholic
State legislative service	House 1987 to present

COMMITTEE ASSIGNMENT HISTORY

1997 Appropriations, Higher Education
1995 Appropriations, Juvenile Justice and Family Issues
1993 Appropriations, Judicial Affairs
1991 Appropriations, Financial Institutions
1989 Local and Consent Calendars, Science and Technology
1987 Business and Commerce, Liquor Regulation

BILL PASSAGE RATES, 1997

	Total	Passed Legislature	Pct. Passed Legislature
Authored	62	20	32%
Sponsored	14	13	93%
Amendments	18	18	100%

ELECTORAL HISTORY IN CURRENT DISTRICT

	1994	1996	1998
Primary Election Opponent(s)	No	No	No
General Election Opponent(s)	No	No	No

House District 43

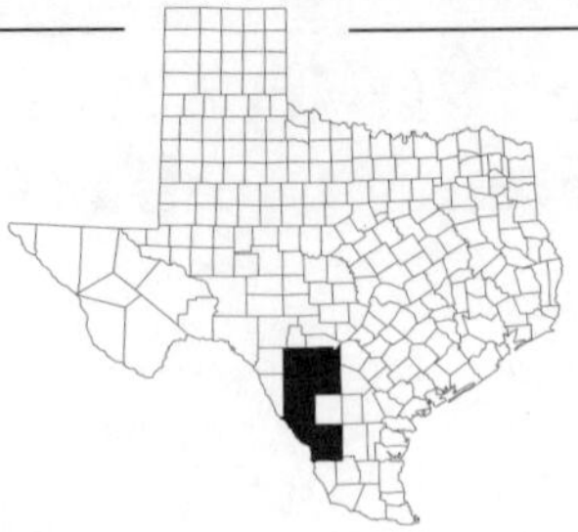

COUNTIES IN DISTRICT

Dimmit, Frio, Medina, Uvalde, Webb (part), Zavala

DEMOGRAPHIC INFORMATION

Population	
Total	108,959
Anglo	28.2%
Black	0.6%
Hispanic	70.7%
Others	0.5%

Education	
High School Graduates	50.3%
College Graduates	9.3%

Age of Population	
5 years or less	10.8%
6-17 years	23.8%
18-64 years	54.4%
65 or older	11.0%

Wealth and Urbanization	
Per capita Income	$7,145
Avg. House Value	$40,569
Percent Poverty	36.9%
Public Assistance	15.4%
Percent Urban	60.5%

Employed	
Percent Employed	88.1%
Private Sector	68.5%

Household Types	
Family households	92.4%
Non-family households	6.1%
Single-parent families	18.7%
Both parents working	48.9%

SENATE DISTRICTS IN HOUSE DISTRICT

Dist 19 Frank Madla (D)
Dist 21 Judith Zaffirini (D)
Dist 25 Jeff Wentworth (R)

DISTRICT ELECTION DATA

House 1996	
Tracy O. King (D)	100.0%

House 1998	
Tracy O. King (D)	100.0%

President 1996	
Bill Clinton (D)	59.4%
Bob Dole (R)	40.6%

Composite Party Vote 1994	
Democratic	59.4%
Republican	40.6%

Registered Voters 1996	**70,969**
Turnout	55,030
Percent of registered voting	77.5%

House District 43
Rep. Tracy O. King (D)

House Office
(512) 463-0742

District Office
210 North High Street
Uvalde, Texas 78801
(210) 278-2519

Personal

Year of birth	1960
Family	Married to Cheryl King, one child
Education	Southwest Texas Junior College Texas A&M University, B.S., Agricultural Engineering
Occupation	Hearing aid specialist
Religion	Methodist
State legislative service	House 1995 to present

COMMITTEE ASSIGNMENT HISTORY

1997 Local and Consent Calendars, Natural Resources, State Recreational Resources
1995 Agriculture and Livestock, Natural Resources

BILL PASSAGE RATES, 1997

	Total	Passed Legislature	Pct. Passed Legislature
Authored	20	11	55%
Sponsored	0	0	NA
Amendments	18	13	72%

ELECTORAL HISTORY IN CURRENT DISTRICT

	1994	1996	1998
Primary Election Opponent(s)	Yes	No	No
General Election Opponent(s)	Rep	No	No

House District 44

COUNTIES IN DISTRICT

Atascosa, Duval, Jim Wells, La Salle, McMullen, Wilson

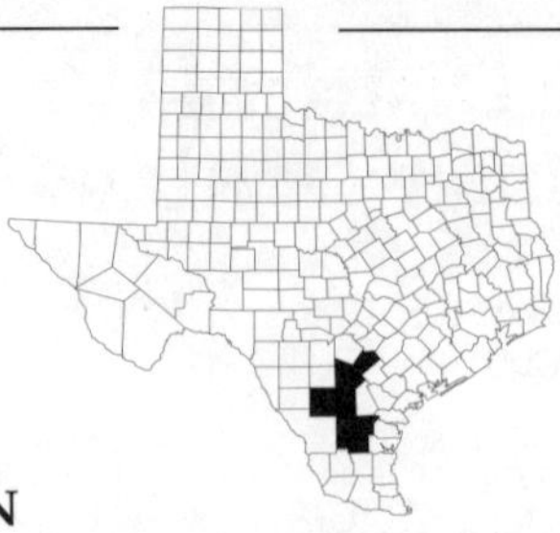

DEMOGRAPHIC INFORMATION

Population	
Total	109,851
Anglo	38.0%
Black	0.6%
Hispanic	61.0%
Others	0.5%

Education	
High School Graduates	56.2%
College Graduates	8.8%

Age of Population	
5 years or less	10.1%
6-17 years	22.0%
18-64 years	55.8%
65 or older	12.2%

Wealth and Urbanization	
Per capita Income	$8,452
Avg. House Value	$41,668
Percent Poverty	29.5%
Public Assistance	13.9%
Percent Urban	49.2%

Employed	
Percent Employed	90.8%
Private Sector	70.1%

Household Types	
Family households	91.8%
Non-family households	7.1%
Single-parent families	17.0%
Both parents working	52.6%

SENATE DISTRICTS IN HOUSE DISTRICT

Dist 19 Frank Madla (D)
Dist 20 Carlos F. Truan (D)
Dist 21 Judith Zaffirini (D)

DISTRICT ELECTION DATA

House 1996	
Richard Raymond (D)	100.0%

House 1998	
Ignacio Salinas (D)	52.8%
Bob Hurley (R)	47.2%

President 1996	
Bill Clinton (D)	61.4%
Bob Dole (R)	38.6%

Composite Party Vote 1994	
Democratic	63.6%
Republican	36.4%

Registered Voters 1996	**76,283**
Turnout	36,787
Percent of registered voting	48.2%

House District 44
Rep. Ignacio Salinas (D)

House Office
(512) 463-0590

District Office
505 S. Victoria St.
San Diego, Texas 78384
(512) 476-5355

Personal

Year of birth	1958
Family	
Education	University of Dalas, B.A. Texas A&I University, M.S. University of Texas at Austin, doctoral studies
Occupation	Educator
Religion	
State legislative service	House 1999 to present

COMMITTEE ASSIGNMENT HISTORY

BILL PASSAGE RATES, 1995

	Total	Passed Legislature	Pct. Passed Legislature
Authored	NA	NA	NA
Sponsored	NA	NA	NA
Amendments	NA	NA	NA

ELECTORAL HISTORY IN CURRENT DISTRICT

	1994	1996	1998
Primary Election Opponent(s)	NA	NA	Yes
General Election Opponent(s)	NA	NA	Rep

House District 45

COUNTIES IN DISTRICT

Comal, Guadalupe

DEMOGRAPHIC INFORMATION

Population

Total	116,705
Anglo	69.1%
Black	3.5%
Hispanic	26.7%
Others	0.9%

Education

High School Graduates	72.5%
College Graduates	16.9%

Age of Population

5 years or less	8.9%
6-17 years	18.3%
18-64 years	58.9%
65 or older	13.8%

Wealth and Urbanization

Per capita Income	$12,249
Avg. House Value	$77,255
Percent Poverty	15.6%
Public Assistance	6.1%
Percent Urban	59.4%

Employed

Percent Employed	93.7%
Private Sector	72.0%

Household Types

Family households	89.3%
Non-family households	8.9%
Single-parent families	18.0%
Both parents working	68.5%

SENATE DISTRICTS IN HOUSE DISTRICT

Dist 18 Kenneth L. Armbrister (D)

Dist 21 Judith Zaffirini (D)

Dist 25 Jeff Wentworth (R)

DISTRICT ELECTION DATA

House 1996

Bill Utterback (L)	11.3%
Edmund Kuempel (R)	88.7%

President 1996

Bill Clinton (D)	32.9%
Bob Dole (R)	67.1%

Composite Party Vote 1994

Democratic	36.7%
Republican	63.3%

Registered Voters 1996	**89,268**
Turnout	50,582
Percent of registered voting	56.7%

House 1998

Edmund Kuempel (R)	100.0%

House District 45
Rep. Edmund Kuempel (R)

House Office
(512) 463-0602

District Office
523 E. Donegan #102
Seguin, Texas 78155
(210) 379-8732

Personal

Year of birth	1942
Family	Married to Birdie Kuempel, two children
Education	Texas Lutheran College, B.A., Business
Occupation	Salesman, Structural Metals, Inc.
Religion	Lutheran
State legislative service	House 1983 to present

COMMITTEE ASSIGNMENT HISTORY

1997 Environmental Regulation, State Recreational Resources (Chair)
1995 Environmental Regulation, State Recreational Resources (Chair)
1993 Energy Resources, Environmental Regulation, House Administration
1991 Environmental Affairs, House Administration (Chair), Retirement and Aging
1989 Environmental Affairs, Retirement and Aging
1987 Environmental Affairs, Retirement and Aging (Chair)
1985 Appropriations, Environmental Affairs
1983 Labor and Employment Relations, Ways and Means

BILL PASSAGE RATES, 1997

	Total	Passed Legislature	Pct. Passed Legislature
Authored	24	12	50%
Sponsored	7	5	71%
Amendments	5	5	100%

ELECTORAL HISTORY IN CURRENT DISTRICT

	1994	1996	1998
Primary Election Opponent(s)	No	Yes	No
General Election Opponent(s)	No	Lib	No

House District 46

COUNTIES IN DISTRICT

Caldwell, Gonzales, Hays

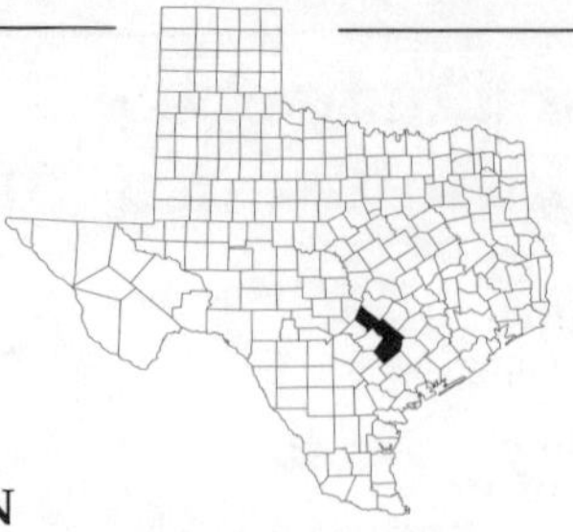

DEMOGRAPHIC INFORMATION

Population		**Wealth and Urbanization**	
Total	109,211	Per capita Income	$10,554
Anglo	61.9%	Avg. House Value	$72,155
Black	6.2%	Percent Poverty	24.8%
Hispanic	31.5%	Public Assistance	7.3%
Others	0.8%	Percent Urban	45.0%

Education		**Employed**	
High School Graduates	68.9%	Percent Employed	92.5%
College Graduates	19.3%	Private Sector	66.2%

Age of Population		**Household Types**	
5 years or less	8.6%	Family households	78.5%
6-17 years	17.8%	Non-family households	14.1%
18-64 years	62.8%	Single-parent families	17.4%
65 or older	10.7%	Both parents working	65.8%

SENATE DISTRICTS IN HOUSE DISTRICT

Dist 14 Gonzalo Barrientos (D)

Dist 18 Kenneth L. Armbrister (D)

DISTRICT ELECTION DATA

House 1996		**House 1998**	
Alec Rhodes(D)	56.4%	Alec Rhodes (D)	50.0%
Ken Fleuriet (R)	43.6%	Rick Green (R)	50.0%

President 1996	
Bill Clinton (D)	48.3%
Bob Dole (R)	51.7%

Composite Party Vote 1994	
Democratic	53.1%
Republican	46.9%

Registered Voters 1996	**75,414**
Turnout	40,788
Percent of registered voting	54.1%

House District 46
Rep. Alec Rhodes (D)*

House Office
(512) 463-0498

District Office
P. O. Box 2910
Austin, Texas 78768
(512) 463-0498

Personal

Year of birth	1942
Family	Married to Charlotte Rhodes, two children
Education	University of North Carolina, B.A., Economics Emory University, M.B.A.
Occupation	Businessman
Religion	Episcopalian
State legislative service	House 1995 to present

COMMITTEE ASSIGNMENT HISTORY

1997 Business and Industry (Vice-Chair), Public Education, Rules and Resolutions

1995 Business and Industry, Rules and Resolutions, State, Federal and International Relations

BILL PASSAGE RATES, 1995

	Total	Passed Legislature	Pct. Passed Legislature
Authored	13	6	46%
Sponsored	4	4	100%
Amendments	6	5	83%

ELECTORAL HISTORY IN CURRENT DISTRICT

	1994	1996	1998
Primary Election Opponent(s)	Yes	No	No
General Election Opponent(s)	No	Rep	Rep

*See also page 403.

House District 47

COUNTIES IN DISTRICT

Travis (part)

DEMOGRAPHIC INFORMATION

Population		**Wealth and Urbanization**	
Total	118,508	Per capita Income	$24,232
Anglo	87.9%	Avg. House Value	$144,542
Black	2.3%	Percent Poverty	5.2%
Hispanic	7.1%	Public Assistance	1.3%
Others	2.7%	Percent Urban	71.7%

Education		**Employed**	
High School Graduates	93.7%	Percent Employed	96.3%
College Graduates	49.9%	Private Sector	68.9%

Age of Population		**Household Types**	
5 years or less	8.6%	Family households	85.6%
6-17 years	16.3%	Non-family households	14.0%
18-64 years	67.6%	Single-parent families	13.6%
65 or older	7.5%	Both parents working	66.4%

SENATE DISTRICTS IN HOUSE DISTRICT

Dist 14 Gonzalo Barrientos (D)

Dist 25 Jeff Wentworth (R)

DISTRICT ELECTION DATA

House 1996		**House 1998**	
John Lindell (D)	29.3%		
Terry Keel (R)	69.0%	Terry Keel (R)	100.0%
John Stern (NLP)	1.7%		

President 1996	
Bill Clinton (D)	39.8%
Bob Dole (R)	60.2%

Composite Party Vote 1994	
Democratic	42.8%
Republican	57.2%

Registered Voters 1996	**124,668**
Turnout	79,052
Percent of registered voting	63.4%

House District 47
Rep. Terry Keel (R)

House Office
(512) 463-0652

DistrictOffice
P. O. Box 2910
Austin, Texas 78768
(512) 463-0652

Personal

Year of birth	1958
Family	Single
Education	University of Texas at Austin, B.A.
	University of Houston, J.D.
Occupation	Attorney at Law
Religion	Catholic
State legislative service	House 1997 to present

COMMITTEE ASSIGNMENT HISTORY

1997 Criminal Jurisprudence, Public Safety

BILL PASSAGE RATES, 1997

	Total	Passed Legislature	Pct. Passed Legislature
Authored	53	10	19%
Sponsored	12	8	67%
Amendments	8	6	75%

ELECTORAL HISTORY IN CURRENT DISTRICT

	1994	1996	1998
Primary Election Opponent(s)	NA	Yes	No
General Election Opponent(s)	NA	Dem, NLP	No

House District 48

COUNTIES IN DISTRICT

Travis (part)

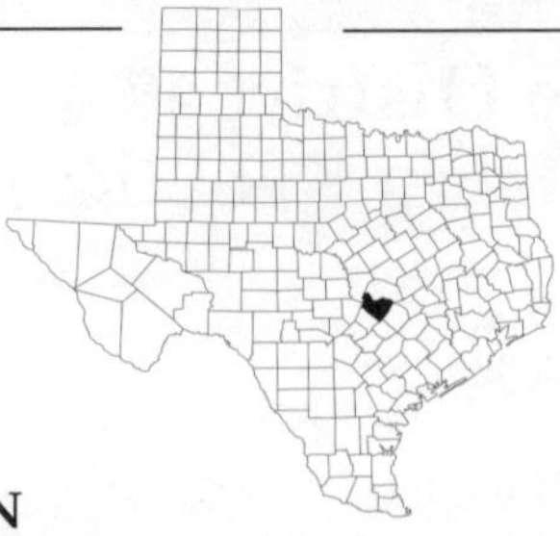

DEMOGRAPHIC INFORMATION

Population

Total	118,325
Anglo	73.2%
Black	4.7%
Hispanic	19.5%
Others	2.9%

Wealth and Urbanization

Per capita Income	$17,700
Avg. House Value	$106,338
Percent Poverty	10.4%
Public Assistance	2.3%
Percent Urban	98.6%

Education

High School Graduates	90.5%
College Graduates	40.0%

Employed

Percent Employed	95.1%
Private Sector	64.4%

Age of Population

5 years or less	9.4%
6-17 years	14.5%
18-64 years	69.4%
65 or older	6.6%

Household Types

Family households	75.9%
Non-family households	22.7%
Single-parent families	24.1%
Both parents working	73.2%

SENATE DISTRICTS IN HOUSE DISTRICT

Dist 14 Gonzalo Barrientos (D)

DISTRICT ELECTION DATA

House 1996

Sherri Greenberg (D)	100.0%

House 1998

Sherri Greenberg (D)	100.0%

President 1996

Bill Clinton (D)	57.0%
Bob Dole (R)	43.0%

Composite Party Vote 1994

Democratic	58.7%
Republican	41.3%

Registered Voters 1996	**94,354**
Turnout	52,266
Percent of registered voting	55.4%

House District 48
Rep. Sherri Greenberg (D)

House Office
(512) 463-0700

District Office
P.O. Box 2910
Austin, Texas 78768
(512) 463-0700

Personal

Year of birth	1958
Family	Married to Cary Ferchill, two children
Education	University of Texas, B.A.
	London School of Economics, M.S.
Occupation	Public finance specialist
Religion	Jewish
State legislative service	House 1991 to present

COMMITTEE ASSIGNMENT HISTORY

1997 Appropriations, Economic Development
1995 Appropriations, Criminal Jurisprudence
1993 Criminal Jurisprudence, Natural Resources
1991 Natural Resources, Science and Technology

BILL PASSAGE RATES, 1997

	Total	Passed Legislature	Pct. Passed Legislature
Authored	69	27	39%
Sponsored	29	22	76%
Amendments	38	35	92%

ELECTORAL HISTORY IN CURRENT DISTRICT

	1994	1996	1998
Primary Election Opponent(s)	No	Yes	No
General Election Opponent(s)	Rep	No	No

House District 49

COUNTIES IN DISTRICT
Travis (part)

DEMOGRAPHIC INFORMATION

Population		**Wealth and Urbanization**	
Total	117,860	Per capita Income	$13,761
Anglo	74.0%	Avg. House Value	$79,514
Black	6.7%	Percent Poverty	16.6%
Hispanic	14.4%	Public Assistance	2.7%
Others	5.1%	Percent Urban	100%

Education		**Employed**	
High School Graduates	87.8%	Percent Employed	94.2%
College Graduates	39.1%	Private Sector	69.5%

Age of Population		**Household Types**	
5 years or less	7.5%	Family households	61.3%
6-17 years	10.6%	Non-family households	29.8%
18-64 years	74.2%	Single-parent families	29.4%
65 or older	7.8%	Both parents working	72.4%

SENATE DISTRICTS IN HOUSE DISTRICT

Dist 14 Gonzalo Barrientos (D)

DISTRICT ELECTION DATA

House 1996		**House 1998**	
Elliott Naishtat (D)	63.2%	Elliott Naishtat (D)	63.3%
Emil Blomquist (R)	36.8%	Emil Blomquist (R)	36.7%

President 1996	
Bill Clinton (D)	61.4%
Bob Dole (R)	38.6%

Composite Party Vote 1994	
Democratic	62.1%
Republican	37.9%

Registered Voters 1996	**93,178**
Turnout	48,877
Percent of registered voting	52.5%

House District 49
Rep. Elliott Naishtat (D)

House Office
(512) 463-0668

District Office
P.O. Box 2910
Austin, Texas 78768
(512) 463-0668

Personal

Year of birth	1945
Family	Single, no children
Education	Queen's College, B.A.
	University of Texas, J.D., M.S.S.W.
Occupation	Attorney
Religion	Jewish
State legislative service	House 1991 to present

COMMITTEE ASSIGNMENT HISTORY

1997 Human Services (Vice-Chair), Juvenile Justice and Family Issues
1995 Human Services (Vice-Chair), Juvenile Justice and Family Issues
1993 Human Services, Urban Affairs
1991 Government Organization, Human Services

BILL PASSAGE RATES, 1995

	Total	Passed Legislature	Pct. Passed Legislature
Authored	158	42	27%
Sponsored	49	44	90%
Amendments	17	15	88%

ELECTORAL HISTORY IN CURRENT DISTRICT

	1994	1996	1998
Primary Election Opponent(s)	No	No	No
General Election Opponent(s)	Rep	Rep	Rep

House District 50

COUNTIES IN DISTRICT
Travis (part)

DEMOGRAPHIC INFORMATION

Population		**Wealth and Urbanization**	
Total	110,145	Per capita Income	$10,901
Anglo	44.2%	Avg. House Value	$61,394
Black	32.4%	Percent Poverty	22.3%
Hispanic	21.9%	Public Assistance	7.8%
Others	2.3%	Percent Urban	92.0%

Education		**Employed**	
High School Graduates	72.6%	Percent Employed	91.8%
College Graduates	20.9%	Private Sector	66.1%

Age of Population		**Household Types**	
5 years or less	9.6%	Family households	77.3%
6-17 years	15.4%	Non-family households	20.5%
18-64 years	66.0%	Single-parent families	34.8%
65 or older	7.8%	Both parents working	72.3%

SENATE DISTRICTS IN HOUSE DISTRICT

Dist 14 Gonzalo Barrientos (D)

DISTRICT ELECTION DATA

House 1996		**House 1998**	
Dawnna M. Dukes (D)	100.0%	Dawnna M. Dukes (D)	100.0%

President 1996	
Bill Clinton (D)	71.3%
Bob Dole (R)	28.7%

Composite Party Vote 1994	
Democratic	70.4%
Republican	29.6%

Registered Voters 1996	**74,425**
Turnout	36,266
Percent of registered voting	48.7%

House District 50
Rep. Dawnna M. Dukes (D)

House Office
(512) 463-0506

District Office
P.O. Box 2910
Austin, Texas 78768-2910
(512) 463-0506

Personal

Year of birth	1963
Family	Single, no children
Education	Texas A&M University, B.S., Psychology
Occupation	Consultant
Religion	Catholic
State legislative service	House 1995 to present

COMMITTEE ASSIGNMENT HISTORY

1997 Business and Industry, Environmental Regulation
1995 Environmental Regulation, State, Federal and International Relations

BILL PASSAGE RATES, 1997

	Total	Passed Legislature	Pct. Passed Legislature
Authored	66	16	24%
Sponsored	5	4	80%
Amendments	15	10	67%

ELECTORAL HISTORY IN CURRENT DISTRICT

	1994	1996	1998
Primary Election Opponent(s)	Yes	No	No
General Election Opponent(s)	Rep	No	No

House District 51

COUNTIES IN DISTRICT
Travis (part)

DEMOGRAPHIC INFORMATION

Population

Total	111,569
Anglo	10.1%
Black	9.5%
Hispanic	44.0%
Others	2.9%

Education

High School Graduates	69.4%
College Graduates	21.1%

Age of Population

5 years or less	9.9%
6-17 years	16.6%
18-64 years	67.4%
65 or older	6.1%

Wealth and Urbanization

Per capita Income	$9,503
Avg. House Value	$60,704
Percent Poverty	26.5%
Public Assistance	7.1%
Percent Urban	92.8%

Employed

Percent Employed	91.9%
Private Sector	67.8%

Household Types

Family households	73.1%
Non-family households	23.2%
Single-parent families	30.3%
Both parents working	66.8%

SENATE DISTRICTS IN HOUSE DISTRICT

Dist 14 Gonzalo Barrientos (D)

DISTRICT ELECTION DATA

House 1996

Glen Maxey (D)	71.8%
David Blakely (R)	24.0%
Dan Wolfe (NLP)	4.2%

President 1996

Bill Clinton (D)	75.5%
Bob Dole (R)	24.5%

Composite Party Vote 1994

Democratic	74.0%
Republican	26.0%

Registered Voters 1996	**72,495**
Turnout	31,413
Percent of registered voting	43.3%

House 1998

Glen Maxey (D)	73.4%
Fred Ebner (R)	26.6%

House District 51
Rep. Glen Maxey (D)

House Office
(512) 463-0552
(512) 463-5896 (Fax)
Glen.Maxey@house.state.tx.us

District Office
P.O. Box 2910
Austin, Texas 78768
(512) 462-0552

Personal

Year of birth	1952
Family	Single, no children
Education	Sam Houston State University, B.S., M.Ed.
Occupation	Information systems executive
Religion	Metropolitan Community Church
State legislative service	House 1991 (part) to present

COMMITTEE ASSIGNMENT HISTORY

1997 House Administration, Human Services, Public Health
1995 Human Services, Public Health
1993 Human Services, Public Health
1991 Cultural and Historical Resources, Retirement and Aging

BILL PASSAGE RATES, 1997

	Total	Passed Legislature	Pct. Passed Legislature
Authored	187	43	23%
Sponsored	24	19	79%
Amendments	33	27	82%

ELECTORAL HISTORY IN CURRENT DISTRICT

	1994	1996	1996
Primary Election Opponent(s)	No	Yes	No
General Election Opponent(s)	Rep	Rep, NLP	Rep

House District 52

COUNTIES IN DISTRICT
Williamson (part)

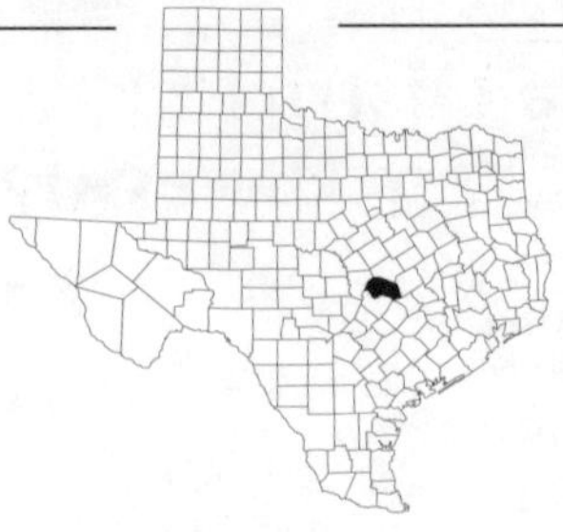

DEMOGRAPHIC INFORMATION

Population

Total	118,276
Anglo	77.9%
Black	5.4%
Hispanic	15.3%
Others	1.6%

Education

High School Graduates	80.1%
College Graduates	23.7%

Age of Population

5 years or less	10.3%
6-17 years	20.3%
18-64 years	61.1%
65 or older	8.3%

Wealth and Urbanization

Per capita Income	$13,193
Avg. House Value	$75,180
Percent Poverty	11.1%
Public Assistance	3.8%
Percent Urban	77.2%

Employed

Percent Employed	95.5%
Private Sector	74.2%

Household Types

Family households	87.6%
Non-family households	10.6%
Single-parent families	18.1%
Both parents working	71.8%

SENATE DISTRICTS IN HOUSE DISTRICT 52

Dist 5 Steve Ogden (R)
Dist 25 Jeff Wentworth (R)

DISTRICT ELECTION DATA

House 1996

Jerry Graham (D)	38.4%
Mike Krusee (R)	61.6%

House 1998

Mike Krusee (R)	100.0%

President 1996

Bill Clinton (D)	40.6%
Bob Dole (R)	59.4%

Composite Party Vote 1994

Democratic	44.1%
Republican	55.9%

Registered Voters 1996	**91,609**
Turnout	54,093
Percent of registered voting	59.0%

House District 52
Rep. Mike Krusee (R)

House Office
(512) 463-0670

District Office
316 North Main Street
Taylor, Texas 76574
(512) 365-8341

Personal

Year of birth	1959
Family	Married to Leigh Krusee, five children
Education	Georgetown University
Occupation	Consultant
Religion	Presbyterian
State legislative service	House 1993 to present

COMMITTEE ASSIGNMENT HISTORY

1997 Human Services, Land and Resource Management
1995 Human Services, Land and Resource Management, Rules and Resolutions
1993 International and Cultural Relations, Public Safety, Rules and Resolutions

BILL PASSAGE RATES, 1997

	Total	Passed Legislature	Pct. Passed Legislature
Authored	31	6	19%
Sponsored	5	4	80%
Amendments	8	8	100%

ELECTORAL HISTORY IN CURRENT DISTRICT

	1994	1996	1998
Primary Election Opponent(s)	Yes	No	No
General Election Opponent(s)	Dem	Dem	No

House District 53

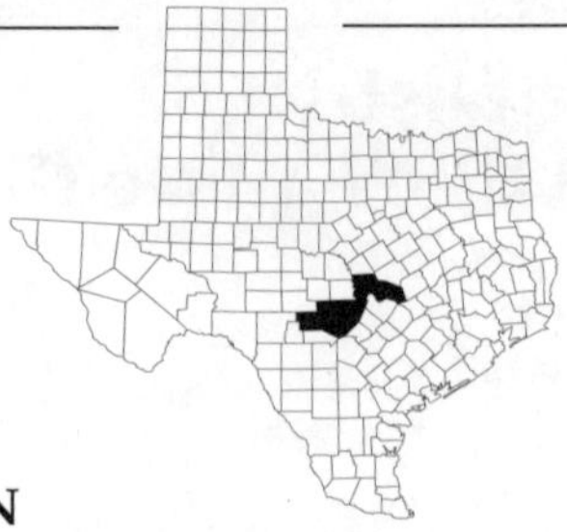

COUNTIES IN DISTRICT
Blanco, Burnet, Gillespie, Kendall, Kerr, Williamson (part)

DEMOGRAPHIC INFORMATION

Population

Total	118,021
Anglo	84.3%
Black	1.4%
Hispanic	13.6%
Others	.9%

Wealth and Urbanization

Per capita Income	$12,825
Avg. House Value	$80,084
Percent Poverty	13.8%
Public Assistance	5.0%
Percent Urban	45.4%

Education

High School Graduates	75.3%
College Graduates	19.3%

Employed

Percent Employed	95.0%
Private Sector	67.6%

Age of Population

5 years or less	8.5%
6-17 years	16.9%
18-64 years	55.1%
65 or older	19.4%

Household Types

Family households	86.3%
Non-family households	10.6%
Single-parent families	17.7%
Both parents working	70.0%

SENATE DISTRICTS IN HOUSE DISTRICT 53

Dist 5 Steve Ogden (R)
Dist 24 Troy Fraser (R)
Dist 25 Jeff Wentworth (R)

DISTRICT ELECTION DATA

House 1996

Jim Franklin (D)	27.3%
Harvey Hildebran (R)	72.7%

House 1998

Harvey Hildebran (R)	100.0%

President 1996

Bill Clinton (D)	31.1%
Bob Dole (R)	68.9%

Composite Party Vote 1994

Democratic	32.7%
Republican	67.3%

Registered Voters 1996	**94,710**
Turnout	61,224
Percent of registered voting	64.6%

House District 53
Rep. Harvey Hilderbran (R)

House Office
(512) 463-0536
(512) 463-5896 (Fax)

District Office
125 Lehmann Drive
Kerrville, Texas 78028
(830) 257-2333

Personal

Year of birth	1960
Family	Married to Tracy Hilderbran, one child
Education	Texas Tech University, B.A., Political Science
Occupation	Businessman
Religion	Episcopalian
State legislative service	House 1989 to present

COMMITTEE ASSIGNMENT HISTORY

1997 Human Services (Chair), State Recreational Resources
1995 Land and Resource Management, Human Services (Chair)
1993 Environmental Regulation, Human Services (Chair)
1991 Human Services, Natural Resources, Rules and Resolutions
1989 Public Education, Retirement and Aging

BILL PASSAGE RATES, 1997

	Total	Passed Legislature	Pct. Passed Legislature
Authored	30	9	30%
Sponsored	11	9	82%
Amendments	19	16	84%

ELECTORAL HISTORY IN CURRENT DISTRICT

	1994	1996	1998
Primary Election Opponent(s)	Yes	No	No
General Election Opponent(s)	Dem	Dem	No

House District 54

COUNTIES IN DISTRICT

Bell, Lampasas, McCulloch, Mills, San Saba

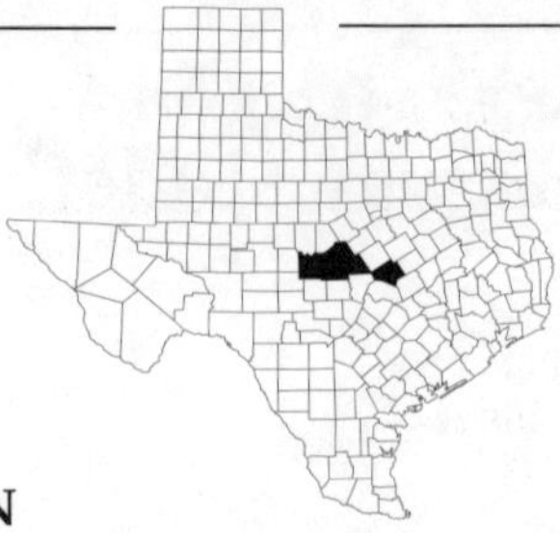

DEMOGRAPHIC INFORMATION

Population		Wealth and Urbanization	
Total	112,346	Per capita Income	$9,973
Anglo	65.5%	Avg. House Value	$56,056
Black	16.4%	Percent Poverty	17.8%
Hispanic	15.1%	Public Assistance	6.1%
Others	3.5%	Percent Urban	67.3%

Education		Employed	
High School Graduates	75.7%	Percent Employed	90.0%
College Graduates	14.0%	Private Sector	61.8%

Age of Population		Household Types	
5 years or less	10.9%	Family households	88.2%
6-17 years	18.0%	Non-family households	10.5%
18-64 years	60.5%	Single-parent families	18.5%
65 or older	10.6%	Both parents working	62.8%

SENATE DISTRICTS IN HOUSE DISTRICT

Dist 24 Troy Fraser (R)

DISTRICT ELECTION DATA

House 1996		House 1998	
Dick Miller (D)	47.3%	Don Armstrong (D)	45.7%
Suzanna Gratia Hupp (R)	52.7%	Suzanna Gratia Hupp (R)	54.3%

President 1996	
Bill Clinton (D)	44.8%
Bob Dole (R)	55.2%

Composite Party Vote 1994	
Democratic	52.3%
Republican	47.7%

Registered Voters 1996	68,933
Turnout	35,338
Percent of registered voting	51.3%

House District 54
Rep. Suzanna Gratia Hupp (R)

House Office
(512) 463-0684

District Office
P.O. Box 751
Lampasas, Texas 76550
(512) 556-8954

Personal

Year of birth	1959
Family	Married to Gregory Hupp, two children
Education	Texas Chiropractor College, D.C.
Occupation	Chiropractor and breeder of Arabian horses
Religion	Christian
State legislative service	House 1996 (part) to present

COMMITTEE ASSIGNMENT HISTORY

1997 Agriculture and Livestock, Corrections
1996 NA

BILL PASSAGE RATES, 1997

	Total	Passed Legislature	Pct. Passed Legislature
Authored	13	3	23%
Sponsored	4	1	25%
Amendments	6	3	50%

ELECTORAL HISTORY IN CURRENT DISTRICT

	1994	1996	1998
Primary Election Opponent(s)	NA	No	No
General Election Opponent(s)	NA	Dem	Dem

House District 55

COUNTIES IN DISTRICT
Bell (part)

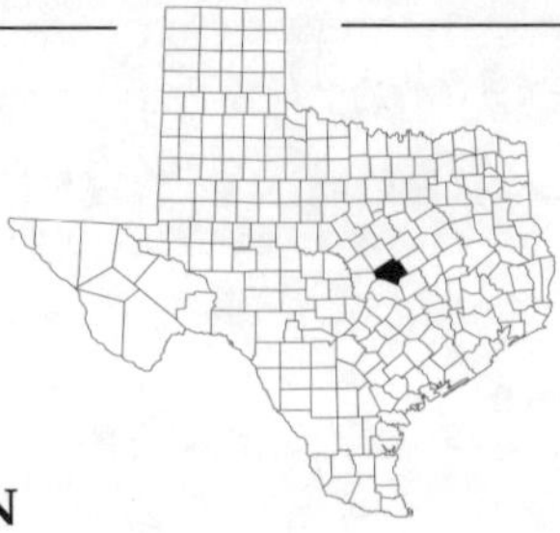

DEMOGRAPHIC INFORMATION

Population	
Total	110,973
Anglo	69.6%
Black	16.3%
Hispanic	12.2%
Others	2.3%

Education	
High School Graduates	79.6%
College Graduates	19.8%

Age of Population	
5 years or less	10.8%
6-17 years	16.9%
18-64 years	61.9%
65 or older	10.4%

Wealth and Urbanization	
Per capita Income	$11,801
Avg. House Value	$67,414
Percent Poverty	14.8%
Public Assistance	6.2%
Percent Urban	85.7%

Employed	
Percent Employed	92.5%
Private Sector	72.5%

Household Types	
Family households	82.2%
Non-family households	10.3%
Single-parent families	19.6%
Both parents working	61.8%

SENATE DISTRICTS IN HOUSE DISTRICT

Dist 24 Troy Fraser (R)

DISTRICT ELECTION DATA

House 1996	
Dianne White Delisi (R)	100.0%

House 1998	
Dianne White Delisi (R)	100.0%

President 1996	
Bill Clinton (D)	40.1%
Bob Dole (R)	59.9%

Composite Party Vote 1994	
Democratic	47.5%
Republican	52.5%

Registered Voters 1996	65,181
Turnout	34,842
Percent of registered voting	53.5%

House District 55
Rep. Dianne White Delisi (R)

House Office
(512) 463-0630
dianne.delisi@house.state.tx.us

District Office
3500 Southwest H. K. Dogen Loop, Suite 100
Temple, Texas 76504
(254) 774-9888

Personal

Year of birth	1943
Family	Single, two children
Education	Southern Methodist University, B.A.
	University of Colorado, M.A.
Occupation	State representative
Religion	Episcopalian
State legislative service	House 1991 to present

COMMITTEE ASSIGNMENT HISTORY

1997 Appropriations (Vice-Chair), Public Health
1995 Appropriations (Vice-Chair), Public Health
1993 Appropriations, Public Health (Vice-Chair), Rules and Resolutions
1991 House Administration, Public Safety, State, Federal and International Affairs

BILL PASSAGE RATES, 1997

	Total	Passed Legislature	Pct. Passed Legislature
Authored	41	15	37%
Sponsored	9	6	67%
Amendments	11	7	64%

ELECTORAL HISTORY IN CURRENT DISTRICT

	1994	1996	1998
Primary Election Opponent(s)	No	No	No
General Election Opponent(s)	No	No	No

House District 56

COUNTIES IN DISTRICT

Falls, Limestone, McLennan

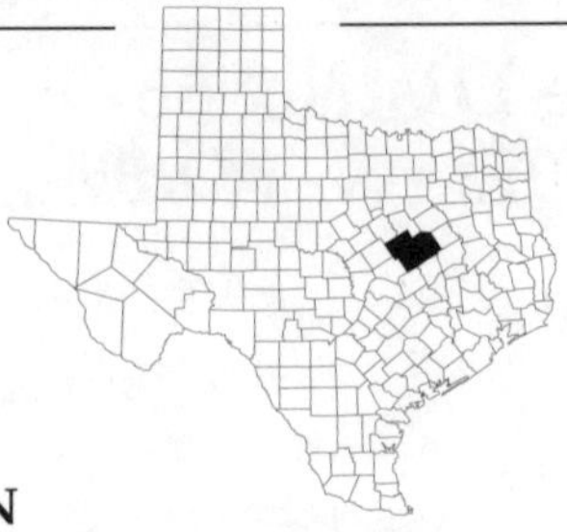

DEMOGRAPHIC INFORMATION

Population	
Total	113,422
Anglo	79.0%
Black	12.2%
Hispanic	7.9%
Others	1.1%

Wealth and Urbanization	
Per capita Income	$12,625
Avg. House Value	$69,651
Percent Poverty	19.5%
Public Assistance	6.0%
Percent Urban	72.7%

Education	
High School Graduates	75.0%
College Graduates	21.6%

Employed	
Percent Employed	95.0%
Private Sector	74.5%

Age of Population	
5 years or less	7.8%
6-17 years	15.1%
18-64 years	62.4%
65 or older	14.7%

Household Types	
Family households	76.9%
Non-family households	17.0%
Single-parent families	20.6%
Both parents working	69.4%

SENATE DISTRICTS IN HOUSE DISTRICT

Dist 5 Steve Ogden (R)

Dist 22 David Sibley (R)

DISTRICT ELECTION DATA

House 1996	
Kip Averitt (R)	100.0%

President 1996	
Bill Clinton (D)	41.4%
Bob Dole (R)	58.6%

Composite Party Vote 1994	
Democratic	46.9%
Republican	53.1%

Registered Voters 1996	**74,670**
Turnout	44,497
Percent of registered voting	59.6%

House 1998	
Charles Rothrock (D)	30.7%
Kip Averitt (R)	69.3%

House District 56
Rep. Kip Averitt (R)

House Office
(512) 463-0712

District Office
6801 Sanger, #199B
Waco, Texas 76710
(254) 772-6225

Personal

Year of birth	1954
Family	Married to Kathy Averitt, four children
Education	Baylor University, B.B.A., M.B.A.
Occupation	Manufacturing
Religion	Baptist
State legislative service	House 1993 to present

COMMITTEE ASSIGNMENT HISTORY

1997 Appropriations, Insurance
1995 Insurance, Pensions and Investments
1993 Business and Industry, Insurance, Rules and Resolutions

BILL PASSAGE RATES, 1997

	Total	Passed Legislature	Pct. Passed Legislature
Authored	16	8	50%
Sponsored	5	4	80%
Amendments	10	10	100%

ELECTORAL HISTORY IN CURRENT DISTRICT

	1994	1996	1998
Primary Election Opponent(s)	No	No	No
General Election Opponent(s)	No	No	Dem

House District 57

COUNTIES IN DISTRICT

McLennan (part)

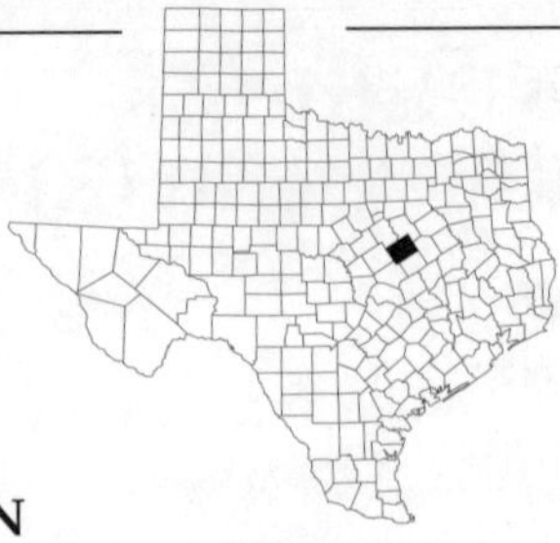

DEMOGRAPHIC INFORMATION

Population	
Total	114,359
Anglo	62.0%
Black	21.6%
Hispanic	15.9%
Others	.7%

Education	
High School Graduates	63.3%
College Graduates	9.0%

Age of Population	
5 years or less	9.7%
6-17 years	19.2%
18-64 years	56.9%
65 or older	14.1%

Wealth and Urbanization	
Per capita Income	$8,919
Avg. House Value	$41,560
Percent Poverty	24.5%
Public Assistance	9.4%
Percent Urban	77.9%

Employed	
Percent Employed	91.7%
Private Sector	77.6%

Household Types	
Family households	84.5%
Non-family households	12.1%
Single-parent families	28.2%
Both parents working	65.2%

SENATE DISTRICTS IN HOUSE DISTRICT

Dist 5 Steve Ogden (R)

Dist 22 David Sibley (R)

DISTRICT ELECTION DATA

House 1996	
Jim Dunnam (D)	58.6%
Barbara Rusling (R)	41.4%

President 1996	
Bill Clinton (D)	58.6%
Bob Dole (R)	41.4%

Composite Party Vote 1994	
Democratic	59.9%
Republican	40.1%

Registered Voters 1996	**65,396**
Turnout	31,821
Percent of registered voting	48.7%

House 1998	
Jim Dunnam (D)	100.0%

House District 57
Rep. Jim Dunnam (D)

House Office
(512) 463-0508

District Office
P.O. Box 1962
Waco, Texas 76703-1962
(254) 753-8546

Personal

Year of birth	1963
Family	Married to Michelle Dunnam, three children
Education	Baylor, B.B.A., J.D.
Occupation	Attorney
Religion	Methodist
State legislative service	House 1997 to present

COMMITTEE ASSIGNMENT HISTORY
1997 Criminal Jurisprudence, Higher Education

BILL PASSAGE RATES, 1997

	Total	Passed Legislature	Pct. Passed Legislature
Authored	14	4	29%
Sponsored	4	4	100%
Amendments	14	10	71%

ELECTORAL HISTORY IN CURRENT DISTRICT

	1994	1996	1998
Primary Election Opponent(s)	NA	No	No
General Election Opponent(s)	NA	Rep	No

House District 58

COUNTIES IN DISTRICT
Bosque, Johnson, Somerville

DEMOGRAPHIC INFORMATION

Population	
Total	117,650
Anglo	88.7%
Black	2.4%
Hispanic	8.2%
Others	.8%

Wealth and Urbanization	
Per capita Income	$11,910
Avg. House Value	$64,994
Percent Poverty	12.4%
Public Assistance	5.1%
Percent Urban	43.1%

Education	
High School Graduates	70.6%
College Graduates	11.5%

Employed	
Percent Employed	93.2%
Private Sector	78.5%

Age of Population	
5 years or less	9.3%
6-17 years	19.4%
18-64 years	59.1%
65 or older	12.2%

Household Types	
Family households	89.8%
Non-family households	8.2%
Single-parent families	15.5%
Both parents working	61.9%

SENATE DISTRICTS IN HOUSE DISTRICT

Dist 10 Chris Harris (R)
Dist 22 David Sibley (R)

DISTRICT ELECTION DATA

House 1996	
Bernard Erickson (D)	45.8%
Arlene Wohlgemuth (R)	54.2%

House 1998	
Gayle Appleby Ledbetter (D)	40.6%
Arlene Wohlgemuth (R)	59.4%

President 1996	
Bill Clinton (D)	44.1%
Bob Dole (R)	55.9%

Composite Party Vote 1994	
Democratic	48.3%
Republican	51.7%

Registered Voters 1996	**76,265**
Turnout	30,635
Percent of registered voting	40.2%

House District 58
Rep. Arlene Wohlgemuth (R)

House Office
(512) 463-0538
Arlene.Wohlgemuth@house.state.tx.us

District Office
344-I S.W. Wilshire Blvd.
Burleson, Texas 76097
(817) 295-5158

Personal

Year of birth	1947
Family	Married to Mikeal Wohlgemuth, two children
Education	Texas Tech University
Occupation	Flight instructor
Religion	Steppingstone Family
State legislative service	House 1995 to present

COMMITTEE ASSIGNMENT HISTORY

1997 Human Services, Urban Affairs
1995 County Affairs, Human Services

BILL PASSAGE RATES, 1997

	Total	Passed Legislature	Pct. Passed Legislature
Authored	29	7	24%
Sponsored	2	2	100%
Amendments	19	15	79%

ELECTORAL HISTORY IN CURRENT DISTRICT

	1994	1996	1998
Primary Election Opponent(s)	No	No	No
General Election Opponent(s)	Dem	Dem	Dem

House District 59

COUNTIES IN DISTRICT

Comanche, Coryell, Erath, Hamilton

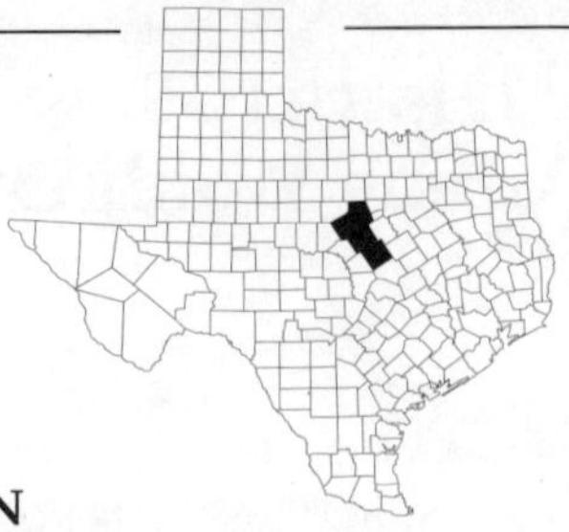

DEMOGRAPHIC INFORMATION

Population		Wealth and Urbanization	
Total	113,318	Per capita Income	$9,640
Anglo	76.1%	Avg. House Value	$49,533
Black	12.2%	Percent Poverty	15.9%
Hispanic	10.0%	Public Assistance	5.2%
Others	2.0%	Percent Urban	68.7%

Education		Employed	
High School Graduates	73.3%	Percent Employed	92.3%
College Graduates	13.2%	Private Sector	61.6%

Age of Population		Household Types	
5 years or less	9.0%	Family households	75.5%
6-17 years	16.1%	Non-family households	9.4%
18-64 years	63.2%	Single-parent families	13.6%
65 or older	11.6%	Both parents working	61.5%

SENATE DISTRICTS IN HOUSE DISTRICT

Dist 22 David Sibley (R)

Dist 24 Troy Fraser (R)

DISTRICT ELECTION DATA

House 1996	
Allen Place (D)	49.7%
Becky Farrar (R)	49.4%
P. C. Wisdom Hanes (NLP)	0.9%

President 1996	
Bill Clinton (D)	44.2%
Bob Dole (R)	55.8%

Composite Party Vote 1994	
Democratic	51.4%
Republican	48.6%

Registered Voters 1996	59,120
Turnout	31,418
Percent of registered voting	53.1%

House 1998	
David Lengefeld (D)	54.6%
Becky Farrar (R)	45.4%

House District 59
Rep. David Lengefeld (D)

House Office
(512) 463-0628

District Office
P.O. Box 471
Hamilton, Texas 76531
(254) 386-3133

Personal

Year of birth	1945
Family	Married to Saundra Lengefeld, three children
Education	Baylor University, B.A.
Occupation	Insurance Agent
Religion	Baptist
State legislative service	House 1999 to present

COMMITTEE ASSIGNMENT HISTORY

BILL PASSAGE RATES, 1997

	Total	Passed Legislature	Pct. Passed Legislature
Authored	NA	NA	NA
Sponsored	NA	NA	NA
Amendments	NA	NA	NA

ELECTORAL HISTORY IN CURRENT DISTRICT

	1994	1996	1998
Primary Election Opponent(s)	NA	NA	Yes
General Election Opponent(s)	NA	NA	Rep

House District 60

COUNTIES IN DISTRICT

Callahan, Eastland, Hood, Palo Pinto, Runnels, Shackleford, Stephens, Taylor (part)

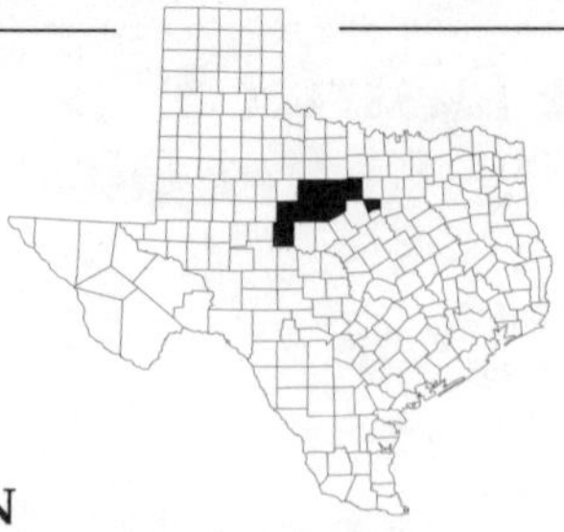

DEMOGRAPHIC INFORMATION

Population		**Wealth and Urbanization**	
Total	112,906	Per capita Income	$11,180
Anglo	89.3%	Avg. House Value	$51,187
Black	1.5%	Percent Poverty	17.2%
Hispanic	8.5%	Public Assistance	7.0%
Others	.8%	Percent Urban	40.1%

Education		**Employed**	
High School Graduates	67.3%	Percent Employed	92.7%
College Graduates	12.1%	Private Sector	71.7%

Age of Population		**Household Types**	
5 years or less	8.3%	Family households	86.7%
6-17 years	17.8%	Non-family households	11.1%
18-64 years	55.5%	Single-parent families	16.7%
65 or older	18.4%	Both parents working	60.2%

SENATE DISTRICTS IN HOUSE DISTRICT

Dist 22 David Sibley (R)

Dist 24 Troy Fraser (R)

DISTRICT ELECTION DATA

House 1996		**House 1998**	
John Cook (D)	49.4%		
Jim Keffer (R)	50.6%	Jim Keffer (R)	100.0%

President 1996	
Bill Clinton (D)	43.3%
Bob Dole (R)	56.7%

Composite Party Vote 1994	
Democratic	49.3%
Republican	50.7%

Registered Voters 1996	**76,201**
Turnout	45,363
Percent of registered voting	59.5%

House District 60
Rep. Jim Keffer (R)

House Office
(512) 463-0656

District Office
P. O. Box 857
Eastland, Texas 76448
(817) 629-1731
(800) 586-4515

Personal

Year of birth	1953
Family	Married to Leslie Bradly Keffer, three children
Education	Texas Tech, B.A., Communications
Occupation	Business executive, sales
Religion	Baptist
State legislative service	House 1997 to present

COMMITTEE ASSIGNMENT HISTORY
1997 Economic Development, Public Safety

BBILL PASSAGE RATES, 1997

	Total	Passed Legislature	Pct. Passed Legislature
Authored	16	2	13%
Sponsored	1	1	100%
Amendments	3	3	100%

ELECTORAL HISTORY IN CURRENT DISTRICT

	1994	1996	1998
Primary Election Opponent(s)	NA	No	No
General Election Opponent(s)	NA	Dem	No

House District 61

COUNTIES IN DISTRICT

Cooke (part), Parker, Wise

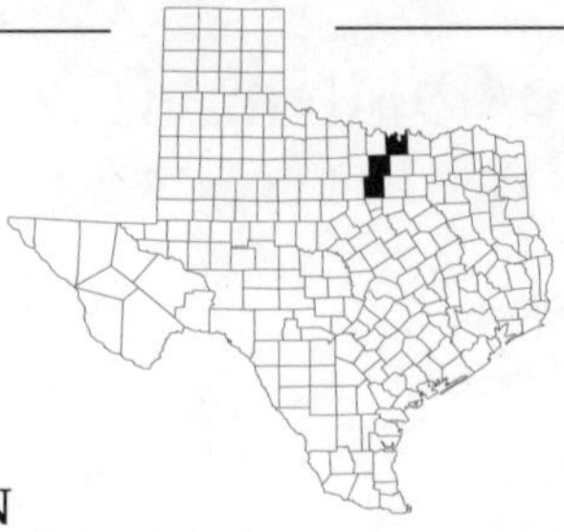

DEMOGRAPHIC INFORMATION

Population

Total	114,864
Anglo	92.5%
Black	1.1%
Hispanic	5.1%
Others	.9%

Wealth and Urbanization

Per capita Income	$12,378
Avg. House Value	$67,975
Percent Poverty	12.1%
Public Assistance	4.9%
Percent Urban	26.6%

Education

High School Graduates	72.2%
College Graduates	12.6%

Employed

Percent Employed	94.5%
Private Sector	74.1%

Age of Population

5 years or less	9.0%
6-17 years	19.4%
18-64 years	59.7%
65 or older	11.9%

Household Types

Family households	89.9%
Non-family households	8.1%
Single-parent families	13.4%
Both parents working	60.3%

SENATE DISTRICTS IN HOUSE DISTRICT

Dist 10 Chris Harris (R)
Dist 22 David Sibley (R)
Dist 30 Tom Haywood (R)

DISTRICT ELECTION DATA

House 1996

Ric Williamson (R)	100.0%

House 1998

Brenda Brown Rotramble (D)	35.4%
Phil King (R)	64.6%

President 1996

Bill Clinton (D)	39.7%
Bob Dole (R)	60.3%

Composite Party Vote 1994

Democratic	44.0%
Republican	56.0%

Registered Voters 1996	**80,284**
Turnout	46,423
Percent of registered voting	57.8%

House District 61
Rep. Phil King (R)

House Office
(512) 463-0738

District Office
P.O. Box 1913
Weatherford, Texas 76234
(817) 596-4796

Personal

Year of birth	1956
Family	Married to Terry King, six children
Education	B.A., M.B.A., J.D.
Occupation	Judge/Attorney
Religion	Christian
State legislative service	House 1999 to present

COMMITTEE ASSIGNMENT HISTORY

BILL PASSAGE RATES, 1997

	Total	Passed Legislature	Pct. Passed Legislature
Authored	NA	NA	NA
Sponsored	NA	NA	NA
Amendments	NA	NA	NA

ELECTORAL HISTORY IN CURRENT DISTRICT

	1994	1996	1998
Primary Election Opponent(s)	NA	NA	No
General Election Opponent(s)	NA	NA	Dem

House District 62

COUNTIES IN DISTRICT

Cooke (part), Grayson

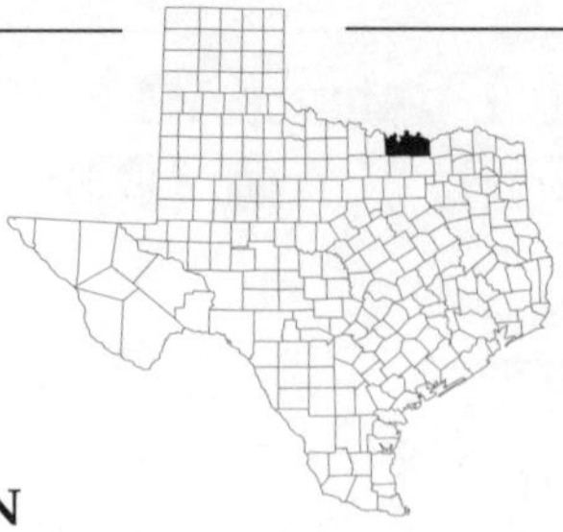

DEMOGRAPHIC INFORMATION

Population	
Total	110,398
Anglo	88.9%
Black	6.4%
Hispanic	3.3%
Others	1.5%

Education	
High School Graduates	72.0%
College Graduates	13.7%

Age of Population	
5 years or less	8.0%
6-17 years	17.7%
18-64 years	57.8%
65 or older	16.5%

Wealth and Urbanization	
Per capita Income	$12,136
Avg. House Value	$55,333
Percent Poverty	14.1%
Public Assistance	6.6%
Percent Urban	60.1%

Employed	
Percent Employed	93.4%
Private Sector	79.6%

Household Types	
Family households	85.7%
Non-family households	11.7%
Single-parent families	20.7%
Both parents working	67.3%

SENATE DISTRICTS IN HOUSE DISTRICT

Dist 30 Tom Haywood (R)

DISTRICT ELECTION DATA

House 1996	
Roger Sanders (D)	46.1%
Ron Clark (R)	53.9%

President 1996	
Bill Clinton (D)	44.2%
Bob Dole (R)	55.8%

Composite Party Vote 1994	
Democratic	46.2%
Republican	53.8%

Registered Voters 1996	**74,213**
Turnout	41,891
Percent of registered voting	56.4%

House 1998	
Sam J. Thorpe (D)	33.9%
Ron Clark (R)	66.1%

House District 62
Rep. Ron Clark (R)

House Office
(512) 463-0474

District Office
200 N. Travis, #400
Sherman, Texas 75090
(903) 893-9426

Personal

Year of birth	1953
Family	Married to Joanna Clark, two children
Education	University of Connecticut, B.A., M.A. University of Texas, J.D.
Occupation	Attorney
Religion	Catholic
State legislative service	House 1997 to present

COMMITTEE ASSIGNMENT HISTORY
1997 Judicial Affairs, Urban Affairs

BILL PASSAGE RATES, 1997

	Total	Passed Legislature	Pct. Passed Legislature
Authored	18	4	22%
Sponsored	3	2	67%
Amendments	15	12	80%

ELECTORAL HISTORY IN CURRENT DISTRICT

	1994	1996	1998
Primary Election Opponent(s)	NA	No	No
General Election Opponent(s)	NA	Dem	Dem

House District 63

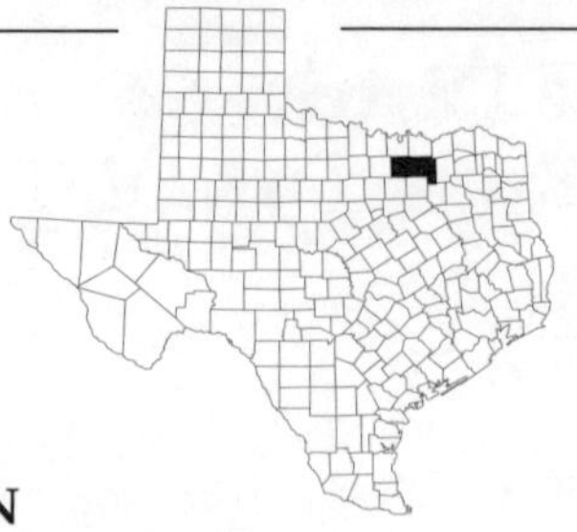

COUNTIES IN DISTRICT
Collin (part) , Denton (part), Rockwall

DEMOGRAPHIC INFORMATION

Population

Total	115,894
Anglo	86.6%
Black	4.6%
Hispanic	7.7%
Others	1.2%

Education

High School Graduates	78.0%
College Graduates	22.5%

Age of Population

5 years or less	9.4%
6-17 years	18.9%
18-64 years	62.1%
65 or older	9.6%

Wealth and Urbanization

Per capita Income	$15,459
Avg. House Value	$96,801
Percent Poverty	10.5%
Public Assistance	4.0%
Percent Urban	53.1%

Employed

Percent Employed	95.5%
Private Sector	75.2%

Household Types

Family households	88.8%
Non-family households	9.1%
Single-parent families	15.0%
Both parents working	66.3%

SENATE DISTRICTS IN HOUSE DISTRICT

Dist 2 David Cain (D)
Dist 8 Florence Shapiro (R)
Dist 9 Jane Nelson (R)
Dist 16 John J. Carona (R)
Dist 22 David Sibley (R)
Dist 30 Tom Haywood (R)

DISTRICT ELECTION DATA

House 1996

Mary Denny (R)	100.0%

President 1996

Bill Clinton (D)	33.3%
Bob Dole (R)	66.7%

Composite Party Vote 1994

Democratic	37.1%
Republican	62.9%

Registered Voters 1996	**91,557**
Turnout	51,486
Percent of registered voting	56.2%

House 1998

Kenneth Bridges (D)	25.6%
Mary Denny (R)	74.4%

House District 63
Rep. Mary Denny (R)

House Office
(512) 463-0688

District Office
416 W. University Drive, #200
Denton, Texas 76201
(817) 565-0083

Personal

Year of birth	1948
Family	Single, one child
Education	University of North Texas, B.S., Education
Occupation	Businesswoman, rancher
Religion	Episcopalian
State legislative service	House 1993 to present

COMMITTEE ASSIGNMENT HISTORY
1997 County Affairs, Elections
1995 Elections, Human Services, Rules and Resolutions
1993 Agriculture and Wildlife Management, Elections

BILL PASSAGE RATES, 1997

	Total	Passed Legislature	Pct. Passed Legislature
Authored	33	11	33%
Sponsored	7	7	100%
Amendments	2	2	100%

ELECTORAL HISTORY IN CURRENT DISTRICT

	1994	1996	1998
Primary Election Opponent(s)	No	No	Yes
General Election Opponent(s)	No	No	Dem

House District 64

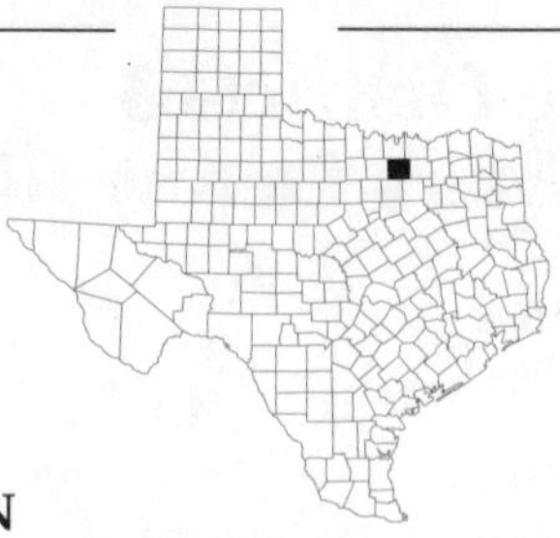

COUNTIES IN DISTRICT
Denton (part)

DEMOGRAPHIC INFORMATION

Population	
Total	113,208
Anglo	84.5%
Black	5.8%
Hispanic	7.2%
Others	2.6%

Wealth and Urbanization	
Per capita Income	$15,271
Avg. House Value	$105,288
Percent Poverty	10.4%
Public Assistance	2.1%
Percent Urban	95.6%

Education	
High School Graduates	86.0%
College Graduates	30.4%

Employed	
Percent Employed	95.2%
Private Sector	80.4%

Age of Population	
5 years or less	9.8%
6-17 years	16.0%
18-64 years	69.9%
65 or older	4.4%

Household Types	
Family households	79.2%
Non-family households	16.0%
Single-parent families	13.5%
Both parents working	68.0%

SENATE DISTRICTS IN HOUSE DISTRICT

Dist 9 Jane Nelson (R)
Dist 22 David Sibley (R)
Dist 30 Tom Haywood (R)

DISTRICT ELECTION DATA

House 1996	
Jim Horn (R)	100.0%

House 1998	
Ronny Crownover (R)	100.0%

President 1996	
Bill Clinton (D)	34.5%
Bob Dole (R)	65.5%

Composite Party Vote 1994	**35,028**
Democratic	33.2%
Republican	66.8%

Registered Voters 1996	**94,297**
Turnout	50,504
Percent of registered voting	53.6%

House District 64
Rep. Ronny Crownover (R)

House Office
(512) 463-0582

District Office
P.O. Box 429
Lake Dallas, Texas 75065
(940) 497-4044

Personal

Year of birth	1945
Family	Married to Myra Crownover, four children
Education	University of North Texas, B.B.A.
	Texas A&M University, B.S., D.V.M.
Occupation	Veterinarian
Religion	Presbyterian
State legislative service	House 1999 to present

COMMITTEE ASSIGNMENT HISTORY

BILL PASSAGE RATES, 1997

	Total	Passed Legislature	Pct. Passed Legislature
Authored	NA	NA	NA
Sponsored	NA	NA	NA
Amendments	NA	NA	NA

ELECTORAL HISTORY IN CURRENT DISTRICT

	1994	1996	1998
Primary Election Opponent(s)	NA	NA	Yes
General Election Opponent(s)	NA	NA	No

House District 65

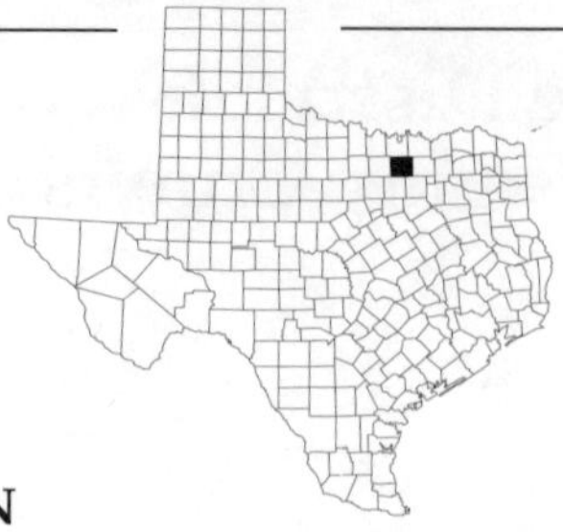

COUNTIES IN DISTRICT

Denton (part)

DEMOGRAPHIC INFORMATION

Population

Total	111,401
Anglo	83.2%
Black	5.3%
Hispanic	7.5%
Others	4.2%

Wealth and Urbanization

Per capita Income	$17,136
Avg. House Value	$95,378
Percent Poverty	5.3%
Public Assistance	1.7%
Percent Urban	92.0%

Education

High School Graduates	90.2%
College Graduates	36.5%

Employed

Percent Employed	96.4%
Private Sector	82.5%

Age of Population

5 years or less	11.3%
6-17 years	16.7%
18-64 years	68.1%
65 or older	3.9%

Household Types

Family households	83.2%
Non-family households	15.5%
Single-parent families	14.5%
Both parents working	69.6%

SENATE DISTRICTS IN HOUSE DISTRICT

Dist 9 Jane Nelson (R)
Dist 22 David Sibley (R)
Dist 30 Tom Haywood (R)

DISTRICT ELECTION DATA

House 1996

Burt Solomons (R)	100.0%

House 1998

Burt Solomons (R)	100.0%

President 1996

Bill Clinton (D)	37.2%
Bob Dole (R)	62.8%

Composite Party Vote 1994

Democratic	35.3%
Republican	64.7%

Registered Voters 1996	**78,770**
Turnout	41,269
Percent of registered voting	52.4%

House District 65
Rep. Burt Solomons (R)

House Office
(512) 463-0478

District Office
1029 Rosemeade Pkwy., Suite 108
Carrollton, Texas 75007
(972) 394-3904

Personal

Year of birth	1950
Family	Married to Jamie Solomons, onechild
Education	Texas Tech University, B.A. Southern Methodist University, M.P.A. University of Tulsa, J.D.
Occupation	Attorney
Religion	Baptist
State legislative service	House 1995 to present

COMMITTEE ASSIGNMENT HISTORY

1997 Business and Industry, Financial Institutions
1995 Business and Industry, Economic Development

BILL PASSAGE RATES, 1997

	Total	Passed Legislature	Pct. Passed Legislature
Authored	40	10	25%
Sponsored	1	1	100%
Amendments	15	14	93%

ELECTORAL HISTORY IN CURRENT DISTRICT

	1994	1996	1998
Primary Election Opponent(s)	NA	No	No
General Election Opponent(s)	Dem	No	No

House District 66

COUNTIES IN DISTRICT

Collin (part)

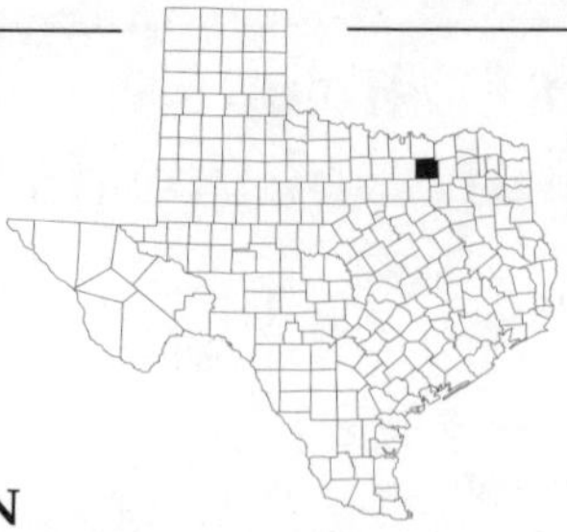

DEMOGRAPHIC INFORMATION

Population	
Total	111,672
Anglo	88.2%
Black	3.0%
Hispanic	4.2%
Others	4.6%

Education	
High School Graduates	95.9%
College Graduates	54.5%

Age of Population	
5 years or less	9.0%
6-17 years	17.8%
18-64 years	70.2%
65 or older	3.0%

Wealth and Urbanization	
Per capita Income	$26,535
Avg. House Value	$167,702
Percent Poverty	2.2%
Public Assistance	.9%
Percent Urban	99.9%

Employed	
Percent Employed	97.5%
Private Sector	87.1%

Household Types	
Family households	86.0%
Non-family households	13.7%
Single-parent families	11.4%
Both parents working	59.1%

SENATE DISTRICTS IN HOUSE DISTRICT

Dist 8 Florence Shapiro (R)

DISTRICT ELECTION DATA

House 1996	
Brian McCall (R)	100.0%

House 1998	
Brian McCall (R)	100.0%

President 1996	
Bill Clinton (D)	29.8%
Bob Dole (R)	70.2%

Composite Party Vote 1994	
Democratic	28.4%
Republican	71.6%

Registered Voters 1996	**105,234**
Turnout	62,702
Percent of registered voting	59.6%

House District 66
Rep. Brian McCall (R)

House Office
(512) 463-0594

District Office
609 W. 15th, #200
Plano, Texas 75075
(972) 881-0890

Personal

Year of birth	1958
Family	Single, no children
Education	Baylor University, B.A.
	Southern Methodist University, M.L.A.
Occupation	Business Owner
Religion	Baptist
State legislative service	House 1991 (part) to present

COMMITTEE ASSIGNMENT HISTORY

1997 Calendars, State Affairs, State Recreational Resources (Vice-Chair)
1995 Pensions and Investments, State Affairs
1993 Human Services, Public Health
1991 Cultural and Historical Resources, Science and Technology

BILL PASSAGE RATES, 1997

	Total	Passed Legislature	Pct. Passed Legislature
Authored	33	9	27%
Sponsored	13	10	77%
Amendments	7	7	100%

ELECTORAL HISTORY IN CURRENT DISTRICT

	1994	1996	1998
Primary Election Opponent(s)	No	No	No
General Election Opponent(s)	No	No	No

House District 67

COUNTIES IN DISTRICT
Collin (part)

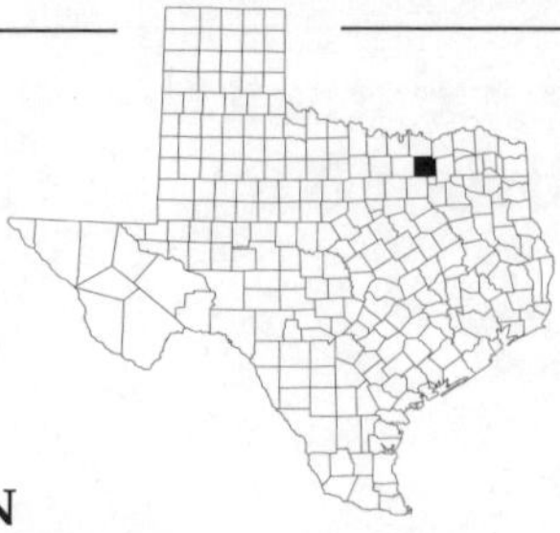

DEMOGRAPHIC INFORMATION

Population		**Wealth and Urbanization**	
Total	110,990	Per capita Income	$17,196
Anglo	86.0%	Avg. House Value	$103,041
Black	3.7%	Percent Poverty	5.9%
Hispanic	7.7%	Public Assistance	2.4%
Others	2.6%	Percent Urban	78.6%

Education		**Employed**	
High School Graduates	86.8%	Percent Employed	96.2%
College Graduates	31.6%	Private Sector	83.4%

Age of Population		**Household Types**	
5 years or less	11.5%	Family households	92.2%
6-17 years	19.3%	Non-family households	7.5%
18-64 years	64.3%	Single-parent families	13.8%
65 or older	5.0%	Both parents working	67.4%

SENATE DISTRICTS IN HOUSE DISTRICT

Dist 8 Florence Shapiro (R)

DISTRICT ELECTION DATA

House 1996		**House 1998**	
Jerry Madden (R)	100.0%	Jerry Madden (R)	100.0%

President 1996	
Bill Clinton (D)	31.6%
Bob Dole (R)	68.4%

Composite Party Vote 1994	
Democratic	31.6%
Republican	68.4%

Registered Voters 1996	**92,645**
Turnout	53,553
Percent of registered voting	57.8%

House District 67
Rep. Jerry Madden (R)

House Office
(512) 463-0544
(512) 463-9974 fax
jerry.madden@house.state.tx.us

District Office
520 E. Central Parkway #236
Plano, Texas 75094
(972) 424-2235

Personal

Year of birth	1943
Family	Married to Barbara Madden, three children
Education	United States Military Academy, B.S., Engineering University of Texas at Dallas, M.I.S.
Occupation	Insurance account executive
Religion	Methodist
State legislative service	House 1993 to present

COMMITTEE ASSIGNMENT HISTORY

1997 Elections, Public Safety, Rules and Resolutions
1995 Elections (Vice-Chair), Public Safety
1993 Elections, Urban Affairs

BILL PASSAGE RATES, 1997

	Total	Passed Legislature	Pct. Passed Legislature
Authored	43	12	28%
Sponsored	3	3	100%
Amendments	57	35	61%

ELECTORAL HISTORY IN CURRENT DISTRICT

	1994	1996	1998
Primary Election Opponent(s)	No	No	No
General Election Opponent(s)	Ind	No	No

House District 68

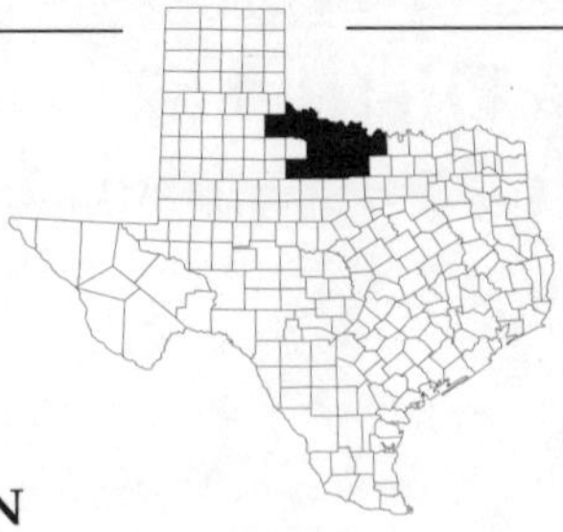

COUNTIES IN DISTRICT

Archer, Baylor, Clay, Cottle, Foard, Hardeman, Haskell, Jack, Montague, Throckmorton, Wichita (part), Wilbarger, Young

DEMOGRAPHIC INFORMATION

Population

Total	108,051
Anglo	89.3%
Black	2.8%
Hispanic	7.3%
Others	0.7%

Wealth and Urbanization

Per capita Income	$10,626
Avg. House Value	$41,116
Percent Poverty	17.9%
Public Assistance	6.8%
Percent Urban	52.2%

Education

High School Graduates	63.5%
College Graduates	10.9%

Employed

Percent Employed	94.3%
Private Sector	66.0%

Age of Population

5 years or less	8.4%
6-17 years	17.4%
18-64 years	54.3%
65 or older	19.9%

Household Types

Family households	86.2%
Non-family households	11.6%
Single-parent families	15.9%
Both parents working	64.1%

SENATE DISTRICTS IN HOUSE DISTRICT

Dist 22 David Sibley (R)
Dist 24 Troy Fraser (R)
Dist 30 Tom Haywood (R)

DISTRICT ELECTION DATA

House 1996

Charles Finnell (D)	100.0%

House 1998

Charles Finnell (D)	49.4%
Rick Hardcastle (R)	50.6%

President 1996

Bill Clinton (D)	45.9%
Bob Dole (R)	54.1%

Composite Party Vote 1994

Democratic	55.3%
Republican	44.7%

Registered Voters 1996	**71,393**
Turnout	40,184
Percent of registered voting	56.3%

House District 68
Rep. Rick Hardcastle (R)*

House Office
(512) 463-0526

District Office
P.O. Box 1614
Vernon, Texas 76385
9407) 552-5990

Personal

Year of birth	1956
Family	Married to Nancy Zeissel, two children
Education	Tarleton State University
Occupation	Terra International, Location Manager
Religion	Catholic
State legislative service	House 1999 to present

COMMITTEE ASSIGNMENT HISTORY

BILL PASSAGE RATES, 1997

	Total	Passed Legislature	Pct. Passed Legislature
Authored	NA	NA	NA
Sponsored	NA	NA	NA
Amendments	NA	NA	NA

ELECTORAL HISTORY IN CURRENT DISTRICT

	1994	1996	1998
Primary Election Opponent(s)	NA	NA	Yes
General Election Opponent(s)	NA	NA	Dem

*See also page 403.

House District 69

COUNTIES IN DISTRICT

Wichita (part)

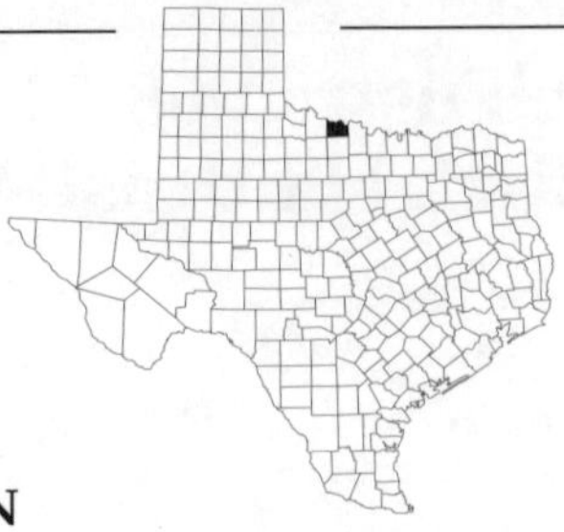

DEMOGRAPHIC INFORMATION

Population	
Total	112,235
Anglo	79.0%
Black	9.9%
Hispanic	9.1%
Others	2.3%

Wealth and Urbanization	
Per capita Income	$11,500
Avg. House Value	$55,000
Percent Poverty	16.5%
Public Assistance	6.3%
Percent Urban	97.4%

Education	
High School Graduates	74.9%
College Graduates	16.8%

Employed	
Percent Employed	92.7%
Private Sector	73.9%

Age of Population	
5 years or less	9.4%
6-17 years	16.8%
18-64 years	61.2%
65 or older	12.5%

Household Types	
Family households	81.7%
Non-family households	12.3%
Single-parent families	22.3%
Both parents working	64.9%

SENATE DISTRICTS IN HOUSE DISTRICT

Dist 30 Tom Haywood (R)

DISTRICT ELECTION DATA

House 1996	
John Hirschi (D)	100.0%

House 1998	
David Farabee (D)	56.1%
Ron Buffum (R)	43.9%

President 1996	
Bill Clinton (D)	43.8%
Bob Dole (R)	56.2%

Composite Party Vote 1994	
Democratic	49.4%
Republican	50.6%

Registered Voters 1996	**67,673**
Turnout	37,118
Percent of registered voting	54.8%

House District 69
Rep. David Farabee (D)

House Office
(512) 463-0534

District Office
P.O. Box 1533
Wichita Falls, Texas 76307
(940) 781-7312

Personal

Year of birth	1964
Family	Married to Terri Farabee, three children
Education	Midwestern State, B.A.
Occupation	Insurance Agent
Religion	Methodist
State legislative service	House 1999 to present

COMMITTEE ASSIGNMENT HISTORY

BILL PASSAGE RATES, 1997

	Total	Passed Legislature	Pct. Passed Legislature
Authored	NA	NA	NA
Sponsored	NA	NA	NA
Amendments	NA	NA	NA

ELECTORAL HISTORY IN CURRENT DISTRICT

	1994	1996	1998
Primary Election Opponent(s)	NA	NA	No
General Election Opponent(s)	NA	NA	Rep

House District 70

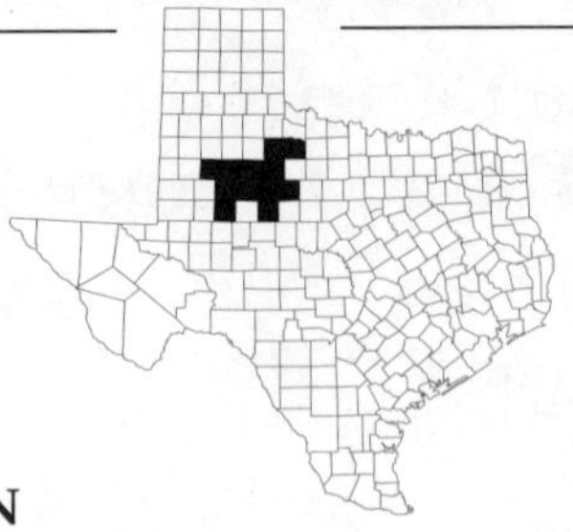

COUNTIES IN DISTRICT

Borden, Fisher, Garza, Howard, Jones, Kent, King, Knox, Lynn, Nolan, Scurry, Stonewall

DEMOGRAPHIC INFORMATION

Population	
Total	109,817
Anglo	70.6%
Black	4.3%
Hispanic	24.6%
Others	0.7%

Wealth and Urbanization	
Per capita Income	$10,169
Avg. House Value	$38,805
Percent Poverty	21.3%
Public Assistance	8.5%
Percent Urban	58.2%

Education	
High School Graduates	62.6%
College Graduates	11.0%

Employed	
Percent Employed	93.3%
Private Sector	65.7%

Age of Population	
5 years or less	9.2%
6-17 years	19.0%
18-64 years	55.7%
65 or older	16.1%

Household Types	
Family households	86.0%
Non-family households	10.0%
Single-parent families	18.4%
Both parents working	58.0%

SENATE DISTRICTS IN HOUSE DISTRICT

Dist 24 Troy Fraser (R)
Dist 28 Robert Duncan (R)
Dist 30 Tom Haywood (R)

DISTRICT ELECTION DATA

House 1996	
David Counts (D)	51.1%
Scott McLaughlin (R)	48.9%

House 1998	
David Counts (D)	53.6%
Scott McLaughlin (R)	46.4%

President 1996	
Bill Clinton (D)	48.0%
Bob Dole (R)	52.0%

Composite Party Vote 1994	
Democratic	54.4%
Republican	45.6%

Registered Voters 1996	**64,210**
Turnout	36,411
Percent of registered voting	56.7%

House District 70
Rep. David Counts (D)

House Office
(512) 463-0480

District Office
P.O. Box 338
Knox City, Texas 79529
(817) 658-5012

Personal

Year of birth	1936
Family	Married to Mary Counts, two children
Education	West Texas State University North Texas State University
Occupation	Insurance, real estate
Religion	Baptist
State legislative service	House 1988 (part) to present

COMMITTEE ASSIGNMENT HISTORY

1997 Natural Resources (Chair), State Affairs
1995 Insurance, (Chair) Natural Resources
1993 Insurance, Natural Resources (Chair), Redistricting
1991 Appropriations, Insurance
1989 Human Services, Insurance
1988 NA

BILL PASSAGE RATES, 1997

	Total	Passed Legislature	Pct. Passed Legislature
Authored	46	23	50%
Sponsored	8	6	75%
Amendments	0	0	NA

ELECTORAL HISTORY IN CURRENT DISTRICT

	1994	1996	1998
Primary Election Opponent(s)	No	No	No
General Election Opponent(s)	Rep	Rep	Rep

House District 71

COUNTIES IN DISTRICT
Taylor (part)

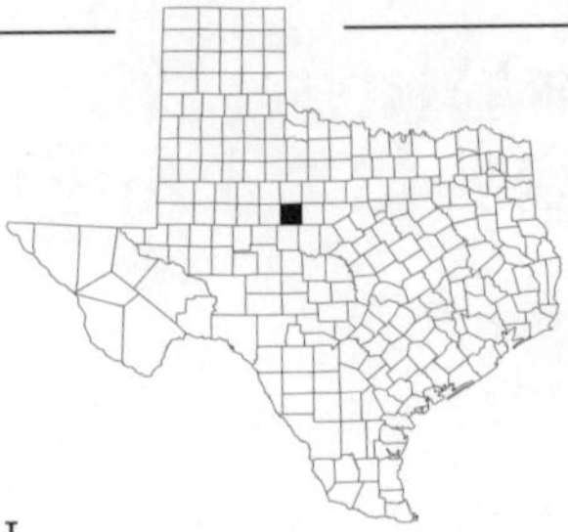

DEMOGRAPHIC INFORMATION

Population	
Total	114,752
Anglo	77.0%
Black	6.6%
Hispanic	15.0%
Others	1.6%

Education	
High School Graduates	75.5%
College Graduates	21.4%

Age of Population	
5 years or less	9.8%
6-17 years	17.3%
18-64 years	61.0%
65 or older	11.8%

Wealth and Urbanization	
Per capita Income	$11,793
Avg. House Value	$53,322
Percent Poverty	15.6%
Public Assistance	5.8%
Percent Urban	96.1%

Employed	
Percent Employed	93.0%
Private Sector	72.8%

Household Types	
Family households	82.0%
Non-family households	12.0%
Single-parent families	18.3%
Both parents working	66.6%

SENATE DISTRICTS IN HOUSE DISTRICT

Dist 24 Troy Fraser (R)
Dist 30 Tom Haywood (R)

DISTRICT ELECTION DATA

House 1996	
Bob Hunter (R)	100.0%

House 1998	
Bob Hunter (R)	100.0%

President 1996	
Bill Clinton (D)	36.0%
Bob Dole (R)	64.0%

Composite Party Vote 1994	
Democratic	43.4%
Republican	56.6%

Registered Voters 1996	**68,411**
Turnout	38,802
Percent of registered voting	56.7%

House District 71
Rep. Bob Hunter (R)

House Office
(512) 463-0718

District Office
P.O. Box 1498
Abilene, Texas 79604
(915) 677-0211

Personal

Year of birth	1928
Family	Married to Shirley Hunter, three children
Education	Abilene Christian University, B.S., M.B.A. Pepperdine University, L.L.D. University of St. Thomas, L.H.D., T.W.C., Lit.D.
Occupation	University administrator
Religion	Church of Christ
State legislative service	House 1985 (part) to present

COMMITTEE ASSIGNMENT HISTORY

1997 Redistricting, State Affairs, State, Federal and International Relations (Chair)
1995 State Affairs, State, Federal and International Relations (Chair)
1993 Higher Education, International and Cultural Relations (Chair)
1991 Higher Education, Rules and Resolutions
1989 Higher Education, State, Federal and International Relations
1987 Elections, Science and Technology
1985 NA

BILL PASSAGE RATES, 1997

	Total	Passed Legislature	Pct. Passed Legislature
Authored	34	11	32%
Sponsored	13	11	85%
Amendments	5	5	100%

ELECTORAL HISTORY IN CURRENT DISTRICT

	1994	1996	1998
Primary Election Opponent(s)	Yes	No	No
General Election Opponent(s)	No	No	No

House District 72

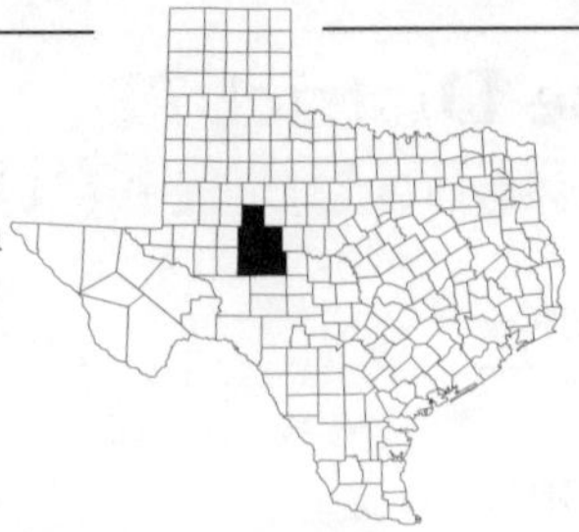

COUNTIES IN DISTRICT
Coke, Irion, Mitchell, Sterling, Tom Green

DEMOGRAPHIC INFORMATION

Population

Total	112,965
Anglo	69.2%
Black	4.0%
Hispanic	25.7%
Others	1.2%

Wealth and Urbanization

Per capita Income	$11,327
Avg. House Value	$55,227
Percent Poverty	17.7%
Public Assistance	6.2%
Percent Urban	79.8%

Education

High School Graduates	69.8%
College Graduates	16.2%

Employed

Percent Employed	92.3%
Private Sector	71.7%

Age of Population

5 years or less	9.1%
6-17 years	17.9%
18-64 years	59.3%
65 or older	13.7%

Household Types

Family households	83.2%
Non-family households	11.6%
Single-parent families	18.8%
Both parents working	67.2%

SENATE DISTRICTS IN HOUSE DISTRICT

Dist 24 Troy Fraser (R)
Dist 25 Jeff Wentworth (R)
Dist 28 Robert Duncan (R)

DISTRICT ELECTION DATA

House 1996

Robert Junell (D)	100.0%

House 1998

Robert Junell (D)	79.3%
Russ Duerstine (R)	20.7%

President 1996

Bill Clinton (D)	40.4%
Bob Dole (R)	59.6%

Composite Party Vote 1994

Democratic	48.2%
Republican	51.8%

Registered Voters 1996	**67,823**
Turnout	38,077
Percent of registered voting	56.1%

House District 72
Rep. Robert Junell (D)

House Office
(512) 463-0472

District Office
P.O. Box 3362
San Angelo, Texas 76902
(915) 657-0197

Personal

Year of birth	1947
Family	Married to Beverly Junell, three children
Education	Texas Tech University, B.S., Education University of Arkansas, M.A., Political Science Texas Tech University, J.D.
Occupation	Attorney
Religion	Presbyterian
State legislative service	House 1989 to present

COMMITTEE ASSIGNMENT HISTORY
1997 Appropriations (Chair), General Investigating
1995 Appropriations (Chair), General Investigating
1993 Appropriations (Chair)
1991 Appropriations, Business and Commerce
1989 House Administration, Natural Resources, Liquor Regulation

BILL PASSAGE RATES, 1997

	Total	Passed Legislature	Pct. Passed Legislature
Authored	54	24	44%
Sponsored	20	13	65%
Amendments	40	38	95%

ELECTORAL HISTORY IN CURRENT DISTRICT

	1994	1996	1998
Primary Election Opponent(s)	No	No	No
General Election Opponent(s)	No	No	Rep

House District 73

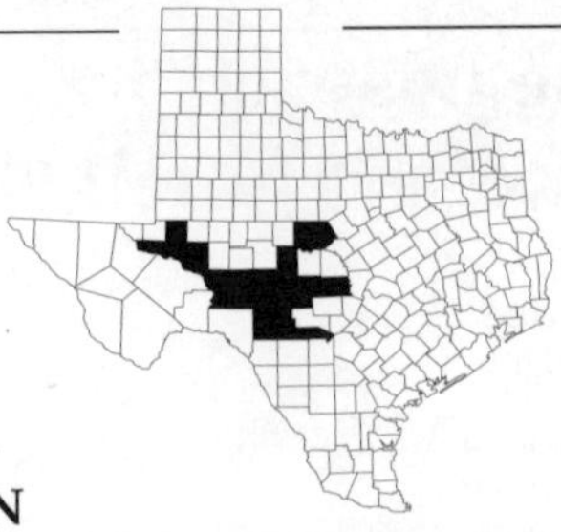

COUNTIES IN DISTRICT

Bandera, Brown, Coleman, Concho, Crane, Crockett, Ector (part), Edwards, Kimble, Llano, Mason, Menard, Real, Schleicher, Sutton, Upton, Ward

DEMOGRAPHIC INFORMATION

Population	
Total	118,043
Anglo	75.8%
Black	2.2%
Hispanic	21.4%
Others	0.6%

Wealth and Urbanization	
Per capita Income	$10,306
Avg. House Value	$49,523
Percent Poverty	20.8%
Public Assistance	7.5%
Percent Urban	42.5%

Education	
High School Graduates	65.9%
College Graduates	13.0%

Employed	
Percent Employed	93.8%
Private Sector	67.6%

Age of Population	
5 years or less	8.2%
6-17 years	18.7%
18-64 years	54.6%
65 or older	18.5%

Household Types	
Family households	85.7%
Non-family households	11.3%
Single-parent families	17.5%
Both parents working	57.9%

SENATE DISTRICTS IN HOUSE DISTRICT

Dist 19 Frank Madla (D)
Dist 24 Troy Fraser (R)
Dist 25 Jeff Wentworth (R)
Dist 28 Robert Duncan (R)

DISTRICT ELECTION DATA

House 1996	
Robert R. (Bob) Turner (D)	100.0%

House 1998	
Robert R. (Bob) Turner (D)	51.7%
Randy C. Leifeste (R)	48.3%

President 1996	
Bill Clinton (D)	39.8%
Bob Dole (R)	60.2%

Composite Party Vote 1994	
Democratic	47.2%
Republican	52.8%

Registered Voters 1996	79,210
Turnout	47,816
Percent of registered voting	60.4%

House District 73
Rep. Robert R. (Bob) Turner (D)

House Office
(512) 463-0644

District Office
P.O. Box 879
Coleman, Texas 76834
(915) 625-3596

Personal

Year of birth	1934
Family	Married to Ann Gale Turner, three children
Education	Liberty University U.S. Army Command and General Staff College U.S. Army Officer Advance Leadership Course
Occupation	Farmer, rancher
Religion	Methodist
State legislative service	House 1991 to present

COMMITTEE ASSIGNMENT HISTORY

1997 Agriculture and Livestock, Land and Resource Management (Vice-Chair)
1995 Land and Resource Management, State Recreational Resources
1993 Agriculture and Wildlife Management, Natural Resources
1991 (part) Cultural and Historical Resources, Labor and Employment Relations, Science and Technology

BILL PASSAGE RATES, 1997

	Total	Passed Legislature	Pct. Passed Legislature
Authored	52	17	33%
Sponsored	3	2	67%
Amendments	12	10	83%

ELECTORAL HISTORY IN CURRENT DISTRICT

	1994	1996	1998
Primary Election Opponent(s)	No	No	No
General Election Opponent(s)	Rep, Ind	No	Rep

House District 74

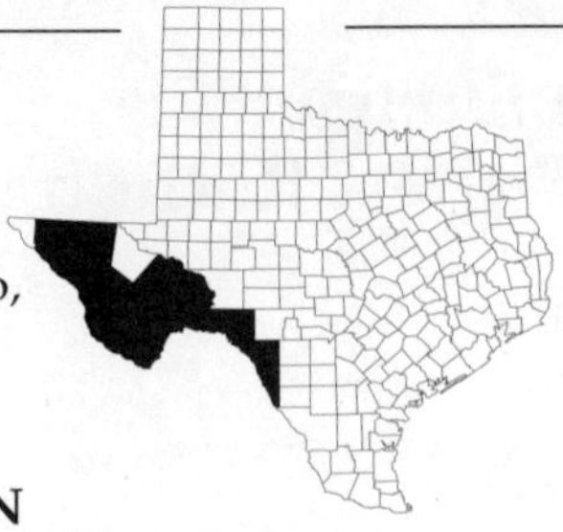

COUNTIES IN DISTRICT

Brewster, Culberson, Hudspeth, Jeff Davis, Kinney, Maverick, Pecos, Presidio, Terrell, Val Verde

DEMOGRAPHIC INFORMATION

Population

Total	117,889
Anglo	24.9%
Black	0.9%
Hispanic	73.1%
Others	1.2%

Education

High School Graduates	51.4%
College Graduates	12.4%

Age of Population

5 years or less	10.6%
6-17 years	23.0%
18-64 years	56.0%
65 or older	10.4%

Wealth and Urbanization

Per capita Income	$7,394
Avg. House Value	$44,049
Percent Poverty	39.2%
Public Assistance	15.5%
Percent Urban	63.1%

Employed

Percent Employed	86.4%
Private Sector	62.4%

Household Types

Family households	91.1%
Non-family households	7.2%
Single-parent families	17.2%
Both parents working	45.9%

SENATE DISTRICTS IN HOUSE DISTRICT

Dist 19 Frank Madla (D)

Dist 28 Robert Duncan (R)

DISTRICT ELECTION DATA

House 1996

Pete P. Gallego (D)	100.0%

House 1998

Pete P. Gallego (D)	100.0%

President 1996

Bill Clinton (D)	62.1%
Bob Dole (R)	37.9%

Composite Party Vote 1994

Democratic	59.3%
Republican	40.7%

Registered Voters 1996	**63,646**
Turnout	31,864
Percent of registered voting	50.1%

House District 74
Rep. Pete P. Gallego (D)

House Office
(512) 463-0566

District Office
P.O. Box 777
Alpine, Texas 79831
(915) 837-7383

Personal

Year of birth	1961
Family	Married to Marie Elena Ramon, no children
Education	Sul Ross State University, B.A.
	University of Texas, J.D.
Occupation	Attorney
Religion	Catholic
State legislative service	House 1991 to present

COMMITTEE ASSIGNMENT HISTORY

1997 Appropriations, Elections, General Investigating (Chair)
1995 General Investigating (Chair), Higher Education
1993 Calendars, Appropriations, Judicial Affairs (Vice-Chair)
1991 Criminal Jurisprudence, State, Federal and International Relations

BILL PASSAGE RATES, 1997

	Total	Passed Legislature	Pct. Passed Legislature
Authored	60	19	32%
Sponsored	12	9	75%
Amendments	21	20	95%

ELECTORAL HISTORY IN CURRENT DISTRICT

	1994	1996	1998
Primary Election Opponent(s)	No	No	No
General Election Opponent(s)	Rep	No	No

House District 75

COUNTIES IN DISTRICT

El Paso (part)

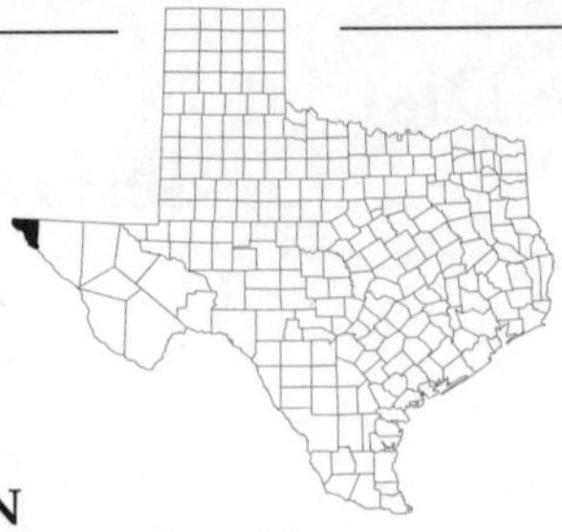

DEMOGRAPHIC INFORMATION

Population	
Total	118,382
Anglo	13.3%
Black	1.1%
Hispanic	85.1%
Others	0.8%

Education	
High School Graduates	50.6%
College Graduates	8.6%

Age of Population	
5 years or less	11.5%
6-17 years	26.4%
18-64 years	56.9%
65 or older	5.3%

Wealth and Urbanization	
Per capita Income	$6,890
Avg. House Value	$57,779
Percent Poverty	33.6%
Public Assistance	12.1%
Percent Urban	91.7%

Employed	
Percent Employed	87.7%
Private Sector	76.2%

Household Types	
Family households	96.0%
Non-family households	3.5%
Single-parent families	20.3%
Both parents working	49.2%

SENATE DISTRICTS IN HOUSE DISTRICT

Dist 28 Robert Duncan (R)

Dist 29 Eliot Shapleigh (D)

DISTRICT ELECTION DATA

House 1996	
Gilbert Serna (D)	68.2%
James Barnett (R)	31.8%

President 1996	
Bill Clinton (D)	74.1%
Bob Dole (R)	25.9%

Composite Party Vote 1994	
Democratic	63.9%
Republican	36.1%

Registered Voters 1996	**56,132**
Turnout	24,307
Percent of registered voting	43.3%

House 1998	
Manny Najera (D)	73.2%
Gerard Sanden (R)	26.8%

House District 75
Rep. Manny Najera (D)

House Office
(512) 463-0954

District Office
1716 Mike Hill
El Paso, Texas 79936
(915) 594-2768

Personal

Year of birth	1935
Family	Married to Maggie Najera, three children
Education	University of Texas El Paso, B.B.A.
Occupation	U.S. Customs District Director, Retired
Religion	Catholic
State legislative service	House 1999 to present

COMMITTEE ASSIGNMENT HISTORY
1997 Corrections, Pensions and Investments
1995 Corrections, State, Federal and International Relations

BILL PASSAGE RATES, 1997

	Total	Passed Legislature	Pct. Passed Legislature
Authored	NA	NA	NA
Sponsored	NA	NA	NA
Amendments	NA	NA	NA

ELECTORAL HISTORY IN CURRENT DISTRICT

	1994	1996	1998
Primary Election Opponent(s)	NA	NA	Yes
General Election Opponent(s)	NA	NA	Rep

House District 76

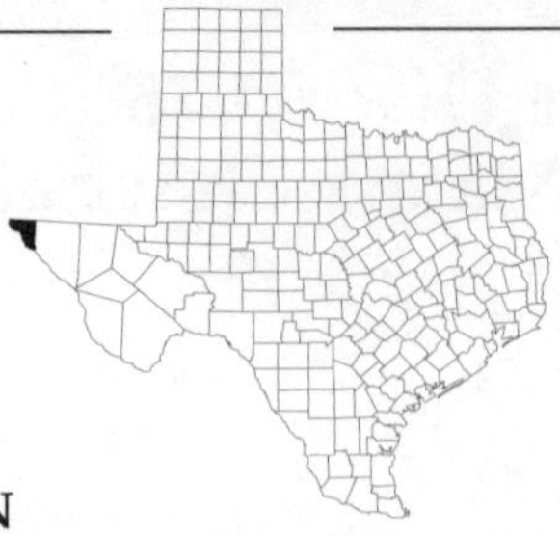

COUNTIES IN DISTRICT

El Paso (part)

DEMOGRAPHIC INFORMATION

Population	
Total	118,293
Anglo	15.0%
Black	2.1%
Hispanic	82.5%
Others	0.6%

Education	
High School Graduates	54.7%
College Graduates	9.3%

Age of Population	
5 years or less	9.6%
6-17 years	21.2%
18-64 years	59.3%
65 or older	9.9%

Wealth and Urbanization	
Per capita Income	$7,566
Avg. House Value	$56,874
Percent Poverty	29.1%
Public Assistance	13.9%
Percent Urban	100%

Employed	
Percent Employed	88.3%
Private Sector	74.7%

Household Types	
Family households	93.9%
Non-family households	5.8%
Single-parent families	28.8%
Both parents working	49.3%

SENATE DISTRICTS IN HOUSE DISTRICT

Dist 29 Eliot Shapleigh (D)

DISTRICT ELECTION DATA

House 1996	
Norma Chavez (D)	100.0%

House 1998	
Norma Chavez (D)	100.0%

President 1996	
Bill Clinton (D)	76.5%
Bob Dole (R)	23.5%

Composite Party Vote 1994	
Democratic	68.5%
Republican	31.5%

Registered Voters 1996	60,420
Turnout	27,999
Percent of registered voting	46.3%

House District 76
Rep. Norma Chavez (D)

House Office
(512) 463-0622

District Office
P.O. Box 2910
Austin, Texas 78768
(512) 463-0622

Personal

Year of birth	1960
Family	Single, no children
Education	San Angelo State University University of Texas at El Paso
Occupation	Business Manager
Religion	Christian
State legislative service	House 1997 to present

COMMITTEE ASSIGNMENT HISTORY

1997 Human Services, Rules and Resolutions, State, Federal and International Relations

BILL PASSAGE RATES, 1997

	Total	Passed Legislature	Pct. Passed Legislature
Authored	35	4	11%
Sponsored	6	5	83%
Amendments	11	7	64%

ELECTORAL HISTORY IN CURRENT DISTRICT

	1994	1996	1998
Primary Election Opponent(s)	NA	Yes	No
General Election Opponent(s)	NA	No	No

House District 77

COUNTIES IN DISTRICT

El Paso (part)

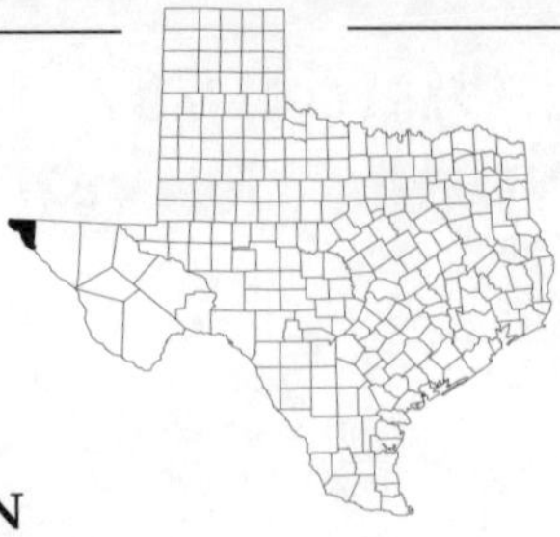

DEMOGRAPHIC INFORMATION

Population

Total	118,279
Anglo	14.6%
Black	2.4%
Hispanic	82.2%
Others	1.0%

Wealth and Urbanization

Per capita Income	$6,653
Avg. House Value	$53,789
Percent Poverty	39.6%
Public Assistance	14.3%
Percent Urban	100%

Education

High School Graduates	48.6%
College Graduates	10.2%

Employed

Percent Employed	86.5%
Private Sector	77.4%

Age of Population

5 years or less	10.9%
6-17 years	19.8%
18-64 years	57.1%
65 or older	12.2%

Household Types

Family households	87.4%
Non-family households	9.8%
Single-parent families	32.3%
Both parents working	47.5%

SENATE DISTRICTS IN HOUSE DISTRICT

Dist 29 Eliot Shapleigh (D)

DISTRICT ELECTION DATA

House 1996

Paul C. Moreno (D)	100.0%

House 1998

Paul C. Moreno (D)	100.0%

President 1996

Bill Clinton (D)	76.9%
Bob Dole (R)	23.1%

Composite Party Vote 1994

Democratic	70.0%
Republican	30.0%

Registered Voters 1996	**49,711**
Turnout	21,665
Percent of registered voting	43.6%

House District 77
Rep. Paul C. Moreno (D)

House Office
(512) 463-0638

District Office
2314 Montana
El Paso, Texas 79903
(915) 544-0789

Personal

Year of birth	1931
Family	Single, one child
Education	Texas Western College, B.B.A. University of Texas, J.D.
Occupation	Attorney, state representative
Religion	Catholic
State legislative service	House 1967-71, 1975 to present

COMMITTEE ASSIGNMENT HISTORY

1997 Appropriations, Redistricting, State, Federal and International Relations (Vice-Chair)
1995 Redistricting(Vice-Chair), Transportation
1993 Higher Education, Redistricting(Vice-Chair), Ways and Means
1991 Higher Education, Judiciary, Redistricting
1989 Appropriations, Labor and Employment Relations, Urban Affairs (Vice-Chair)
1987 Labor and Employment Relations, Urban Affairs
1985 Liquor Regulations, Retirement and Aging
1983 Cultural and Historical Resources, Retirement and Aging
1981 Appropriations, Judicial Affairs
1979 Employment Practices, Judiciary
1977 Judiciary, Labor
1975 Intergovernmental Affairs, Judiciary
1971 Banks and Banking, Criminal Jurisprudence, Highways and Roads, Mental Health and Mental Retardation, State Finance
1969 Judicial Districts, Labor, Motor Transportation, Youth
1967 Aeronautics, Enrolled Bills, Labor, Military and Veterans' Affairs

BILL PASSAGE RATES, 1997

	Total	Passed Legislature	Pct. Passed Legislature
Authored	10	1	10%
Sponsored	2	2	100%
Amendments	2	0	0%

ELECTORAL HISTORY IN CURRENT DISTRICT

	1994	1996	1998
Primary Election Opponent(s)	No	No	Yes
General Election Opponent(s)	No	No	No

House District 78

COUNTIES IN DISTRICT

El Paso (part)

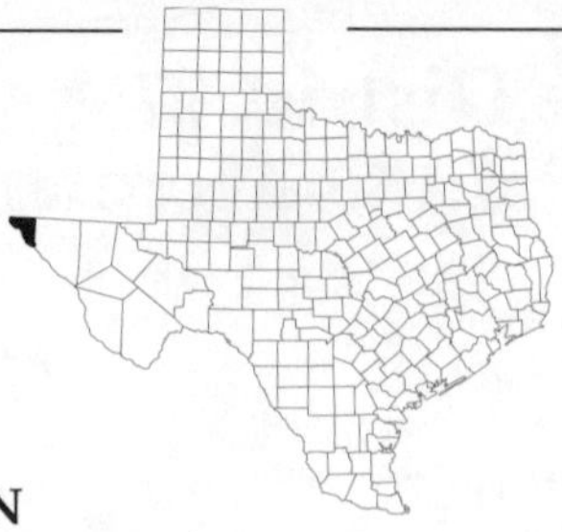

DEMOGRAPHIC INFORMATION

Population		**Wealth and Urbanization**	
Total	118,282	Per capita Income	$16,834
Anglo	57.6%	Avg. House Value	$107,730
Black	7.5%	Percent Poverty	9.1%
Hispanic	32.5%	Public Assistance	2.8%
Others	2.7%	Percent Urban	100%

Education		**Employed**	
High School Graduates	90.2%	Percent Employed	94.5%
College Graduates	35.8%	Private Sector	69.2%

Age of Population		**Household Types**	
5 years or less	9.4%	Family households	83.9%
6-17 years	17.7%	Non-family households	9.4%
18-64 years	64.9%	Single-parent families	14.7%
65 or older	8.0%	Both parents working	58.5%

SENATE DISTRICTS IN HOUSE DISTRICT

Dist 28 Robert Duncan (R)

Dist 29 Eliot Shapleigh (D)

DISTRICT ELECTION DATA

House 1996		**House 1998**	
		John Cook (D)	35.2%
Pat Haggerty (R)	100.0%	Pat Haggerty (R)	64.8%

President 1996	
Bill Clinton (D)	47.1%
Bob Dole (R)	52.9%

Composite Party Vote 1994	
Democratic	45.0%
Republican	55.0%

Registered Voters 1996	**73,679**
Turnout	39,711
Percent of registered voting	53.9%

House District 78
Rep. Pat Haggerty (R)

House Office
(512) 463-0728

District Office
4849 North Mesa, #206
El Paso, Texas 79912
(915) 532-1391

Personal

Year of birth	1944
Family	Married to Yvonne Haggerty, no children
Education	University of Texas at El Paso, B.A., M.A.
Occupation	Real estate broker
Religion	Catholic
State legislative service	House 1989 to present

COMMITTEE ASSIGNMENT HISTORY

1997 Appropriations, Licensing and Administrative Procedures
1995 Appropriations, Pensions and Investments
1993 Investments and Banking, Ways and Means
1991 Business and Commerce, Natural Resources
1989 Cultural and Historical Resources, Urban Affairs

BILL PASSAGE RATES, 1997

	Total	Passed Legislature	Pct. Passed Legislature
Authored	10	4	40%
Sponsored	2	2	100%
Amendments	9	7	78%

ELECTORAL HISTORY IN CURRENT DISTRICT

	1994	1996	1998
Primary Election Opponent(s)	No	No	No
General Election Opponent(s)	Dem	No	Dem

House District 79

COUNTIES IN DISTRICT

El Paso (part)

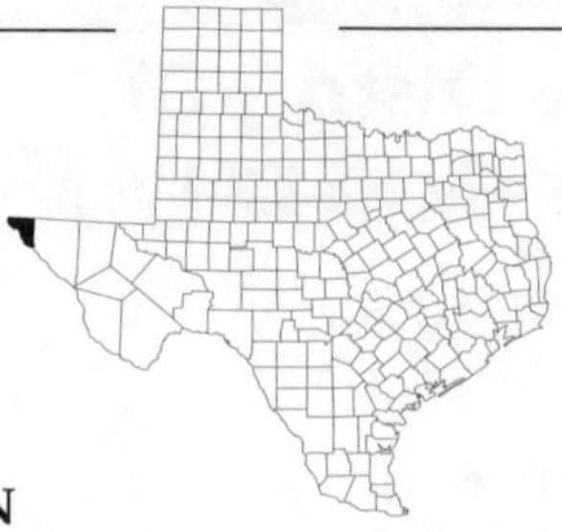

DEMOGRAPHIC INFORMATION

Population		**Wealth and Urbanization**	
Total	118,374	Per capita Income	$8,491
Anglo	27.3%	Avg. House Value	$59,252
Black	5.7%	Percent Poverty	20.5%
Hispanic	65.6%	Public Assistance	8.3%
Others	1.8%	Percent Urban	94.6%

Education		**Employed**	
High School Graduates	70.5%	Percent Employed	90.2%
College Graduates	13.5%	Private Sector	72.7%

Age of Population		**Household Types**	
5 years or less	12.8%	Family households	93.2%
6-17 years	23.5%	Non-family households	4.7%
18-64 years	59.1%	Single-parent families	19.9%
65 or older	4.6%	Both parents working	56.0%

SENATE DISTRICTS IN HOUSE DISTRICT

Dist 28 Robert Duncan (R)

Dist 29 Eliot Shapleigh (D)

DISTRICT ELECTION DATA

House 1996		**House 1998**	
Joseph C. Pickett (D)	100.0%	Joseph C. Pickett (D)	100.0%

President 1996	
Bill Clinton (D)	66.9%
Bob Dole (R)	33.1%

Composite Party Vote 1994	
Democratic	57.3%
Republican	42.7%

Registered Voters 1996	**56,000**
Turnout	24,565
Percent of registered voting	43.9%

House District 79
Rep. Joseph C. Pickett (D)

House Office
(512) 463-0596

District Office
1790 Lee Trevino, Suite 307
El Paso, Texas 79936
(915) 590-4349

Personal

Year of birth	1956
Family	Married to Denise Pickett, four children
Education	Attended University of Texas at El Paso
Occupation	State Representative
Religion	Catholic
State legislative service	House 1995 to present

COMMITTEE ASSIGNMENT HISTORY

1997 Licensing and Administrative Procedures, Transportation
1995 Criminal Jurisprudence, Licensing and Administrative Procedures

BILL PASSAGE RATES, 1997

	Total	Passed Legislature	Pct. Passed Legislature
Authored	28	5	18%
Sponsored	5	4	80%
Amendments	17	12	71%

ELECTORAL HISTORY IN CURRENT DISTRICT

	1994	1996	1998
Primary Election Opponent(s)	Yes	No	No
General Election Opponent(s)	No	No	No

House District 80

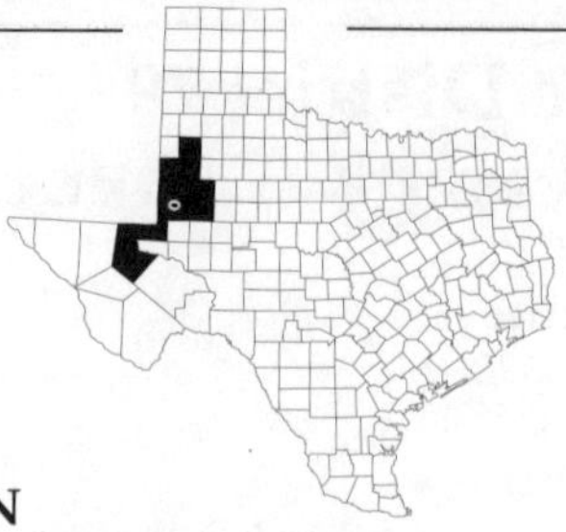

COUNTIES IN DISTRICT

Andrews, Dawson, Gaines, Hockley, Loving, Martin, Reeves, Terry, Winkler, Yoakum

DEMOGRAPHIC INFORMATION

Population	
Total	118,554
Anglo	56.0%
Black	2.9%
Hispanic	40.5%
Others	0.7%

Wealth and Urbanization	
Per capita Income	$9,851
Avg. House Value	$43,277
Percent Poverty	23.8%
Public Assistance	8.7%
Percent Urban	65.8%

Education	
High School Graduates	57.3%
College Graduates	9.8%

Employed	
Percent Employed	92.0%
Private Sector	69.2%

Age of Population	
5 years or less	10.7%
6-17 years	22.9%
18-64 years	55.3%
65 or older	11.2%

Household Types	
Family households	91.4%
Non-family households	7.1%
Single-parent families	14.7%
Both parents working	49.3%

SENATE DISTRICTS IN HOUSE DISTRICT

Dist 19 Frank Madla (D)
Dist 28 Robert Duncan (R)
Dist 31 Teel Bivins (R)

DISTRICT ELECTION DATA

House 1996	
Gary L. Walker (R)	100.0%

House 1998	
Gary L. Walker (R)	100.0%

President 1996	
Bill Clinton (D)	40.6%
Bob Dole (R)	59.4%

Composite Party Vote 1994	
Democratic	47.7%
Republican	52.3%

Registered Voters 1996	**61,718**
Turnout	33,056
Percent of registered voting	53.6%

House District 80
Rep. Gary L. Walker (R)

House Office
(512) 463-0678

District Office
P.O. Box 750
Plains, Texas 79355
(806) 456-7470

Personal

Year of birth	1946
Family	Married to Frankie Walker, two children
Education	Texas A&M University, B.S., Animal Science
Occupation	Water conservation, landfill consultant
Religion	Baptist
State legislative service	House 1995 to present

COMMITTEE ASSIGNMENT HISTORY

1997 Appropriations, Natural Resources (Vice-Chair)
1995 Agriculture and Livestock, Natural Resources

BILL PASSAGE RATES, 1997

	Total	Passed Legislature	Pct. Passed Legislature
Authored	17	1	6%
Sponsored	7	5	71%
Amendments	10	10	100%

ELECTORAL HISTORY IN CURRENT DISTRICT

	1994	1996	1998
Primary Election Opponent(s)	No	No	Yes
General Election Opponent(s)	Dem	No	No

House District 81

COUNTIES IN DISTRICT
Ector (part)

DEMOGRAPHIC INFORMATION

Population	
Total	118,101
Anglo	63.2%
Black	4.7%
Hispanic	31.1%
Others	1.2%

Wealth and Urbanization	
Per capita Income	$10,868
Avg. House Value	$51,316
Percent Poverty	20.4%
Public Assistance	6.7%
Percent Urban	95.6%

Education	
High School Graduates	66.8%
College Graduates	11.4%

Employed	
Percent Employed	92.2%
Private Sector	77.8%

Age of Population	
5 years or less	11.1%
6-17 years	20.8%
18-64 years	58.8%
65 or older	9.3%

Household Types	
Family households	89.4%
Non-family households	9.9%
Single-parent families	21.4%
Both parents working	53.1%

SENATE DISTRICTS IN HOUSE DISTRICT

Dist 28 Robert Duncan (R)
Dist 31 Teel Bivins (R)

DISTRICT ELECTION DATA

House 1996	
G. E. (Buddy) West (R)	100.0%

House 1998	
G. E. (Buddy) West (R)	100.0%

President 1996	
Bill Clinton (D)	40.3%
Bob Dole (R)	59.7%%

Composite Party Vote 1994	
Democratic	39.9%
Republican	60.1%

Registered Voters 1996	**61,886**
Turnout	33,251
Percent of registered voting	53.7%

House District 81
Rep. G. E. (Buddy) West (R)

House Office
(512) 463-0546

District Office
4526 E. Univ. Bldg. 5, Suite G
Odessa, Texas 79762
(915) 367-2721

Personal

Year of birth	1936
Family	Married to Shirley West, three children
Education	University of Texas of the Permian Basin, B.B.A.
Occupation	Safety engineer-Retired
Religion	Baptist
State legislative service	House 1993 to present

COMMITTEE ASSIGNMENT HISTORY

1997 Appropriations, House Administration, State, Federal and International Relations

1995 Energy Resources (Vice-Chair), House Administration, Public Education

1993 Energy Resources, Public Education

BILL PASSAGE RATES, 1997

	Total	Passed Legislature	Pct. Passed Legislature
Authored	33	10	30%
Sponsored	3	3	100%
Amendments	3	2	67%

ELECTORAL HISTORY IN CURRENT DISTRICT

	1994	1996	1998
Primary Election Opponent(s)	No	No	No
General Election Opponent(s)	No	No	No

House District 82

COUNTIES IN DISTRICT

Glasscock, Midland, Regan

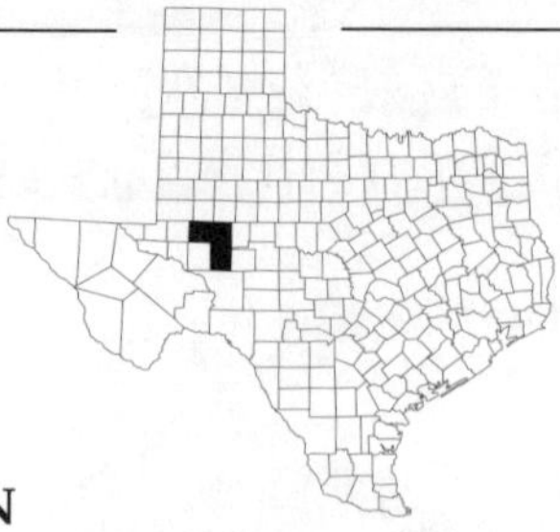

DEMOGRAPHIC INFORMATION

Population		**Wealth and Urbanization**	
Total	112,572	Per capita Income	$15,220
Anglo	69.3%	Avg. House Value	$72,521
Black	7.5%	Percent Poverty	14.4%
Hispanic	22.3%	Public Assistance	4.9%
Others	1.2%	Percent Urban	85.8%

Education		**Employed**	
High School Graduates	76.2%	Percent Employed	93.8%
College Graduates	25.6%	Private Sector	76.5%

Age of Population		**Household Types**	
5 years or less	11.6%	Family households	88.6%
6-17 years	20.1%	Non-family households	10.5%
18-64 years	59.4%	Single-parent families	17.5%
65 or older	8.9%	Both parents working	58.7%

SENATE DISTRICTS IN HOUSE DISTRICT

Dist 28 Robert Duncan (R)

Dist 31 Teel Bivins (R)

DISTRICT ELECTION DATA

House 1996		**House 1998**	
Tom Craddick (R)	100.0%	Tom Craddick (R)	100.0%

President 1996	
Bill Clinton (D)	27.4%
Bob Dole (R)	72.6%

Composite Party Vote 1994	
Democratic	29.4%
Republican	70.6%

Registered Voters 1996	**67,147**
Turnout	39,234
Percent of registered voting	58.4%

House District 82
Rep. Tom Craddick (R)

House Office
(512) 463-0500

District Office
408 West Wall
Midland, Texas 79701
(915) 682-3000

Personal

Year of birth	1943
Family	Married to Nadine Craddick, two children
Education	Texas Tech University, B.B.A., M.B.A.
Occupation	Sales Representative Mustang Mud, Inc.
Religion	Catholic
State legislative service	House 1969 to present

COMMITTEE ASSIGNMENT HISTORY

1997 State Affairs, Ways and Means (Chair)
1995 Calendars, State Affairs, Ways and Means (Chair)
1993 Calendars, Ways and Means (Chair)
1991 Energy, Public Health(Chair), Redistricting
1989 Energy (Vice-Chair), Ways and Means
1987 Energy, Ways and Means
1985 Energy, (Chair) Natural Resources
1983 Calendars, Energy, (Chair) Natural Resources
1981 Energy Resources, Natural Resources (Chair)
1979 Energy Resources, Natural Resources (Chair)
1977 Energy Resources, Natural Resources (Chair)
1975 Natural Resources (Chair), Energy Resources
1973 Agriculture and Livestock, Insurance, Natural Resources
1971 Agriculture, Enrolled and Engrossed Bills, Liquor Regulation, Public Health
1969 Congressional and Legislative Districts, Insurance, Liquor Regulation, Public Health

BILL PASSAGE RATES, 1997

	Total	Passed Legislature	Pct. Passed Legislature
Authored	27	13	48%
Sponsored	3	3	100%
Amendments	11	10	91%

ELECTORAL HISTORY IN CURRENT DISTRICT

	1994	1996	1998
Primary Election Opponent(s)	No	No	No
General Election Opponent(s)	No	No	No

House District 83

COUNTIES IN DISTRICT
Lubbock (part)

DEMOGRAPHIC INFORMATION

Population	
Total	107,306
Anglo	49.5%
Black	13.0%
Hispanic	36.4%
Others	1.5%

Education	
High School Graduates	60.2%
College Graduates	13.0%

Age of Population	
5 years or less	10.4%
6-17 years	20.0%
18-64 years	60.3%
65 or older	9.3%

Wealth and Urbanization	
Per capita Income	$8,800
Avg. House Value	$45,704
Percent Poverty	26.8%
Public Assistance	9.9%
Percent Urban	81.0%

Employed	
Percent Employed	90.9%
Private Sector	74.5%

Household Types	
Family households	85.2%
Non-family households	12.6%
Single-parent families	22.9%
Both parents working	59.8%

SENATE DISTRICTS IN HOUSE DISTRICT

Dist 28 Robert Duncan (R)

DISTRICT ELECTION DATA

House 1996	
Brad Clardy (L)	17.0%
Delwin Jones (R)	83.0%

House 1998	
Delwin Jones (R)	100.0%

President 1996	
Bill Clinton (D)	44.9%
Bob Dole (R)	55.1%

Composite Party Vote 1994	
Democratic	47.9%
Republican	52.1%

Registered Voters 1996	**60,643**
Turnout	27,950
Percent of registered voting	46.1%

House District 83
Rep. Delwin Jones (R)

House Office
(512) 463-0542
(512) 463-0671 (Fax)

District Office
5609-A Villa Drive
Lubbock, Texas 79412
(806) 763-4468
(806) 763-1201 (Fax)

Personal

Year of birth	1924
Family	Married to Reta Jones, two children
Education	Texas Tech University, B.B.A., Accounting
Occupation	Investor
Religion	Methodist
State legislative service	House 1965-71, 1989 to present

COMMITTEE ASSIGNMENT HISTORY

1997 Licensing and Administrative Procedures, Redistricting (Chair), State Affairs
1995 Licensing and Administrative Procedures, Redistricting (Chair), State Affairs
1993 Licensing and Administrative Procedures, Redistricting (Chair), State Affairs
1991 County Affairs, General Investigating, Redistricting (Vice-Chair), State Affairs
1989 County Affairs, Redistricting (Vice-Chair), State Affairs
1971 Agriculture, Congressional and Legislative Districts (Chair), Elections, Governmental Affairs and Efficiency, Mental Health and Mental Retardation
1969 Agriculture (Chair), Governmental Affairs and Efficiency, Labor, School Districts, Youth
1967 Agriculture (Vice-Chair), Conservation and Reclamation, Labor, Mental Health and Mental Retardation
1965 Agriculture, Appropriations, Examination of Comptroller's and Treasurer's Accounts, Municipal and Private Corporations

BILL PASSAGE RATES, 1997

	Total	Passed Legislature	Pct. Passed Legislature
Authored	33	7	21%
Sponsored	8	8	100%
Amendments	3	1	33%

ELECTORAL HISTORY IN CURRENT DISTRICT

	1994	1996	1998
Primary Election Opponent(s)	No	No	No
General Election Opponent(s)	Dem	Lib	No

House District 84

COUNTIES IN DISTRICT

Lubbock (part)

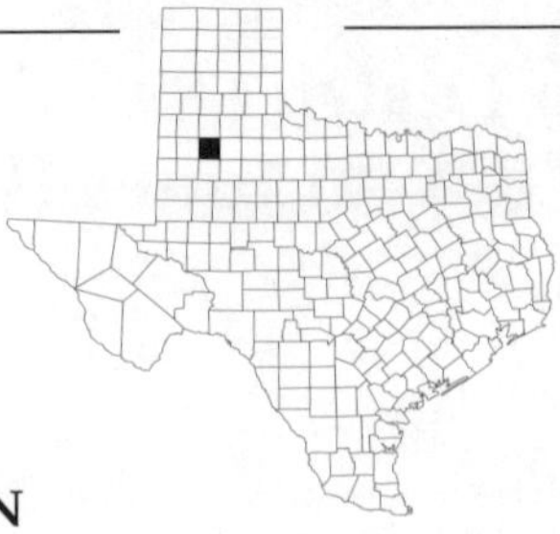

DEMOGRAPHIC INFORMATION

Population

Total	115,330
Anglo	85.2%
Black	2.8%
Hispanic	10.2%
Others	1.7%

Education

High School Graduates	86.8%
College Graduates	33.2%

Age of Population

5 years or less	7.8%
6-17 years	14.8%
18-64 years	67.1%
65 or older	10.3%

Wealth and Urbanization

Per capita Income	$15,096
Avg. House Value	$75,205
Percent Poverty	11.6%
Public Assistance	3.4%
Percent Urban	95.2%

Employed

Percent Employed	95.3%
Private Sector	69.2%

Household Types

Family households	77.3%
Non-family households	16.3%
Single-parent families	16.5%
Both parents working	68.3%

SENATE DISTRICTS IN HOUSE DISTRICT

Dist 28 Robert Duncan (R)

DISTRICT ELECTION DATA

House 1996

Don R. Richards (D)	42.1%
Carl H. Isett (R)	57.9%

President 1996

Bill Clinton (D)	25.2%
George Bush (R)	68.3%

Composite Party Vote 1994

Democratic	33.5%
Republican	52.1%

Registered Voters 1996	**78,081**
Turnout	47,120
Percent of registered voting	60.3%

House 1998

Carl H. Isett (R)	100.0%

House District 84
Rep. Carl H. Isett (R)

House Office
(512) 463-0676

District Office
P.O. Box 2910
Austin, Texas 78768
(512) 463-0676

Personal

Year of birth	1957
Family	Married to Cheri N. Isett, four children
Education	Texas Tech University, B.A., Accounting and Finance, M.S., Finance
Occupation	Accountant
Religion	Catholic
State legislative service	House 1997 to present

COMMITTEE ASSIGNMENT HISTORY
1997 Elections, State, Federal and International Relations

BILL PASSAGE RATES, 1997

	Total	Passed Legislature	Pct. Passed Legislature
Authored	17	1	6%
Sponsored	6	5	83%
Amendments	8	3	38%

ELECTORAL HISTORY IN CURRENT DISTRICT

	1994	1996	1998
Primary Election Opponent(s)	NA	NA	No
General Election Opponent(s)	NA	Dem	No

House District 85

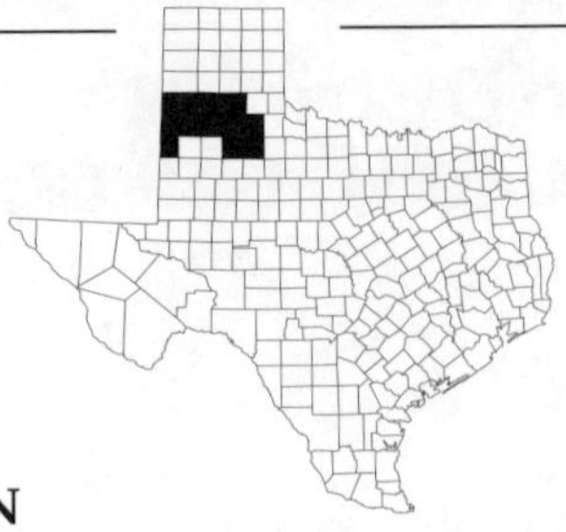

COUNTIES IN DISTRICT

Bailey, Briscoe, Castro, Cochran, Crosby, Dickens, Floyd, Hale, Lamb, Motley, Parmer, Swisher

DEMOGRAPHIC INFORMATION

Population

Total	110,125
Anglo	56.5%
Black	4.2%
Hispanic	38.9%
Others	0.6%

Education

High School Graduates	58.8%
College Graduates	11.0%

Age of Population

5 years or less	10.3%
6-17 years	21.2%
18-64 years	54.0%
65 or older	14.5%

Wealth and Urbanization

Per capita Income	$9,351
Avg. House Value	$40,870
Percent Poverty	25.5%
Public Assistance	8.7%
Percent Urban	49.1%

Employed

Percent Employed	93.2%
Private Sector	69.5%

Household Types

Family households	89.7%
Non-family households	8.9%
Single-parent families	15.0%
Both parents working	54.1%

SENATE DISTRICTS IN HOUSE DISTRICT

Dist 28 Robert Duncan (R)
Dist 30 Tom Haywood (R)
Dist 31 Teel Bivins (R)

DISTRICT ELECTION DATA

House 1996

James E. (Pete) Laney (D)	64.5%
Hollis Cain (R)	35.5%

President 1996

Bill Clinton (D)	39.9%
Bob Dole (R)	60.1%

Composite Party Vote 1994

Democratic	50.7%
Republican	49.3%

Registered Voters 1996	**60,691**
Turnout	34,225
Percent of registered voting	56.4%

House 1998

James E. (Pete) Laney (D)	73.5%
Hollis Cain (R)	26.5%

House District 85
Rep. James E. (Pete) Laney (D)

House Office
Room 2W.13, Capitol Building
Austin, Texas 78701
(512) 463-1000

District Office
P.O. Drawer 900
Hale Center, Texas 79041
(806) 839-2478

Personal

Year of birth	1943
Family	Married to Nelda Laney, three children
Education	Texas Tech University, B.S.
Occupation	Farmer
Religion	Church of Christ
State legislative service	House 1973 to present

COMMITTEE ASSIGNMENT HISTORY

1997 Speaker
1995 Speaker
1993 Speaker
1991 State Affairs (Chair)
1989 State Affairs (Chair)
1987 Government Organization, Science and Technology (Chair)
1985 Elections, House Administration, State Affairs (Chair)
1983 House Administration, State Affairs (Chair)
1981 Agriculture and Livestock, House Administration (Chair), Natural Resources
1979 Criminal Jurisprudence, Government Organization, House Administration (Chair)
1977 Criminal Jurisprudence, Environmental Affairs, House Administration (Chair)
1975 Elections, House Administration (Chair), Revenue and Taxation
1973 Agriculture and Livestock, Environmental Affairs

BILL PASSAGE RATES, 1997

	Total	Passed Legislature	Pct. Passed Legislature
Authored	0	0	NA
Sponsored	0	0	NA
Amendments	0	0	NA

ELECTORAL HISTORY IN CURRENT DISTRICT

	1994	1996	1998
Primary Election Opponent(s)	No	No	No
General Election Opponent(s)	No	Rep	Rep

House District 86

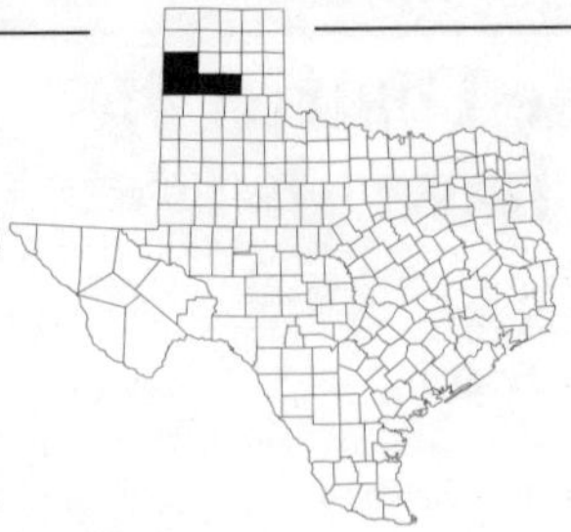

COUNTIES IN DISTRICT

Armstrong, Deaf Smith, Oldham, Randall

DEMOGRAPHIC INFORMATION

Population

Total	113,125
Anglo	83.8%
Black	1.3%
Hispanic	13.9%
Others	1.1%

Wealth and Urbanization

Per capita Income	$14,170
Avg. House Value	$69.616
Percent Poverty	12.3%
Public Assistance	4.1%
Percent Urban	81.6%

Education

High School Graduates	81.0%
College Graduates	23.7%

Employed

Percent Employed	95.1%
Private Sector	72.4%

Age of Population

5 years or less	9.2%
6-17 years	19.9%
18-64 years	60.7%
65 or older	10.2%

Household Types

Family households	87.1%
Non-family households	10.9%
Single-parent families	17.3%
Both parents working	66.3%

SENATE DISTRICTS IN HOUSE DISTRICT

Dist 30 Tom Haywood (R)

Dist 31 Teel Bivins (R)

DISTRICT ELECTION DATA

House 1996

John Smithee (R)	100.0%

House 1998

John Smithee (R)	100.0%

President 1996

Bill Clinton (D)	25.8%
Bob Dole (R)	74.2%

Composite Party Vote 1994

Democratic	36.0%
Republican	64.0%

Registered Voters 1996	**76,869**
Turnout	46,543
Percent of registered voting	60.5%

House District 86
Rep. John Smithee (R)

House Office
(512) 463-0702

District Office
P.O. Box 12076
Amarillo, Texas 79101
(806) 372-3327

Personal

Year of birth	1951
Family	Married to Becky Smithee, three children
Education	West Texas State University, B.B.A.
	Texas Tech University, J.D.
Occupation	Attorney
Religion	Christian
State legislative service	House 1985 to present

COMMITTEE ASSIGNMENT HISTORY

1997 Energy Resources, Insurance (Chair)
1995 Energy Resources, Insurance (Chair)
1993 Economic Development, Insurance (Chair)
1991 Government Organization, Judiciary (Vice-Chair)
1989 Business and Commerce, Judicial Affairs
1987 Energy, Judicial Affairs
1985 Judicial Affairs, Science and Technology

BILL PASSAGE RATES, 1997

	Total	Passed Legislature	Pct. Passed Legislature
Authored	27	8	30%
Sponsored	14	9	64%
Amendments	25	20	80%

ELECTORAL HISTORY IN CURRENT DISTRICT

	1994	1996	1998
Primary Election Opponent(s)	No	No	No
General Election Opponent(s)	No	No	No

House District 87

COUNTIES IN DISTRICT
Moore, Potter

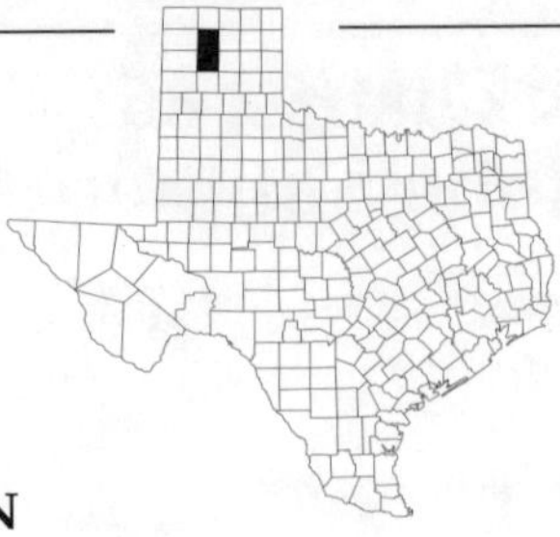

DEMOGRAPHIC INFORMATION

Population	
Total	115,739
Anglo	67.9%
Black	7.6%
Hispanic	21.5%
Others	3.2%

Wealth and Urbanization	
Per capita Income	$10,379
Avg. House Value	$48,926
Percent Poverty	21.1%
Public Assistance	7.1%
Percent Urban	90.3%

Education	
High School Graduates	66.9%
College Graduates	11.4%

Employed	
Percent Employed	92.2%
Private Sector	79.2%

Age of Population	
5 years or less	10.8%
6-17 years	18.4%
18-64 years	58.2%
65 or older	12.6%

Household Types	
Family households	85.4%
Non-family households	12.8%
Single-parent families	26.3%
Both parents working	62.3%

SENATE DISTRICTS IN HOUSE DISTRICT
Dist 31 Teel Bivins (R)

DISTRICT ELECTION DATA

House 1996	
David Swinford (R)	100.0%

House 1998	
David Swinford (R)	100.0%

President 1996	
Bill Clinton (D)	36.7%
Bob Dole (R)	63.3%

Composite Party Vote 1994	
Democratic	43.7%
Republican	56.3%

Registered Voters 1996	**59,517**
Turnout	31,735
Percent of registered voting	53.3%

House District 87
Rep. David Swinford (R)

House Office
(512) 463-0470

District Office
701 S. Taylor, #322
Amarillo, Texas 79101
(806) 374-8787

Personal

Year of birth	1941
Family	Married to Joyce Swinford, two children
Education	Texas Tech University, B.S.
Occupation	Agribusiness
Religion	Church of Christ
State legislative service	House 1991 to present

COMMITTEE ASSIGNMENT HISTORY

1997 Agriculture and Livestock (Vice-Chair), Appropriations, Local and Consent Calendars
1995 Agriculture and Livestock, Appropriations, Local and Consent Calendars
1993 Agriculture and Wildlife Management, Appropriations
1991 Agriculture and Livestock, Cultural and Historical Resources

BILL PASSAGE RATES, 1997

	Total	Passed Legislature	Pct. Passed Legislature
Authored	30	11	37%
Sponsored	5	4	80%
Amendments	23	21	91%

ELECTORAL HISTORY IN CURRENT DISTRICT

	1994	1996	1998
Primary Election Opponent(s)	No	No	No
General Election Opponent(s)	No	No	No

House District 88

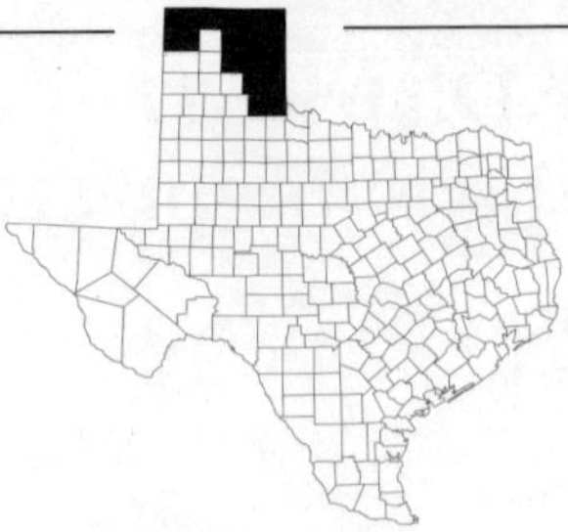

COUNTIES IN DISTRICT

Carson, Childress, Collingsworth, Dallam, Donley, Gray, Hall, Hansford, Hartley, Hemphill, Hutchinson, Lipscomb, Ochiltree, Roberts, Sherman, Wheeler

DEMOGRAPHIC INFORMATION

Population

Total	114,055
Anglo	85.0%
Black	2.5%
Hispanic	11.4%
Others	1.2%

Wealth and Urbanization

Per capita Income	$11,742
Avg. House Value	$43,673
Percent Poverty	15.5%
Public Assistance	5.4%
Percent Urban	50.6%

Education

High School Graduates	70.4%
College Graduates	12.6%

Employed

Percent Employed	95.2%
Private Sector	70.9%

Age of Population

5 years or less	8.5%
6-17 years	19.8%
18-64 years	55.0%
65 or older	16.7%

Household Types

Family households	88.0%
Non-family households	10.6%
Single-parent families	14.8%
Both parents working	57.9%

SENATE DISTRICTS IN HOUSE DISTRICT

Dist 30 Tom Haywood (R)

Dist 31 Teel Bivins (R)

DISTRICT ELECTION DATA

House 1996

Warren Chisum (R)	100.0%

House 1998

Warren Chisum (R)	100.0%

President 1996

Bill Clinton (D)	29.0%
Bob Dole (R)	71.0%

Composite Party Vote 1994

Democratic	40.1%
Republican	59.9%

Registered Voters 1996	**69,607**
Turnout	43,488
Percent of registered voting	62.5%

House District 88
Rep. Warren Chisum (R)

House Office
(512) 463-0736

District Office
P.O. Box 2061
Pampa, Texas 79066
(806) 665-3552

Personal

Year of birth	1938
Family	Married to Omega Chisum, two children
Education	High School
Occupation	Oil and gas producer, Rancher
Religion	Baptist
State legislative service	House 1989 to present

COMMITTEE ASSIGNMENT HISTORY

1997 County Affairs, Environmental Regulation (Chair), House Administration
1995 County Affairs, Environmental Regulation (Chair), House Administration
1993 County Affairs, Environmental Regulation (Chair), House Administration
1991 Corrections, County Affairs
1989 Corrections, County Affairs

BILL PASSAGE RATES, 1997

	Total	Passed Legislature	Pct. Passed Legislature
Authored	52	19	37%
Sponsored	9	5	56%
Amendments	38	26	68%

ELECTORAL HISTORY IN CURRENT DISTRICT

	1994	1996	1998
Primary Election Opponent(s)	No	No	No
General Election Opponent(s)	No	No	No

House District 89

COUNTIES IN DISTRICT

Tarrant (part)

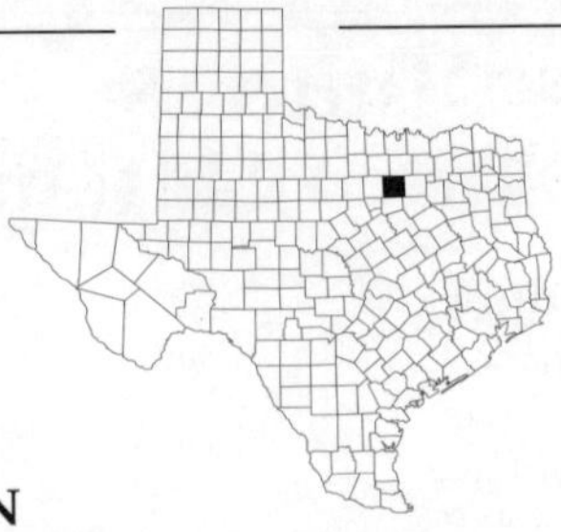

DEMOGRAPHIC INFORMATION

Population	
Total	117,840
Anglo	82.4%
Black	3.6%
Hispanic	11.9%
Others	2.2%

Education	
High School Graduates	74.0%
College Graduates	15.5%

Age of Population	
5 years or less	9.8%
6-17 years	16.4%
18-64 years	62.2%
65 or older	11.6%

Wealth and Urbanization	
Per capita Income	$13,011
Avg. House Value	$68,644
Percent Poverty	11.7%
Public Assistance	4.3%
Percent Urban	96.4%

Employed	
Percent Employed	93.2%
Private Sector	80.0%

Household Types	
Family households	84.1%
Non-family households	14.0%
Single-parent families	22.5%
Both parents working	66.1%

SENATE DISTRICTS IN HOUSE DISTRICT

Dist 9 Jane Nelson (R)
Dist 12 Mike Moncrief (D)
Dist 22 David Sibley (R)

DISTRICT ELECTION DATA

House 1996	
Homer Pete Dear (D)	44.9%
Sue Palmer (R)	55.1%

President 1996	
Bill Clinton (D)	48.6%
Bob Dole (R)	51.4%

Composite Party Vote 1994	
Democratic	49.8%
Republican	50.2%

Registered Voters 1996	**67,080**
Turnout	36,194
Percent of registered voting	54.0%

House 1998	
S. L. "Serge" De Leon (D)	37.6%
Sue Palmer (R)	62.4%

House District 89
Rep. Sue Palmer (R)

House Office
(512) 463-0610

District Office
P.O. Box 4590
Fort Worth, Texas 76164
(817) 740-7400

Personal

Year of birth	1942
Family	Married to Duke Palmer, five children
Education	Tarrant County Junior College
Occupation	President, Lucky Lady Oil
Religion	Methodist
State legislative service	House 1997 to present

COMMITTEE ASSIGNMENT HISTORY

1997 Rules and Resolutions, State, Federal and International Relations, State Recreational Resources

BILL PASSAGE RATES, 1997

	Total	Passed Legislature	Pct. Passed Legislature
Authored	11	4	36%
Sponsored	2	1	50%
Amendments	5	4	80%

ELECTORAL HISTORY IN CURRENT DISTRICT

	1994	1996	1998
Primary Election Opponent(s)	NA	Yes	No
General Election Opponent(s)	NA	Dem	Dem

House District 90

COUNTIES IN DISTRICT

Tarrant (part)

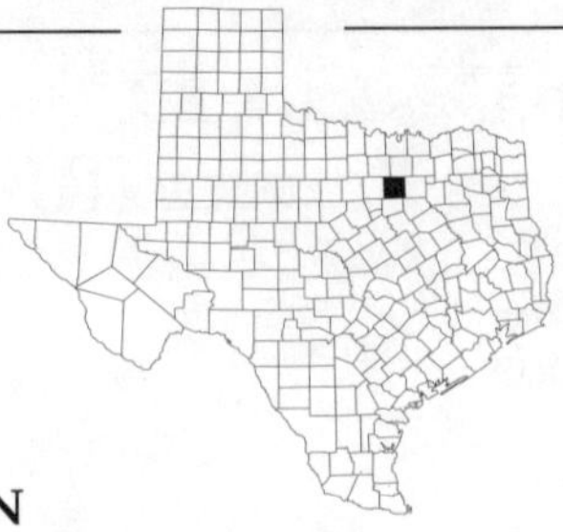

DEMOGRAPHIC INFORMATION

Population	
Total	114,291
Anglo	35.1%
Black	15.9%
Hispanic	47.2%
Others	2.3%

Education	
High School Graduates	48.1%
College Graduates	8.6%

Age of Population	
5 years or less	11.6%
6-17 years	19.0%
18-64 years	57.8%
65 or older	11.6%

Wealth and Urbanization	
Per capita Income	$7,695
Avg. House Value	$41,757
Percent Poverty	27.8%
Public Assistance	9.8%
Percent Urban	100%

Employed	
Percent Employed	89.3%
Private Sector	85.7%

Household Types	
Family households	83.5%
Non-family households	11.1%
Single-parent families	27.9%
Both parents working	55.2%

SENATE DISTRICTS IN HOUSE DISTRICT

Dist 12 Mike Moncrief (D)

DISTRICT ELECTION DATA

House 1996	
Lon Burnam (D)	100.0%

House 1998	
Lon Burnam (D)	100.0%

President 1996	
Bill Clinton (D)	73.6%
Bob Dole (R)	26.4%

Composite Party Vote 1994	
Democratic	69.7%
Republican	30.3%

Registered Voters 1996	**45,778**
Turnout	20,810
Percent of registered voting	45.5%

House District 90
Rep. Lon Burnam (D)

House Office
(512) 463-0740

District Office
P.O. Box 1894
Fort Worth, Texas 76101
(817) 877-5577

Personal

Year of birth	1953
Family	Married to Carol Roark, no children
Education	University of Texas, B.A., Government University of Texas at Arlington, M.A. Regional Planning
Occupation	Consultant
Religion	Quaker
State legislative service	House 1997 to present

COMMITTEE ASSIGNMENT HISTORY
1997 Insurance, Urban Affairs

BILL PASSAGE RATES, 1997

	Total	Passed Legislature	Pct. Passed Legislature
Authored	27	6	22%
Sponsored	6	5	83%
Amendments	18	8	44%

ELECTORAL HISTORY IN CURRENT DISTRICT

	1994	1996	1998
Primary Election Opponent(s)	NA	Yes	No
General Election Opponent(s)	NA	No	No

House District 91

COUNTIES IN DISTRICT

Tarrant (part)

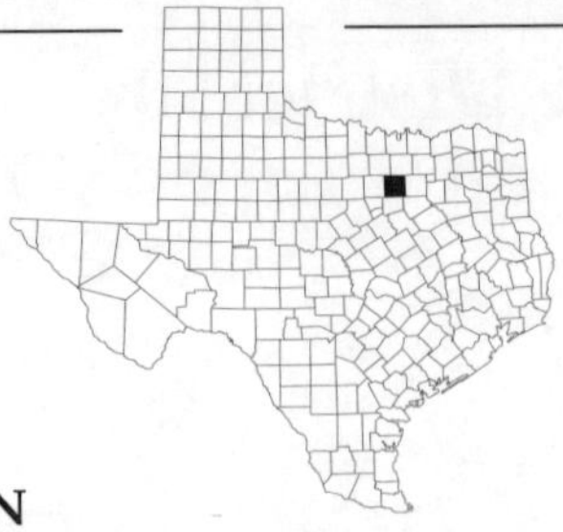

DEMOGRAPHIC INFORMATION

Population		Wealth and Urbanization	
Total	115,377	Per capita Income	$16,070
Anglo	83.7%	Avg. House Value	$86,900
Black	8.3%	Percent Poverty	6.2%
Hispanic	5.8%	Public Assistance	2.2%
Others	2.3%	Percent Urban	100%

Education		Employed	
High School Graduates	23.2%	Percent Employed	95.4%
College Graduates	86.2%	Private Sector	81.2%

Age of Population		Household Types	
5 years or less	10.5%	Family households	86.0%
6-17 years	16.1%	Non-family households	13.7%
18-64 years	65.6%	Single-parent families	19.2%
65 or older	7.8%	Both parents working	71.3%

SENATE DISTRICTS IN HOUSE DISTRICT

Dist 10 Chris Harris (R)

Dist 12 Mike Moncrief (D)

DISTRICT ELECTION DATA

House 1996		House 1998	
Bill G. Carter (R)	100.0%	Bill G. Carter (R)	100.0%

President 1996

Bill Clinton (D)	39.9%
Bob Dole (R)	60.1%

Composite Party Vote 1994

Democratic	38.0%
Republican	62.0%

Registered Voters 1996	**77,772**
Turnout	43,717
Percent of registered voting	56.2%

House District 91
Rep. Bill G. Carter (R)

House Office
(512) 463-0482

District Office
3525 Denton Highway, Suite A
Fort Worth, Texas 76117
(817) 834-1144

Personal

Year of birth	1928
Family	Married to Virginia Carter, six children
Education	Texas A&M University
Occupation	Insurance agent
Religion	Methodist
State legislative service	House 1984 (part) to present

COMMITTEE ASSIGNMENT HISTORY

1997 Local and Consent Calendars (Vice-Chair), Public Safety, State Affairs
1995 Public Safety, State Affairs
1993 Licensing and Administrative Procedures
1991 Public Safety, Rules and Resolutions (Chair), State, Federal and International Affairs
1989 Appropriations, Public Safety
1987 Corrections (Vice-Chair), Transportation
1985 Elections, Insurance
1984 County Affairs, Urban Affairs

BILL PASSAGE RATES, 1997

	Total	Passed Legislature	Pct. Passed Legislature
Authored	22	7	32%
Sponsored	7	5	71%
Amendments	29	28	97%

ELECTORAL HISTORY IN CURRENT DISTRICT

	1994	1996	1998
Primary Election Opponent(s)	No	No	No
General Election Opponent(s)	Dem	No	No

House District 92

COUNTIES IN DISTRICT
Tarrant (part)

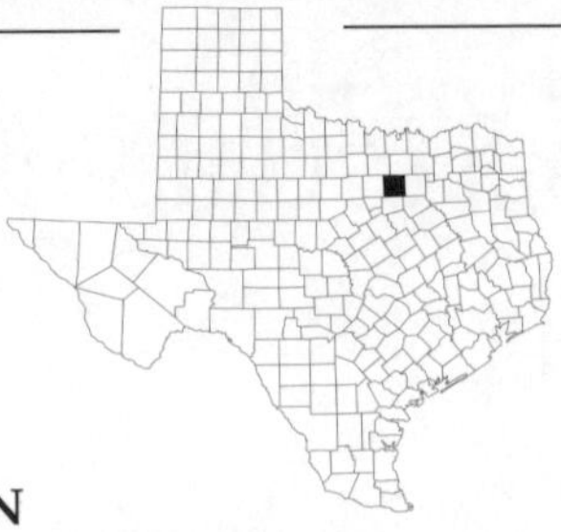

DEMOGRAPHIC INFORMATION

Population	
Total	118,313
Anglo	86.7%
Black	3.9%
Hispanic	6.0%
Others	3.6%

Wealth and Urbanization	
Per capita Income	$17,662
Avg. House Value	$93,142
Percent Poverty	5.7%
Public Assistance	1.8%
Percent Urban	100%

Education	
High School Graduates	88.6%
College Graduates	27.6%

Employed	
Percent Employed	95.8%
Private Sector	86.4%

Age of Population	
5 years or less	8.8%
6-17 years	15.4%
18-64 years	70.1%
65 or older	5.7%

Household Types	
Family households	81.9%
Non-family households	17.4%
Single-parent families	21.7%
Both parents working	71.4%

SENATE DISTRICTS IN HOUSE DISTRICT

Dist 9 Jane Nelson (R)
Dist 10 Chris Harris (R)
Dist 12 Mike Moncrief (D)

DISTRICT ELECTION DATA

House 1996	
Todd Smith (R)	100.0%

House 1998	
Todd Smith (R)	100.0%

President 1996	
Bill Clinton (D)	37.6%
Bob Dole (R)	62.4%

Composite Party Vote 1994	
Democratic	35.1%
Republican	64.9%

Registered Voters 1996	**79,690**
Turnout	43,995
Percent of registered voting	55.2%

House District 92
Rep. Todd Smith (R)

House Office
(512) 463-0522

District Office
1404 Brown Trail
Bedford, Texas 76022
(817) 285-9797

Personal

Year of birth	1963
Family	Married to Nancy McKinney Smith, two children
Education	Southern Methodist University, B.A. University of Texas at Austin, J.D.
Occupation	Attorney
Religion	Baptist
State legislative service	House 1997 to present

COMMITTEE ASSIGNMENT HISTORY
1997 Financial Institutions, Juvenile Justice and Family Issues

BILL PASSAGE RATES, 1997

	Total	Passed Legislature	Pct. Passed Legislature
Authored	20	2	10%
Sponsored	3	1	33%
Amendments	7	7	100%

ELECTORAL HISTORY IN CURRENT DISTRICT

	1994	1996	1998
Primary Election Opponent(s)	NA	Yes	No
General Election Opponent(s)	NA	No	No

House District 93

COUNTIES IN DISTRICT
Tarrant (part)

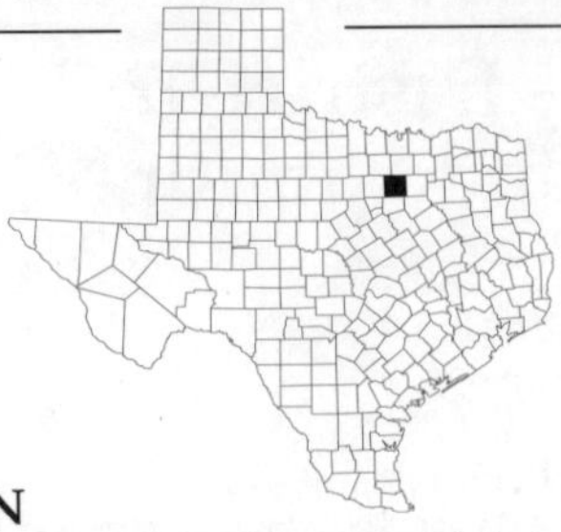

DEMOGRAPHIC INFORMATION

Population		Wealth and Urbanization	
Total	118,561	Per capita Income	$14,679
Anglo	70.4%	Avg. House Value	$80,697
Black	12.2%	Percent Poverty	11.2%
Hispanic	12.9%	Public Assistance	3.2%
Others	4.7%	Percent Urban	100%

Education		Employed	
High School Graduates	83.9%	Percent Employed	94.7%
College Graduates	24.2%	Private Sector	85.6%

Age of Population		Household Types	
5 years or less	10.9%	Family households	79.0%
6-17 years	15.2%	Non-family households	20.4%
18-64 years	69.7%	Single-parent families	23.7%
65 or older	4.3%	Both parents working	66.5%

SENATE DISTRICTS IN HOUSE DISTRICT

Dist 9 Jane Nelson (R)
Dist 10 Chris Harris (R)
Dist 23 Royce West (D)

DISTRICT ELECTION DATA

House 1996		House 1998	
Toby Goodman (R)	100%	Toby Goodman (R)	100.0%

President 1996	
Bill Clinton (D)	45.9%
Bob Dole (R)	54.1%

Composite Party Vote 1994	
Democratic	41.0%
Republican	59.0%

Registered Voters 1996	**69,289**
Turnout	33,399
Percent of registered voting	48.2%

House District 93
Rep. Toby Goodman (R)

House Office
(512) 463-0562

District Office
1600 East Lamar, Suite 115
Arlington, Texas 76011
(817) 460-8290

Personal

Year of birth	1948
Family	Married to Gloria Goodman, three children
Education	Texas Christian University, B.S.
	Baylor University, J.D.
Occupation	Attorney
Religion	Baptist
State legislative service	House 1991 to present

COMMITTEE ASSIGNMENT HISTORY

1997 Civil Practices, Juvenile Justice and Family Issues (Chair)
1995 Judicial Affairs, Juvenile Justice and Family Issues (Chair)
1993 Judicial Affairs, State Affairs
1991 Judicial Affairs, Judiciary

BILL PASSAGE RATES, 1997

	Total	Passed Legislature	Pct. Passed Legislature
Authored	51	13	25%
Sponsored	27	25	93%
Amendments	25	24	96%

ELECTORAL HISTORY IN CURRENT DISTRICT

	1994	1996	1998
Primary Election Opponent(s)	No	No	No
General Election Opponent(s)	No	No	No

House District 94

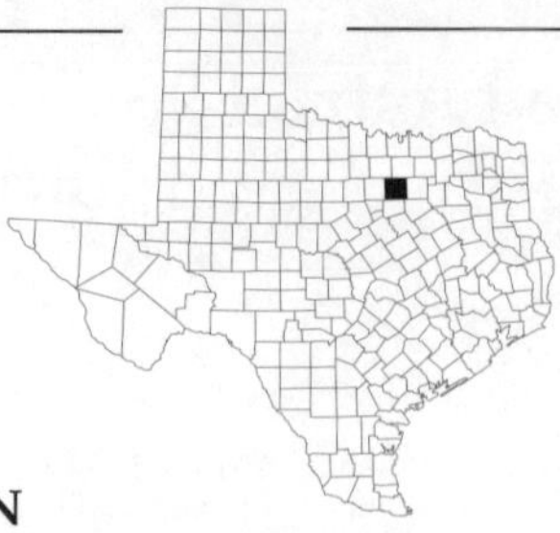

COUNTIES IN DISTRICT

Tarrant (part)

DEMOGRAPHIC INFORMATION

Population	
Total	117,538
Anglo	84.1%
Black	5.4%
Hispanic	6.2%
Others	4.4%

Wealth and Urbanization	
Per capita Income	$17,439
Avg. House Value	$105,518
Percent Poverty	8.0%
Public Assistance	2.8%
Percent Urban	100%

Education	
High School Graduates	89.8%
College Graduates	34.6%

Employed	
Percent Employed	95.0%
Private Sector	79.5%

Age of Population	
5 years or less	8.6%
6-17 years	17.2%
18-64 years	67.1%
65 or older	7.1%

Household Types	
Family households	85.9%
Non-family households	12.7%
Single-parent families	19.6%
Both parents working	68.8%

SENATE DISTRICTS IN HOUSE DISTRICT

Dist 10 Chris Harris (R)

DISTRICT ELECTION DATA

House 1996	
David Offutt (NLP)	11.3%
Kent Grusendorf (R)	88.7%

House 1998	
Kent Grusendorf (R)	100.0%

President 1996	
Bill Clinton (D)	36.6%
Bob Dole (R)	63.4%

Composite Party Vote 1994	
Democratic	35.0%
Republican	65.0%

Registered Voters 1996	**79,798**
Turnout	46,795
Percent of registered voting	58.6%

House District 94
Rep. Kent Grusendorf (R)

House Office
(512) 463-0624
Kent.Grusendorf@house.state.tx.us

District Office
1221 West Nathan Lowe Road
Arlington, Texas 76017
(817) 465-9411

Personal

Year of birth	1939
Family	Single, no children
Education	University of Texas at Arlington, B.B.A.
Occupation	President, Cyco Manufacturing
Religion	Baptist
State legislative service	House 1987 to present

COMMITTEE ASSIGNMENT HISTORY

1997 Financial Institutions, Redistricting, Ways and Means
1995 Financial Institutions, Public Education, Redistricting
1993 Elections, Public Education
1991 Public Education, Redistricting, Transportation
1989 Corrections, Public Education, Redistricting
1987 Human Services, Public Education

BILL PASSAGE RATES, 1997

	Total	Passed Legislature	Pct. Passed Legislature
Authored	10	3	30%
Sponsored	0	0	NA
Amendments	33	21	64%

ELECTORAL HISTORY IN CURRENT DISTRICT

	1994	1996	1998
Primary Election Opponent(s)	No	No	Yes
General Election Opponent(s)	Dem	NLP	No

House District 95

COUNTIES IN DISTRICT
Tarrant (part)

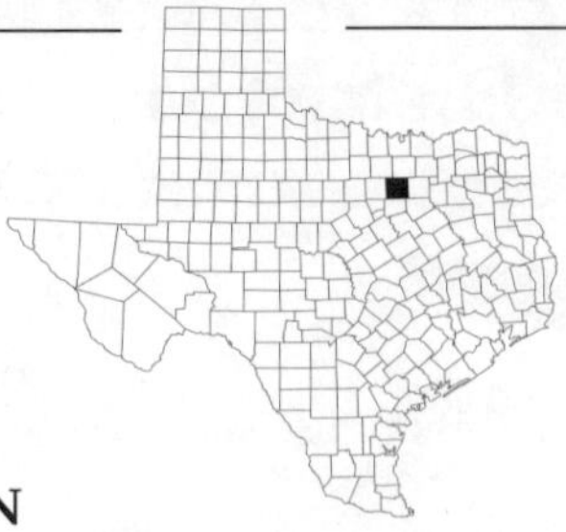

DEMOGRAPHIC INFORMATION

Population		**Wealth and Urbanization**	
Total	113,674	Per capita Income	$8,649
Anglo	31.2%	Avg. House Value	$45,837
Black	57.7%	Percent Poverty	25.0%
Hispanic	10.6%	Public Assistance	11.8%
Others	1.2%	Percent Urban	99.9%

Education		**Employed**	
High School Graduates	62.3%	Percent Employed	88.5%
College Graduates	8.2%	Private Sector	79.6%

Age of Population		**Household Types**	
5 years or less	10.6%	Family households	88.2%
6-17 years	19.6%	Non-family households	9.6%
18-64 years	58.7%	Single-parent families	38.7%
65 or older	11.1%	Both parents working	66.4%

SENATE DISTRICTS IN HOUSE DISTRICT

Dist 12 Mike Moncrief (D)

DISTRICT ELECTION DATA

House 1996		**House 1998**	
Glenn O. Lewis (D)	100.0%	Glenn O. Lewis (D)	100.0%

President 1996	
Bill Clinton (D)	84.5%
Bob Dole (R)	15.5%

Composite Party Vote 1994	
Democratic	81.5%
Republican	18.5%

Registered Voters 1996	**63,789**
Turnout	31,633
Percent of registered voting	49.6%

House District 95
Rep. Glenn O. Lewis (D)

House Office
(512) 463-0716
Glenn.Lewis@house.state.tx.us

District Office
100 Circle Drive, #200
Fort Worth, Texas 76119
(817) 536-6772

Personal

Year of birth	1954
Family	Married to Arveda Lewis, two children
Education	Tarrant County Junior College, A.A. Texas Wesleyan College, B.A. University of Texas, J.D.
Occupation	Attorney
Religion	Baptist
State legislative service	House 1995 to present

COMMITTEE ASSIGNMENT HISTORY

1997 County Affairs, Insurance, Rules and Resolutions
1995 County Affairs, Insurance

BILL PASSAGE RATES, 1997

	Total	Passed Legislature	Pct. Passed Legislature
Authored	52	11	21%
Sponsored	5	3	60%
Amendments	16	11	69%

ELECTORAL HISTORY IN CURRENT DISTRICT

	1994	1996	1998
Primary Election Opponent(s)	Yes	No	No
General Election Opponent(s)	No	No	No

House District 96

COUNTIES IN DISTRICT

Tarrant (part)

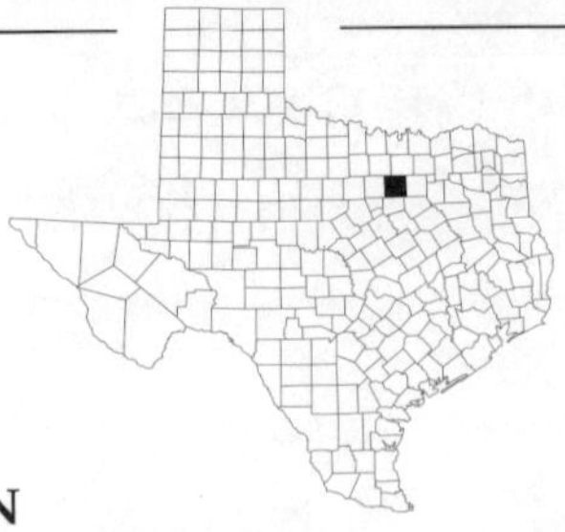

DEMOGRAPHIC INFORMATION

Population		**Wealth and Urbanization**	
Total	118,517	Per capita Income	$15,994
Anglo	82.2%	Avg. House Value	$88,441
Black	7.8%	Percent Poverty	4.5%
Hispanic	7.1%	Public Assistance	1.7%
Others	3.1%	Percent Urban	97.7%

Education		**Employed**	
High School Graduates	86.9%	Percent Employed	95.8%
College Graduates	28.1%	Private Sector	80.6%

Age of Population		**Household Types**	
5 years or less	11.8%	Family households	91.1%
6-17 years	18.9%	Non-family households	8.4%
18-64 years	64.7%	Single-parent families	13.0%
65 or older	4.6%	Both parents working	67.3%

SENATE DISTRICTS IN HOUSE DISTRICT

Dist 10 Chris Harris (R)

Dist 12 Mike Moncrief (D)

DISTRICT ELECTION DATA

House 1996		**House 1998**	
Kenneth (Kim) Brimer (R)	100.0%	Kenneth (Kim) Brimer (R)	100.0%

President 1996	
Bill Clinton (D)	41.1%
Bob Dole (R)	58.9%

Composite Party Vote 1994	
Democratic	38.9%
Republican	61.1%

Registered Voters 1996	**84,081**
Turnout	47,931
Percent of registered voting	57.0%

House District 96
Rep. Kenneth (Kim) Brimer (R)

House Office
(512) 463-0632

District Office
P.O. Box 170154
Arlington, Texas 76003
(817) 483-9793

Personal

Year of birth	1945
Family	Married to Janna Brimer, two children
Education	Stephen F. Austin State University, B.S.
Occupation	Insurance agent
Religion	Methodist
State legislative service	House 1989 to present

COMMITTEE ASSIGNMENT HISTORY

1997 Business and Industry (Chair), Calendars, State Affairs
1995 Business and Industry (Chair), Calendars, Licensing and Administrative Procedures
1993 Business and Industry (Chair), Calendars, Insurance
1991 Business and Commerce, Insurance, Local and Consent Calendars (Vice-Chair)
1989 Cultural and Historic Resources, Insurance

BILL PASSAGE RATES, 1997

	Total	Passed Legislature	Pct. Passed Legislature
Authored	55	14	25%
Sponsored	16	11	69%
Amendments	14	13	93%

ELECTORAL HISTORY IN CURRENT DISTRICT

	1994	1996	1998
Primary Election Opponent(s)	No	No	No
General Election Opponent(s)	No	No	No

House District 97

COUNTIES IN DISTRICT

Tarrant (part)

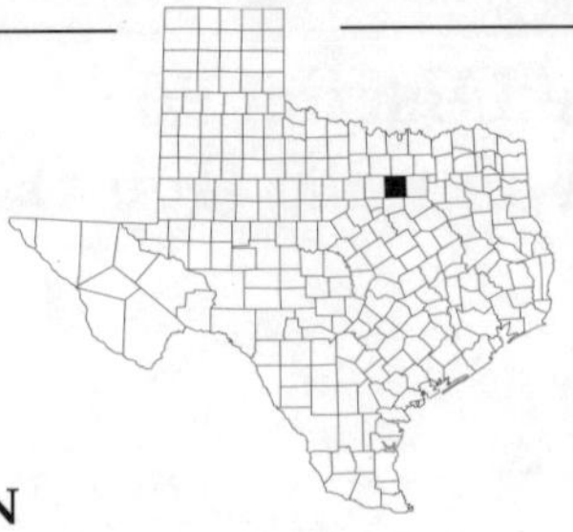

DEMOGRAPHIC INFORMATION

Population

Total	118,332
Anglo	86.5%
Black	5.0%
Hispanic	6.1%
Others	2.5%

Wealth and Urbanization

Per capita Income	$22,855
Avg. House Value	$123,663
Percent Poverty	6.0%
Public Assistance	2.1%
Percent Urban	99.0%

Education

High School Graduates	90.7%
College Graduates	40.6%

Employed

Percent Employed	96.3%
Private Sector	79.3%

Age of Population

5 years or less	7.4%
6-17 years	12.7%
18-64 years	66.1%
65 or older	13.8%

Household Types

Family households	78.9%
Non-family households	18.5%
Single-parent families	17.7%
Both parents working	64.2%

SENATE DISTRICTS IN HOUSE DISTRICT

Dist 10 Chris Harris (R)

Dist 12 Mike Moncrief (D)

DISTRICT ELECTION DATA

House 1996

Anna Mowery (R)	100.0%

House 1998

Anna Mowery (R)	100.0%

President 1996

Bill Clinton (D)	38.4%
Bob Dole (R)	61.6%

Composite Party Vote 1994

Democratic	38.1%
Republican	61.9%

Registered Voters 1996	**85,094**
Turnout	54,347
Percent of registered voting	63.9%

House District 97
Rep. Anna Mowery (R)

House Office
(512) 463-0608

District Office
4100 International Plaza Tower II, #534
Fort Worth, Texas 76109
(817) 732-1372

Personal

Year of birth	1931
Family	Married to Wesley Mowery, four children
Education	Baylor University, B.A., Drama/Speech, Political Science Central State University, Master of Teaching
Occupation	State representative
Religion	Baptist
State legislative service	House 1988 (part) to present

COMMITTEE ASSIGNMENT HISTORY

1997 Appropriations, Land and Resource Management
1995 Appropriations, (Vice-Chair) Land and Resource Management (Vice-Chair)
1993 Appropriations, Business and Industry (Vice-Chair), House Administration
1991 Elections (Vice-Chair), Labor and Employment Relations
1989 Elections, Labor and Employment Relations
1988 NA

BILL PASSAGE RATES, 1997

	Total	Passed Legislature	Pct. Passed Legislature
Authored	11	1	9%
Sponsored	2	2	100%
Amendments	3	3	100%

ELECTORAL HISTORY IN CURRENT DISTRICT

	1994	1996	1998
Primary Election Opponent(s)	Yes	No	No
General Election Opponent(s)	Dem	No	No

House District 98

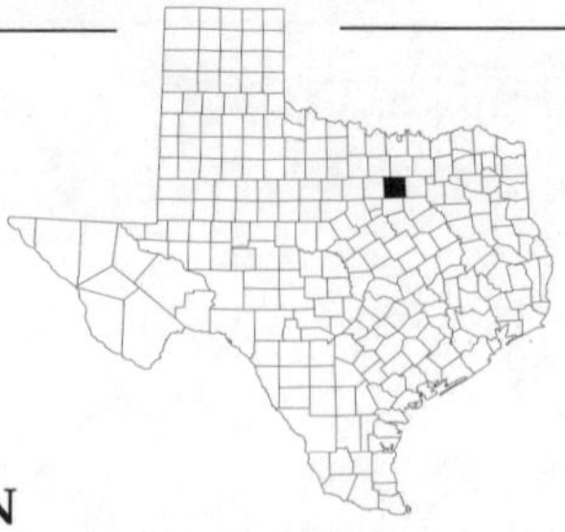

COUNTIES IN DISTRICT

Tarrant (part)

DEMOGRAPHIC INFORMATION

Population

Total	117,660
Anglo	87.9%
Black	2.2%
Hispanic	6.7%
Others	3.2%

Wealth and Urbanization

Per capita Income	$16,614
Avg. House Value	$100,643
Percent Poverty	6.5%
Public Assistance	2.7%
Percent Urban	97.3%

Education

High School Graduates	81.7%
College Graduates	24.0%

Employed

Percent Employed	95.9%
Private Sector	84.3%

Age of Population

5 years or less	10.6%
6-17 years	18.1%
18-64 years	64.5%
65 or older	6.8%

Household Types

Family households	88.8%
Non-family households	9.8%
Single-parent families	14.6%
Both parents working	67.0%

SENATE DISTRICTS IN HOUSE DISTRICT

Dist 9 Jane Nelson (R)

Dist 10 Chris Harris (R)

Dist 12 Mike Moncrief (D)

DISTRICT ELECTION DATA

House 1996

Nancy Moffat (R)	100.0%

House 1998

Gene Mitchell (D)	23.5%
Vicki Truitt (R)	76.5%

President 1996

Bill Clinton (D)	33.9%
Bob Dole (R)	66.1%

Composite Party Vote 1994

Democratic	33.0%
Republican	67.0%

Registered Voters 1996	**89,844**
Turnout	52,666
Percent of registered voting	58.6%

House District 98
Rep. Vicki Truitt (R)

House Office
(512) 463-0690

District Office
1342 Johnson Road
Keller, Texas 76248-4205
(817) 379-5727

Personal

Year of birth	1954
Family	Married to Jim Truitt, two children
Education	High School
Occupation	Health Care Consultant
Religion	Catholic
State legislative service	House 1999 to present

COMMITTEE ASSIGNMENT HISTORY

BILL PASSAGE RATES, 1997

	Total	Passed Legislature	Pct. Passed Legislature
Authored	NA	NA	NA
Sponsored	NA	NA	NA
Amendments	NA	NA	NA

ELECTORAL HISTORY IN CURRENT DISTRICT

	1994	1996	1998
Primary Election Opponent(s)	NA	NA	Yes
General Election Opponent(s)	NA	NA	Dem

House District 99

COUNTIES IN DISTRICT
Dallas (part)

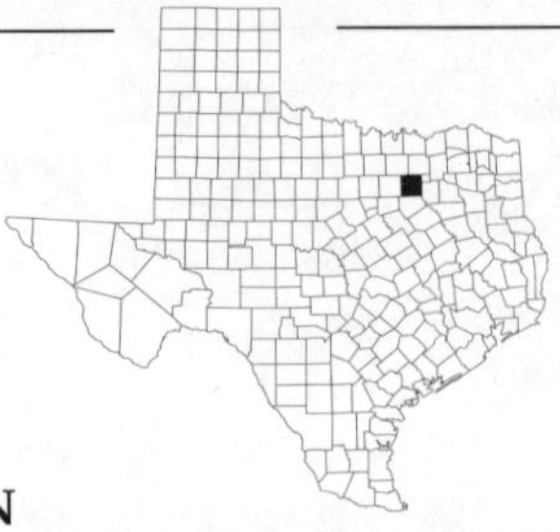

DEMOGRAPHIC INFORMATION

Population	
Total	118,397
Anglo	75.0%
Black	6.1%
Hispanic	14.0%
Others	5.1%

Wealth and Urbanization	
Per capita Income	$21,639
Avg. House Value	$131,606
Percent Poverty	7.0%
Public Assistance	1.6%
Percent Urban	100%

Education	
High School Graduates	87.9%
College Graduates	37.6%

Employed	
Percent Employed	95.9%
Private Sector	86.8%

Age of Population	
5 years or less	9.2%
6-17 years	12.2%
18-64 years	73.3%
65 or older	5.4%

Household Types	
Family households	77.3%
Non-family households	22.5%
Single-parent families	20.2%
Both parents working	70.1%

SENATE DISTRICTS IN HOUSE DISTRICT

Dist 8 Florence Shapiro (R)
Dist 9 Jane Nelson (R)

DISTRICT ELECTION DATA

House 1996	
Ken Marchant (R)	100.0%

House 1998	
Ken Marchant (R)	100.0%

President 1996	
Bill Clinton (D)	33.7%
Bob Dole (R)	66.3%

Composite Party Vote 1994	
Democratic	29.8%
Republican	69.1%

Registered Voters 1996	**84,626**
Turnout	46,391
Percent of registered voting	54.8%

House District 99
Rep. Ken Marchant (R)

House Office
(512) 463-0468

District Office
1452 Halsey Way, Suite 102
Carrollton, Texas 75007
(972) 418-6100

Personal

Year of birth	1951
Family	Married to Donna Marchant, four children
Education	Southern Nazarene, B.A. Nazarene Theological Seminary
Occupation	Investor
Religion	Nazarene
State legislative service	House 1987 to present

COMMITTEE ASSIGNMENT HISTORY

1997 Corrections, Financial Institutions (Chair), Redistricting
1995 Financial Institutions (Chair), Redistricting, Ways and Means
1993 Investments and Banking (Chair), Redistricting, State Affairs
1991 Financial Institutions, Redistricting, State Affairs
1989 Financial Institutions, State, Federal and International Relations
1987 Financial Institutions, Urban Affairs

BILL PASSAGE RATES, 1997

	Total	Passed Legislature	Pct. Passed Legislature
Authored	20	6	30%
Sponsored	7	6	86%
Amendments	10	9	90%

ELECTORAL HISTORY IN CURRENT DISTRICT

	1994	1996	1998
Primary Election Opponent(s)	No	No	No
General Election Opponent(s)	No	No	No

House District 100

COUNTIES IN DISTRICT

Dallas (part)

DEMOGRAPHIC INFORMATION

Population	
Total	107,320
Anglo	34.0%
Black	50.1%
Hispanic	14.7%
Others	2.0%

Education	
High School Graduates	63.1%
College Graduates	15.0%

Age of Population	
5 years or less	9.5%
6-17 years	16.4%
18-64 years	61.1%
65 or older	13.0%

Wealth and Urbanization	
Per capita Income	$10,684
Avg. House Value	$66,586
Percent Poverty	29.9%
Public Assistance	12.8%
Percent Urban	100%

Employed	
Percent Employed	87.7%
Private Sector	81.4%

Household Types	
Family households	78.5%
Non-family households	16.3%
Single-parent families	47.6%
Both parents working	59.2%

SENATE DISTRICTS IN HOUSE DISTRICT

Dist 2 David Cain (D)
Dist 3 Drew Nixon (R)
Dist 8 Florence Shapiro (R)
Dist 16 John J. Carona (R)
Dist 23 Royce West (D)

DISTRICT ELECTION DATA

House 1996	
Terri Hodge (D)	68.6%
Joe Granado (R)	29.3%
Mike Neder (L)	2.1%

President 1996	
Bill Clinton (D)	71.4%
Bob Dole (R)	28.6%

Composite Party Vote 1994	
Democratic	65.3%
Republican	32.3%

Registered Voters 1996	**58,380**
Turnout	27,126
Percent of registered voting	46.5%

House 1998	
Terri Hodge (D)	100.0%

House District 100
Rep. Terri Hodge (D)

House Office
(512) 463-0586

District Office
4032 Swiss Ave.
Dallas, Texas 75231
(214) 824-1996
(214) 828-2330 (Fax)

Personal

Year of birth	1940
Family	Single, one child
Education	High school graduate
Occupation	Retired
Religion	Lutheran
State legislative service	House 1997 to present

COMMITTEE ASSIGNMENT HISTORY
1997 Elections, Urban Affairs

BILL PASSAGE RATES, 1997

	Total	Passed Legislature	Pct. Passed Legislature
Authored	12	5	42%
Sponsored	3	3	100%
Amendments	1	1	100%

ELECTORAL HISTORY IN CURRENT DISTRICT

	1994	1996	1998
Primary Election Opponent(s)	NA	Yes	Yes
General Election Opponent(s)	NA	Rep, Lib	No

House District 101

COUNTIES IN DISTRICT
Dallas (part)

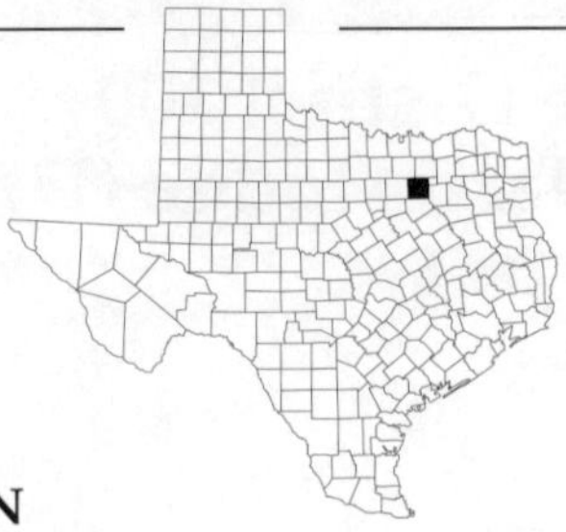

DEMOGRAPHIC INFORMATION

Population	
Total	118,405
Anglo	81.6%
Black	6.0%
Hispanic	8.9%
Others	3.6%

Wealth and Urbanization	
Per capita Income	$15,442
Avg. House Value	$77,580
Percent Poverty	5.5%
Public Assistance	2.7%
Percent Urban	97.9%

Education	
High School Graduates	83.9%
College Graduates	21.3%

Employed	
Percent Employed	95.6%
Private Sector	81.0%

Age of Population	
5 years or less	10.6%
6-17 years	17.9%
18-64 years	66.3%
65 or older	5.2%

Household Types	
Family households	88.2%
Non-family households	11.4%
Single-parent families	19.1%
Both parents working	72.3%

SENATE DISTRICTS IN HOUSE DISTRICT

Dist 16 John J. Carona (R)

DISTRICT ELECTION DATA

House 1996	
Elvira Reyna (R)	100.0%

House 1998	
Elvira Reyna (R)	100.0%

President 1996	
Bill Clinton (D)	41.5%
Bob Dole (R)	58.5%

Composite Party Vote 1994	
Democratic	35.1%
Republican	63.7%

Registered Voters 1996	**69,082**
Turnout	36,361
Percent of registered voting	52.6%

House District 101
Rep. Elvira Reyna (R)

House Office
(512) 463-0464

District Office
18601 LBJ Freeway, Ste. 700
Mesquite, Texas 75150
(972) 279-7030

Personal

Year of birth	1950
Family	Married to J. A. Reyna, two children
Education	Eastfield Community College, A.A.
	University of Texas Arlington, B.A.
Occupation	State representative
Religion	Baptist
State legislative service	1993 (part) to present

COMMITTEE ASSIGNMENT HISTORY
1997 Higher Education, Public Safety
1995 Higher Education, State, Federal and International Relations
1993 NA

BILL PASSAGE RATES, 1997

	Total	Passed Legislature	Pct. Passed Legislature
Authored	11	5	45%
Sponsored	5	5	100%
Amendments	3	3	100%

ELECTORAL HISTORY IN CURRENT DISTRICT

	1994	1996	1998
Primary Election Opponent(s)	Yes	No	Yes
General Election Opponent(s)	Dem	No	No

House District 102

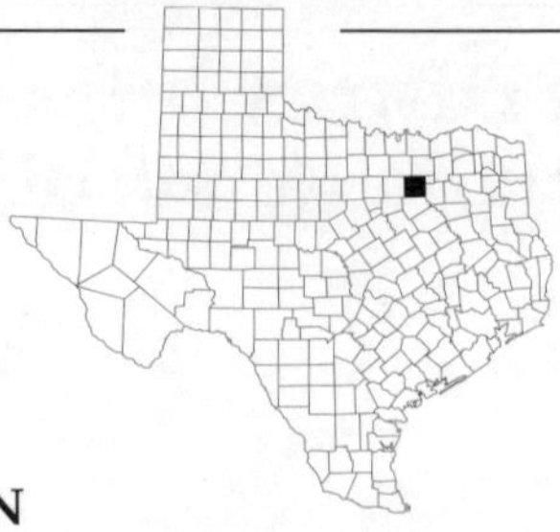

COUNTIES IN DISTRICT
Dallas (part)

DEMOGRAPHIC INFORMATION

Population

Total	118,514
Anglo	75.0%
Black	10.5%
Hispanic	8.7%
Others	6.0%

Wealth and Urbanization

Per capita Income	$25,609
Avg. House Value	$184,566
Percent Poverty	7.4%
Public Assistance	2.0%
Percent Urban	100.0%

Education

High School Graduates	91.7%
College Graduates	46.2%

Employed

Percent Employed	95.7%
Private Sector	84.2%

Age of Population

5 years or less	8.0%
6-17 years	14.4%
18-64 years	70.0%
65 or older	7.5%

Household Types

Family households	78.1%
Non-family households	21.9%
Single-parent families	23.7%
Both parents working	64.8%

SENATE DISTRICTS IN HOUSE DISTRICT

Dist 8 Florence Shapiro (R)
Dist 16 John J. Carona (R)

DISTRICT ELECTION DATA

House 1996

Tony Goolsby (R)	100.0%

House 1998

Tony Goolsby (R)	100.0%

President 1996

Bill Clinton (D)	37.2%
Bob Dole (R)	62.8%

Composite Party Vote 1994

Democratic	32.9%
Republican	66.0%

Registered Voters 1996	**71,606**
Turnout	41,931
Percent of registered voting	58.6%

House District 102
Rep. Tony Goolsby (R)

House Office
(512) 463-0454

District Office
9696 Skillman, Suite 210
Dallas, Texas 75243
(214) 503-1900

Personal

Year of birth	1933
Family	Married to Toppy Goolsby, three children
Education	University of North Texas, B.S.
Occupation	Insurance investments
Religion	Methodist
State legislative service	House 1989 to present

COMMITTEE ASSIGNMENT HISTORY

1997 House Administration (Chair), Licensing and Administrative Procedures, Pensions and Investments

1995 Higher Education, House Administration (Vice-Chair), Licensing and Administrative Procedures

1993 Higher Education, House Administration (Vice-Chair), Licensing and Administrative Procedures

1991 House Administration, Liquor Regulation, Retirement and Aging

1989 Elections, Liquor Regulation

BILL PASSAGE RATES, 1997

	Total	Passed Legislature	Pct. Passed Legislature
Authored	39	11	28%
Sponsored	8	6	75%
Amendments	10	9	90%

ELECTORAL HISTORY IN CURRENT DISTRICT

	1994	1996	1998
Primary Election Opponent(s)	No	No	No
General Election Opponent(s)	No	No	No

House District 103

COUNTIES IN DISTRICT

Dallas (part)

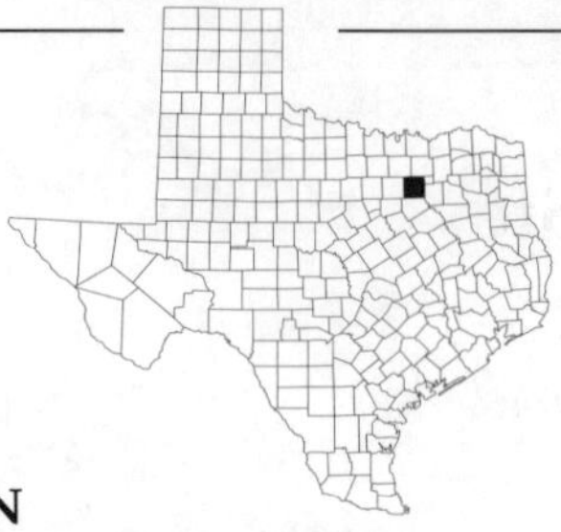

DEMOGRAPHIC INFORMATION

Population		**Wealth and Urbanization**	
Total	115,993	Per capita Income	$13,215
Anglo	44.1%	Avg. House Value	$110,407
Black	15.9%	Percent Poverty	21.0%
Hispanic	36.8%	Public Assistance	5.2%
Others	4.1%	Percent Urban	100.0%

Education		**Employed**	
High School Graduates	68.1%	Percent Employed	92.0%
College Graduates	20.5%	Private Sector	86.6%

Age of Population		**Household Types**	
5 years or less	10.7%	Family households	74.6%
6-17 years	14.0%	Non-family households	24.6%
18-64 years	67.7%	Single-parent families	34.5%
65 or older	7.6%	Both parents working	65.6%

SENATE DISTRICTS IN HOUSE DISTRICT

Dist 2 David Cain (D)
Dist 8 Florence Shapiro (R)
Dist 9 Jane Nelson (R)
Dist 23 Royce West (D)

DISTRICT ELECTION DATA

House 1996		**House 1998**	
Steve Wolens (D)	100.0%	Steve Wolens (D)	100.0%

President 1996	
Bill Clinton (D)	59.8%
Bob Dole (R)	40.2%

Composite Party Vote 1994	
Democratic	54.3%
Republican	43.7%

Registered Voters 1996	**47,924**
Turnout	22,501
Percent of registered voting	47.0%

House District 103
Rep. Steve Wolens (D)

House Office
(512) 463-0746

District Office
3102 Oak Lawn Ave., #1100
Dallas, Texas 75219-4281
(214) 528-5566

Personal

Year of birth	1950
Family	Married to Laura Wolens, three children
Education	Stanford University, B.A.
	Southern Methodist University, J.D.
Occupation	Attorney
Religion	Jewish
State legislative service	House 1981 to present

COMMITTEE ASSIGNMENT HISTORY

1997 State Affairs (Chair)
1995 Calendars, State Affairs, Ways and Means (Vice-Chair)
1993 Calendars, State Affairs, Ways and Means
1991 Business and Commerce (Chair), Ways and Means
1989 Business and Commerce (Chair), Ways and Means
1987 Business and Commerce (Chair), Ways and Means
1985 Appropriations, Local and Consent Calendars, Transportation
1983 Appropriations, Urban Affairs
1981 Business and Industry, Higher Education

BILL PASSAGE RATES, 1997

	Total	Passed Legislature	Pct. Passed Legislature
Authored	14	2	14%
Sponsored	7	6	86%
Amendments	18	15	83%

ELECTORAL HISTORY IN CURRENT DISTRICT

	1994	1996	1998
Primary Election Opponent(s)	No	No	No
General Election Opponent(s)	No	No	No

House District 104

COUNTIES IN DISTRICT

Dallas (part)

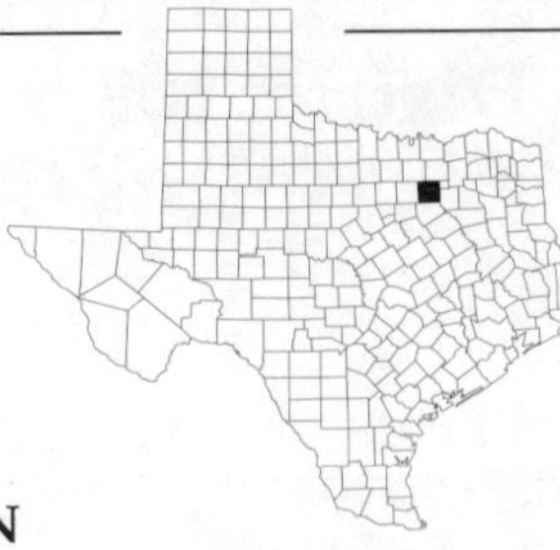

DEMOGRAPHIC INFORMATION

Population	
Total	109,378
Anglo	25.5%
Black	10.0%
Hispanic	63.1%
Others	2.0%

Wealth and Urbanization	
Per capita Income	$8,038
Avg. House Value	$50,376
Percent Poverty	25.4%
Public Assistance	8.2%
Percent Urban	100.0%

Education	
High School Graduates	41.6%
College Graduates	5.0%

Employed	
Percent Employed	89.9%
Private Sector	85.8%

Age of Population	
5 years or less	12.6%
6-17 years	22.0%
18-64 years	57.5%
65 or older	7.9%

Household Types	
Family households	87.8%
Non-family households	8.4%
Single-parent families	23.3%
Both parents working	57.6%

SENATE DISTRICTS IN HOUSE DISTRICT

Dist 2 David Cain (D)
Dist 9 Jane Nelson (R)
Dist 23 Royce West (D)

DISTRICT ELECTION DATA

House 1996	
Domingo Garcia (D)	72.4%
Monty O. Weddell (R)	27.7%

House 1998	
Domingo Garcia (D)	69.8%
Monty Weddell (R)	30.2%

President 1996	
Bill Clinton (D)	73.9%
Bob Dole (R)	26.1%

Composite Party Vote 1994	
Democratic	63.7%
Republican	34.1%

Registered Voters 1996	**36,786**
Turnout	14,772
Percent of registered voting	40.2%

House District 104
Rep. Domingo Garcia (D)

House Office
(512) 463-0654

District Office
1107 W. Jefferson
Dallas, Texas 75208
(214) 941-8300

Personal

Year of birth	1958
Family	Married to Dr. Elba Garcia, two children
Education	University of North Texas, B.A.
	Texas Southern University, J.D.
Occupation	Attorney
Religion	Catholic
State legislative service	House 1997 to present

COMMITTEE ASSIGNMENT HISTORY
1997 Judicial Affairs, Urban Affairs

BILL PASSAGE RATES, 1997

	Total	Passed Legislature	Pct. Passed Legislature
Authored	32	5	16%
Sponsored	2	1	50%
Amendments	7	3	43%

ELECTORAL HISTORY IN CURRENT DISTRICT

	1994	1996	1998
Primary Election Opponent(s)	NA	Yes	Yes
General Election Opponent(s)	NA	Rep	Rep

House District 105

COUNTIES IN DISTRICT

Dallas (part)

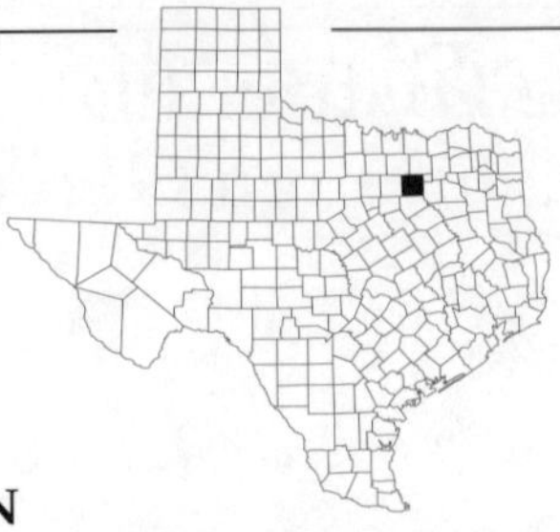

DEMOGRAPHIC INFORMATION

Population	
Total	118,413
Anglo	68.3%
Black	14.3%
Hispanic	15.9%
Others	1.7%

Education	
High School Graduates	64.5%
College Graduates	9.4%

Age of Population	
5 years or less	11.3%
6-17 years	19.3%
18-64 years	60.3%
65 or older	9.0%

Wealth and Urbanization	
Per capita Income	$10,698
Avg. House Value	$57,721
Percent Poverty	14.6%
Public Assistance	6.0%
Percent Urban	97.4%

Employed	
Percent Employed	93.0%
Private Sector	81.5%

Household Types	
Family households	88.2%
Non-family households	10.1%
Single-parent families	25.3%
Both parents working	64.8%

SENATE DISTRICTS IN HOUSE DISTRICT

Dist 2 David Cain (D)
Dist 9 Jane Nelson (R)
Dist 16 John J. Carona (R
Dist 23 Royce West (D)

DISTRICT ELECTION DATA

House 1996	
Dale B. Tillery (D)	61.8%
Richard Stokley (R)	35.3%
Jack W. Borninski (IND)	2.9%

President 1996	
Bill Clinton (D)	61.9%
Bob Dole (R)	38.1%

Composite Party Vote 1994	
Democratic	53.0%
Republican	45.2%

Registered Voters 1996	**54,816**
Turnout	24,840
Percent of registered voting	45.3%

House 1998	
Dale B. Tillery (D)	100.0%

House District 105
Rep. Dale B. Tillery (D)

House Office
(512) 463-0548

District Office
8035 E. R. L. Thornton Fwy. #519
Dallas, Texas 75228
(214) 324-9010

Personal

Year of birth	1957
Family	Married to Melanie Tillery, four children
Education	North Texas State University, B.A.
	Texas Tech University, J.D.
Occupation	Attorney
Religion	Methodist
State legislative service	House 1995 to present

COMMITTEE ASSIGNMENT HISTORY
1997 Appropriations, House Administration, Pensions and Investments
1995 Civil Practices, Urban Affairs

BILL PASSAGE RATES, 1997

	Total	Passed Legislature	Pct. Passed Legislature
Authored	43	4	9%
Sponsored	4	3	75%
Amendments	11	9	82%

ELECTORAL HISTORY IN CURRENT DISTRICT

	1994	1996	1998
Primary Election Opponent(s)	Yes	No	No
General Election Opponent(s)	Rep	Rep, Ind	No

House District 106

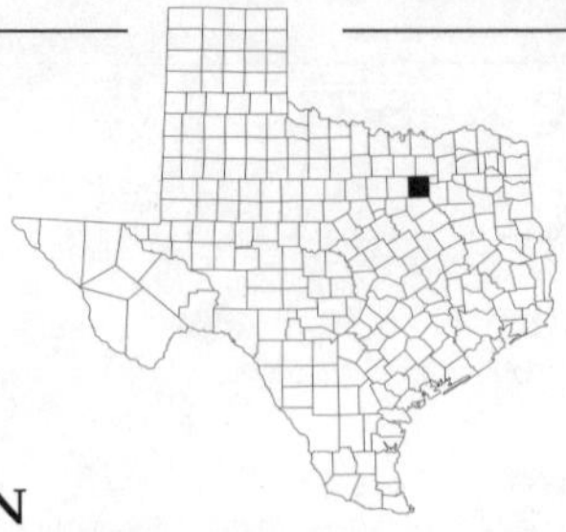

COUNTIES IN DISTRICT
Dallas (part)

DEMOGRAPHIC INFORMATION

Population	
Total	118,070
Anglo	72.7%
Black	7.8%
Hispanic	15.9%
Others	3.9%

Wealth and Urbanization	
Per capita Income	$14,305
Avg. House Value	$77,299
Percent Poverty	8.6%
Public Assistance	3.7%
Percent Urban	100.0%

Education	
High School Graduates	78.4%
College Graduates	19.0%

Employed	
Percent Employed	94.5%
Private Sector	82.5%

Age of Population	
5 years or less	10.5%
6-17 years	18.4%
18-64 years	64.8%
65 or older	6.3%

Household Types	
Family households	88.2%
Non-family households	11.5%
Single-parent families	20.8%
Both parents working	71.3%

SENATE DISTRICTS IN HOUSE DISTRICT

Dist 8 Florence Shapiro (R)
Dist 9 Jane Nelson (R)
Dist 23 Royce West (D)

DISTRICT ELECTION DATA

House 1996	
J. David Gutierrez (D)	40.9%
Ray Allen (R)	59.1%

House 1998	
John J. Lopez (D)	35.0%
Ray Allen (R)	65.0%

President 1996	
Bill Clinton (D)	45.9%
Bob Dole (R)	54.1%

Composite Party Vote 1994	
Democratic	39.9%
Republican	58.7%

Registered Voters 1996	**65,428**
Turnout	34,122
Percent of registered voting	52.2%

House District 106
Rep. Ray Allen (R)

House Office
(512) 463-0694

District Office
2321 S. Beltline #145
Grand Prairie, Texas 75051
(972) 264-4231

Personal

Year of birth	1950
Family	Married to Debbie Allen, five children
Education	American Christian College, B.A., History, Political Science
Occupation	Publishing
Religion	Christian
State legislative service	House 1993 to present

COMMITTEE ASSIGNMENT HISTORY

1997 Corrections (Vice-Chair), Environmental Regulation
1995 Corrections, Public Safety
1993 Criminal Jurisprudence, Public Safety

BILL PASSAGE RATES, 1997

	Total	Passed Legislature	Pct. Passed Legislature
Authored	44	12	27%
Sponsored	13	9	69%
Amendments	16	14	88%

ELECTORAL HISTORY IN CURRENT DISTRICT

	1994	1996	1998
Primary Election Opponent(s)	No	No	No
General Election Opponent(s)	Dem, Lib	Dem	Dem

House District 107

COUNTIES IN DISTRICT
Dallas (part)

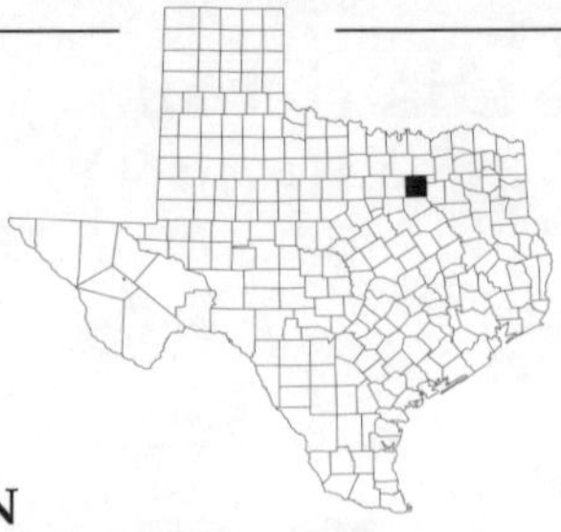

DEMOGRAPHIC INFORMATION

Population	
Total	117,308
Anglo	51.8%
Black	14.4%
Hispanic	31.5%
Others	3.1%

Wealth and Urbanization	
Per capita Income	$15,956
Avg. House Value	$109,597
Percent Poverty	21.3%
Public Assistance	3.5%
Percent Urban	100.0%

Education	
High School Graduates	73.7%
College Graduates	31.7%

Employed	
Percent Employed	93.3%
Private Sector	85.4%

Age of Population	
5 years or less	8.4%
6-17 years	11.2%
18-64 years	70.9%
65 or older	9.5%

Household Types	
Family households	64.1%
Non-family households	34.8%
Single-parent families	29.8%
Both parents working	60.5%

SENATE DISTRICTS IN HOUSE DISTRICT

Dist 2 David Cain (D)
Dist 8 Florence Shapiro (R)
Dist 16 John J. Carona (R)
Dist 23 Royce West (D)

DISTRICT ELECTION DATA

House 1996	
Harryette B. Ehrhardt (D)	58.1%
Ernest Leonard (R)	38.6%
Steven May (L)	2.5%
Charles R. Baker (NLP)	0.9%

House 1998	
Harryette B. Ehrhardt (D)	57.7%
John Alvis (R)	42.3%

President 1996	
Bill Clinton (D)	58.9%
Bob Dole (R)	41.1%

Composite Party Vote 1994	
Democratic	52.0%
Republican	46.2%

Registered Voters 1996	**60,889**
Turnout	29,956
Percent of registered voting	49.2%

House District 107
Rep. Harryette Ehrhardt (D)

House Office
(512) 463-0476

District Office
6333 Prospect Ave.
Dallas, Texas 75214
(214) 824-3107

Personal

Year of birth	1934
Family	Married to John Ehrhardt, five children
Education	Southern Methodist University, B.S., M.Ed. University of Houston, D.Ed.
Occupation	Teacher
Religion	Episcopalian
State legislative service	House 1995 to present

COMMITTEE ASSIGNMENT HISTORY

1997 Financial Institutions, Rules and Resolutions, Urban Affairs
1995 Elections, Rules and Resolutions, Urban Affairs

BILL PASSAGE RATES, 1997

	Total	Passed Legislature	Pct. Passed Legislature
Authored	21	7	33%
Sponsored	1	0	0%
Amendments	9	8	89%

ELECTORAL HISTORY IN CURRENT DISTRICT

	1994	1996	1998
Primary Election Opponent(s)	No	No	No
General Election Opponent(s)	Rep, Lib	Rep, Lib, NLP	Rep

House District 108

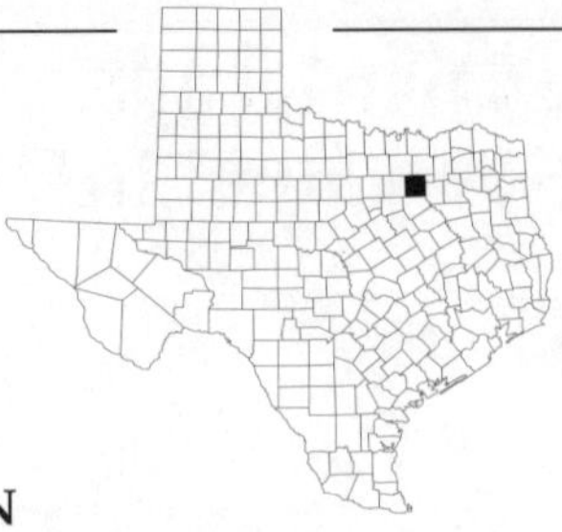

COUNTIES IN DISTRICT

Dallas (part)

DEMOGRAPHIC INFORMATION

Population

Total	118,320
Anglo	87.8%
Black	5.4%
Hispanic	4.6%
Others	2.3%

Education

High School Graduates	94.0%
College Graduates	55.6%

Age of Population

5 years or less	6.9%
6-17 years	11.1%
18-64 years	69.0%
65 or older	13.0%

Wealth and Urbanization

Per capita Income	$31,040
Avg. House Value	$226,612
Percent Poverty	6.1%
Public Assistance	1.4%
Percent Urban	100.0%

Employed

Percent Employed	96.6%
Private Sector	82.3%

Household Types

Family households	68.8%
Non-family households	28.0%
Single-parent families	22.5%
Both parents working	56.4%

SENATE DISTRICTS IN HOUSE DISTRICT

Dist 8 Florence Shapiro (R)

Dist 16 John J. Carona (R)

DISTRICT ELECTION DATA

House 1996

Phil Bird (D)	24.3%
Carolyn Galloway (R)	73.8%
Clifton M. Murphy (L)	1.9%

President 1996

Bill Clinton (D)	30.9%
Bob Dole (R)	69.1%

Composite Party Vote 1994

Democratic	28.8%
Republican	70.2%

Registered Voters 1996	**86,202**
Turnout	55,201
Percent of registered voting	64.0%

House 1998

Kenn George (R)	100.0%

House District 108
Rep. Kenn George (R)

House Office
(512) 463-0560

District Office
8080 North Central Expressway, Suite 1600
Dallas, Texas 75206
(214) 891-8096

Personal

Year of birth	1948
Family	Married to Patricia George, four children
Education	Washington and Lee, B.A.
	University of Texas at Austin, M.B.A.
Occupation	CEO
Religion	Catholic
State legislative service	House 1999 to present

COMMITTEE ASSIGNMENT HISTORY

BILL PASSAGE RATES, 1997

	Total	Passed Legislature	Pct. Passed Legislature
Authored	NA	NA	NA
Sponsored	NA	NA	NA
Amendments	NA	NA	NA

ELECTORAL HISTORY IN CURRENT DISTRICT

	1994	1996	1998
Primary Election Opponent(s)	NA	NA	Yes
General Election Opponent(s)	NA	NA	No

House District 109

COUNTIES IN DISTRICT

Dallas (part)

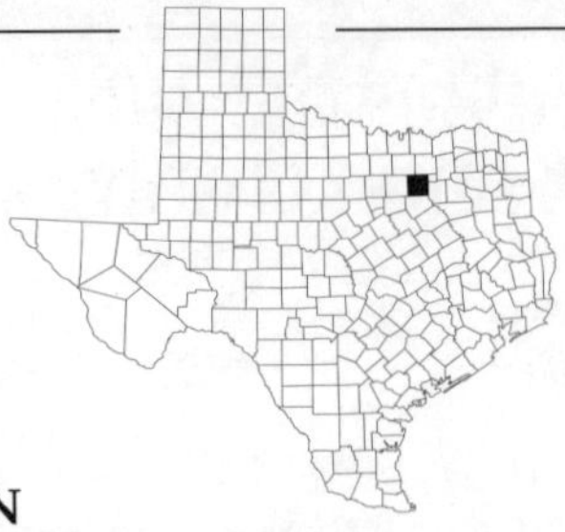

DEMOGRAPHIC INFORMATION

Population	
Total	117,068
Anglo	34.6%
Black	53.5%
Hispanic	11.7%
Others	0.8%

Education	
High School Graduates	67.0%
College Graduates	12.5%

Age of Population	
5 years or less	10.8%
6-17 years	21.8%
18-64 years	59.4%
65 or older	8.0%

Wealth and Urbanization	
Per capita Income	$10,323
Avg. House Value	$68,553
Percent Poverty	21.7%
Public Assistance	11.5%
Percent Urban	99.5%

Employed	
Percent Employed	89.9%
Private Sector	78.7%

Household Types	
Family households	91.5%
Non-family households	7.7%
Single-parent families	35.5%
Both parents working	68.7%

SENATE DISTRICTS IN HOUSE DISTRICT

Dist 2 David Cain (D)

Dist 9 Jane Nelson (R)

Dist 23 Royce West (D)

DISTRICT ELECTION DATA

House 1996	
Helen Giddings (D)	100.0%

President 1996	
Bill Clinton (D)	75.5%
Bob Dole (R)	24.5%

Composite Party Vote 1994	
Democratic	68.2%
Republican	29.3%

Registered Voters 1996	**65,500**
Turnout	31,645
Percent of registered voting	48.3%

House 1998	
Helen Giddings (D)	100.0%

House District 109
Rep. Helen Giddings (D)

House Office
(512) 463-0953

District Office
1510 North Hampton #220
De Soto, Texas 75115
(972) 224-6795

Personal

Year of birth	
Family	Married to Donald Giddings, no children
Education`	University of Texas at Arlington
Occupation	Small business owner
Religion	Methodist
State legislative service	House 1993 to present

COMMITTEE ASSIGNMENT HISTORY

1997 Business and Industry, Financial Institutions, Redistricting
1995 Business and Industry, Financial Institutions, Redistricting
1993 Business and Industry, Investments and Banking

BILL PASSAGE RATES, 1997

	Total	Passed Legislature	Pct. Passed Legislature
Authored	24	6	25%
Sponsored	5	5	100%
Amendments	9	8	89%

ELECTORAL HISTORY IN CURRENT DISTRICT

	1994	1996	1998
Primary Election Opponent(s)	No	No	No
General Election Opponent(s)	No	No	No

House District 110

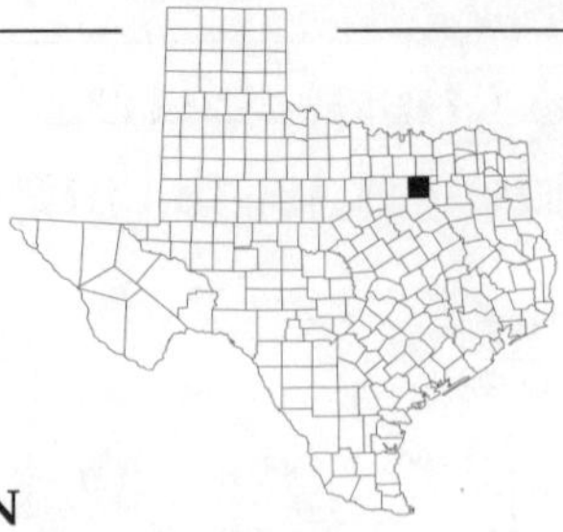

COUNTIES IN DISTRICT

Dallas (part)

DEMOGRAPHIC INFORMATION

Population	
Total	111,270
Anglo	34.5%
Black	57.5%
Hispanic	7.4%
Others	1.1%

Wealth and Urbanization	
Per capita Income	$12,603
Avg. House Value	$74,989
Percent Poverty	12.1%
Public Assistance	5.1%
Percent Urban	100.0%

Education	
High School Graduates	79.2%
College Graduates	19.3%

Employed	
Percent Employed	91.9%
Private Sector	75.7%

Age of Population	
5 years or less	9.3%
6-17 years	19.7%
18-64 years	63.6%
65 or older	7.3%

Household Types	
Family households	88.9%
Non-family households	10.3%
Single-parent families	33.7%
Both parents working	75.1%

SENATE DISTRICTS IN HOUSE DISTRICT

Dist 9 Jane Nelson (R)

Dist 23 Royce West (D)

DISTRICT ELECTION DATA

House 1996	
Jesse W. Jones (D)	92.9%
Howard B. Bridges, Jr. (L)	7.1%

House 1998	
Jesse W. Jones (D)	100.0%

President 1996	
Bill Clinton (D)	74.3%
Bob Dole (R)	25.7%

Composite Party Vote 1994	
Democratic	66.8%
Republican	30.8%

Registered Voters 1996	**68,914**
Turnout	36,481
Percent of registered voting	52.9%

House District 110
Rep. Jesse Jones (D)

House Office
(512) 463-0664

District Office
1266 East Ledbetter Dr.
Dallas, Texas 75216
(214) 375-3773

Personal

Year of birth	1931
Family	Married to Labelle Jones, seven children
Education	Texas College, B.S., M.S. New Mexico Highland University Arizona State University, Ph.D. Chemistry
Occupation	Professor
Religion	Baptist
State legislative service	House 1993 to present

COMMITTEE ASSIGNMENT HISTORY

1997 Elections (Vice-Chair), Juvenile Justice and Family Issues, Local and Consent Calendars
1995 Elections, Human Services, Rules and Resolutions
1993 Elections, Higher Education

BILL PASSAGE RATES, 1997

	Total	Passed Legislature	Pct. Passed Legislature
Authored	41	9	22%
Sponsored	4	4	100%
Amendments	3	3	100%

ELECTORAL HISTORY IN CURRENT DISTRICT

	1994	1996	1998
Primary Election Opponent(s)	Yes	No	No
General Election Opponent(s)	No	Lib	No

House District 111

COUNTIES IN DISTRICT

Dallas (part)

DEMOGRAPHIC INFORMATION

Population	
Total	109,144
Anglo	33.1%
Black	55.4%
Hispanic	10.7%
Others	1.7%

Education	
High School Graduates	69.5%
College Graduates	16.8%

Age of Population	
5 years or less	10.8%
6-17 years	20.5%
18-64 years	60.4%
65 or older	8.3%

Wealth and Urbanization	
Per capita Income	$11,356
Avg. House Value	$74,093
Percent Poverty	18.3%
Public Assistance	9.1%
Percent Urban	99.8%

Employed	
Percent Employed	90.9%
Private Sector	77.3%

Household Types	
Family households	91.3%
Non-family households	7.8%
Single-parent families	31.5%
Both parents working	68.6%

SENATE DISTRICTS IN HOUSE DISTRICT

Dist 2 David Cain (D)
Dist 9 Jane Nelson (R)
Dist 23 Royce West (D)

DISTRICT ELECTION DATA

House 1996	
Yvonne Davis (D)	100.0%

House 1998	
Yvonne Davis (D)	100.0%

President 1996	
Bill Clinton (D)	71.1%
Bob Dole (R)	28.9%

Composite Party Vote 1994	
Democratic	67.4%
Republican	30.2%

Registered Voters 1996	**67,822**
Turnout	34,665
Percent of registered voting	51.1%

House District 111
Rep. Yvonne Davis (D)

House Office
(512) 463-0598

District Office
400 S. Zang Blvd., #801
Dallas, Texas 75208
(214) 941-3895

Personal

Year of birth	1955
Family	Single, no children
Education	University of Houston, B.S.
Occupation	Small business owner
Religion	Baptist
State legislative service	House 1993 to present

COMMITTEE ASSIGNMENT HISTORY

1997 Appropriations, Energy Resources, Local and Consent Calendars
1995 Appropriations, Economic Development
1993 International and Cultural Relations, Rules and Resolutions

BILL PASSAGE RATES, 1997

	Total	Passed Legislature	Pct. Passed Legislature
Authored	13	3	23%
Sponsored	0	0	NA
Amendments	18	15	83%

ELECTORAL HISTORY IN CURRENT DISTRICT

	1994	1996	1998
Primary Election Opponent(s)	Yes	No	No
General Election Opponent(s)	Rep	No	No

House District 112

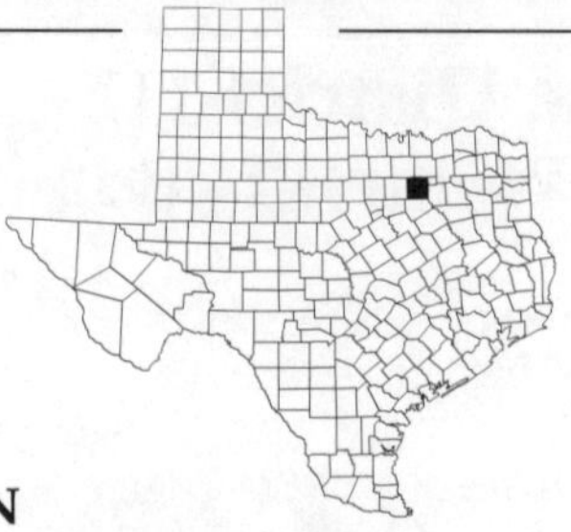

COUNTIES IN DISTRICT
Dallas (part)

DEMOGRAPHIC INFORMATION

Population		**Wealth and Urbanization**	
Total	118,526	Per capita Income	$17,268
Anglo	80.3%	Avg. House Value	$90,417
Black	4.4%	Percent Poverty	6.0%
Hispanic	9.0%	Public Assistance	2.4%
Others	6.4%	Percent Urban	100.0%

Education		**Employed**	
High School Graduates	85.5%	Percent Employed	95.8%
College Graduates	31.8%	Private Sector	83.1%

Age of Population		**Household Types**	
5 years or less	9.8%	Family households	90.3%
6-17 years	17.6%	Non-family households	9.0%
18-64 years	64.6%	Single-parent families	17.6%
65 or older	8.0%	Both parents working	69.5%

SENATE DISTRICTS IN HOUSE DISTRICT

Dist 8 Florence Shapiro (R)

Dist 16 John J. Carona (R)

DISTRICT ELECTION DATA

House 1996		**House 1998**	
Fred Hill (R)	100.0%	Fred Hill (R)	100.0%

President 1996	
Bill Clinton (D)	36.4%
Bob Dole (R)	63.6%

Composite Party Vote 1994	
Democratic	32.9%
Republican	65.9%

Registered Voters 1996	**69,698**
Turnout	40,498
Percent of registered voting	58.1%

House District 112
Rep. Fred Hill (R)

House Office
(512) 463-0486

District Office
770 N. Coit Rd. #2485
Richardson, Texas 75080
(972) 234-8980

Personal

Year of birth	1939
Family	Married to Jeannine Hill, five children
Education	California Polytechnic University, B.S.
Occupation	Businessman
Religion	Baptist
State legislative service	House 1989 to present

COMMITTEE ASSIGNMENT HISTORY

1997 Transportation, Urban Affairs (Chair)
1995 Elections, Urban Affairs (Chair)
1993 International and Cultural Relations, Urban Affairs (Chair)
1991 Higher Education, House Administration, Public Safety
1989 Cultural and Historical Resources, Judicial Affairs

BILL PASSAGE RATES, 1997

	Total	Passed Legislature	Pct. Passed Legislature
Authored	24	2	8%
Sponsored	9	5	56%
Amendments	5	4	80%

ELECTORAL HISTORY IN CURRENT DISTRICT

	1994	1996	1998
Primary Election Opponent(s)	No	No	No
General Election Opponent(s)	No	No	No

House District 113

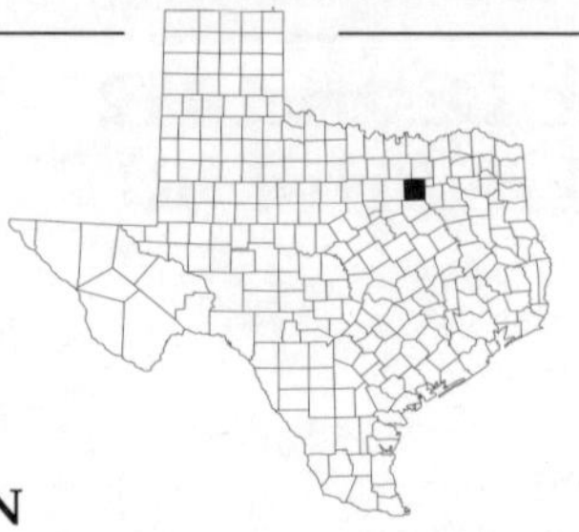

COUNTIES IN DISTRICT
Dallas (part)

DEMOGRAPHIC INFORMATION

Population		**Wealth and Urbanization**	
Total	118,528	Per capita Income	$15,778
Anglo	76.5%	Avg. House Value	$86,703
Black	9.9%	Percent Poverty	6.7%
Hispanic	10.2%	Public Assistance	2.5%
Others	3.6%	Percent Urban	99.0%

Education		**Employed**	
High School Graduates	85.4%	Percent Employed	95.5%
College Graduates	26.0%	Private Sector	83.6%

Age of Population		**Household Types**	
5 years or less	11.8%	Family households	92.0%
6-17 years	19.9%	Non-family households	7.9%
18-64 years	64.6%	Single-parent families	16.3%
65 or older	3.6%	Both parents working	72.1%

SENATE DISTRICTS IN HOUSE DISTRICT

Dist 16 John J. Carona (R)

DISTRICT ELECTION DATA

House 1996		**House 1998**	
Joe Driver (R)	100.0%	Joe Driver (R)	100.0%

President 1996	
Bill Clinton (D)	38.9%
Bob Dole (R)	61.1%

Composite Party Vote 1994	
Democratic	33.3%
Republican	65.5%

Registered Voters 1996	**74,146**
Turnout	39,614
Percent of registered voting	53.4%

House District 113
Rep. Joe Driver (R)

House Office
(512) 463-0574

District Office
201 South Glenbrook
Garland, Texas 75040
(972) 276-1556

Personal

Year of birth	1946
Family	Married to DeAnne Driver, two children
Education	University of North Texas, B.B.A.
Occupation	Insurance
Religion	Methodist
State legislative service	House 1993 to present

COMMITTEE ASSIGNMENT HISTORY

1997 Energy Resources, Public Safety (Vice-Chair)
1995 Insurance, Local and Consent Calendars, Public Safety
1993 Energy Resources, Insurance

BILL PASSAGE RATES, 1997

	Total	Passed Legislature	Pct. Passed Legislature
Authored	21	6	29%
Sponsored	4	3	75%
Amendments	1	1	100%

ELECTORAL HISTORY IN CURRENT DISTRICT

	1994	1996	1998
Primary Election Opponent(s)	No	No	No
General Election Opponent(s)	No	No	No

House District 114

COUNTIES IN DISTRICT

Dallas (part)

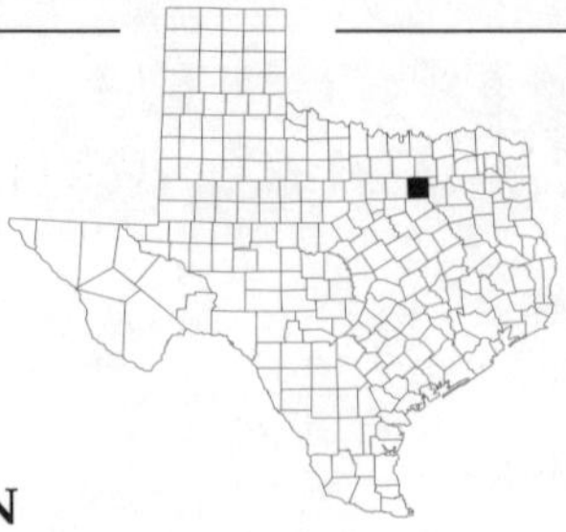

DEMOGRAPHIC INFORMATION

Population

Total	118,156
Anglo	78.8%
Black	5.1%
Hispanic	12.2%
Others	4.0%

Education

High School Graduates	87.3%
College Graduates	37.8%

Age of Population

5 years or less	8.2%
6-17 years	13.3%
18-64 years	68.8%
65 or older	9.7%

Wealth and Urbanization

Per capita Income	$23,732
Avg. House Value	$148,410
Percent Poverty	7.2%
Public Assistance	2.0%
Percent Urban	100.0%

Employed

Percent Employed	95.4%
Private Sector	84.3%

Household Types

Family households	82.0%
Non-family households	17.0%
Single-parent families	18.6%
Both parents working	66.6%

SENATE DISTRICTS IN HOUSE DISTRICT

Dist 8 Florence Shapiro (R)

Dist 9 Jane Nelson (R)

DISTRICT ELECTION DATA

House 1996

Will Hartnett (R)	88.3%
Matthew A. Trotter (L)	11.7%

House 1998

Will Hartnett (R)	100.0%

President 1996

Bill Clinton (D)	35.1%
Bob Dole (R)	64.9%

Composite Party Vote 1994

Democratic	31.8%
Republican	67.0%

Registered Voters 1996	**76,939**
Turnout	46,147
Percent of registered voting	60.0%

House District 114
Rep. Will Hartnett (R)

House Office
(512) 463-0576

District Office
1601 Elm Street, #4900
Dallas, Texas 75201-7210
(214) 698-1776

Personal

Year of birth	1956
Family	Married to Tammy L. Hartnett, no children
Education	Harvard University, B.A.
	University of Texas, J.D.
Occupation	Probate Attorney
Religion	Catholic
State legislative service	House 1991 to present

COMMITTEE ASSIGNMENT HISTORY

1997 Judicial Affairs (Vice-Chair), Transportation
1995 Civil Practices, Judicial Affairs (Vice-Chair), Local and Consent Calendars
1993 Judicial Affairs, Criminal Jurisprudence (Vice-Chair), Local and Consent Calendars
1991 Government Organization, Judiciary

BILL PASSAGE RATES, 1997

	Total	Passed Legislature	Pct. Passed Legislature
Authored	19	9	47%
Sponsored	5	5	100%
Amendments	19	14	74%

ELECTORAL HISTORY IN CURRENT DISTRICT

	1994	1996	1998
Primary Election Opponent(s)	No	No	No
General Election Opponent(s)	Lib	Lib	No

House District 115

COUNTIES IN DISTRICT
Bexar (part)

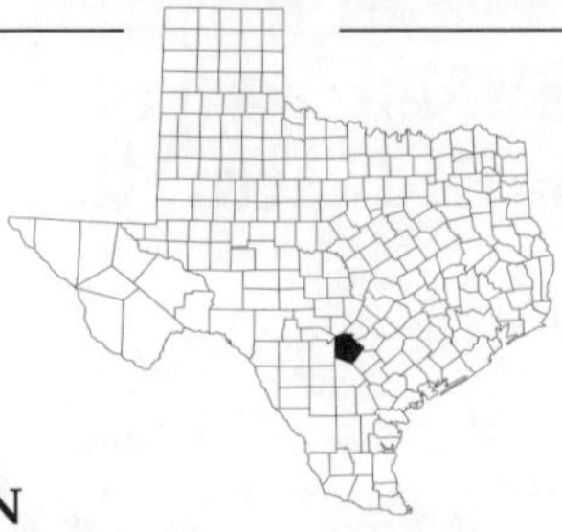

DEMOGRAPHIC INFORMATION

Population

Total	107,373
Anglo	27.5%
Black	2.8%
Hispanic	68.9%
Others	1.0%

Wealth and Urbanization

Per capita Income	$8,040
Avg. House Value	$48,764
Percent Poverty	35.4%
Public Assistance	15.1%
Percent Urban	100.0%

Education

High School Graduates	57.2%
College Graduates	11.5%

Employed

Percent Employed	88.1%
Private Sector	77.2%

Age of Population

5 years or less	10.5%
6-17 years	17.1%
18-64 years	58.1%
65 or older	14.3%

Household Types

Family households	80.4%
Non-family households	15.2%
Single-parent families	37.6%
Both parents working	50.8%

SENATE DISTRICTS IN HOUSE DISTRICT

Dist 25 Jeff Wentworth (R)
Dist 26 Gregory Luna (D)

DISTRICT ELECTION DATA

House 1996

Leticia Van de Putte (D)	100.0%

House 1998

Leticia Van de Putte (D)	100.0%

President 1996

Bill Clinton (D)	66.3%
Bob Dole (R)	33.7%

Composite Party Vote 1994

Democratic	61.3%
Republican	38.7%

Registered Voters 1996	**58,006**
Turnout	25,934
Percent of registered voting	44.7%

House District 115
Rep. Leticia Van de Putte (D)

House Office
(512) 463-0532

District Office
3718-A Blanco Rd., #2
San Antonio, Texas 78212
(210) 733-6604

Personal

Year of birth	1954
Family	Married to Pete "Henry" Van de Putte, Jr., six children
Education	University of Texas, B.S., Pharmacy
Occupation	Pharmacist
Religion	Catholic
State legislative service	House 1991 to present

COMMITTEE ASSIGNMENT HISTORY

1997 Economic Development, Insurance (Vice-Chair)
1995 Economic Development, Juvenile Justice and Family Issues
1993 Human Services, International and Cultural Relations
1991 Human Services, Labor and Employment Relations

BILL PASSAGE RATES, 1997

	Total	Passed Legislature	Pct. Passed Legislature
Authored	57	15	26%
Sponsored	24	17	71%
Amendments	26	23	88%

ELECTORAL HISTORY IN CURRENT DISTRICT

	1994	1996	1998
Primary Election Opponent(s)	Yes	No	No
General Election Opponent(s)	No	No	No

House District 116

COUNTIES IN DISTRICT
Bexar (part)

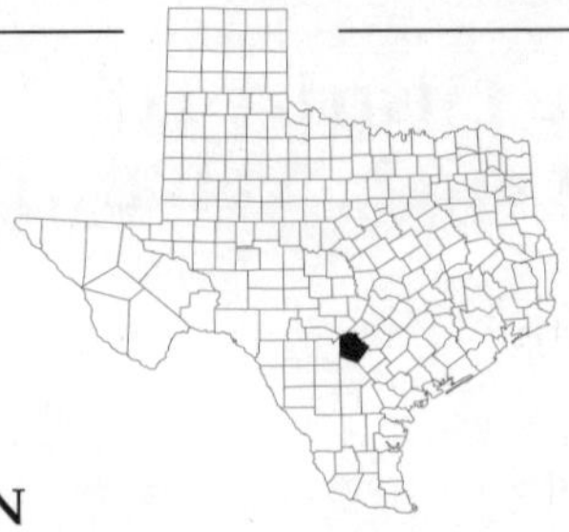

DEMOGRAPHIC INFORMATION

Population	
Total	107,320
Anglo	26.6%
Black	4.1%
Hispanic	68.5%
Others	1.2%

Wealth and Urbanization	
Per capita Income	$9,612
Avg. House Value	$51,581
Percent Poverty	24.3%
Public Assistance	10.3%
Percent Urban	100.0%

Education	
High School Graduates	66.7%
College Graduates	14.4%

Employed	
Percent Employed	91.0%
Private Sector	74.9%

Age of Population	
5 years or less	9.9%
6-17 years	17.2%
18-64 years	58.9%
65 or older	14.0%

Household Types	
Family households	82.8%
Non-family households	15.7%
Single-parent families	35.5%
Both parents working	59.9%

SENATE DISTRICTS IN HOUSE DISTRICT

Dist 25 Jeff Wentworth (R)
Dist 26 Gregory Luna (D)

DISTRICT ELECTION DATA

House 1996	
Leo G. Alvarado Jr. (D)	70.1%
Donald D. Varella (R)	29.9%

President 1996	
Bill Clinton (D)	69.4%
Bob Dole (R)	30.6%

Composite Party Vote 1994	
Democratic	64.0%
Republican	36.0%

Registered Voters 1996	**60,574**
Turnout	27,195
Percent of registered voting	44.9%

House 1998	
Leo G. Alvarado Jr. (D)	100.0%

House District 116
Rep. Leo G. Alvarado Jr. (D)

House Office
(512) 463-0616

District Office
115 Camaron #200
San Antonio, Texas 78205
(210) 229-1884

Personal

Year of birth	1939
Family	Single, four children
Education	St. Mary's University, B.A., J.D.
Occupation	Attorney
Religion	Catholic
State legislative service	House 1993 to present

COMMITTEE ASSIGNMENT HISTORY
1997 Civil Practices, House Administration, State Affairs
1995 Civil Practices, Redistricting, State Affairs
1993 Insurance, Judicial Affairs, Redistricting

BILL PASSAGE RATES, 1997

	Total	Passed Legislature	Pct. Passed Legislature
Authored	16	3	19%
Sponsored	2	2	100%
Amendments	4	3	75%

ELECTORAL HISTORY IN CURRENT DISTRICT

	1994	1996	1998
Primary Election Opponent(s)	No	No	No
General Election Opponent(s)	Rep	Rep	No

House District 117

COUNTIES IN DISTRICT
Bexar (part)

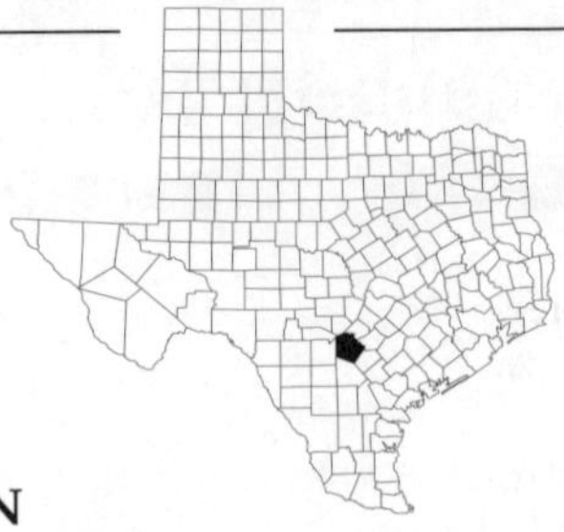

DEMOGRAPHIC INFORMATION

Population	
Total	107,307
Anglo	29.4%
Black	6.2%
Hispanic	63.0%
Others	1.8%

Wealth and Urbanization	
Per capita Income	$7,671
Avg. House Value	$42,674
Percent Poverty	25.7%
Public Assistance	11.2%
Percent Urban	92.6%

Education	
High School Graduates	64.5%
College Graduates	8.4%

Employed	
Percent Employed	88.5%
Private Sector	68.7%

Age of Population	
5 years or less	11.9%
6-17 years	22.4%
18-64 years	60.7%
65 or older	5.0%

Household Types	
Family households	87.9%
Non-family households	4.9%
Single-parent families	23.2%
Both parents working	55.1%

SENATE DISTRICTS IN HOUSE DISTRICT

Dist 19 Frank Madla (D)
Dist 25 Jeff Wentworth (R)
Dist 26 Gregory Luna (D)

DISTRICT ELECTION DATA

House 1996	
John A. Longoria (D)	100.0%

House 1998	
John A. Longoria (D)	100.0%

President 1996	
Bill Clinton (D)	63.7%
Bob Dole (R)	36.3%

Composite Party Vote 1994	
Democratic	58.3%
Republican	41.7%

Registered Voters 1996	**53,349**
Turnout	21,830
Percent of registered voting	40.9%

House District 117
Rep. John A. Longoria (D)

House Office
(512) 463-0618

District Office
1007 Poteet Jourdanton Hwy. #110
San Antonio, Texas 78224
(210) 921-0839

Personal

Year of birth	1945
Family	Married to Patty Longoria, five children
Education	St. Mary's University, B.A., J.D.
Occupation	Attorney
Religion	Catholic
State legislative service	House 1993 to present

COMMITTEE ASSIGNMENT HISTORY

1997 State Affairs, State Recreational Resources
1995 Corrections, County Affairs
1993 Corrections, County Affairs

BILL PASSAGE RATES, 1997

	Total	Passed Legislature	Pct. Passed Legislature
Authored	42	2	5%
Sponsored	3	3	100%
Amendments	7	5	71%

ELECTORAL HISTORY IN CURRENT DISTRICT

	1994	1996	1998
Primary Election Opponent(s)	No	No	No
General Election Opponent(s)	No	No	No

House District 118

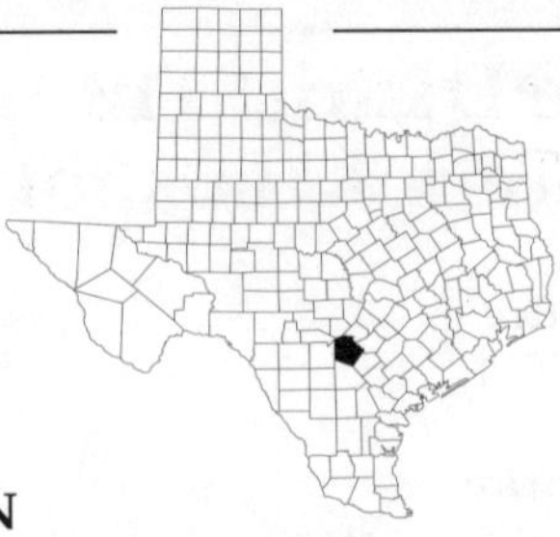

COUNTIES IN DISTRICT

Bexar (part)

DEMOGRAPHIC INFORMATION

Population	
Total	107,282
Anglo	31.2%
Black	2.1%
Hispanic	66.1%
Others	0.8%

Education	
High School Graduates	55.9%
College Graduates	4.7%

Age of Population	
5 years or less	10.5%
6-17 years	22.1%
18-64 years	58.7%
65 or older	8.6%

Wealth and Urbanization	
Per capita Income	$7,410
Avg. House Value	$40,818
Percent Poverty	24.8%
Public Assistance	10.8%
Percent Urban	79.4%

Employed	
Percent Employed	88.6%
Private Sector	72.8%

Household Types	
Family households	91.7%
Non-family households	6.0%
Single-parent families	23.8%
Both parents working	56.1%

SENATE DISTRICTS IN HOUSE DISTRICT

Dist 19 Frank Madla (D)

Dist 21 Judith Zaffirini (D)

DISTRICT ELECTION DATA

House 1996	
Ciro D. Rodriguez (D)	100.0%

House 1998	
Carlos "Charlie" Uresti (D)	100.0%

President 1996	
Bill Clinton (D)	67.5%
Bob Dole (R)	32.5%

Composite Party Vote 1994	
Democratic	64.0%
Republican	36.0%

Registered Voters 1996	**58,134**
Turnout	24,466
Percent of registered voting	42.1%

House District 118
Rep. Carlos Uresti (D)

House Office
(512) 463-0714

District Office
1114 SW Military Dr., #103
San Antonio, Texas 78221
(210) 932-2568

Personal

Year of birth	1946
Family	Married to Yolanda Uresti, one child
Education	St. Mary's University, B.A., J.D.
Occupation	Attorney
Religion	Catholic
State legislative service	House 1998 to present

COMMITTEE ASSIGNMENT HISTORY

1997 Higher Education, Public Health

BILL PASSAGE RATES, 1997

	Total	Passed Legislature	Pct. Passed Legislature
Authored	NA	NA	NA
Sponsored	NA	NA	NA
Amendments	NA	NA	NA

ELECTORAL HISTORY IN CURRENT DISTRICT

	1994	1996	1997	1998
Primary Election Opponent(s)	NA	NA	NA	Yes
General Election Opponent(s)	NA	NA	NA	No
Special Election Opponent(s)	NA	NA	Dems, Rep	NA

House District 119

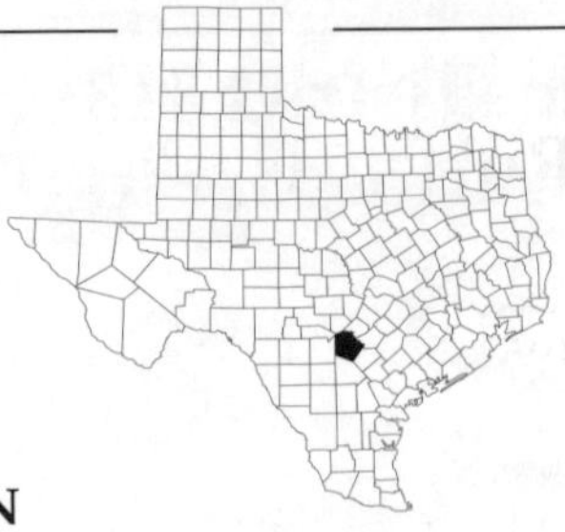

COUNTIES IN DISTRICT
Bexar (part)

DEMOGRAPHIC INFORMATION

Population

Total	107,261
Anglo	30.0%
Black	7.2%
Hispanic	61.9%
Others	1.2%

Education

High School Graduates	61.3%
College Graduates	9.3%

Age of Population

5 years or less	10.7%
6-17 years	20.5%
18-64 years	56.2%
65 or older	12.5%

Wealth and Urbanization

Per capita Income	$8,725
Avg. House Value	$47,111
Percent Poverty	24.6%
Public Assistance	12.5%
Percent Urban	97.6%

Employed

Percent Employed	88.9%
Private Sector	71.9%

Household Types

Family households	90.0%
Non-family households	9.0%
Single-parent families	25.4%
Both parents working	58.0%

SENATE DISTRICTS IN HOUSE DISTRICT

Dist 19 Frank Madla (D)
Dist 21 Judith Zaffirini (D)
Dist 26 Gregory Luna (D)

DISTRICT ELECTION DATA

House 1996

Robert R. Puente (D)	100.0%

House 1998

Robert R. Puente (D)	100.0%

President 1996

Bill Clinton (D)	67.4%
Bob Dole (R)	32.6%

Composite Party Vote 1994

Democratic	64.2%
Republican	35.8%

Registered Voters 1996	**62,666**
Turnout	28,120
Percent of registered voting	44.9%

House District 119
Rep. Robert R. Puente (D)

House Office
(512) 463-0452

District Office
2931 E. Southcross, #201
San Antonio, Texas 78223
(210) 532-8899

Personal

Year of birth	1958
Family	Married to Carmen Puente, three children
Education	St. Mary's University, B.A.
	University of Texas, J.D.
Occupation	Attorney
Religion	Catholic
State legislative service	House 1991 to present

COMMITTEE ASSIGNMENT HISTORY

1997 Environmental Regulation, Local and Consent Calendars, Natural Resources
1995 Juvenile Justice and Family Issues, Local and Consent Calendars, Natural Resources
1993 Judicial Affairs, Natural Resources
1991 Natural Resources, Urban Affairs

BILL PASSAGE RATES, 1997

	Total	Passed Legislature	Pct. Passed Legislature
Authored	33	5	15%
Sponsored	7	6	86%
Amendments	60	44	73%

ELECTORAL HISTORY IN CURRENT DISTRICT

	1994	1996	1998
Primary Election Opponent(s)	No	Yes	No
General Election Opponent(s)	No	No	No

House District 120

COUNTIES IN DISTRICT
Bexar (part)

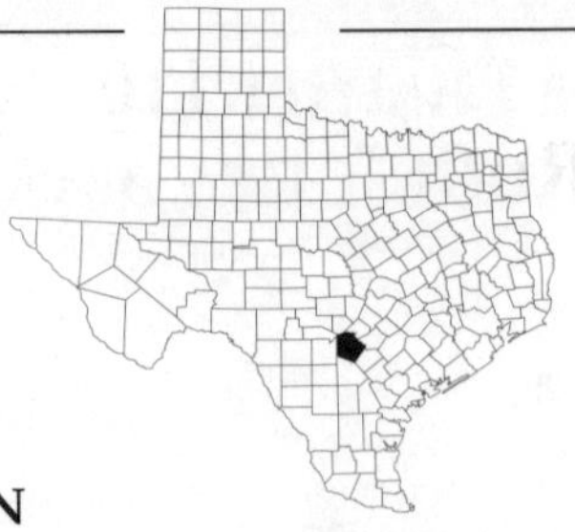

DEMOGRAPHIC INFORMATION

Population	
Total	107,393
Anglo	32.2%
Black	34.9%
Hispanic	31.8%
Others	1.9%

Education	
High School Graduates	68.2%
College Graduates	11.3%

Age of Population	
5 years or less	10.5%
6-17 years	19.4%
18-64 years	59.8%
65 or older	10.3%

Wealth and Urbanization	
Per capita Income	$8,875
Avg. House Value	$47,052
Percent Poverty	25.3%
Public Assistance	12.8%
Percent Urban	99.8%

Employed	
Percent Employed	88.0%
Private Sector	72.4%

Household Types	
Family households	83.7%
Non-family households	10.0%
Single-parent families	34.0%
Both parents working	58.4%

SENATE DISTRICTS IN HOUSE DISTRICT

Dist 19 Frank Madla (D)
Dist 21 Judith Zaffirini (D)
Dist 25 Jeff Wentworth (R)
Dist 26 Gregory Luna (D)

DISTRICT ELECTION DATA

House 1996	
Ruth Jones McClendon (D)	100.0%

House 1998	
Ruth Jones McClendon (D)	100.0%

President 1996	
Bill Clinton (D)	70.5%
Bob Dole (R)	29.5%

Composite Party Vote 1994	
Democratic	66.9%
Republican	33.1%

Registered Voters 1996	**59,368**
Turnout	25,919
Percent of registered voting	43.7%

House District 120
Rep. Ruth Jones McClendon (D)

House Office
(512) 463-0708

District Office
1149 E. Commerce, Suite 210
San Antonio, Texas 78205
(210) 225-2107
(210) 225-2796 Fax

Personal

Year of birth	
Family	Married to Denver McClendon
Education	Texas Southern University, B.A.
	Webster University, M.A.
Occupation	State Representative
Religion	Catholic
State legislative service	House 1996 (part) to present

COMMITTEE ASSIGNMENT HISTORY

1997 Juvenile Justice and Family Issues, Public Safety
1996 NA

BILL PASSAGE RATES, 1997

	Total	Passed Legislature	Pct. Passed Legislature
Authored	44	12	27%
Sponsored	10	10	100%
Amendments	6	6	100%

ELECTORAL HISTORY IN CURRENT DISTRICT

	1994	1996	1998
Primary Election Opponent(s)	NA	NA	No
General Election Opponent(s)	NA	No	No
Special Election Opponent(s)	NA	No	NA

House District 121

COUNTIES IN DISTRICT

Bexar (part)

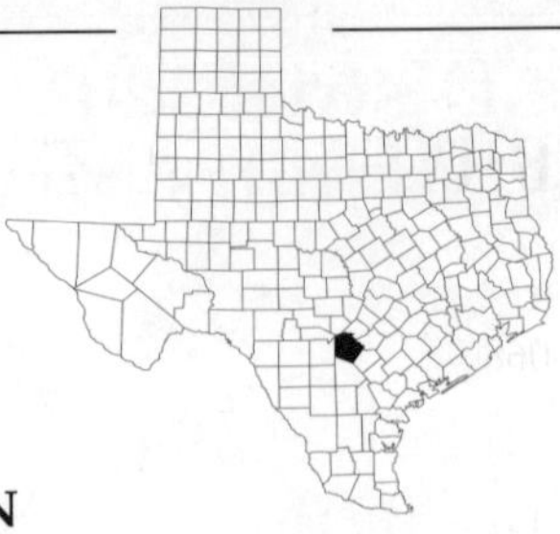

DEMOGRAPHIC INFORMATION

Population	
Total	107,936
Anglo	73.4%
Black	6.5%
Hispanic	17.9%
Others	2.4%

Education	
High School Graduates	89.5%
College Graduates	32.9%

Age of Population	
5 years or less	8.0%
6-17 years	15.5%
18-64 years	62.8%
65 or older	13.8%

Wealth and Urbanization	
Per capita Income	$19,022
Avg. House Value	$100,686
Percent Poverty	8.2%
Public Assistance	3.1%
Percent Urban	100.0%

Employed	
Percent Employed	94.6%
Private Sector	70.8%

Household Types	
Family households	83.6%
Non-family households	15.5%
Single-parent families	22.0%
Both parents working	66.1%

SENATE DISTRICTS IN HOUSE DISTRICT

Dist 19 Frank Madla (D)
Dist 21 Judith Zaffirini (D)
Dist 25 Jeff Wentworth (R)

DISTRICT ELECTION DATA

House 1996	
Bette Graham White (D)	33.8%
Bill Siebert (R)	66.2%

House 1998	
Bill Siebert (R)	100.0%

President 1996	
Bill Clinton (D)	34.7%
Bob Dole (R)	65.3%

Composite Party Vote 1994	
Democratic	33.6%
Republican	66.4%

Registered Voters 1996	**77,917**
Turnout	45,155
Percent of registered voting	58.0%

House District 121
Rep. Bill Siebert (R)

House Office
(512) 463-0686

District Office
1777 N.E. Loop 410, #910
San Antonio, Texas 78217
(210) 824-8821

Personal

Year of birth	1947
Family	Single, three children
Education	Pacific Western University, B.S.
Occupation	Businessman
Religion	Episcopalian
State legislative service	House 1993 to present

COMMITTEE ASSIGNMENT HISTORY

1997 Economic Development, Local and Consent Calendars, Transportation (Vice-Chair)
1995 Local and Consent Calendars, State Recreational Resources (Vice-Chair), Transportation
1993 Insurance, Rules and Resolutions, Transportation

BILL PASSAGE RATES, 1997

	Total	Passed Legislature	Pct. Passed Legislature
Authored	29	12	41%
Sponsored	7	7	100%
Amendments	16	14	88%

ELECTORAL HISTORY IN CURRENT DISTRICT

	1994	1996	1998
Primary Election Opponent(s)	No	Yes	No
General Election Opponent(s)	Dem	Dem	No

House District 122

COUNTIES IN DISTRICT

Bexar (part)

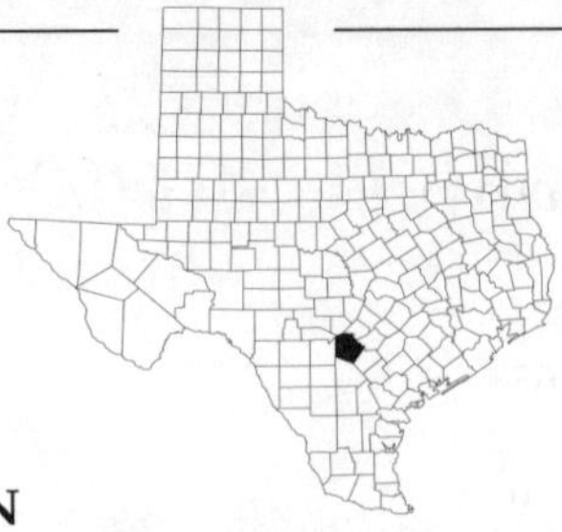

DEMOGRAPHIC INFORMATION

Population	
Total	107,718
Anglo	77.7%
Black	3.1%
Hispanic	17.6%
Others	1.8%

Wealth and Urbanization	
Per capita Income	$19,014
Avg. House Value	$105,406
Percent Poverty	4.5%
Public Assistance	2.1%
Percent Urban	96.7%

Education	
High School Graduates	94.0%
College Graduates	38.4%

Employed	
Percent Employed	95.9%
Private Sector	74.7%

Age of Population	
5 years or less	9.3%
6-17 years	18.3%
18-64 years	66.8%
65 or older	5.6%

Household Types	
Family households	87.1%
Non-family households	12.6%
Single-parent families	17.0%
Both parents working	66.9%

SENATE DISTRICTS IN HOUSE DISTRICT

Dist 21 Judith Zaffirini (D)
Dist 25 Jeff Wentworth (R)
Dist 26 Gregory Luna (D)

DISTRICT ELECTION DATA

House 1996	
John H. Shields (R)	100.0%

House 1998	
John H. Shields (R)	100.0%

President 1996	
Bill Clinton (D)	31.6%
Bob Dole (R)	68.4%

Composite Party Vote 1994	
Democratic	29.8%
Republican	70.2%

Registered Voters 1996	**90,961**
Turnout	53,391
Percent of registered voting	58.7%

House District 122
Rep. John H. Shields (R)

House Office
(512) 463-0658

District Office
16414 San Pedro, Suite 432
San Antonio, Texas 78232-2260
(210) 545-1221

Personal

Year of birth	1954
Family	Married to Marsha Shields, two children
Education	Duke University, B.A.
	Trinity University, M.A.
	St. Mary's University, J.D.
Occupation	Business attorney, consultant
Religion	Christian
State legislative service	House 1993 to present

COMMITTEE ASSIGNMENT HISTORY
1997 Judicial Affairs, Urban Affairs
1995 Economic Development, Insurance
1993 Economic Development, Insurance, Local and Consent Calendars

BILL PASSAGE RATES, 1997

	Total	Passed Legislature	Pct. Passed Legislature
Authored	19	3	16%
Sponsored	4	4	100%
Amendments	24	13	54%

ELECTORAL HISTORY IN CURRENT DISTRICT

	1994	1996	1998
Primary Election Opponent(s)	No	No	No
General Election Opponent(s)	Dem	No	No

House District 123

COUNTIES IN DISTRICT

Bexar (part)

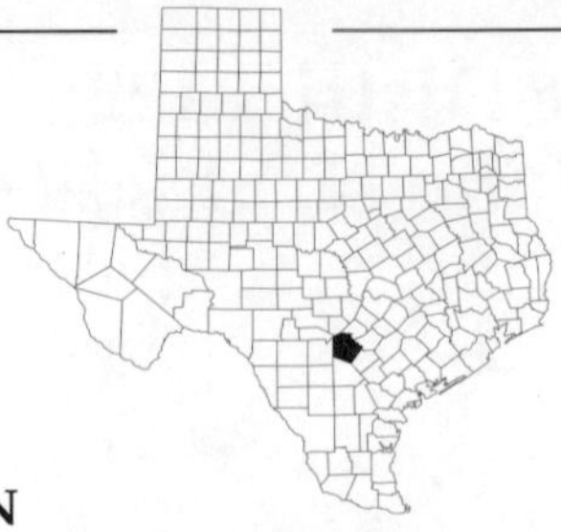

DEMOGRAPHIC INFORMATION

Population		Wealth and Urbanization	
Total	107,381	Per capita Income	$20,922
Anglo	72.6%	Avg. House Value	$123,299
Black	2.2%	Percent Poverty	7.3%
Hispanic	23.0%	Public Assistance	2.0%
Others	2.3%	Percent Urban	86.4%

Education		Employed	
High School Graduates	92.1%	Percent Employed	95.6%
College Graduates	40.0%	Private Sector	72.7%

Age of Population		Household Types	
5 years or less	8.0%	Family households	82.4%
6-17 years	15.4%	Non-family households	15.9%
18-64 years	66.7%	Single-parent families	18.6%
65 or older	9.9%	Both parents working	68.7%

SENATE DISTRICTS IN HOUSE DISTRICT

Dist 25 Jeff Wentworth (R)

Dist 26 Gregory Luna (D)

DISTRICT ELECTION DATA

House 1996		House 1998	
Frank J. Corte (R)	100.0%	Frank J. Corte (R)	100.0%

President 1996

Bill Clinton (D)	35.4%
Bob Dole (R)	64.6%

Composite Party Vote 1994

Democratic	34.0%
Republican	66.0%

Registered Voters 1996	**88,217**
Turnout	51,756
Percent of registered voting	58.7%

House District 123
Rep. Frank J. Corte (R)

House Office
(512) 463-0646

District Office
5410 Fredericksburg #302
San Antonio, Texas 78229
(210) 349-0320

Personal

Year of birth	1959
Family	Married to Valerie Corte, three children
Education	Texas A&M University, B.S., Building Construction
Occupation	Businessman
Religion	Baptist
State legislative service	House 1993 to present

COMMITTEE ASSIGNMENT HISTORY

1997 Business and Industry, Natural Resources
1995 Business and Industry, Natural Resources, Rules and Resolutions
1993 Business and Industry, County Affairs

BILL PASSAGE RATES, 1997

	Total	Passed Legislature	Pct. Passed Legislature
Authored	40	5	13%
Sponsored	1	1	100%
Amendments	34	24	71%

ELECTORAL HISTORY IN CURRENT DISTRICT

	1994	1996	1998
Primary Election Opponent(s)	No	Yes	Yes
General Election Opponent(s)	No	No	No

House District 124

COUNTIES IN DISTRICT

Bexar (part)

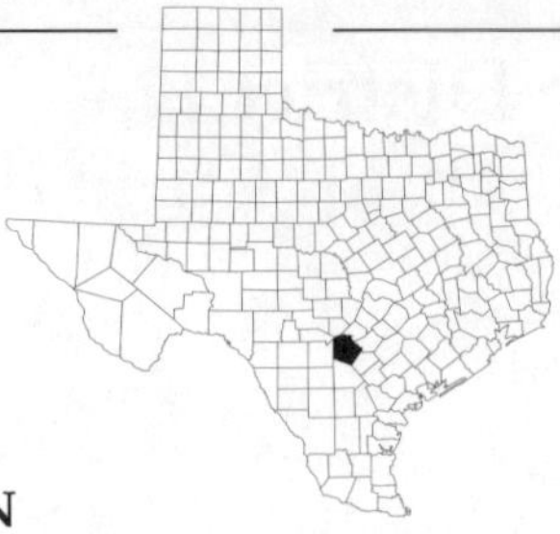

DEMOGRAPHIC INFORMATION

Population

Total	107,558
Anglo	28.0%
Black	5.7%
Hispanic	65.0%
Others	1.6%

Education

High School Graduates	66.3%
College Graduates	14.3%

Age of Population

5 years or less	11.9%
6-17 years	22.0%
18-64 years	59.5%
65 or older	6.6%

Wealth and Urbanization

Per capita Income	$9,140
Avg. House Value	$53,598
Percent Poverty	23.0%
Public Assistance	10.3%
Percent Urban	92.6%

Employed

Percent Employed	90.6%
Private Sector	68.3%

Household Types

Family households	93.6%
Non-family households	6.1%
Single-parent families	21.9%
Both parents working	57.7%

SENATE DISTRICTS IN HOUSE DISTRICT

Dist 19 Frank Madla (D)
Dist 25 Jeff Wentworth (R)
Dist 26 Gregory Luna (D)

DISTRICT ELECTION DATA

House 1996

Christine Hernandez (D)	100.0%

House 1998

Juan F. Solis III (D)	100.0%

President 1996

Bill Clinton (D)	63.6%
Bob Dole (R)	36.4%

Composite Party Vote 1994

Democratic	59.1%
Republican	40.9%

Registered Voters 1996	**68,042**
Turnout	31,210
Percent of registered voting	45.9%

House District 124
Rep. Juan F. Solis, III (D)

House Office
(512) 463-0634

District Office
907 W. Kirk Pl.
San Antonio, Texas 78278
(210) 679-8500

Personal

Year of birth	1961
Family	Married to Mariz Coraida, two children
Education	Sam Houston State University, B.B.A.
Occupation	Consultant and Small Businessman
Religion	Catholic
State legislative service	House 1999 to present

COMMITTEE ASSIGNMENT HISTORY

BILL PASSAGE RATES, 1997

	Total	Passed Legislature	Pct. Passed Legislature
Authored	NA	NA	NA
Sponsored	NA	NA	NA
Amendments	NA	NA	NA

ELECTORAL HISTORY IN CURRENT DISTRICT

	1994	1996	1998
Primary Election Opponent(s)	NA	NA	Yes
General Election Opponent(s)	NA	NA	No

House District 125

COUNTIES IN DISTRICT

Bexar (part)

DEMOGRAPHIC INFORMATION

Population

Total	110,865
Anglo	31.9%
Black	3.9%
Hispanic	62.9%
Others	1.5%

Education

High School Graduates	71.4%
College Graduates	19.9%

Age of Population

5 years or less	10.7%
6-17 years	20.7%
18-64 years	61.7%
65 or older	6.9%

Wealth and Urbanization

Per capita Income	$10,370
Avg. House Value	$58,255
Percent Poverty	19.1%
Public Assistance	8.2%
Percent Urban	100.0%

Employed

Percent Employed	91.5%
Private Sector	70.7%

Household Types

Family households	90.5%
Non-family households	8.2%
Single-parent families	22.7%
Both parents working	61.3%

SENATE DISTRICTS IN HOUSE DISTRICT

Dist 25 Jeff Wentworth (R)

Dist 26 Gregory Luna (D)

DISTRICT ELECTION DATA

House 1996

Arthur (Art) Reyna (D)	61.1%
David J. Kirk (R)	38.9%

President 1996

Bill Clinton (D)	60.5%
Bob Dole (R)	39.5%

Composite Party Vote 1994

Democratic	56.9%
Republican	43.1%

Registered Voters 1996	**67,414**
Turnout	30,801
Percent of registered voting	45.7%

House 1998

Arthur (Art) Reyna (D)	100.0%

House District 125
Rep. Arthur (Art) Reyna (D)

House Office
(512) 463-0642

District Office
P.O. Box 681435
San Antonio, Texas 78268
(210) 680-8683

Personal

Year of birth	1956
Family	Married to Sylvia Reyna, two children
Education	St. Mary's University, B.A., J.D.
Occupation	Attorney
Religion	Catholic
State legislative service	House 1997 to present

COMMITTEE ASSIGNMENT HISTORY
1997 Criminal Jurisprudence, Juvenile Justice and Family Issues

BILL PASSAGE RATES, 1997

	Total	Passed Legislature	Pct. Passed Legislature
Authored	7	3	43%
Sponsored	43	3	100%
Amendments	5	5	100%

ELECTORAL HISTORY IN CURRENT DISTRICT

	1994	1996	1998
Primary Election Opponent(s)	NA	Yes	No
General Election Opponent(s)	NA	Rep	No

House District 126

COUNTIES IN DISTRICT

Harris (part)

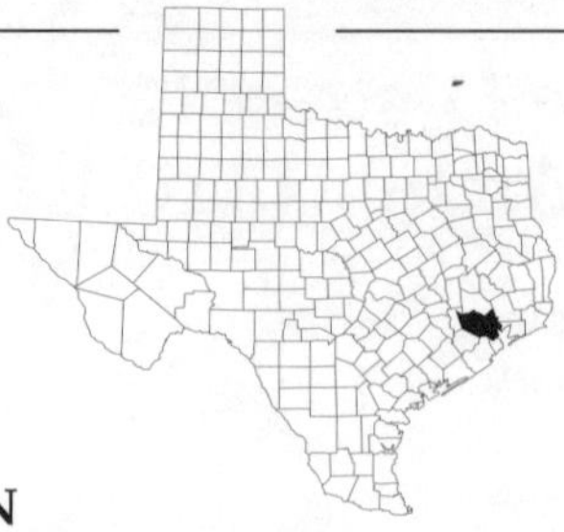

DEMOGRAPHIC INFORMATION

Population		**Wealth and Urbanization**	
Total	117,884	Per capita Income	$22,992
Anglo	81.6%	Avg. House Value	$125,794
Black	5.5%	Percent Poverty	3.6%
Hispanic	8.5%	Public Assistance	1.7%
Others	4.4%	Percent Urban	98.2%

Education		**Employed**	
High School Graduates	91.9%	Percent Employed	96.2%
College Graduates	44.6%	Private Sector	83.8%

Age of Population		**Household Types**	
5 years or less	9.1%	Family households	91.4%
6-17 years	21.1%	Non-family households	8.4%
18-64 years	65.7%	Single-parent families	12.5%
65 or older	4.1%	Both parents working	59.9%

SENATE DISTRICTS IN HOUSE DISTRICT

Dist 7 Jon Lindsay (R)

Dist 15 John Whitmire (D)

DISTRICT ELECTION DATA

House 1996		**House 1998**	
Peggy Hamric (R)	100.0%	Peggy Hamric (R)	100.0%

President 1996	
Bill Clinton (D)	26.4%
Bob Dole (R)	73.6%

Composite Party Vote 1994	
Democratic	23.5%
Republican	75.1%

Registered Voters 1996	**81,392**
Turnout	51,590
Percent of registered voting	63.4%

House District 126
Rep. Peggy Hamric (R)

House Office
(512) 463-0496

District Office
7915 FM 1960 West, Ste. 325
Houston, Texas 77070
(281) 890-1200

Personal

Year of birth	1940
Family	Married to Burt Hamric, two children
Education	University of Oklahoma, B.S., Education
Occupation	State representative, small business owner
Religion	Presbyterian
State legislative service	House 1991 (part) to present

COMMITTEE ASSIGNMENT HISTORY

1997 House Administration, Land and Resource Management, Licensing and Administrative Procedures
1995 County Affairs, Land and Resource Management, Redistricting
1993 Corrections, County Affairs, Redistricting
1991 Cultural and Historical Resources, Urban Affairs

BILL PASSAGE RATES, 1997

	Total	Passed Legislature	Pct. Passed Legislature
Authored	39	6	15%
Sponsored	4	2	50%
Amendments	9	8	89%

ELECTORAL HISTORY IN CURRENT DISTRICT

	1994	1996	1998
Primary Election Opponent(s)	Yes	Yes	No
General Election Opponent(s)	No	No	No

House District 127

COUNTIES IN DISTRICT
Harris (part)

DEMOGRAPHIC INFORMATION

Population		**Wealth and Urbanization**	
Total	113,436	Per capita Income	$18,289
Anglo	85.2%	Avg. House Value	$99,035
Black	5.9%	Percent Poverty	6.8%
Hispanic	7.6%	Public Assistance	3.1%
Others	1.6%	Percent Urban	71.7%

Education		**Employed**	
High School Graduates	87.1%	Percent Employed	95.4%
College Graduates	30.9%	Private Sector	83.4%

Age of Population		**Household Types**	
5 years or less	9.9%	Family households	92.4%
6-17 years	21.9%	Non-family households	7.3%
18-64 years	62.8%	Single-parent families	15.4%
65 or older	5.3%	Both parents working	58.2%

SENATE DISTRICTS IN HOUSE DISTRICT

Dist 4 Michael L. Galloway (R)
Dist 7 Jon Lindsay (R)
Dist 11 Mike Jackson (R)
Dist 15 John Whitmire (D)
Dist 17 J. E. (Buster) Brown (R)

DISTRICT ELECTION DATA

House 1996		**House 1998**	
Joe Crabb (R)	100.0%	Joe Crabb (R)	100.0%

President 1996	
Bill Clinton (D)	28.3%
Bob Dole (R)	71.7%

Composite Party Vote 1994	
Democratic	26.6%
Republican	72.0%

Registered Voters 1996	**76,542**
Turnout	45,028
Percent of registered voting	58.8%

House District 127
Rep. Joe Crabb (R)

House Office
(512) 463-0520

District Office
2240 North Park Dr., #101
Kingwood, Texas 77339
(281) 359-1270

Personal

Year of birth	1939
Family	Married to Nancy Crabb, five children
Education	University of Texas, B.A., J.D. University of St. Thomas, Master of Theology Texas Christian University, Doctor of Ministry
Occupation	Minister, Attorney
Religion	Methodist
State legislative service	House 1993 to present

COMMITTEE ASSIGNMENT HISTORY

1997 General Investigating (Vice-Chair), Judicial Affairs, Land and Resource Management
1995 Business and Industry, Elections, General Investigating (Vice-Chair)
1993 Business and Industry, Elections

BILL PASSAGE RATES, 1997

	Total	Passed Legislature	Pct. Passed Legislature
Authored	15	3	20%
Sponsored	2	0	0%
Amendments	1	1	100%

ELECTORAL HISTORY IN CURRENT DISTRICT

	1994	1996	1998
Primary Election Opponent(s)	No	No	No
General Election Opponent(s)	Dem	No	No

House District 128

COUNTIES IN DISTRICT
Harris (part)

DEMOGRAPHIC INFORMATION

Population

Total	118,153
Anglo	60.7%
Black	15.7%
Hispanic	22.0%
Others	2.2%

Wealth and Urbanization

Per capita Income	$11,800
Avg. House Value	$52,719
Percent Poverty	13.9%
Public Assistance	5.6%
Percent Urban	94.7%

Education

High School Graduates	67.2%
College Graduates	10.5%

Employed

Percent Employed	92.2%
Private Sector	82.9%

Age of Population

5 years or less	10.5%
6-17 years	21.2%
18-64 years	61.2%
65 or older	7.1%

Household Types

Family households	90.4%
Non-family households	9.2%
Single-parent families	19.9%
Both parents working	58.0%

SENATE DISTRICTS IN HOUSE DISTRICT

Dist 6 Mario V. Gallegos (D)
Dist 11 Mike Jackson (R)
Dist 15 John Whitmire (D)

DISTRICT ELECTION DATA

House 1996

Fred M. Bosse (D)	100.0%

House 1998

Fred M. Bosse (D)	62.6%
Dwayne Andries (R)	37.4%

President 1996

Bill Clinton (D)	53.6%
Bob Dole (R)	43.7%

Composite Party Vote 1994

Democratic	51.8%
Republican	46.8%

Registered Voters 1996	**58,460**
Turnout	28,085
Percent of registered voting	48.0%

House District 128
Rep. Fred M. Bosse (D)

House Office
(512) 463-0660

District Office
855 Uvalde Rd. #A
Houston, Texas 77015
(713) 453-6336

Personal

Year of birth	1947
Family	Single, two children
Education	Texas A&M University, B.S.
	University of Houston, J.D.
Occupation	Attorney
Religion	Catholic
State legislative service	House 1991 to present

COMMITTEE ASSIGNMENT HISTORY

1997 Civil Practices, Land and Resource Management (Chair)
1995 Calendars, State Affairs
1993 Natural Resources (Vice-Chair), Transportation (Vice-Chair)
1991 Natural Resources, Science and Technology

BILL PASSAGE RATES, 1997

	Total	Passed Legislature	Pct. Passed Legislature
Authored	37	11	30%
Sponsored	14	12	86%
Amendments	17	14	82%

ELECTORAL HISTORY IN CURRENT DISTRICT

	1994	1996	1998
Primary Election Opponent(s)	No	No	No
General Election Opponent(s)	No	No	Rep

House District 129

COUNTIES IN DISTRICT
Harris (part)

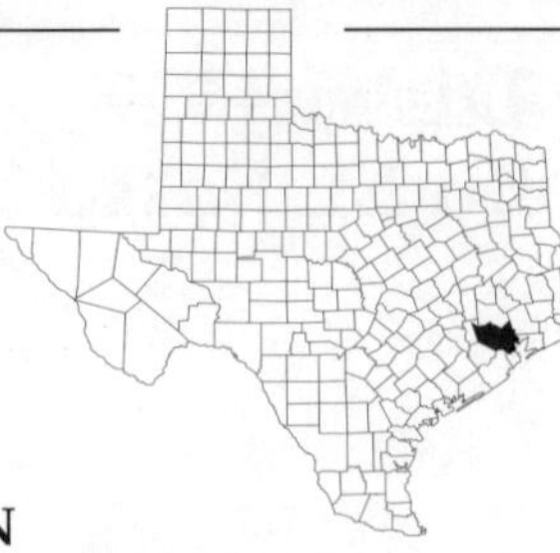

DEMOGRAPHIC INFORMATION

Population

Total	117,198
Anglo	83.2%
Black	3.8%
Hispanic	9.3%
Others	3.7%

Wealth and Urbanization

Per capita Income	$19,352
Avg. House Value	$87,486
Percent Poverty	5.8%
Public Assistance	2.3%
Percent Urban	99.9%

Education

High School Graduates	88.1%
College Graduates	30.2%

Employed

Percent Employed	95.7%
Private Sector	81.3%

Age of Population

5 years or less	8.9%
6-17 years	18.9%
18-64 years	66.9%
65 or older	5.3%

Household Types

Family households	87.8%
Non-family households	11.6%
Single-parent families	15.0%
Both parents working	63.0%

SENATE DISTRICTS IN HOUSE DISTRICT

Dist 6 Mario V. Gallegos (D)
Dist 11 Mike Jackson (R)
Dist 15 John Whitmire (D)
Dist 17 J. E. (Buster) Brown (R)

DISTRICT ELECTION DATA

House 1996

Mike Jackson (R)	100.0%

President 1996

Bill Clinton (D)	33.3%
Bob Dole (R)	66.7%

Composite Party Vote 1994

Democratic	31.0%
Republican	67.6%

Registered Voters 1996	**83,541**
Turnout	49,511
Percent of registered voting	59.3%

House 1998

Rick O'Sullivan (D)	27.7%
John Davis (R)	70.6%
Kevin J. Hagen (Lib)	1.7%

House District 129
Rep. John Davis (R)

House Office
(512) 463-0734

District Office
1314B Underwood
La Porte, Texas 77571
(281) 476-4364

Personal

Year of birth	1960
Family	Jayne Davis, three children
Education	Baylor University, B.B.A.
	University of Houston Clear Lake, B.A.
Occupation	Business Owner
Religion	Christian
State legislative service	House 1999 to present

COMMITTEE ASSIGNMENT HISTORY

BILL PASSAGE RATES, 1997

	Total	Passed Legislature	Pct. Passed Legislature
Authored	NA	NA	NA
Sponsored	NA	NA	NA
Amendments	NA	NA	NA

ELECTORAL HISTORY IN CURRENT DISTRICT

	1994	1996	1998
Primary Election Opponent(s)	NA	NA	Yes
General Election Opponent(s)	NA	NA	Dem, Lib

House District 130

COUNTIES IN DISTRICT
Harris (part)

DEMOGRAPHIC INFORMATION

Population

Total	118,415
Anglo	81.7%
Black	4.1%
Hispanic	10.6%
Others	3.7%

Wealth and Urbanization

Per capita Income	$19,038
Avg. House Value	$92,402
Percent Poverty	4.5%
Public Assistance	1.7%
Percent Urban	88.6%

Education

High School Graduates	90.7%
College Graduates	36.3%

Employed

Percent Employed	96.7%
Private Sector	83.8%

Age of Population

5 years or less	11.4%
6-17 years	19.8%
18-64 years	65.0%
65 or older	3.8%

Household Types

Family households	89.6%
Non-family households	10.1%
Single-parent families	13.6%
Both parents working	65.3%

SENATE DISTRICTS IN HOUSE DISTRICT

Dist 7 Jon Lindsay (R)
Dist 17 J. E. (Buster) Brown (R)

DISTRICT ELECTION DATA

House 1996

John Culberson (R)	100.0%

House 1998

John Culberson (R)	100.0%

President 1996

Bill Clinton (D)	27.5%
Bob Dole (R)	72.5%

Composite Party Vote 1994

Democratic	24.4%
Republican	74.2%

Registered Voters 1996	**85,615**
Turnout	54,316
Percent of registered voting	63.4%

House District 130
Rep. John Culberson (R)

House Office
(512) 463-0528

District Office
15119 Memorial Dr., # 216
Houston, Texas 77079
(281) 558-7018

Personal

Year of birth	1956
Family	Married to Belinda Culberson, one child
Education	Southern Methodist University, B.A.
	South Texas Law, J.D.
Occupation	Attorney
Religion	Protestant
State legislative service	House 1987 to present

COMMITTEE ASSIGNMENT HISTORY

1997 Natural Resources, Public Education
1995 Civil Practices, Corrections
1993 Energy Resources, Urban Affairs
1991 Judicial Affairs, Corrections (Vice-Chair)
1989 Natural Resources, Science and Technology
1987 Public Education, Science and Technology

BILL PASSAGE RATES, 1997

	Total	Passed Legislature	Pct. Passed Legislature
Authored	33	3	9%
Sponsored	2	2	100%
Amendments	16	13	81%

ELECTORAL HISTORY IN CURRENT DISTRICT

	1994	1996	1998
Primary Election Opponent(s)	No	No	No
General Election Opponent(s)	Dem	No	No

House District 131

COUNTIES IN DISTRICT
Harris (part)

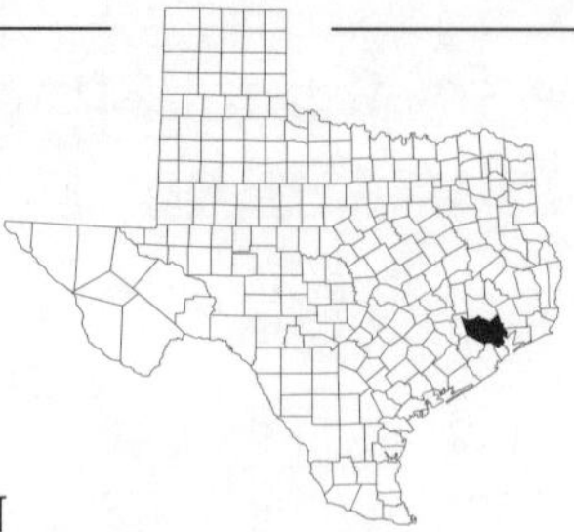

DEMOGRAPHIC INFORMATION

Population		Wealth and Urbanization	
Total	107,848	Per capita Income	$13,182
Anglo	28.6%	Avg. House Value	$61,131
Black	53.0%	Percent Poverty	16.1%
Hispanic	14.3%	Public Assistance	6.3%
Others	5.0%	Percent Urban	99.2%

Education		Employed	
High School Graduates	79.3%	Percent Employed	91.5%
College Graduates	27.4%	Private Sector	79.1%

Age of Population		Household Types	
5 years or less	10.4%	Family households	86.1%
6-17 years	18.2%	Non-family households	13.6%
18-64 years	65.1%	Single-parent families	35.9%
65 or older	6.3%	Both parents working	70.4%

SENATE DISTRICTS IN HOUSE DISTRICT

Dist 13 Rodney Ellis (D)

Dist 17 J. E. (Buster) Brown (R)

DISTRICT ELECTION DATA

House 1996		House 1998	
Ron Wilson (D)	100.0%	Ron Wilson (D)	100.0%

President 1996	
Bill Clinton (D)	76.4%
Bob Dole (R)	23.6%

Composite Party Vote 1994	
Democratic	70.2%
Republican	28.4%

Registered Voters 1996	**55,775**
Turnout	29,644
Percent of registered voting	53.1%

House District 131
Rep. Ron Wilson (D)

House Office
(512) 463-0744

District Office
5039 Reed Rd.
Houston, Texas 77033
(713) 731-2400

Personal

Year of birth	1953
Family	Married to Treina Wilson, two children
Education	University of Texas, B.A., J.D.
Occupation	Attorney
Religion	Church of Christ
State legislative service	House 1977 to present

COMMITTEE ASSIGNMENT HISTORY

1997 Energy Resources, Licensing and Administrative Procedures (Chair), Redistricting
1995 Licensing and Administrative Procedures (Chair), Pensions and Investments, Redistricting
1993 Licensing and Administrative Procedures (Chair), Redistricting, State Affairs
1991 Liquor Regulation (Chair), Redistricting, Ways and Means
1989 Liquor Regulation (Chair), Ways and Means
1987 Liquor Regulation (Chair), Ways and Means
1985 Calendars, Government Organization (Vice-Chair)
1983 Judiciary, Public Health
1981 Calendars, Energy Resources, Health Services (Chair)
1979 Calendars, Financial Institutions, Higher Education
1977 Energy Resources, Financial Institutions

BILL PASSAGE RATES, 1997

	Total	Passed Legislature	Pct. Passed Legislature
Authored	74	2	3%
Sponsored	5	2	40%
Amendments	11	9	82%

ELECTORAL HISTORY IN CURRENT DISTRICT

	1994	1996	1998
Primary Election Opponent(s)	No	No	Yes
General Election Opponent(s)	No	No	No

House District 132

COUNTIES IN DISTRICT
Harris (part)

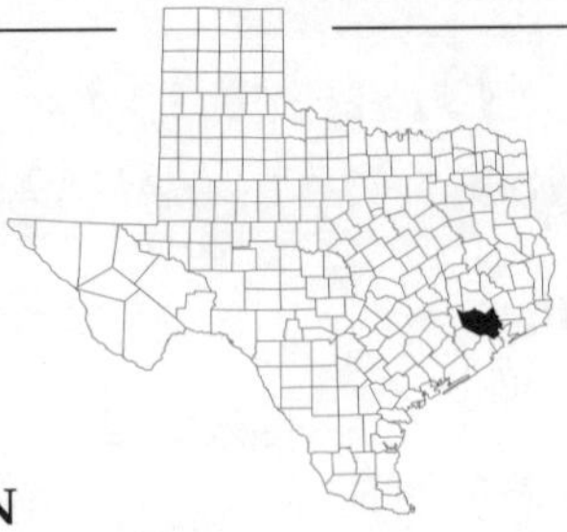

DEMOGRAPHIC INFORMATION

Population

Total	107,853
Anglo	52.8%
Black	30.2%
Hispanic	13.0%
Others	4.8%

Education

High School Graduates	85.8%
College Graduates	42.7%

Age of Population

5 years or less	8.5%
6-17 years	13.8%
18-64 years	66.8%
65 or older	10.8%

Wealth and Urbanization

Per capita Income	$20,278
Avg. House Value	$112,528
Percent Poverty	13.0%
Public Assistance	4.3%
Percent Urban	100.0%

Employed

Percent Employed	94.2%
Private Sector	77.3%

Household Types

Family households	77.9%
Non-family households	19.1%
Single-parent families	29.8%
Both parents working	69.1%

SENATE DISTRICTS IN HOUSE DISTRICT

Dist 13 Rodney Ellis (D)

Dist 17 J. E. (Buster) Brown (R)

DISTRICT ELECTION DATA

House 1996

Scott Hochberg (D)	63.9%
Ken Zimmern (R)	36.1%

President 1996

Bill Clinton (D)	58.7%
Bob Dole (R)	41.3%

Composite Party Vote 1994

Democratic	53.4%
Republican	45.0%

Registered Voters 1996	**67,725**
Turnout	41,979
Percent of registered voting	62.0%

House 1998

Scott Hochberg (D)	100.0%

House District 132
Rep. Scott Hochberg (D)

House Office
(512) 463-0492

District Office
4660 Beechnut #245
Houston, Texas 77096
(713) 660-7783

Personal

Year of birth	1953
Family	Married to Kathryn Elek, no children
Education	Rice University, B.A., Master of Electrical Engineering
Occupation	Electronics consultant
Religion	Jewish
State legislative service	House 1993 to present

COMMITTEE ASSIGNMENT HISTORY

1997 Appropriations, Public Education
1995 Public Education, State Affairs
1993 Natural Resources, Public Education,

BILL PASSAGE RATES, 1997

	Total	Passed Legislature	Pct. Passed Legislature
Authored	29	9	31%
Sponsored	4	3	75%
Amendments	22	21	95%

ELECTORAL HISTORY IN CURRENT DISTRICT

	1994	1996	1998
Primary Election Opponent(s)	Yes	No	No
General Election Opponent(s)	No	Rep	No

House District 133

COUNTIES IN DISTRICT

Harris (part)

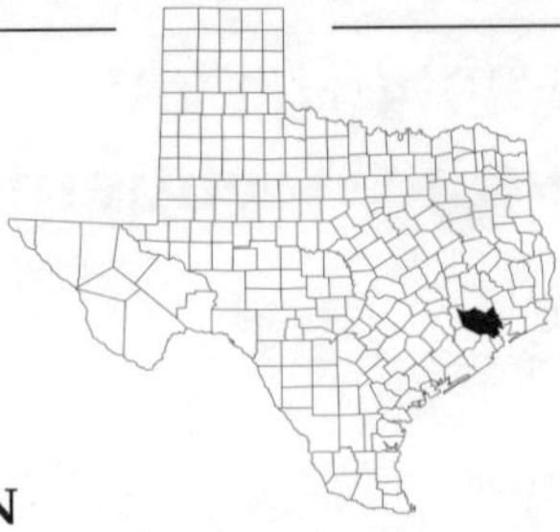

DEMOGRAPHIC INFORMATION

Population		**Wealth and Urbanization**	
Total	118,575	Per capita Income	$27,177
Anglo	76.6%	Avg. House Value	$153,206
Black	4.4%	Percent Poverty	7.2%
Hispanic	13.0%	Public Assistance	1.8%
Others	6.2%	Percent Urban	100.0%

Education		**Employed**	
High School Graduates	92.1%	Percent Employed	96.1%
College Graduates	51.2%	Private Sector	84.6%

Age of Population		**Household Types**	
5 years or less	7.2%	Family households	76.2%
6-17 years	12.2%	Non-family households	23.1%
18-64 years	71.2%	Single-parent families	20.5%
65 or older	9.5%	Both parents working	59.2%

SENATE DISTRICTS IN HOUSE DISTRICT

Dist 6 Mario V. Gallegos Jr. (D)
Dist 7 Jon Lindsay (R)
Dist 13 Rodney Ellis (D)
Dist 17 J. E. (Buster) Brown (R)

DISTRICT ELECTION DATA

House 1996		**House 1998**	
Joe M. Nixon (R)	100.0%	Joe M. Nixon (R)	100.0%

President 1996	
Bill Clinton (D)	28.9%
Bob Dole (R)	71.1%

Composite Party Vote 1994	
Democratic	27.7%
Republican	70.9%

Registered Voters 1996	**77,834**
Turnout	48,411
Percent of registered voting	62.2%

House District 133
Rep. Joe M. Nixon (R)

House Office
(512) 463-0514

District Office
P.O. Box 2910
Austin, Texas 78768
(713) 785-7373
(800) 643-7329

Personal

Year of birth	1956
Family	Married to Allyson Nixon, three children
Education	Texas A&M University, B.S., Economics St. Mary's University, J.D.
Occupation	Attorney
Religion	Catholic
State legislative service	House 1995 to present

COMMITTEE ASSIGNMENT HISTORY

1997 Civil Practices, Criminal Jurisprudence
1995 Criminal Jurisprudence, Judicial Affairs

BILL PASSAGE RATES, 1997

	Total	Passed Legislature	Pct. Passed Legislature
Authored	37	2	5%
Sponsored	1	0	0%
Amendments	8	5	63%

ELECTORAL HISTORY IN CURRENT DISTRICT

	1994	1996	1998
Primary Election Opponent(s)	Yes	No	No
General Election Opponent(s)	Dem	No	No

House District 134

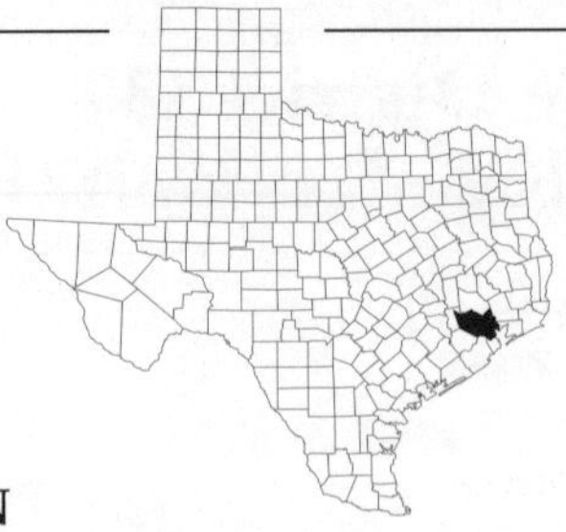

COUNTIES IN DISTRICT

Harris (part)

DEMOGRAPHIC INFORMATION

Population

Total	118,523
Anglo	55.5%
Black	17.3%
Hispanic	21.7%
Others	6.3%

Wealth and Urbanization

Per capita Income	$19,441
Avg. House Value	$149,169
Percent Poverty	14.5%
Public Assistance	3.4%
Percent Urban	100.0%

Education

High School Graduates	84.0%
College Graduates	40.5%

Employed

Percent Employed	94.2%
Private Sector	83.4%

Age of Population

5 years or less	10.7%
6-17 years	12.3%
18-64 years	68.5%
65 or older	8.5%

Household Types

Family households	76.5%
Non-family households	23.1%
Single-parent families	27.8%
Both parents working	66.0%

SENATE DISTRICTS IN HOUSE DISTRICT

Dist 6 Mario V. Gallegos Jr. (D)
Dist 7 Jon Lindsay (R)
Dist 13 Rodney Ellis (D)
Dist 17 J. E. (Buster) Brown (R)

DISTRICT ELECTION DATA

House 1996

Kyle Janek (R)	100.0%

House 1998

Mike Laster (D)	39.7%
Kyle Janek (R)	60.3%

President 1996

Bill Clinton (D)	44.6%
Bob Dole (R)	55.4%

Composite Party Vote 1994

Democratic	40.4%
Republican	58.2%

Registered Voters 1996	**60,423**
Turnout	35,245
Percent of registered voting	58.3%

House District 134
Rep. Kyle Janek (R)

House Office
(512) 463-0748

District Office
7777 SW Freeway, #102
Houston, Texas 77074
(713) 272-8929

Personal

Year of birth	1958
Family	Married, no children
Education	Texas A&M University, B.S., Zoology University of Texas Medical Branch, M.D.
Occupation	Physician
Religion	Episcopalian
State legislative service	House 1995 to present

COMMITTEE ASSIGNMENT HISTORY

1997 Business and Industry, Public Health
1995 Business and Industry, Public Health

BILL PASSAGE RATES, 1997

	Total	Passed Legislature	Pct. Passed Legislature
Authored	28	6	21%
Sponsored	13	9	69%
Amendments	13	9	69%

ELECTORAL HISTORY IN CURRENT DISTRICT

	1994	1996	1998
Primary Election Opponent(s)	Yes	No	No
General Election Opponent(s)	Dem, Lib	No	Dem

House District 135

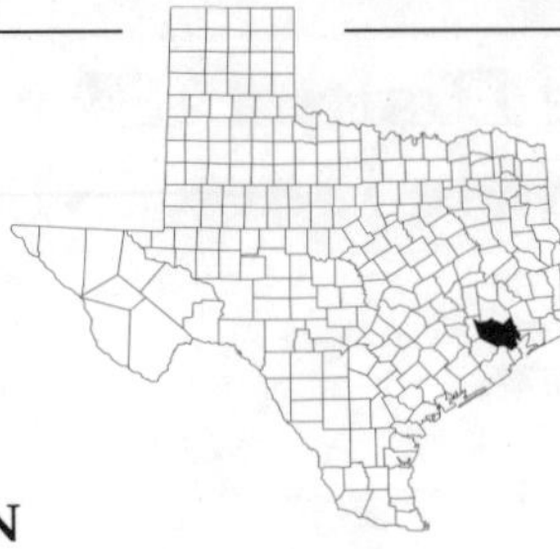

COUNTIES IN DISTRICT
Harris (part)

DEMOGRAPHIC INFORMATION

Population		**Wealth and Urbanization**	
Total	117,668	Per capita Income	$16,839
Anglo	75.5%	Avg. House Value	$78,706
Black	6.3%	Percent Poverty	5.1%
Hispanic	12.4%	Public Assistance	2.1%
Others	6.0%	Percent Urban	98.4%

Education		**Employed**	
High School Graduates	88.6%	Percent Employed	95.9%
College Graduates	32.0%	Private Sector	84.0%

Age of Population		**Household Types**	
5 years or less	12.3%	Family households	90.5%
6-17 years	19.7%	Non-family households	9.5%
18-64 years	65.0%	Single-parent families	15.0%
65 or older	3.0%	Both parents working	66.3%

SENATE DISTRICTS IN HOUSE DISTRICT

Dist 6 Mario V. Gallegos Jr. (D)
Dist 7 Jon Lindsay (R)
Dist 15 John Whitmire (D)

DISTRICT ELECTION DATA

House 1996		**House 1998**	
Gary Elkins (R)	100.0%	Gary Elkins (R)	100.0%

President 1996	
Bill Clinton (D)	31.2%
Bob Dole (R)	68.8%

Composite Party Vote 1994	
Democratic	27.4%
Republican	71.1%

Registered Voters 1996	**75,422**
Turnout	46,834
Percent of registered voting	62.1%

House District 135
Rep. Gary Elkins (R)

House Office
(512) 463-0722

District Office
9219 Katy Freeway, #223
Houston, Texas 77024
(713) 468-1990

Personal

Year of birth	1955
Family	Married to Julie Elkins, four children
Education	Southwestern Assemblies of God College, B.S.
Occupation	Businessman, Consultant
Religion	Assembly of God
State legislative service	House 1995 to present

COMMITTEE ASSIGNMENT HISTORY

1997 Business and Industry, Financial Institutions
1995 Financial Institutions, Rules and Resolutions, State, Federal and International Relations

BILL PASSAGE RATES, 1997

	Total	Passed Legislature	Pct. Passed Legislature
Authored	11	2	18%
Sponsored	2	2	100%
Amendments	0	0	NA

ELECTORAL HISTORY IN CURRENT DISTRICT

	1994	1996	1998
Primary Election Opponent(s)	Yes	No	No
General Election Opponent(s)	Lib	No	No

House District 136

COUNTIES IN DISTRICT

Harris (part)

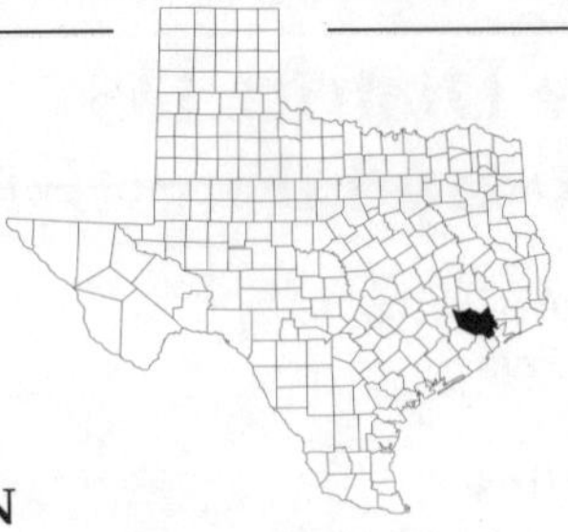

DEMOGRAPHIC INFORMATION

Population	
Total	118,251
Anglo	75.8%
Black	4.3%
Hispanic	15.3%
Others	4.8%

Education	
High School Graduates	86.9%
College Graduates	45.1%

Age of Population	
5 years or less	7.6%
6-17 years	13.1%
18-64 years	68.0%
65 or older	11.3%

Wealth and Urbanization	
Per capita Income	$34,871
Avg. House Value	$245,685
Percent Poverty	9.8%
Public Assistance	3.0%
Percent Urban	100.0%

Employed	
Percent Employed	95.8%
Private Sector	83.2%

Household Types	
Family households	77.3%
Non-family households	21.7%
Single-parent families	23.6%
Both parents working	57.6%

SENATE DISTRICTS IN HOUSE DISTRICT

Dist 6 Mario V. Gallegos Jr. (D)
Dist 7 Jon Lindsay (R)
Dist 13 Rodney Ellis (D)
Dist 15 John Whitmire (D)
Dist 17 J. E. (Buster) Brown (R)

DISTRICT ELECTION DATA

House 1996	
Beverly Woolley (R)	92.4%
Gary William Moore (L)	7.6%

President 1996	
Bill Clinton (D)	27.0%
Bob Dole (R)	73.0%

Composite Party Vote 1994	
Democratic	28.3%
Republican	70.2%

Registered Voters 1996	77,159
Turnout	49,881
Percent of registered voting	64.6%

House 1998	
Beverly Woolley (R)	92.1%
Ben Easton (L)	7.9%

House District 136
Rep. Beverly Woolley (R)

House Office
(512) 463-0696

District Office
2200 Post Oak Blvd. #625
Houston, Texas 77056
(713) 629-6313

Personal

Year of birth	1939
Family	Married to Lynn A. Woolley, three children
Education	University of Houston, B.A., Political Science
Occupation	Small business owner
Religion	Catholic
State legislative service	House 1995 to present

COMMITTEE ASSIGNMENT HISTORY

1997 Business and Industry, Pensions and Investments (Vice-Chair)
1995 Local and Consent Calendars, State Recreational Resources, Urban Affairs

BILL PASSAGE RATES, 1997

	Total	Passed Legislature	Pct. Passed Legislature
Authored	25	8	32%
Sponsored	3	1	33%
Amendments	6	6	100%

ELECTORAL HISTORY IN CURRENT DISTRICT

	1994	1996	1998
Primary Election Opponent(s)	Yes	No	No
General Election Opponent(s)	Lib	Lib	Lib

House District 137

COUNTIES IN DISTRICT

Harris (part)

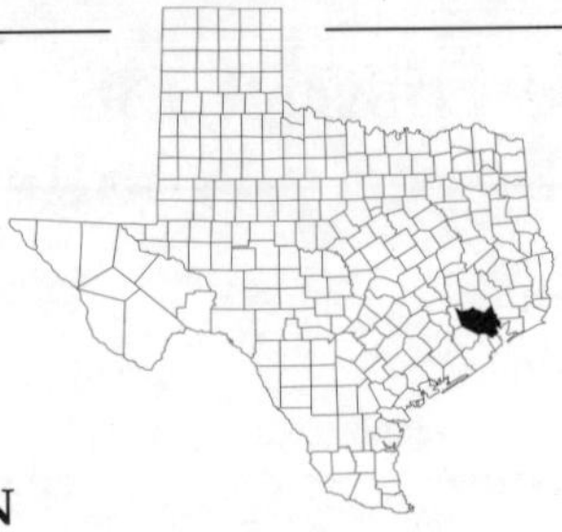

DEMOGRAPHIC INFORMATION

Population

Total	111,406
Anglo	47.1%
Black	9.6%
Hispanic	39.8%
Others	4.2%

Education

High School Graduates	71.4%
College Graduates	35.2%

Age of Population

5 years or less	8.5%
6-17 years	11.3%
18-64 years	73.9%
65 or older	6.3%

Wealth and Urbanization

Per capita Income	$16,549
Avg. House Value	$123,060
Percent Poverty	24.7%
Public Assistance	4.2%
Percent Urban	100.0%

Employed

Percent Employed	93.0%
Private Sector	83.4%

Household Types

Family households	61.8%
Non-family households	36.6%
Single-parent families	28.8%
Both parents working	64.1%

SENATE DISTRICTS IN HOUSE DISTRICT

Dist 6 Mario V. Gallegos Jr. (D)
Dist 7 Jon Lindsay (R)
Dist 13 Rodney Ellis (D)
Dist 15 John Whitmire (D)
Dist 17 J. E. (Buster) Brown (R)

DISTRICT ELECTION DATA

House 1996

Debra Danburg (D)	64.7%
Chris LaRue (R)	35.3%

President 1996

Bill Clinton (D)	59.6%
Bob Dole (R)	40.4%

Composite Party Vote 1994

Democratic	56.5%
Republican	42.0%

Registered Voters 1996	**55,7514**
Turnout	30,372
Percent of registered voting	54.5%

House 1998

Debra Danburg (D)	63.2%
Ben Domingues, II (R)	36.8%

House District 137
Rep. Debra Danburg (D)

House Office
(512) 463-0504

District Office
P.O. Box 66602
Houston, Texas 77266
(713) 520-8068

Personal

Year of birth	1951
Family	Single, no children
Education	University of Houston, B.A., Sociology Texas Law Center, Bates College of Law, J.D.
Occupation	Attorney
Religion	Jewish
State legislative service	House 1981 to present

COMMITTEE ASSIGNMENT HISTORY

1997 Calendars, Elections (Chair), State Affairs
1995 Elections (Chair), State Affairs
1993 Elections (Chair), State Affairs
1991 Elections (Chair), State Affairs
1989 Appropriations, Cultural and Historical Resources
1987 Criminal Jurisprudence, Rules and Resolutions, State Affairs
1985 Criminal Jurisprudence, Cultural and Historical Resources (Vice-Chair), Rules and Resolutions
1983 Criminal Jurisprudence, Environmental Affairs (Vice-Chair)
1981 Business and Industry, Elections

BILL PASSAGE RATES, 1997

	Total	Passed Legislature	Pct. Passed Legislature
Authored	61	14	23%
Sponsored	12	11	92%
Amendments	7	5	71%

ELECTORAL HISTORY IN CURRENT DISTRICT

	1994	1996	1998
Primary Election Opponent(s)	No	No	No
General Election Opponent(s)	Lib	Rep	Rep

House District 138

COUNTIES IN DISTRICT
Harris (part)

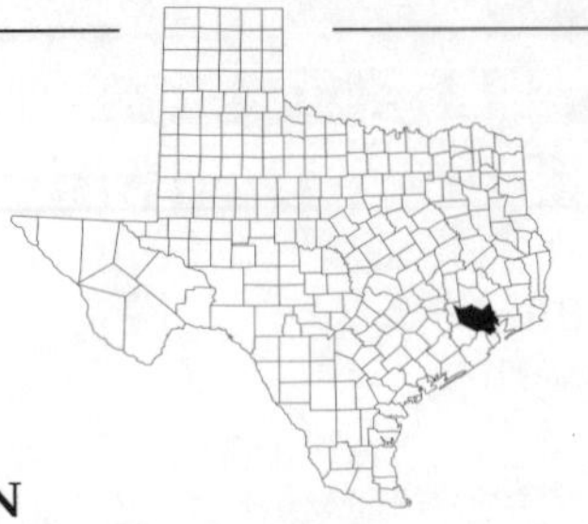

DEMOGRAPHIC INFORMATION

Population	
Total	111,559
Anglo	50.7%
Black	21.0%
Hispanic	26.5%
Others	2.3%

Wealth and Urbanization	
Per capita Income	$12,040
Avg. House Value	$59,230
Percent Poverty	18.5%
Public Assistance	7.0%
Percent Urban	100.0%

Education	
High School Graduates	66.6%
College Graduates	13.4%

Employed	
Percent Employed	92.1%
Private Sector	83.6%

Age of Population	
5 years or less	9.7%
6-17 years	16.5%
18-64 years	62.5%
65 or older	11.3%

Household Types	
Family households	85.1%
Non-family households	14.1%
Single-parent families	30.3%
Both parents working	63.3%

SENATE DISTRICTS IN HOUSE DISTRICT

Dist 6 Mario V. Gallegos Jr. (D)
Dist 15 John Whitmire (D)

DISTRICT ELECTION DATA

House 1996	
Ken Yarbrough (D)	51.0%
Dwayne Bohac (R)	49.0%

House 1998	
Ken Yarbrough (D)	50.4%
Dwayne Bohac (R)	49.6%

President 1996	
Bill Clinton (D)	54.9%
Bob Dole (R)	45.1%

Composite Party Vote 1994	
Democratic	50.9%
Republican	47.7%

Registered Voters 1996	**58,085**
Turnout	30,881
Percent of registered voting	53.2%

House District 138
Rep. Ken Yarbrough (D)*

House Office
(512) 463-0648

District Office
1412 W. 43rd Street
Houston, Texas 77018
(713) 263-1516
(713) 263-9665 fax

Personal

Year of birth	1937
Family	Single, four children
Education	Houston Community College Purdue University
Occupation	Executive director of Plumbing Education Council of Texas
Religion	Catholic
State legislative service	House 1991 to present

COMMITTEE ASSIGNMENT HISTORY

1997 Economic Development (Vice-Chair), Licensing and Administrative Procedures
1995 Economic Development (Vice-Chair), Licensing and Administrative Procedures
1993 Economic Development (Vice-Chair), Licensing and Administrative Procedures
1991 Labor and Employment Relations, Urban Affairs

BILL PASSAGE RATES, 1997

	Total	Passed Legislature	Pct. Passed Legislature
Authored	43	10	23%
Sponsored	5	4	80%
Amendments	21	17	81%

ELECTORAL HISTORY IN CURRENT DISTRICT

	1994	1996	1998
Primary Election Opponent(s)	No	Yes	No
General Election Opponent(s)	Rep, Lib	Rep	Rep

*See also page 403.

House District 139

COUNTIES IN DISTRICT

Harris (part)

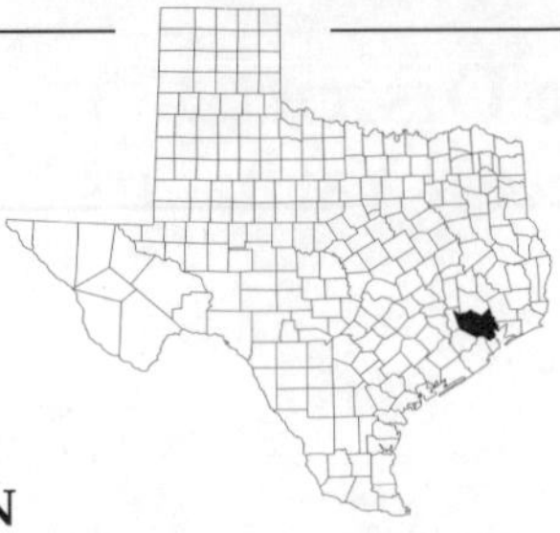

DEMOGRAPHIC INFORMATION

Population	
Total	109,819
Anglo	30.1%
Black	48.2%
Hispanic	16.2%
Others	6.2%

Wealth and Urbanization	
Per capita Income	$10,820
Avg. House Value	$50,867
Percent Poverty	19.2%
Public Assistance	7.6%
Percent Urban	100.0%

Education	
High School Graduates	70.6%
College Graduates	15.2%

Employed	
Percent Employed	90.7%
Private Sector	80.8%

Age of Population	
5 years or less	11.1%
6-17 years	21.2%
18-64 years	62.8%
65 or older	5.0%

Household Types	
Family households	89.6%
Non-family households	10.4%
Single-parent families	29.8%
Both parents working	66.7%

SENATE DISTRICTS IN HOUSE DISTRICT

Dist 6 Mario V. Gallegos Jr. (D)

Dist 15 John Whitmire (D)

DISTRICT ELECTION DATA

House 1996	
Sylvester Turner (D)	100.0%

House 1998	
Sylvester Turner (D)	100.0%

President 1996	
Bill Clinton (D)	76.2%
Bob Dole (R)	23.8%

Composite Party Vote 1994	
Democratic	71.7%
Republican	26.8%

Registered Voters 1996	**51,880**
Turnout	23,982
Percent of registered voting	46.2%

House District 139
Rep. Sylvester Turner (D)

House Office
(512) 463-0554

District Office
6915 Antoine, Ste. E
Houston, Texas 77091
(713) 683-6363

Personal

Year of birth	1954
Family	Single, one child
Education	University of Houston, B.A.
	Harvard University, J.D.
Occupation	Attorney
Religion	Baptist
State legislative service	House 1989 to present

COMMITTEE ASSIGNMENT HISTORY

1997 Appropriations, Calendars, State Affairs (Vice-Chair)
1995 Appropriations, Calendars, State Affairs (Vice-Chair)
1993 Calendars (Vice-Chair), Corrections, State Affairs
1991 Energy, House Administration
1989 Energy, Labor and Employment Relations

BILL PASSAGE RATES, 1997

	Total	Passed Legislature	Pct. Passed Legislature
Authored	43	10	23%
Sponsored	6	5	83%
Amendments	15	13	87%

ELECTORAL HISTORY IN CURRENT DISTRICT

	1994	1996	1998
Primary Election Opponent(s)	No	No	No
General Election Opponent(s)	No	No	No

House District 140

COUNTIES IN DISTRICT

Harris (part)

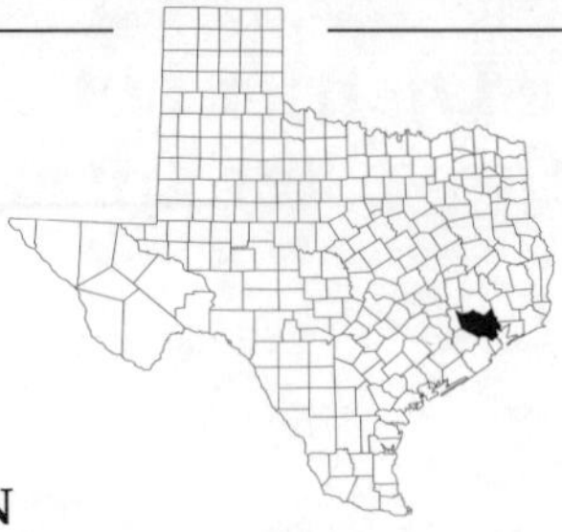

DEMOGRAPHIC INFORMATION

Population		Wealth and Urbanization	
Total	107,265	Per capita Income	$7,723
Anglo	37.0%	Avg. House Value	$39,621
Black	12.0%	Percent Poverty	25.7%
Hispanic	49.9%	Public Assistance	9.3%
Others	1.8%	Percent Urban	100.0%

Education		Employed	
High School Graduates	47.8%	Percent Employed	90.3%
College Graduates	3.8%	Private Sector	82.4%

Age of Population		Household Types	
5 years or less	11.3%	Family households	92.6%
6-17 years	22.8%	Non-family households	7.3%
18-64 years	58.9%	Single-parent families	23.6%
65 or older	6.9%	Both parents working	49.0%

SENATE DISTRICTS IN HOUSE DISTRICT

Dist 6 Mario V. Gallegos Jr. (D)
Dist 13 Rodney Ellis (D)
Dist 15 John Whitmire (D)

DISTRICT ELECTION DATA

House 1996		House 1998	
Kevin Bailey (D)	100.0%	Kevin Bailey (D)	100.0%

President 1996	
Bill Clinton (D)	65.4%
Bob Dole (R)	34.6%

Composite Party Vote 1994	
Democratic	57.3%
Republican	41.3%

Registered Voters 1996	**43,572**
Turnout	17,968
Percent of registered voting	41.2%

House District 140
Rep. Kevin Bailey (D)

House Office
(512) 463-0924

District Office
507 Sam Houston Parkway
Houston, Texas 77060
(281) 847-9000

Personal

Year of birth	1951
Family	Single, two children
Education	University of Texas at El Paso, B.A.
	Sam Houston State University, M.A.
Occupation	College teacher
Religion	Methodist
State legislative service	House 1991 to present

COMMITTEE ASSIGNMENT HISTORY

1997 Higher Education, House Administration, Urban Affairs (Vice-Chair)
1995 House Administration, Public Safety (Vice-Chair), Urban Affairs
1993 House Administration, Public Safety (Vice-Chair), Urban Affairs
1991 Public Safety, Urban Affairs

BILL PASSAGE RATES, 1997

	Total	Passed Legislature	Pct. Passed Legislature
Authored	39	3	8%
Sponsored	5	2	40%
Amendments	10	8	80%

ELECTORAL HISTORY IN CURRENT DISTRICT

	1994	1996	1998
Primary Election Opponent(s)	Yes	Yes	No
General Election Opponent(s)	No	No	No

House District 141

COUNTIES IN DISTRICT
Harris (part)

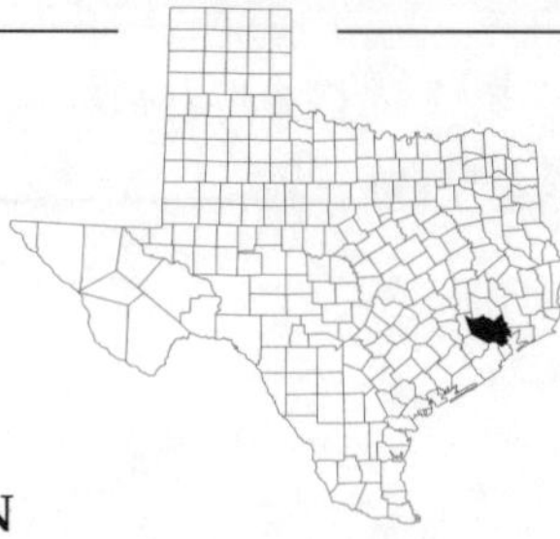

DEMOGRAPHIC INFORMATION

Population

Total	108,371
Anglo	31.0%
Black	53.3%
Hispanic	15.2%
Others	1.3%

Wealth and Urbanization

Per capita Income	$9,481
Avg. House Value	$46,705
Percent Poverty	21.6%
Public Assistance	10.2%
Percent Urban	84.1%

Education

High School Graduates	64.2%
College Graduates	9.5%

Employed

Percent Employed	88.6%
Private Sector	79.4%

Age of Population

5 years or less	10.2%
6-17 years	21.4%
18-64 years	61.2%
65 or older	7.1%

Household Types

Family households	90.1%
Non-family households	8.2%
Single-parent families	32.5%
Both parents working	59.8%

SENATE DISTRICTS IN HOUSE DISTRICT

Dist 6 Mario V. Gallegos Jr. (D)
Dist 7 Jon Lindsay (R)
Dist 13 Rodney Ellis (D)
Dist 15 John Whitmire (D)

DISTRICT ELECTION DATA

House 1996

Senfronia Thompson (D)	100.0%

House 1998

Senfronia Thompson (D)	100.0%

President 1996

Bill Clinton (D)	76.1%
Bob Dole (R)	23.9%

Composite Party Vote 1994

Democratic	73.8%
Republican	24.8%

Registered Voters 1996	**67,401**
Turnout	31,703
Percent of registered voting	47.0%

House District 141
Rep. Senfronia Thompson (D)

House Office
(512) 463-0720

District Office
10527 Homestead
Houston, Texas 77016
(713) 633-3390
(713) 633-7830 (Fax)

Personal

Year of birth	
Family	Single, two children
Education	Texas Southern University, B.S., J.D.
	Prairie View A&M University, M.Ed.
Occupation	Attorney
Religion	Nondenominational
State legislative service	House 1973 to present

COMMITTEE ASSIGNMENT HISTORY

1997 Judicial Affairs (Chair), Ways and Means
1995 Judicial Affairs (Chair), Local and Consent Calendars, Urban Affairs
1993 International and Cultural Relations, Judicial Affairs (Chair)
1991 Judicial Affairs (Chair), Retirement and Aging
1989 Insurance, Judiciary (Chair), Redistricting
1987 Insurance, Judicial Affairs, Rules and Resolutions (Chair),
1985 Appropriations, Elections
1983 Appropriations, Labor and Employment Relations,
1981 Appropriations, Environmental Affairs, Rules
1979 Appropriations, Business and Industry, Local and Consent Calendars
1977 Local and Consent Calendars
1975 Constitutional Revision, Higher Education
1973 Business and Industry, Education, Labor

BILL PASSAGE RATES, 1997

	Total	Passed Legislature	Pct. Passed Legislature
Authored	74	23	31%
Sponsored	18	15	83%
Amendments	18	15	83%

ELECTORAL HISTORY IN CURRENT DISTRICT

	1994	1996	1998
Primary Election Opponent(s)	No	No	Yes
General Election Opponent(s)	No	No	No

House District 142

COUNTIES IN DISTRICT
Harris (part)

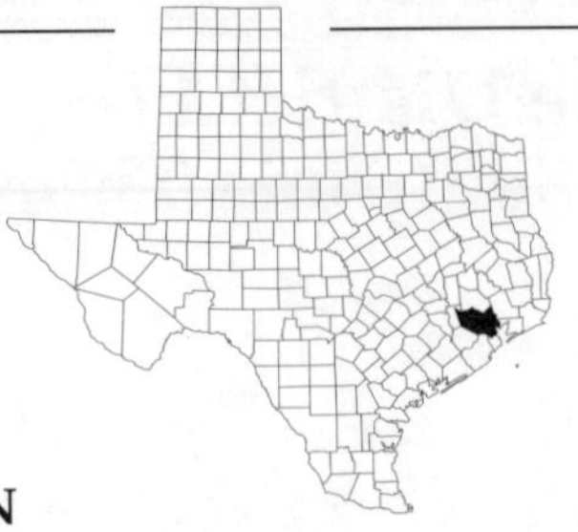

DEMOGRAPHIC INFORMATION

Population	
Total	107,302
Anglo	24.4%
Black	55.3%
Hispanic	18.9%
Others	2.3%

Education	
High School Graduates	58.6%
College Graduates	9.8%

Age of Population	
5 years or less	10.9%
6-17 years	18.9%
18-64 years	61.4%
65 or older	8.7%

Wealth and Urbanization	
Per capita Income	$8,776
Avg. House Value	$41,039
Percent Poverty	30.8%
Public Assistance	14.6%
Percent Urban	98.8%

Employed	
Percent Employed	87.2%
Private Sector	80.2%

Household Types	
Family households	85.0%
Non-family households	14.3%
Single-parent families	41.5%
Both parents working	58.5%

SENATE DISTRICTS IN HOUSE DISTRICT

Dist 6 Mario V. Gallegos Jr. (D)
Dist 7 Jon Lindsay (R)
Dist 13 Rodney Ellis (D)
Dist 15 John Whitmire (D)

DISTRICT ELECTION DATA

House 1996	
Harold V. Dutton Jr. (D)	100.0%

House 1998	
Harold V. Dutton Jr. (D)	100.0%

President 1996	
Bill Clinton (D)	81.6%
Bob Dole (R)	18.4%

Composite Party Vote 1994	
Democratic	79.8%
Republican	18.7%

Registered Voters 1996	**61,925**
Turnout	27,554
Percent of registered voting	44.5%

House District 142
Rep. Harold V. Dutton (D)

House Office
(512) 463-0510

District Office
9111 Eastex Freeway, Ste. 336
Houston, Texas 77093
(713) 692-9192

Personal

Year of birth	1945
Family	Single, seven children
Education	Texas Southern University, B.B.A., Accounting Thurgood Marshall School of Law, J.D.
Occupation	Attorney
Religion	Catholic
State legislative service	House 1985 to present

COMMITTEE ASSIGNMENT HISTORY

1997 Calendars, Civil Practices, Public Education (Vice-Chair)
1995 Calendars, Energy Resources, Insurance
1993 Energy Resources, Urban Affairs (Vice-Chair)
1991 Appropriations, Energy
1989 Business and Commerce (Vice-Chair), Judiciary, Rules and Resolutions
1987 Judiciary (Vice-Chair), Public Education,
1985 Judiciary, Retirement and Aging

BILL PASSAGE RATES, 1997

	Total	Passed Legislature	Pct. Passed Legislature
Authored	49	8	16%
Sponsored	6	4	67%
Amendments	28	21	75%

ELECTORAL HISTORY IN CURRENT DISTRICT

	1994	1996	1998
Primary Election Opponent(s)	Yes	Yes	No
General Election Opponent(s)	No	No	No

House District 143

COUNTIES IN DISTRICT
Harris (part)

DEMOGRAPHIC INFORMATION

Population

Total	110,172
Anglo	30.0%
Black	3.5%
Hispanic	65.8%
Others	1.0%

Education

High School Graduates	43.2%
College Graduates	3.9%

Age of Population

5 years or less	11.4%
6-17 years	22.2%
18-64 years	57.6%
65 or older	8.8%

Wealth and Urbanization

Per capita Income	$7,785
Avg. House Value	$36,805
Percent Poverty	25.0%
Public Assistance	9.0%
Percent Urban	100.0%

Employed

Percent Employed	89.8%
Private Sector	84.7%

Household Types

Family households	91.9%
Non-family households	7.7%
Single-parent families	19.8%
Both parents working	45.2%

SENATE DISTRICTS IN HOUSE DISTRICT

Dist 6 Mario V. Gallegos Jr. (D)
Dist 11 Mike Jackson (R)
Dist 13 Rodney Ellis (D)
Dist 15 John Whitmire (D)

DISTRICT ELECTION DATA

House 1996

Gerard Torres (D)	71.6%
David McCullough (R)	28.4%

President 1996

Bill Clinton (D)	70.9%
Bob Dole (R)	29.1%

Composite Party Vote 1994

Democratic	65.3%
Republican	33.3%

Registered Voters 1996	**46,337**
Turnout	19,997
Percent of registered voting	43.2%

House 1998

Joe Moreno (D)	70.8%
K. E. Glucksmann (R)	29.2%

House District 143
Rep. Joe Moreno (D)

House Office
(512) 463-0614

District Office
7001 Abeline
Houston, Texas 77020
(713) 764-2257

Personal

Year of birth	1964
Family	Single, no children
Education	Attended Texas Southern University, University of St. Thomas
Occupation	Businessman
Religion	Catholic
State legislative service	House 1998 to present

COMMITTEE ASSIGNMENT HISTORY

BILL PASSAGE RATES, 1997

	Total	Passed Legislature	Pct. Passed Legislature
Authored	NA	NA	NA
Sponsored	NA	NA	NA
Amendments	NA	NA	NA

ELECTORAL HISTORY IN CURRENT DISTRICT

	1994	1996	1998
Primary Election Opponent(s)	NA	NA	No
General Election Opponent(s)	NA	NA	Rep
Special Election Opponent(s)	NA	NA	Rep

House District 144

COUNTIES IN DISTRICT

Harris (part)

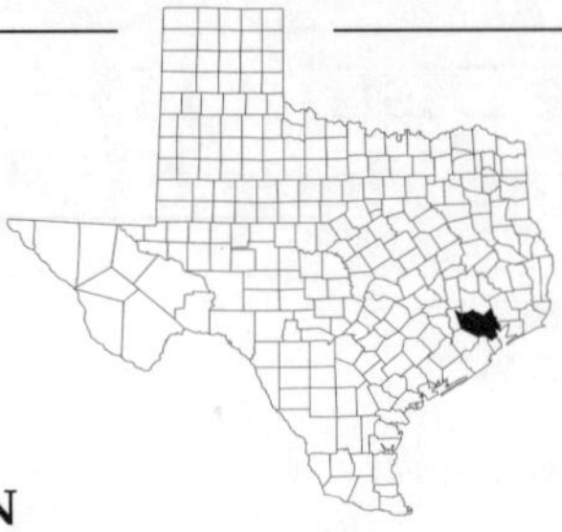

DEMOGRAPHIC INFORMATION

Population	
Total	110,924
Anglo	75.8%
Black	2.7%
Hispanic	18.5%
Others	3.0%

Wealth and Urbanization	
Per capita Income	$14,583
Avg. House Value	$63,350
Percent Poverty	11.3%
Public Assistance	4.0%
Percent Urban	100.0%

Education	
High School Graduates	79.4%
College Graduates	20.0%

Employed	
Percent Employed	94.5%
Private Sector	84.1%

Age of Population	
5 years or less	10.2%
6-17 years	18.6%
18-64 years	65.3%
65 or older	6.0%

Household Types	
Family households	86.6%
Non-family households	12.9%
Single-parent families	21.9%
Both parents working	59.9%

SENATE DISTRICTS IN HOUSE DISTRICT

Dist 6 Mario V. Gallegos Jr. (D)
Dist 11 Mike Jackson (R)
Dist 17 J. E. (Buster) Brown (R)

DISTRICT ELECTION DATA

House 1996	
Brooks T. Harrison (D)	36.2%
Robert E. Talton (R)	61.2%
Clifford Lee Messina (L)	2.6%

House 1998	
Robert E. Talton (R)	88.0%
Clifford Lee Messina (L)	12.0%

President 1996	
Bill Clinton (D)	41.3%
Bob Dole (R)	58.7%

Composite Party Vote 1994	
Democratic	37.5%
Republican	61.2%

Registered Voters 1996	**61,543**
Turnout	32,986
Percent of registered voting	53.6%

House District 144
Rep. Robert E. Talton (R)

House Office
(512) 463-0460

District Office
P.O. Box 5661
Pasadena, Texas 77508
(713) 472-0539

Personal

Year of birth	1945
Family	Married to Sue Talton, two children
Education	University of Houston, B.B.A.
	South Texas College of Law, J.D.
Occupation	Attorney
Religion	Baptist
State legislative service	House 1993 to present

COMMITTEE ASSIGNMENT HISTORY

1997 Criminal Jurisprudence (Vice-Chair), Environmental Regulation
1995 Criminal Jurisprudence (Vice-Chair), Environmental Regulation
1993 Criminal Jursiprudence, Environmental Regulation

BILL PASSAGE RATES, 1997

	Total	Passed Legislature	Pct. Passed Legislature
Authored	41	4	10%
Sponsored	10	6	60%
Amendments	19	19	100%

ELECTORAL HISTORY IN CURRENT DISTRICT

	1994	1996	1998
Primary Election Opponent(s)	No	No	No
General Election Opponent(s)	Dem	Dem, Lib	Lib

House District 145

COUNTIES IN DISTRICT

Harris (part)

DEMOGRAPHIC INFORMATION

Population	
Total	107,958
Anglo	26.9%
Black	4.8%
Hispanic	66.1%
Others	2.8%

Education	
High School Graduates	47.1%
College Graduates	7.4%

Age of Population	
5 years or less	12.5%
6-17 years	20.9%
18-64 years	58.3%
65 or older	8.3%

Wealth and Urbanization	
Per capita Income	$8,133
Avg. House Value	$44,258
Percent Poverty	25.7%
Public Assistance	7.9%
Percent Urban	100.0%

Employed	
Percent Employed	90.1%
Private Sector	86.5%

Household Types	
Family households	89.7%
Non-family households	9.9%
Single-parent families	23.1%
Both parents working	50.2%

SENATE DISTRICTS IN HOUSE DISTRICT

Dist 6 Mario V. Gallegos Jr. (D)

Dist 11 Mike Jackson (R)

DISTRICT ELECTION DATA

House 1996	
Diana Davila (D)	70.9%
Michael Bunch (R)	29.1%

President 1996	
Bill Clinton (D)	66.5%
Bob Dole (R)	33.5%

Composite Party Vote 1994	
Democratic	59.5%
Republican	39.1%

Registered Voters 1996	**39,569**
Turnout	17,132
Percent of registered voting	43.3%

House 1998	
Rick Noreiga (D)	67.1%
Michael Bunch (R)	32.9%

House District 145
Rep. Rick Noriega (D)

House Office
(512) 463-0732

District Office
P.O. Box 230324
Houston, Texas 77504
(713) 921-1213

Personal

Year of birth	1958
Family	Married to Melissa Noriega, two children
Education	University of Houston, B.A. Harvard University, M.P.A.
Occupation	Businessman
Religion	Catholic
State legislative service	House 1999 to present

COMMITTEE ASSIGNMENT HISTORY

BILL PASSAGE RATES, 1997

	Total	Passed Legislature	Pct. Passed Legislature
Authored	NA	NA	NA
Sponsored	NA	NA	NA
Amendments	NA	NA	NA

ELECTORAL HISTORY IN CURRENT DISTRICT

	1994	1996	1998
Primary Election Opponent(s)	NA	NA	Yes
General Election Opponent(s)	NA	NA	Rep

House District 146

COUNTIES IN DISTRICT
Harris (part)

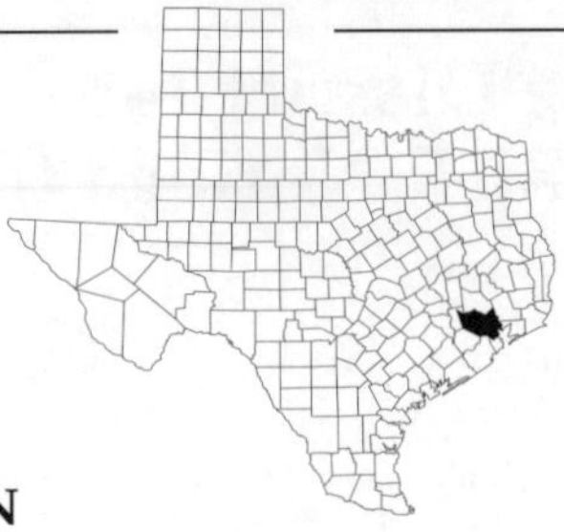

DEMOGRAPHIC INFORMATION

Population		**Wealth and Urbanization**	
Total	107,911	Per capita Income	$9,978
Anglo	30.7%	Avg. House Value	$45,836
Black	54.4%	Percent Poverty	25.4%
Hispanic	11.1%	Public Assistance	13.5%
Others	4.3%	Percent Urban	100.0%

Education		**Employed**	
High School Graduates	66.0%	Percent Employed	87.5%
College Graduates	17.3%	Private Sector	79.0%

Age of Population		**Household Types**	
5 years or less	9.5%	Family households	86.4%
6-17 years	18.4%	Non-family households	12.3%
18-64 years	62.6%	Single-parent families	40.8%
65 or older	9.4%	Both parents working	62.7%

SENATE DISTRICTS IN HOUSE DISTRICT

Dist 11 Mike Jackson (R)
Dist 13 Rodney Ellis (D)
Dist 17 J. E. (Buster) Brown (R)

DISTRICT ELECTION DATA

House 1996		**House 1998**	
Al Edwards (D)	73.0%	Al Edwards (D)	75.9%
David Lee Fuson (R)	27.0%	David Fuson (R)	24.1%

President 1996	
Bill Clinton (D)	72.9%
Bob Dole (R)	27.1%

Composite Party Vote 1994	
Democratic	70.4%
Republican	28.2%

Registered Voters 1996	**72,373**
Turnout	36,787
Percent of registered voting	50.8%

House District 146
Rep. Al Edwards (D)

House Office
(512) 463-0518

District Office
4913 Griggs Rd.
Houston, Texas 77021
(713) 741-8800

Personal

Year of birth	1937
Family	Single, three children
Education	Texas Southern University, B.S.
Occupation	Real Estate
Religion	Baptist
State legislative service	House 1979 to present

COMMITTEE ASSIGNMENT HISTORY

1997 Corrections, Rules and Resolutions (Chair), Transportation
1995 Rules and Resolutions (Chair), Public Safety, Transportation
1993 Public Safety, Rules and Resolutions (Chair), Transportation
1991 Retirement and Aging, Rules and Resolutions (Chair), Transportation
1989 Transportation, Urban Affairs
1987 Transportation, Urban Affairs
1985 Transportation (Vice-Chair), Urban Affairs
1983 Transportation (Vice-Chair), Urban Affairs
1981 Intergovernmental Affairs, Transportation
1979 Human Services, Intergovernmental Relations

BILL PASSAGE RATES, 1997

	Total	Passed Legislature	Pct. Passed Legislature
Authored	8	2	25%
Sponsored	1	0	0%
Amendments	3	2	67%

ELECTORAL HISTORY IN CURRENT DISTRICT

	1994	1996	1998
Primary Election Opponent(s)	No	No	No
General Election Opponent(s)	Rep	Rep	Rep

House District 147

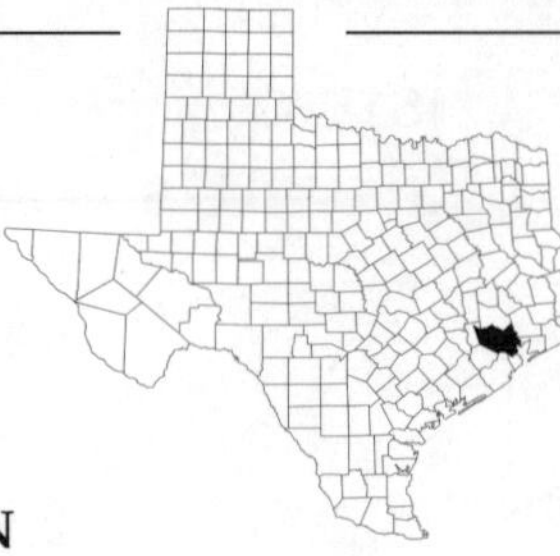

COUNTIES IN DISTRICT

Harris (part)

DEMOGRAPHIC INFORMATION

Population		**Wealth and Urbanization**	
Total	107,290	Per capita Income	$9,507
Anglo	28.5%	Avg. House Value	$55,097
Black	51.3%	Percent Poverty	28.7%
Hispanic	17.9%	Public Assistance	12.8%
Others	3.5%	Percent Urban	100.0%

Education		**Employed**	
High School Graduates	66.1%	Percent Employed	87.7%
College Graduates	15.8%	Private Sector	77.3%

Age of Population		**Household Types**	
5 years or less	9.9%	Family households	78.5%
6-17 years	16.4%	Non-family households	15.8%
18-64 years	63.5%	Single-parent families	43.1%
65 or older	10.2%	Both parents working	60.4%

SENATE DISTRICTS IN HOUSE DISTRICT

Dist 6 Mario V. Gallegos Jr. (D)
Dist 11 Mike Jackson (R)
Dist 13 Rodney Ellis (D)
Dist 15 John Whitmire (D)

DISTRICT ELECTION DATA

House 1996		**House 1998**	
Garnet F. Coleman (D)	100.0%	Garnet F. Coleman (D)	100.0%

President 1996	
Bill Clinton (D)	77.5%
Bob Dole (R)	22.5%

Composite Party Vote 1994	
Democratic	74.0%
Republican	24.6%

Registered Voters 1996	**54,103**
Turnout	25,611
Percent of registered voting	47.3%

House District 147
Rep. Garnet F. Coleman (D)

House Office
(512) 463-0524

District Office
P.O. Box 88140
Houston, Texas 77288
(713) 520-5355

Personal

Year of birth	1961
Family	Married to Angelique Coleman, two children
Education	University of St. Thomas, B.A., Political Science
Occupation	Small business owner
Religion	Episcopalian
State legislative service	House 1991 (part) to present

COMMITTEE ASSIGNMENT HISTORY
1997 Appropriations, Public Health
1995 Appropriations, Public Health
1993 Appropriations, Public Health
1991 NA

BILL PASSAGE RATES, 1997

	Total	Passed Legislature	Pct. Passed Legislature
Authored	78	14	18%
Sponsored	16	13	81%
Amendments	15	14	93%

ELECTORAL HISTORY IN CURRENT DISTRICT

	1994	1996	1998
Primary Election Opponent(s)	No	Yes	No
General Election Opponent(s)	No	No	No

House District 148

COUNTIES IN DISTRICT
Harris (part)

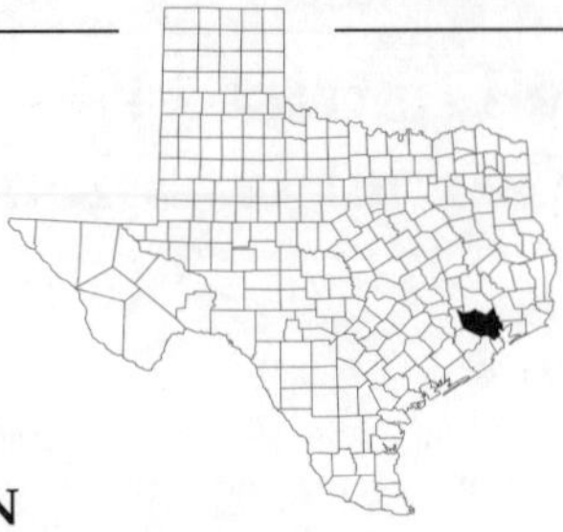

DEMOGRAPHIC INFORMATION

Population	
Total	107,881
Anglo	26.3%
Black	7.9%
Hispanic	63.8%
Others	2.5%

Wealth and Urbanization	
Per capita Income	$8,560
Avg. House Value	$50,065
Percent Poverty	32.5%
Public Assistance	10.0%
Percent Urban	100.0%

Education	
High School Graduates	44.2%
College Graduates	9.8%

Employed	
Percent Employed	90.5%
Private Sector	85.3%

Age of Population	
5 years or less	11.9%
6-17 years	19.8%
18-64 years	59.6%
65 or older	8.7%

Household Types	
Family households	87.5%
Non-family households	11.6%
Single-parent families	27.3%
Both parents working	50.6%

SENATE DISTRICTS IN HOUSE DISTRICT

Dist 6 Mario V. Gallegos Jr. (D)
Dist 7 Jon Lindsay (R)
Dist 13 Rodney Ellis (D)
Dist 15 John Whitmire (D)

DISTRICT ELECTION DATA

House 1996	
Jessica Cristina Farrar (D)	100.0%

House 1998	
Jessica Cristina Farrar (D)	100.0%

President 1996	
Bill Clinton (D)	66.7%
Bob Dole (R)	33.3%

Composite Party Vote 1994	
Democratic	60.9%
Republican	37.7%

Registered Voters 1996	**45,907**
Turnout	21,933
Percent of registered voting	47.8%

House District 148
Rep. Jessica Cristina Farrar (D)

House Office
(512) 463-0620

District Office
5311 Irvington Blvd., Ste. B
Houston, Texas 77009
(713) 691-6912

Personal

Year of birth	1966
Family	Single, no children
Education	University of Houston, B. Arch.
Occupation	Architectural intern
Religion	Catholic
State legislative service	House 1995 to present

COMMITTEE ASSIGNMENT HISTORY
1997 Corrections, Criminal Jurisprudence, Rules and Resolutions
1995 Corrections, Criminal Jurisprudence

BILL PASSAGE RATES, 1997

	Total	Passed Legislature	Pct. Passed Legislature
Authored	18	3	17%
Sponsored	0	0	NA
Amendments	3	2	67%

ELECTORAL HISTORY IN CURRENT DISTRICT

	1994	1996	1998
Primary Election Opponent(s)	Yes	Yes	No
General Election Opponent(s)	No	No	No

House District 149

COUNTIES IN DISTRICT

Harris (part)

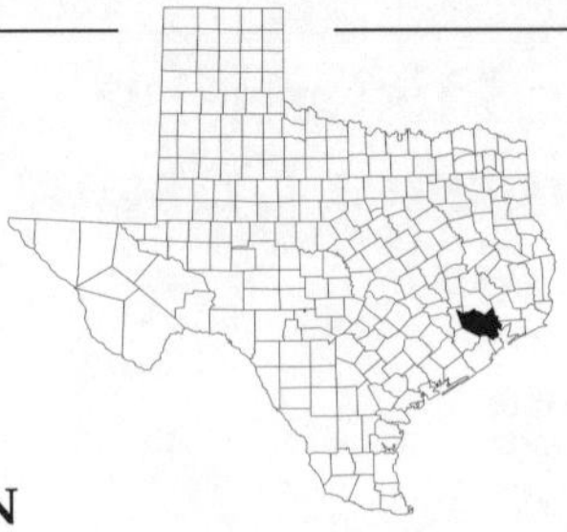

DEMOGRAPHIC INFORMATION

Population

Total	118,164
Anglo	57.2%
Black	11.5%
Hispanic	14.6%
Others	17.1%

Wealth and Urbanization

Per capita Income	$15,341
Avg. House Value	$70,875
Percent Poverty	7.7%
Public Assistance	2.9%
Percent Urban	100.0%

Education

High School Graduates	88.7%
College Graduates	33.9%

Employed

Percent Employed	95.1%
Private Sector	83.9%

Age of Population

5 years or less	10.7%
6-17 years	19.0%
18-64 years	67.4%
65 or older	2.8%

Household Types

Family households	86.8%
Non-family households	13.1%
Single-parent families	21.1%
Both parents working	68.3%

SENATE DISTRICTS IN HOUSE DISTRICT

Dist 7 Jon Lindsay (R)
Dist 13 Rodney Ellis (D)
Dist 17 J. E. (Buster) Brown (R)

DISTRICT ELECTION DATA

House 1996

Bob Schneider (NLP)	18.4%
Talmadge L. Heflin (R)	81.6%

House 1998

Talmadge L. Heflin (R)	100.0%

President 1996

Bill Clinton (D)	44.1%
Bob Dole (R)	55.9%

Composite Party Vote 1994

Democratic	35.4%
Republican	63.1%

Registered Voters 1996	**59,380**
Turnout	31,934
Percent of registered voting	53.8%

House District 149
Rep. Talmadge L. Heflin (R)

House Office
(512) 463-0568

District Office
7419 S. Kirkwood, Ste. B
Houston, Texas 77072
(281) 498-6343

Personal

Year of birth	1940
Family	Married to Janice Heflin, one child
Education	Louisiana Tech University
Occupation	Businessman, management consultant
Religion	Baptist
State legislative service	House 1983 to present

COMMITTEE ASSIGNMENT HISTORY

1997 Appropriations, Ways and Means
1995 Appropriations, Ways and Means
1993 Appropriations, Ways and Means
1991 Local and Consent Calendars, Retirement and Aging (Vice-Chair), Ways and Means
1989 Retirement and Aging, Ways and Means
1987 Public Health, Retirement and Aging
1985 Science and Technology (Vice-Chair), Ways and Means
1983 Cultural and Historical Resources, Public Education

BILL PASSAGE RATES, 1997

	Total	Passed Legislature	Pct. Passed Legislature
Authored	11	2	18%
Sponsored	3	3	100%
Amendments	11	7	64%

ELECTORAL HISTORY IN CURRENT DISTRICT

	1994	1996	1998
Primary Election Opponent(s)	No	No	No
General Election Opponent(s)	No	NLP	No

House District 150

COUNTIES IN DISTRICT

Harris (part)

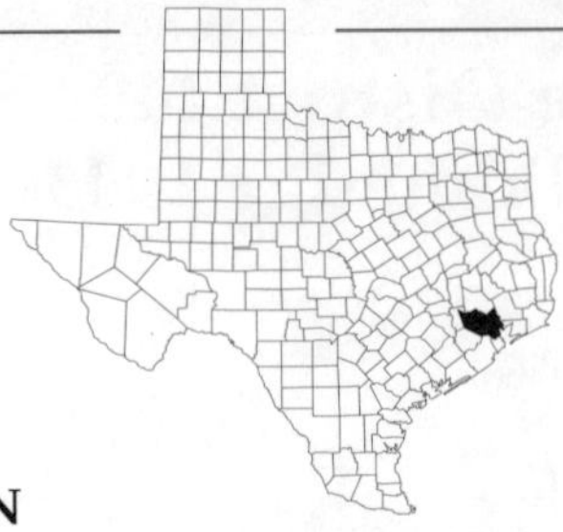

DEMOGRAPHIC INFORMATION

Population	
Total	118,373
Anglo	83.9%
Black	5.9%
Hispanic	8.4%
Others	1.8%

Wealth and Urbanization	
Per capita Income	$15,841
Avg. House Value	$78,581
Percent Poverty	6.2%
Public Assistance	2.7%
Percent Urban	76.8%

Education	
High School Graduates	86.4%
College Graduates	24.2%

Employed	
Percent Employed	95.3%
Private Sector	81.8%

Age of Population	
5 years or less	10.4%
6-17 years	20.6%
18-64 years	64.4%
65 or older	4.6%

Household Types	
Family households	90.9%
Non-family households	8.8%
Single-parent families	18.0%
Both parents working	64.6%

SENATE DISTRICTS IN HOUSE DISTRICT

Dist 7 Jon Lindsay (R)

Dist 15 John Whitmire (D)

DISTRICT ELECTION DATA

House 1996	
Paul J. Hilbert (R)	100.0%

House 1998	
Paul J. Hilbert (R)	100.0%

President 1996	
Bill Clinton (D)	28.2%
Bob Dole (R)	71.8%

Composite Party Vote 1994	
Democratic	26.2%
Republican	72.3%

Registered Voters 1996	**74,855**
Turnout	42,292
Percent of registered voting	56.5%

House District 150
Rep. Paul J. Hilbert (R)

House Office
(512) 463-0572

District Office
2301 FM 1960 West, #204
Houston, Texas 77068
(281) 537-5252

Personal

Year of birth	1949
Family	Single, no children
Education	Xavier University, B.A., M.B.A. South Texas College of Law, J.D.
Occupation	Attorney
Religion	Catholic
State legislative service	House 1983 to present

COMMITTEE ASSIGNMENT HISTORY

1997 Calendars (Vice-Chair), Civil Practices (Vice-Chair), State Affairs
1995 Calendars, Civil Practices (Vice-Chair), State Affairs
1993 Judicial Affairs, Licensing and Administrative Procedures, Local and Consent Calendars
1991 Appropriations, Cultural and Historical Resources, Local and Consent Calendars
1989 Business and Commerce, Rules and Resolutions, State Affairs
1987 Elections (Vice-Chair), Rules and Resolutions, Ways and Means
1985 Judiciary, Urban Affairs
1983 Cultural and Historical Resources, Urban Affairs

BILL PASSAGE RATES, 1997

	Total	Passed Legislature	Pct. Passed Legislature
Authored	46	3	7%
Sponsored	4	3	75%
Amendments	24	21	88%

ELECTORAL HISTORY IN CURRENT DISTRICT

	1994	1996	1998
Primary Election Opponent(s)	No	Yes	No
General Election Opponent(s)	No	No	No

PART III
Supplementary Material

ELECTION RECOUNTS

In three house districts, the results of the general election of 1998 were so close that recounts were likely. In house district 46, challenger Republican Rick Green lost to incumbent Democrat Alec Rhodes by 20 votes out of a total of 25,753 votes cast. In house district 68, incumbent Democrat Charles Finnell lost to challenger Republican Rick Hardcastle by 350 votes out of a total of 29,314 cast. In house district 138, challenger Republican Dwayne Bohac lost to incumbent Democrat Ken Yarbrough by 153 votes out of a total of 20,227 cast.

At the press deadline for this volume, all three losing candidates had indicated that they would probably seek recounts. Historically, general election outcomes in Texas are rarely changed by recounts. However, in the interest of completeness, we present member pages for these three individuals as they would appear in this volume if each were successful in his recount challenge.

House District 46
Rep. Rick Green (R)

House Office
(512) 463-0498

District Office
P.O. Box 900
Dripping Springs, Texas 78620
(512) 894-3098

Personal

Year of birth	1971
Family	Married to Kara Green, one child
Education	Angelo State University, B.B.A. Finance University of Texas Law School, J.D.
Occupation	Small Business Owner
Religion	Baptist
State legislative service	House 1999 to present

COMMITTEE ASSIGNMENT HISTORY

BILL PASSAGE RATES, 1997

	Total	Passed Legislature	Pct. Passed Legislature
Authored	NA	NA	NA
Sponsored	NA	NA	NA
Amendments	NA	NA	NA

ELECTORAL HISTORY IN CURRENT DISTRICT

	1994	1996	1998
Primary Election Opponent(s)	NA	NA	No
General Election Opponent(s)	NA	NA	Dem

House District 68
Rep. Charles Finnell (D)

House Office
(512) 463-0526
(512) 463-6003 (Fax)

District Office
P.O. Box 468
Holliday, Texas 76366
(817) 586-1245
(817) 586-0316 (Fax)

Personal

Year of birth	1943
Family	Married to Kay Finnell, no children
Education	University of Texas, B.A.
Occupation	Small businessman
Religion	Protestant
State legislative service	House 1967-74, 1977 to present

COMMITTEE ASSIGNMENT HISTORY

1997 Appropriations, Transportation
1995 Agriculture & Livestock, Rules & Resolutions (Vice-Chair), Ways and Means
1993 Agriculture and Wildlife Management, County Affairs, Rules & Resolutions
1991 Agriculture & Livestock, Government Organization (Vice-Chair), Redistricting
1989 (Vice-Chair) Government Organization, Rules and Resolutions (Chair)
1987 County Affairs, General Investigating (Chair), Retirement and Aging
1985 Appropriations, Financial Institutions
1983 Retirement and Aging (Chair), Transportation
1981 Health Services, Regions, Compacts and Districts
1979 Appropriative Matters (Vice-Chair), Appropriations, Transportation
1977 Business and Industry, Transportation
1973 Agriculture and Livestock, Elections, Reapportionment
1971 Aeronautics, Agriculture, Congressional and Legislative Districts, Constitutional Amendments, Oil, Gas and Mining
1969 Agriculture, Higher Education, Interstate Cooperation (Vice-Chair), Motor Transportation
1967 Agriculture, Congressional and Legislative Districts, Federal Relations, Highways and Roads, Oil, Gas and Mining

BILL PASSAGE RATES, 1997

	Total	Passed Legislature	Pct. Passed Legislature
Authored	20	9	45%
Sponsored	3	2	67%
Amendments	4	2	50%

ELECTORAL HISTORY IN CURRENT DISTRICT

	1994	1996	1998
Primary Election Opponent(s)	No	No	No
General Election Opponent(s)	No	No	Rep

House District 138
Rep. Dwayne Bohac (R)

House Office
(512) 463-0648

District Office
4415 Lorinda
Houston, Texas 77018
(713) 681-0556

Personal

Year of birth	1966
Family	Married to Darlene Forker, no children
Education	Texas A&M University, B.B.A. Marketing, B. S. Political Science
Occupation	Executive director of Plumbing Education Self-employed, Retail Business
Religion	Baptist
State legislative service	House 1999 to present

COMMITTEE ASSIGNMENT HISTORY

BILL PASSAGE RATES, 1997

	Total	Passed Legislature	Pct. Passed Legislature
Authored	NA	NA	NA
Sponsored	NA	NA	NA
Amendments	NA	NA	NA

ELECTORAL HISTORY IN CURRENT DISTRICT

	1994	1996	1998
Primary Election Opponent(s)	NA	NA	No
General Election Opponent(s)	NA	NA	Dem

ORGANIZATION AND PROCEDURE OF THE TEXAS LEGISLATURE

THE TEXAS LEGISLATURE

The legislature of the state of Texas is the state's law making body. Its primary function is to enact laws to provide for the health, welfare, education, environment, economy, and general well-being of the citizens of Texas. It also establishes public policy through the passage of bills and resolutions and proposes amendments to the state constitution, which then are submitted to the voters for approval or disapproval.

Like most other states, Texas employs a bicameral system in its legislative branch of state government. The Texas Legislature consists of two separate chambers, a 31-member Senate and a 150-member House of Representatives. State senators and representatives are elected from single-member districts to serve four-year and two-year terms, respectively.

As required by law, district boundaries were redrawn after the 1990 census, and each state senator now represents a senatorial district of more than 500,000 residents, while the average house district is composed of more than 115,000 people. The rich diversity of Texas is mirrored in the composition of the two chambers, as 181 men and women from all walks of life unite to represent the 19,500,000 people of the Lone Star State.

In accordance with the Texas Constitution, the legislature meets in a regular legislative session in Austin every two years. By statute, the legislature convenes in a regular session on the second Tuesday in January of every odd-numbered year. These biennial sessions are limited to 140 days' duration. The Constitution also allows the governor to call additional special sessions as necessary. During a called session, which cannot exceed 30 days, the legislature may consider legislation only on matters specified in proclamations issued by the governor.

HOW A BILL BECOMES LAW

How a Bill Originates

A legislator wishing to pass a bill may draft the legislation personally or obtain the professional staff services of a state legislative service agency, such as the Texas Legislative Council, which generally is regarded as the bill-writing arm of the legislature. Bills also may be prepared by attorneys retained for this purpose by organizations or individuals with a particular interest in certain legislation. All bills, except for general appropriations bills, are limited to a single subject.

A bill also may grow out of the recommendations of a special committee created by the legislature to conduct interim studies on specific issues of legislative interest. Interim committees are appointed by the presiding officers of the House and the Senate, who specify each committee's charge and any additional authority and duties necessary to carry out the charge. Interim study committees may consist entirely of members from one chamber or, in the case of a joint committee, of members from both the House and Senate. A presiding officer may also appoint citizen members and other public officials of state and local governments to an interim committee to augment its legislative membership for the purpose of conducting a special study. A special study committee expires upon release of its final report or when the next legislature convenes, whichever occurs first.

Introducing a Bill

A bill may be introduced by any member of the legislature in the member's own chamber. The steps in a bill's progress in both houses are basically the same. The legislator introducing the bill is called the "author" of the bill. A bill passed by one house must proceed to the other for final passage before going to the governor for approval or veto.

To introduce a bill in the House of Representatives, a state representative must first submit the required number of copies of the bill for filing to the chief clerk of the House, who sequentially numbers each document according to the order in which it is received. The House rules of procedure permit unrestricted introduction of bills during the first sixty calendar days of each regular session. After the sixty-day deadline, the introduction of any bill other than a local bill or a bill relating to a matter declared by the governor to be an emergency requires the consent of at least four-fifths of those members present and voting.

To introduce a bill in the Senate, a senator first must submit the required number of copies of the bill to the secretary of the Senate, who sequentially numbers each document according to the order in which it is received. The Senate rules of procedure also permit unrestricted introduction of bills during the first sixty calendar days of each regular session. After the sixty-day deadline in the Senate, the introduction of any bill other than a local bill or a bill relating to a matter declared by the governor to be an emergency requires the consent of at least four-fifths of the membership of the senate.

The Role of Committees

The size of the legislature and the volume of work confronting it in each session make it impossible for the entire membership to deliberate thoughtfully on the many proposed measures. For this reason, the basic business in both houses is conducted according to the committee system whereby permanent, general, and special bodies, determined and formed by the rules of the respective chambers, are appointed to consider bills introduced in the legislature and to advise on their disposition. The committee stage in the deliberative process is at the core of legislative politics since the fate of bills under consideration hinges upon committee action. A large percentage of all legislation never is reported out of committee. Thus, committee action is the first crucial step in the process by which a bill becomes law.

Referral to a Standing Committee

The Texas Constitution provides that no bill may be considered on the floor of a chamber by its members unless the bill first has been referred to a committee and the committee has issued its report on the bill. When a bill is introduced or received from the opposite chamber for consideration, it is read for the first time by its caption and referred by the Speaker or lieutenant governor to an appropriate committee. Known as standing committees, these bodies are created in the rules of the respective houses at the beginning of each regular session and typically consist of seven to fifteen members.

In the House rules, each committee is assigned jurisdiction over a specific subject matter, and the Speaker refers legislation to House committees based on those subject matter jurisdictions. In its rules, the Senate does not provide subject matter jurisdictions for its committees. Although the lieutenant governor is free to refer legislation in the Senate to any standing committee, unofficial subject matter jurisdictions usually are established and followed to prevent duplication of effort by committees.

In the House of Representatives, committee membership is determined in part by seniority and in part by appointments by the Speaker. Each representative sits on at least one committee, and most representatives sit on two or three committees. For the 74th Texas Legislature, the house had thirty-six standing committees. Under past Senate rules, committee membership is determined entirely by appointment by the lieutenant governor. Each senator typically sits on three or four committees. For the 74th Texas Legislature, the Senate had fourteen standing committees.

Immediately after a bill has been referred to committee, a determination must be made as to whether a fiscal note or other impact statement is required; if so, a copy of the bill is sent to the appropriate state agency (e.g., the Legislative Budget Board, the State Pension Review Board, or the Texas Natural Resource Conservation Commission) for preparation of the note or statement. In the House, that document must be attached to the affected bill before a public hearing on the bill may be held, and if the bill is reported from committee, the fiscal note or other impact statement must be attached to the bill when it is printed and distributed to the members of the House. In practice, the Senate merely requires that a copy of the fiscal note or other impact statement be provided to each senator before the bill is considered by the full Senate. A bill requiring extensive analysis often is assigned to a subcommittee of the standing committee to which the bill has been referred. Subcommittees are appointed by the committee chair from the standing committee's membership. After careful scrutiny of the bill under consideration, the subcommittee makes a report to the full committee.

The Committee Process

All committee business is required to be conducted in public meetings. No official action may be made or vote taken except in a meeting that is open to the public. The House rules permit a House committee or subcommittee to meet (1) in a public hearing where testimony is heard and where official action may be taken on bills, resolutions, or other matters; (2) in a formal meeting where the members may discuss and take official action without hearing public testimony; or (3) in a work session for discussion of matters before the committee without taking formal action. The Senate rules do not provide for different types of meetings. Therefore testimony may be heard and official action may be taken at any meeting of a Senate committee or subcommittee. Although a committee is not required to solicit public testimony on any bill, public testimony almost always is solicited on bills of outstanding importance, allowing citizens the opportunity to present arguments on different sides of an issue.

A House committee or subcommittee holding a public hearing during a legislative session must post notice of the hearing at least five calendar days before the hearing during a regular session and at least twenty-four hours in advance of the hearing during a special session. If a House committee or subcommittee is convening for a formal meeting or a work session, written notice must be posted and transmitted to each member of the committee two hours in advance of the meeting, or an announcement must be filed with the journal clerk and read in the House while the House is in session. A Senate committee or subcommittee must post notice of a meeting at least twenty-four hours before the meeting.

Committee Reports

After considering a bill, a committee may choose to take no action or may issue a report on the bill to the House or Senate. The committee report, expressing the committee's recommendations regarding House or Senate action on a bill, includes a record of the committee's vote on the report, the text of the bill as reported by the committee, a detailed bill analysis, and a fiscal note or other impact statement, as necessary.

In the House, all parts of the committee report are assembled and printed and distributed to the members as a single document. In the Senate, the various parts of the committee report are printed and distributed separately to the senators. Committee reports are advisory only and may take several forms. The committee may recommend passage of the bill without amendments, or it may recommend amendments to the bill or even substitute a new bill for the original document.

In the House, all committee reports are referred to the chief clerk, who forwards them to the printer. After being printed, a copy of the House committee report printing (which includes bill text, the committee's recommendation and vote on the bill, the bill analysis, the fiscal note, and other necessary impact statements) is placed in the post office box of each member of the House. The chief clerk then delivers a certified copy of the committee report to the appropriate calendars committee (e.g., the Committee on Calendars or the Committee on Local and Consent Calendars) for placement of the bill on a calendar for consideration by the full House. Calendars committees are given wide discretion in scheduling bills for floor action.

The Senate rules also require committee reports to be printed. After being printed, a copy of the Senate committee report printing (which includes bill text and the committee's recommendation and vote on the bill) is placed in the bill book on each senator's desk in the Senate chamber. When the bill analysis, the fiscal note, and other necessary impact statements have been completed and printed, a copy of those documents is also placed in each senator's bill book. Except for the role of the Committee on Administration in scheduling local and noncontroversial bills for consideration, there is no equivalent to a calendars committee in the Senate. Bills are placed on the regular order of business for consideration by the full Senate in the order in which the printed committee reports are received by the secretary of the Senate for placement in the senators' bill books. For all practical purposes, the regular order of business is merely a listing of bills that are eligible for consideration, because the Senate rules provide that a bill on the regular order of business may not be brought up for floor consideration unless the Senate sponsor of the bill has filed with the secretary of the Senate a written notice of intent to suspend the regular order of business for consideration of the bill.

House Calendars and Lists of Items Eligible for Consideration

House calendars

After a bill or resolution has been reported favorably by a standing committee and the committee report has been printed, the chief clerk forwards the measure to the appropriate calendars committee for placement on a calendar. The House rules provide for four types of calendars:

1. The Daily House Calendar, which contains a list of new bills and resolutions scheduled by the Committee on Calendars for consideration by the House, must be distributed to the members thirty-six hours before the House convenes during regular sessions and twenty-four hours before the House convenes during special sessions.

2. The Supplemental House Calendar (prepared by the Committee on Calendars) must be distributed two hours before the house convenes. It may contain:
   a. measures passed to third reading on the previous day
   b. measures on the Daily House Calendar for a previous day which were not reached for consideration
   c. measures on the Daily House Calendar for the current day
   d. business postponed from a previous day and/or
   e. notice to call from the table a measure laid on the table subject to call on a previous day.

3. The Local, Consent, and Resolutions Calendar must be distributed to the members forth-eight hours before the House convenes. It contains a list of local or noncontroversial bills scheduled by the Committee on Local and Consent Calendars for consideration by the House.

4. The Congratulatory and Memorial Calendar must be distributed twenty-four hours before the House convenes. It contains a list of congratulatory and memorial resolutions and motions scheduled by the Committee on Rules and Resolutions for consideration by the House.

The Supplemental House Calendar, because it includes the measures listed on the Daily House Calendar, is the primary agenda followed by the House during its deliberations. The Local, Consent, and Resolutions Calendar and the Congratulatory and Memorial Calendar are special calendars that are prepared approximately once a week during the last half of a regular session.

In addition to the four calendars listed above, the House rules provide for nine *categories* which may be used to group bills and resolutions on those calendars. Those categories, listed in order of priority, are: (1) emergency calendar (2) major state calendar (3) constitutional amendments calendar (4) general state calendar (5) local calendar (6) consent calendar (7) resolutions calendar (8) congratulatory and memorial resolutions calendar and (9) motions calendar. Within each category, Senate bills and resolutions are required to be listed on the calendars separately from House bills and resolutions, and consideration of Senate bills and resolutions on Senate bill days (Wednesdays and Thursdays) has priority in the order specified by House rule.

Except during the latter part of the regular session when calendars become especially lengthy, the House normally considers all measures listed on its calendars before adjourning or recessing for the day.

List of Items Eligible for Consideration

This list is prepared by the chief clerk of the House, upon request of the Speaker, when the volume of legislation warrants (normally during the last few weeks of a regular session). The list must be distributed six hours before it may be considered. It contains: (1) House bills with Senate amendments eligible to be considered (2) Senate bills for which the Senate has requested the appointment of a conference committee and (3) conference committee reports eligible to be considered.

Floor Action

The first real floor consideration of a bill occurs on its second reading. After it is read the second time, again by caption only, the measure is subject to debate and amendment by the entire membership of the chamber. On second reading, a bill may be amended by a simple majority. If no amendment is made, or if those proposed are disposed of, the final action on second reading of a bill is a vote on its passage to engrossment, if the bill is being considered in the chamber in which it was introduced; or passage to third reading, if the bill is being considered in the opposite chamber. The bill is then laid before the body for a third reading and final passage. A bill may be amended again on third reading, but amendments at this stage require a two-thirds majority for adoption.

Although the Texas Constitution requires a bill to be read on three separate days in each house before it can have the force of law, this constitutional rule may be suspended by a four-fifths vote of the House in which the bill is pending. In such cases, the bill is given an immediate third reading following the vote to pass the bill to engrossment or third reading. The Senate routinely suspends this constitutional provision in order to give a bill an immediate third reading. The House, however, rarely suspends this provision, and third reading consideration of a bill in the House normally occurs on the day following second reading consideration.

After a bill has been read a third time, it is voted on for final passage. If the bill receives a simple majority vote, it is considered passed, and the chief clerk of the House or the secretary of the Senate, as appropriate, certifies the bill's final passage, noting on it the date of its passage and the vote by which it passed. When the bill is passed in the originating chamber, the bill is engrossed, and an exact and accurate copy of the bill, with all corrections and amendments incorporated into it, is prepared and sent to the opposite chamber for consideration. When the bill is passed in the opposite chamber, a new copy of the bill is not prepared. Rather, the bill is immediately returned to the originating chamber with any amendments simply attached to the bill.

Consideration of Local and Noncontroversial Bills

The House and Senate rules both provide for special calendars for the consideration of local and noncontroversial bills. The calendar used for consideration of these bills in the House is the Local, Consent, and Resolutions Calendar, which is set by the Committee on Local and Consent Calendars. A standing committee may recommend, when reporting a bill or resolution, that the measure be sent to the Committee on Local and Consent Calendars for placement on an appropriate calendar. Such a recommendation requires the unanimous consent of all the committee members present when the measure is reported from committee. Measures that are eligible for consideration by the Committee on Local and Consent Calendars are bills that are local as defined by the House rules, and bills and resolutions to which no opposition is anticipated. If it determines that a measure is not eligible for placement on the Local, Consent, and Resolutions Calendar, the Committee on Local and Consent Calendars has the power to transfer the measure to the Committee on Calendars. Local, Consent, and Resolutions Calendars normally are prepared for consideration by the house once a week during the last half of the regular session. These calendars normally are lengthy, but consideration of them is expedited because debate is limited and amendments to measures on these calendars may not be offered unless they first have been approved by the Committee on Local and Consent Calendars. A measure may be removed from the Local, Consent, and Resolutions Calendar if debate exceeds ten minutes or if five or more representatives object to the consideration of the measure.

The calendar used for consideration of local and noncontroversial bills in the senate is the Local and Uncontested Calendar, which is set by the Committee on Administration. A measure may not be considered by the Committee on Administration for placement on the Local and Uncontested Calendar unless both the sponsor of the measure and the chair of the committee from which the measure was reported file a written request with the Committee on Administration for placement on the Local and Uncontested Calendar. Measures that are eligible for consideration by the Committee on Administration are bills that are local as defined by the Senate rules and bills and resolutions to which no opposition is anticipated. Local and Uncontested Calendars normally are prepared for consideration by the senate once or twice a week during the last half of the regular session. Measures on the Local and Uncontested Calendar may be considered without a suspension of the regular order of business, which normally is required for consideration of legislation in the Senate. As in the House, consideration of Local and Uncontested Calendars in the Senate is expedited because the measures on these calendars normally are not debated and amendments to measures on these calendars are prohibited. A measure may be removed from the Local and Uncontested Calendar if two or more senators object to consideration of the measure.

Return of a Bill to the Originating Chamber—Action on Amendments

After a bill has passed through three readings in the opposite chamber, the bill is sent back to the originating chamber and, if there have been no amendments, the bill is enrolled. The enrolled bill is then signed by both presiding officers in the presence of their respective chambers and sent to the governor. When a bill that has been amended by the opposite chamber is returned to the originating chamber, the originating chamber must concur with all of the amendments made by the opposite chamber before the bill can be enrolled. If the originating chamber does not concur with any or all of the opposite chamber's amendments, it may request the appointment of a conference committee to resolve the differences between the House and Senate versions of the bill.

Conference Committee

If a conference committee is called for, the two presiding officers appoint five members each from their respective chambers to serve on the committee. A conference committee's charge is limited to reconciling differences between the two houses, and the committee, unless so directed, may not alter, amend, or omit text that is not in disagreement. Nor may the committee add text on any matter that is not in disagreement or that is not included in either version of the bill in question. After the committee has met and reached an agreement, a report is submitted to both houses for approval or disapproval. The report must be approved by at least three conferees from each house and must contain: the text of the bill as approved by the conference committee, an analysis comparing the text of the compromise bill to both the House and Senate versions, and the signatures of those members of the conference committee who approved the report. A conference committee report is not subject to amendment but must be accepted or rejected in its entirety.

Should the proposed compromise remain unacceptable to either house, it may be returned to the same conference committee for further deliberation, with or without specific instructions; or appointment of a new conference committee may be requested. Failure of the conference committee to reach agreement kills the measure. If the conference committee report is acceptable to both houses, the bill is enrolled, signed by both presiding officers in the presence of their respective chambers, and sent to the governor.

Governor's Action

Upon receiving a bill, the governor has ten days in which to sign the bill, veto it, or allow it to become law without a signature. If the governor elects to veto the bill and the legislature is still in session, the bill is returned to the house in which it originated with an explanation of the governor's objections. A two-thirds majority in each house is required to override the veto. If the governor neither vetoes nor signs the bill within the allotted time period, the bill becomes a law. If a bill is sent to the governor within ten days of final adjournment, the governor has until twenty days after final adjournment to sign the bill, veto it, or allow it to become law without a signature.

Other Types of Legislation

Resolutions

A resolution is a legislative document used to express the collective will of the members of the legislature or of either house. Resolutions are used to handle specific activities of the legislature and commonly are used to propose amendments to the Texas Constitution, take care of housekeeping functions, convey congratulations or condolences to individuals or groups in the state, express legislative intent, express an opinion or sentiment on matters of public interest, give direction to a state agency or official, or call upon certain governmental agencies, offices, or units (such as the U.S. Congress) to take a specific course of action. Resolutions are legislative instruments that must be introduced, assigned numbers, and acted on by the legislature. Except for concurrent resolutions, the governor need not sign and cannot veto them. There are three types of resolutions: joint resolutions, concurrent resolutions, and simple resolutions.

Joint Resolutions

Joint resolutions are used to propose amendments to the Texas Constitution, ratify proposed amendments to the U.S. Constitution, or request a constitutional convention to propose amendments to the U.S. Constitution. Joint resolutions proposing amendments to the Texas Constitution require a vote of two-thirds of the total membership of each house for adoption. Other joint resolutions require a simple majority vote in each house for adoption. A joint resolution takes the same course through both houses as a bill and is like a bill in all respects, except that if it receives the required number of votes at any reading after the first in the house, the resolution is passed. Three readings still are required to pass a joint resolution in the senate. Joint resolutions passed by the legislature are not submitted to the governor for signing but are filed directly with the secretary of state. An amendment to the Texas Constitution proposed by an adopted joint resolution does not become effective until it is approved by Texas voters at a general election.

Concurrent Resolutions

A concurrent resolution is used when both houses have an interest in a particular matter. Such resolutions may originate in either house but must be adopted by both. A concurrent resolution passed by both houses may be used for matters affecting operations and procedures of the legislature, such as joint sessions or adjournment *sine die*. Frequently, concurrent resolutions are used to memorialize the U.S. Congress, give directions to a state agency or officer, or express views of the legislature. Concurrent resolutions, except those that pertain solely to procedural matters between the two houses, must be submitted to the governor for approval.

Simple Resolutions

House or senate resolutions pertain to matters considered by the house of origin only. Numbered separately from other types of resolutions or bills, they are used for such purposes as adopting or changing rules of procedure or expressing congratulations or condolences.

SPEAKER OF THE HOUSE

The presiding officer of the House of Representatives is the Speaker of the House. The Texas Constitution provides that the House of

Representatives shall elect its own Speaker from among its members.

The Speaker of the Texas House of Representatives occupies a powerful position, first as presiding officer of the 150-member body and then through the authority given to the Speaker in the House rules of procedure to appoint House committees and committee chairs. As presiding officer, the Speaker maintains order during floor debate, recognizing legislators who wish to speak and ruling on procedural matters. The strength wielded through the Speaker's committee appointments is derived from the constitutional requirement that a bill must be approved by a committee before it can be brought before the full House membership for a vote. Besides appointing the members of each standing House committee, subject to rules on seniority, and designating the chair and vice-chair for each committee, the Speaker is also responsible for referring all proposed legislation to the appropriate standing committee. As a state representative, the Speaker of the House may vote on all questions before the House.

THE LIEUTENANT GOVERNOR

The lieutenant governor in Texas is unique in that he is part of both the executive and legislative branches.

As in most states, in Texas the lieutenant governor assumes the powers and duties of the governor when the governor is unable to serve or is absent from the state. But in Texas, the lieutenant governor is elected separately from the governor, and they can be members of different political parties.

The Texas Constitution names the lieutenant governor the constitutional president of the Senate, but the constitution also gives the Senate the authority to write its own rules. From that provision the office of lieutenant governor derives most its power.

These rules, adopted by a majority of senators at the beginning of each legislative session, set down in great detail how business is conducted in the Senate. Powers granted the lieutenant governor by Senate rules can determine whether the lieutenant governor is one of the most powerful state officials or merely a figurehead.

Senate rules give the current lieutenant governor a great deal of influence in shaping state policy and influencing laws that eventually may be passed by the Senate.

At the same time, the power granted by Senate rules also can be taken away by the Senate. If the lieutenant governor offends or loses the confidence of a majority of the senators, they can vote to strip these powers, leaving the constitutional title of "President of the Senate" but little or no authority.

The rules allow the present lieutenant governor to decide all parliamentary questions and to use discretion in following Senate procedural rules. The lieutenant governor can set up standing and special committees and appoint committee chairpersons and individual members. The lieutenant governor is given life-and-death power over proposed legislation because rules allow that person to refer all bills to any committee—a powerful way to control what happens to those bills. The order in which bills are considered also is set by the lieutenant governor under Senate rules.

Another important source of power is the lieutenant governor's leadership role in the Senate. Leadership ability and the faith and confidence inspired in the senators will determine how the lieutenant governor is treated when the Senate writes its rules. With favorable rules, the lieutenant governor and the team of committee chairs can accomplish almost any legislative objective.

The Texas Constitution gives the lieutenant governor the right to debate and vote on all issues when the Senate sits as a Committee of the Whole. The constitutional role as president of the Senate also gives the lieutenant governor the right to cast the deciding vote in the case of a Senate tie.

Like the Speaker of the House, the lieutenant governor is required to sign all bills and resolutions. The Constitution also names the lieutenant governor to the five-member Legislative Redistricting Board, which apportions the state into senatorial and representative districts in the event the legislature is unable to do so.

These powers are fundamental since the Constitution can be changed only by a two-thirds vote in both the House of Representatives and the Senate, followed by approval by a majority vote of the people in a statewide election.

The lieutenant governor derives other powers and responsibilities from state statute. By statute, the lieutenant governor is a member of several legislative branch boards and committees: the Legislative Budget Board, the Legislative Council, the Legislative Audit Committee, and the Legislative Education Board. The lieutenant governor is designated chair of the Legislative Budget Board and the Legislative Council, which have considerable sway over state programs, the budget, and policy.

The Legislative Budget Board, for example, provides the legislature with a recommended budget at the beginning of every session. In many states, budgeting is done only in the executive branch. The authority of the Legislative Budget Board is broad, and its influence on spending is significant. Because the lieutenant governor is chair of the board and possesses the power to make appointments to the board, the lieutenant governor exerts a powerful influence on public policy.

The lieutenant governor is also a member of two executive branch boards created by statute, the Cash Management Committee and the Bond Review Board.

THE LEGISLATIVE BUDGET BOARD

The Legislative Budget Board (LBB) is a permanent, joint committee of the Texas House and Senate. Its principle functions, as provided by statutes, are to examine and make recommendations on spending by state government and on opportunities to maximize federal funding; to analyze and report on the operational efficiency and program performance of each agency and institution; to implement a system of fiscal notes on cost implications of legislation pending before the legislature; and to establish the constitutional limit on the rate of growth of spending from certain state funds.

The budget system in Texas is unique in that the primary budget submitted to the legislature is prepared by the Legislative Budget Board, an agency of the legislature. The membership of the Legislative Budget Board, as provided by law, consists of: the lieutenant governor (chair); the Speaker of the House (vice-chair); the chairs of the House Appropriations, Ways and Means, Senate Finance, and State Affairs Committees; and at-large two members of each house. The Legislative Budget Board's staff is headed by a director who is appointed by the board.

The LBB staff drafts a General Appropriations Bill and companion Legislative Budget Estimates to present to the legislature when it convenes. During the legislative session, the LBB staff serves the Senate Finance Committee and the House Appropriations Committee by scheduling hearings, processing bills, and developing information necessary for the writing of each committee's version of the General Appropriations Bill. If, as is usually the case, each house passes its own version of the General Appropriations Bill, a conference committee is appointed by the presiding officers to work out the differences between the two budgets. The LBB staff prepares a document containing all the differences to be resolved. When the conference committee has completed its deliberations, the staff then prepares the resolution to be presented to both houses for approval.

Since the Texas Constitution requires a balanced budget, appropriations bills must go the comptroller of public accounts for certification as to the availability of state funds. Once the comptroller states that anticipated revenues will be adequate to fund the bill, it is sent to the governor for approval. Through line-item veto authority, the governor may strike out items of appropriation, or the entire budget may be vetoed.

After approval and/or line-item veto of the General Appropriations Bill by the governor, the LBB staff prepares the bill for publication and distribution, including the governor's vetoes when applicable.

THE TEXAS LEGISLATIVE COUNCIL

The Texas Legislative Council, established by statute in 1949, is a nonpartisan legislative branch agency that provides legal and bill-drafting assistance, impartial research and information, and administrative and technical services.

The agency's enabling statute, as amended in 1983, assigns to the council the following duties:

1. To investigate departments, agencies, and officers of the state and to study their functions and problems.
2. To make studies for the use of the legislative branch.
3. To gather information for the use of the legislature.
4. To make any other investigations, studies, and reports that may be considered useful to the legislative branch.
5. To meet and perform its duties in the interim between sessions.
6. To report to the Legislature its recommendations from time to time and to accompany its reports with any drafts of legislation that it considers proper.
7. To assist the Legislature in drafting proposed legislation and
8. To provide data processing services to aid the members and committees in accomplishing their legislative duties.

In 1963, the legislature broadened the scope of the council's duties by creating a permanent statutory revision program and assigning responsibility for execution of the formal revision to the council.

The agency is directed by a council composed of seventeen members —the lieutenant governor and four senators appointed by the lieutenant governor; the Speaker of the House and nine representatives appointed by the Speaker and the chairs of the Senate Administration Committee and the House Administration Committee. The lieutenant governor serves as the chair of the council and the Speaker of the House serves as vice-chair.

The staff of the council is under the direct supervision of its executive director. The council's professional and administrative staff assists legislators in drafting proposed legislation and assists the legislature and individual members in obtaining information on legislative matters.

The staff also has implemented data processing systems to streamline and speed up the printing, processing, and distribution of legislative documents; to report the history and status of legislation; and to automate the administrative operations of members' offices.

In addition, council resources are available in the event of special legislative responsibilities, such as redistricting.

TEXAS LEGISLATIVE REFERENCE LIBRARY

The Texas Legislative Reference Library is a source of data and information about current and past legislatures. Located in Room 2N.3 (second floor, north wing, room 3) of the state capitol building the library is open Monday through Friday from 8:00 a.m. to 5:00 p.m, with extended hours during the legislative session. The library is the legal custodian of the legislative bill files from 1973 to the present. Copies of the original files are available to the public on microfilm, paper, and since 1995, on the legislative Gopher.

The Legislative Reference Library has an extensive collection of documents published by Texas state agencies and universities. In addition, the library contains collections of interim reports and minutes from state agency meetings. These documents are available for photocopying and use in the library but are not available for circulation to the general public.

Resources of the library are located by using the library's online catalogue (TINLAW). The catalogue lists all library holdings by author, title, subject, and keywords. These holdings can be classified as books and reports published by private vendors, statutes of all fifty states, Texas law books, federal law books, and law reviews from all Texas and selected out-of-state schools.

The library maintains a clipping service produced daily by the library staff from approximately forty newspapers. These files are available for viewing and printing in the library on the library's computer network. Clippings are arranged by subject, columnist, newspapers, and date. The library provides information on using this service at each workstation.

Computer terminals are available in the library for public use in searching three databases. FYI (Find Your Incumbent) lists all elected officials for any Texas address. LIS (Legislative Information System) contains bill text and bill history information for the 71st legislative session from 1989 to the present. Information on the current legislature is available on the legislative Gopher. Finally, the TAS (Texas Appointment System) contains detailed information about state agencies and appointments to agencies, boards, and commissions.

CD-ROM databases are available for use in the library. They include the following: American Law Report, Code of Federal Regulations, Encyclopedia Britannica, Shepard's Texas Citations, Shepard's U.S. Citations for the Supreme Court, Social Sciences Index, Texas Administrative Code, Texas Registrar, Texas Cases, Texas Jurisprudence 3d, United States Code Annotated, and Vernon's Texas Statutes and Code Annotated.

THE TEXAS LEGISLATIVE WEB SITE

The Texas Legislative Council Information Systems division is responsible for the Texas Legislature's Internet Web site.

This source has been created so that the public can obtain information about the Texas Legislature. Initial House and Senate information provided includes text for all bill versions, calendars, committee calendars, committee membership, master and supplemental bill lists by subject, or author/sponsor, capitol and district office information, and session times. Information is also provided about legislative districts, legislative terms, the Texas Capitol, and the legislative branch of government.

The Internet address for the Texas Legislative Council's World Wide Web page is: http://www.tlc.state.tx.us.

TEXAS LEGISLATIVE GLOSSARY

ACT — A public law enacted by the Texas Legislature. A bill that has been passed by both houses of the legislature and presented to the governor becomes law if it is signed by the governor, if it is not signed by the governor within a specified period of time, or if the governor vetoes the bill and the veto is overridden by a two-thirds vote in each house.

ACTION — A description of a step that a bill undergoes as it moves through the legislative process.

ADJOURNMENT — The termination of a meeting. Adjournment occurs at the close of each legislative day upon completion of business, with the hour and day of the next meeting set before adjournment.

ADJOURNMENT SINE DIE — Final adjournment of a legislative session. Literally, the phrase means adjournment "without a day" specified to reconvene.

AMENDMENT — Any proposed alteration to a bill or resolution as it moves through the legislative process. Amendments to a measure may be proposed by members in their assigned committees or by any member of a chamber during that chamber's second reading or third reading consideration of the measure.

APPORTIONMENT — The proportionate distribution of elected representatives, either among the states in the case of U.S. Congress or within the state in the case of the state legislature. The division of the state into congressional and state Senate and House districts of equal population for purposes of representation.

APPROPRIATION — An authorization by the legislature for the expenditure of money for a public purpose during a fiscal year or a biennium. In most instances, money cannot be withdrawn from the state treasury except through a specific appropriation. The appropriations for most state government operations are made for two-year periods in one bill passed by the legislature each biennium and referred to as the Appropriations Act.

AUTHOR — The legislator who files a bill and guides it through the legislative process.

BILL — A type of legislative measure that requires passage by both chambers of the legislature and action by the governor. A bill is the primary means used to create and change the laws of the state. The term "bill" generically is used to refer to the various types of legislative measures that may be introduced during a legislative session. Bill types include: Senate and House bills, Senate and House joint resolutions, Senate and House concurrent resolutions, Senate and House resolutions, House memorial motions, and House congratulatory motions.

BILL ANALYSIS — A document that explains in nonlegal language what a bill will do. A bill analysis may include background information on the measure, a statement of purpose, and a section-by-section analysis. Generally, bill analyses are prepared and distributed to the members for the House and Senate committee report versions of a bill. Bill analyses are not routinely prepared for other versions of a bill.

CALENDAR — A list of bills or resolutions that is scheduled or eligible to be taken up for consideration on a specified date by the members of a chamber.

CALLED SESSION — The period during which the legislature meets. There are two types of sessions. The regular session convenes every two years and may last no more than 140 days. A called session is so designated because it must be called by the governor. A called session may last no more than 30 days.

CAPTION — For bills and joint resolutions, the first sentence of the text that summarizes the contents of the bill or resolution. For other types of resolutions and motions, a brief description of the contents of the resolution or motion. The rules of procedure of each house require that the subject of each bill be expressed in a caption that gives the legislature and the public reasonable notice of the subject.

CHAIR — A legislator appointed to preside over a legislative committee.

CHAMBER — The place in which the Senate or House of Representatives meet. Also a generic way to refer to a house of the legislature.

CHIEF CLERK — The chief clerical officer of the House of Representatives. The chief clerk is the custodian of all bills and resolutions in the possession of the House and is responsible for keeping a complete record of their introduction and all subsequent House actions taken on them throughout the legislative process.

COAUTHOR — A legislator authorized by the primary author to join in the authorship of a bill or resolution. A coauthor must be a member of the chamber in which the bill was filed.

COMMITTEE — A group of legislators, appointed by the presiding officer of the House or Senate, to which proposed legislation is referred. A committee may review, discuss, and hold public hearings on a bill that has been referred to it before the committee votes on whether the bill should be reported out of committee for further consideration by the members of the chamber.

COMMITTEE REPORT — The text of a bill or resolution and its required attachments that is prepared when the measure is reported from a committee for further consideration by the members of the chamber. The committee report includes the recommendations of the committee regarding action on the measure by the full House or Senate.

COMMITTEE SUBSTITUTE — When considering a bill or resolution in committee, the committee may make a substantial number of amendments to the original measure, in which case the committee may adopt and report a complete, germane committee substitute in lieu of the original measure. The complete substitute is laid before the chamber, and if the substitute is defeated at any stage, the measure is considered not passed.

CONCURRENCE — When the originating chamber votes to accept, or concur in, the amendments made by the opposite chamber.

CONCURRENT RESOLUTION — A type of legislative measure that requires passage by both chambers of the legislature and action by the governor. A concurrent resolution is used to convey the sentiment of the legislature and may offer a commendation, a memorial, a statement of congratulations, a welcome, or a request for action by another governmental entity. (Concurrent resolutions are also used for administrative matters that require the concurrence of both chambers such as providing for adjournment or a joint session. These types of concurrent resolutions do not require action by the governor.)

CONFERENCE COMMITTEE — A committee composed of five members from each house appointed by the respective presiding officers to resolve the differences between the house and senate versions of a measure when the originating chamber refuses to concur in the changes made by the opposite chamber. Upon reaching an agreement, the conferees issue a report which is then considered for approval by both houses.

CONFERENCE COMMITTEE REPORT — The text of a bill and its required attachments that is issued when a conference committee has completed its work in resolving the differences between the house and senate versions of a measure.

CONSTITUTIONAL AMENDMENT — The legislature may propose a change to the state
constitution by means of a joint resolution. If the joint resolution passes the legislature by a two-thirds vote of both houses, it is placed on the ballot and must be approved by a majority of the voters to become effective.

COSPONSOR — A legislator who joins with the primary sponsor to guide a bill or resolution through the legislative process in the opposite chamber. A cosponsor must be a member of the opposite chamber from the one in which the bill was filed.

DAILY HOUSE CALENDAR — A list of new bills and resolutions scheduled by the Committee on Calendars for consideration by the House which must be distributed to the members thrity-six hours before the House convenes during regular sessions and twenty-four hours before the House convenes during special sessions.

EMERGENCY CLAUSE — Normally the last paragraph of a bill. Neither house of the legislature can suspend the constitutional rule requiring a bill to be read on three separate days if a bill does not have an emergency clause. The specific language of the emergency clause also determines whether a bill that receives a two-thirds record vote in both houses can take effect immediately after the governor signs the bill or files it without a signature.

ENACTING CLAUSE — A clause required by the Texas Constitution to precede the body of each bill. The enacting clause follows the caption.

ENGROSSED — The stage in a bill's legislative progress when it has been passed by the chamber in which it was filed.

ENROLLED — The stage in a bill's legislative progress when it has been passed by both chambers of the legislature. If the bill is not passed in identical form by both, any changes made by the opposite chamber must be accepted by the originating chamber, or a conference committee report must be adopted by both chambers before the bill may be enrolled.

FILED — The stage in a bill's legislative progress when it is given a bill number and introduced into the legislative process. Members of the House of Representatives file bills with the chief clerk of the House. Senators file bills with the secretary of the Senate.

FLOOR — A traditional term for the chamber of either house.

FLOOR ACTION — Action taken by either house on a bill reported by a committee. Subject to rules adopted by the house, members may propose amendments, enter debate, seek to promote or prevent a bill's passage, and vote on its final passage in that house.

FORMAL MEETING — A meeting of a house committee or subcommittee during which formal action may be taken on any measure or matter before the committee or subcommittee. Public testimony cannot be heard during a formal meeting.

INTENT CALENDAR — A list of bills and resolutions for which senators have filed with the secretary of the Senate written notice to suspend the regular order of business for consideration. Normally, a bill may not be brought up for consideration by the full Senate unless it is listed on the Intent Calendar.

INTERIM — The period between regular legislative sessions.

INTRODUCED — The version of a bill or resolution as it was filed in the House or the Senate.

JOINT RESOLUTION — A type of legislative measure that requires passage by both chambers of the legislature but does not require action by the governor. A joint resolution is used to propose amendments to the Texas Constitution, to ratify amendments to the U.S. Constitution, or to request a convention to propose amendments to the U.S. Constitution. Before becoming effective, the provisions of joint resolutions proposing amendments to the Texas Constitution must be approved by the voters of Texas.

JOURNAL — The publication that records the legislative proceedings of each chamber, including record vote information. Each chamber publishes a daily journal for each day that the chamber meets. These daily journals are prepared and distributed to each legislator on the day following each meeting or as soon as practicable. The permanent journal is published in a certified, indexed, and bound volume at the end of a session. The journal indicates the disposition of each motion and point of order made during debate but does not indicate all the members who speak for or against a measure or the text of their remarks.

LEGISLATIVE DAY — That period from a convening after an adjournment until the next adjournment. The House or the Senate may convene for a daily session in the morning, recess for lunch, and adjourn that same evening, completing a legislative day on the same calendar day. However, if a chamber recesses at the end of the day, that particular legislative day continues. Thus, a legislative day may span several calendar days. Also, parts of two legislative days may fall on a single calendar day, as when a chamber adjourns and convenes again on the same calendar day.

LEGISLATURE — The law-making body of the state of Texas. It consists of two chambers, the House of Representatives and the Senate. The Texas Legislature convenes in regular session at noon on the second Tuesday in January of each odd-numbered year for no more than 140 days.

LIST OF ITEMS ELIGIBLE FOR CONSIDERATION — Prepared by the chief clerk of the House, upon request of the Speaker, when the volume of legislation warrants (normally during the last few weeks of a regular session). The list must be distributed six hours before it may be considered and contains: (1) House bills with Senate amendments eligible to be considered; (2) Senate bills for which the Senate has requested the appointment of a conference committee; and (3) conference committee reports eligible to be considered.

LOCAL AND UNCONTESTED CALENDAR — A list of local or non-controversial bills scheduled by the Committee on Administration for consideration by the senate which must be distributed to the senators by noon of the day preceding the day the calendar is to be considered.

LOCAL, CONSENT, AND RESOLUTIONS CALENDAR — A list of local or non-controversial bills scheduled by the Committee on Local and Consent Calendars for consideration by the house which must be distributed to the members forty-eight hours before the house convenes.

MAJORITY — A number of members that is greater than half of the total membership of a group and that has the power to make decisions binding on the whole. There are two types of majorities that may be required for legislative approval of bills and other actions—a simple majority and an absolute majority. A simple majority consists of more than half of those members present and voting. An absolute majority consists of more than half of those members entitled to vote, whether present or absent. Some actions require at least a two-thirds majority vote, while others may require a three-fourths or four-fifths majority vote for adoption or passage.

MOTION — A formal suggestion offered while a house of the legislature or a legislative committee is meeting.

POINT OF ORDER — A motion calling attention to a breach of the procedural rules adopted by the members of the House or Senate at the beginning of a session.

PRESIDENT OF THE SENATE — The presiding officer of the Senate. The state constitution provides that the lieutenant governor shall serve as the president of the Senate.

PUBLIC HEARING — A meeting of a House or Senate committee or subcommittee during which public testimony may be heard and formal action may be taken on any measure or matter before the committee or subcommittee.

QUORUM — The number of members required to conduct business. Two-thirds of the elected members constitutes a quorum in each house. A majority of the appointed members of a committee forms a quorum for the purpose of conducting committee business.

READING — The presentation of a bill before either house by the recital of the bill's caption. The Texas Constitution requires that every bill be read in each house on three separate days. Until a bill is finally passed, it will be in the process of a first, second, or third reading. The first reading of a bill is the point in the process when the bill is referred to committee by the appropriate presiding officer. The second reading of a bill is the first point in the process when the entire membership of a chamber has the opportunity to debate the bill and amend it by majority vote. The third reading of a bill is the next point in the process when the entire membership of a chamber may debate a bill and the final opportunity the members of a chamber have to offer amendments to the bill.

RECESS — A temporary termination of a meeting. Recesses are called for short breaks (e.g., for lunch or dinner) or occasionally at the close of a daily session without ending the legislative day. *See* ADJOURNMENT.

RECORD VOTE — A listing of the individual vote of each member of a committee or the full House or Senate. Committee record votes are conducted by the committee clerk who calls each member's name. Record votes in the House are conducted electronically with each member pushing a button at the member's assigned desk. Senate record votes are conducted by the secretary of the Senate who reads each senator's name in alphabetical order.

REDISTRICTING — A geographical division of the state into congressional, state representative, senatorial, or other legislative districts on the basis of the relative distribution of the state's total population. District boundaries are redrawn every ten years following the publication of the U.S. population.

REGULAR SESSION — The period during which the legislature meets. There are two types of sessions. The regular session convenes every two years and may last no more than 140 days. A called session is so designated because it must be called by the governor. A called session may last no more than 30 days.

RESOLUTION — A formal expression of opinion or decision, other than a proposed law, that may be offered for approval to one or both houses of the legislature by a member of the House or Senate.

ROLL CALL — A registration of the members present at a meeting of a committee or of the full House or Senate. Committee roll calls are conducted by the committee clerk who calls each member's name. Roll calls in the House are conducted electronically with each member pushing a button at the member's assigned desk. Senate roll calls are conducted by the secretary of the Senate who reads each senator's name in alphabetical order.

SECRETARY OF THE SENATE — The chief administrative officer of the Senate, responsible for the day-to-day operations of the Senate and its departments.

SENATE AGENDA — The document prepared daily for the senators and the public which contains the following information: (1) the intent calendar; (2) a list of Senate bills returned from the House with amendments; (3) the status of bills in conference committee; (4) the local and uncontested calendar; (5) gubernatorial appointments reported favorably from the Committee on Nominations and awaiting confirmation by the Senate; (6) committee hearings scheduled, with a list of measures to be considered by the committees; (7) the regular order of business, listing bills that have been reported favorably from committee; (8) Senate floor action from the previous day; and (9) Senate committee action from the previous day.

SESSION — The period during which the legislature meets. There are two types of sessions. The regular session convenes every two years and may last no more than 140 days. A called session is so designated because it must be called by the governor. A called session may last no more than 30 days.

SIMPLE RESOLUTION — The type of legislative measure that is considered only within the chamber in which it is filed. It can offer a commendation, a memorial, a statement of congratulations, a welcome, or other statement of legislative sentiment.

SPEAKER OF THE HOUSE — The presiding officer of the House of Representatives elected from and by the membership of the House at the beginning of each regular session.

SPONSOR — The legislator who guides the bill through the legislative process after the bill has passed the originating chamber. The sponsor must be a member of the opposite chamber of the one in which the bill was filed.

STANDING COMMITTEE — A committee created in the rules of either house that meets during the legislative session and/or an interim to consider and report on measures referred to it by the respective presiding officers.

SUBCOMMITTEE — A group of committee members, appointed by the chair of a committee of the House or the Senate, to which proposed legislation is referred. A subcommittee may review, discuss, and hold public hearings on a bill that has been referred to it before the subcommittee votes on whether the bill should be considered by the full committee.

SUPPLEMENTAL HOUSE CALENDAR — The primary agenda followed by the house during its deliberations. It is prepared by the Committee on Calendars and required to be distributed two hours before the House convenes. The Supplemental House Calendar contains: (a) measures passed to third reading on the previous day; (b) measures on the Daily House Calendar for a previous day which were not reached for consideration; (c) measures on the Daily House Calendar for the current day; and (d) postponed business from a previous day.

VETO — The rejection of an enrolled bill by the governor.

WORK SESSION — A meeting of a house committee or subcommittee during which the members may only discuss measures or matters before the committee or subcommittee. Public testimony cannot be heard and formal action cannot be taken during a work session.